ISBN 978-1-330-11457-5
PIBN 10029280

This book is a reproduction of an important historical work. Forgotten Books uses
state-of-the-art technology to digitally reconstruct the work, preserving the original format
whilst repairing imperfections present in the aged copy. In rare cases, an imperfection in
the original, such as a blemish or missing page, may be replicated in our edition. We do,
however, repair the vast majority of imperfections successfully; any imperfections that
remain are intentionally left to preserve the state of such historical works.

LEGENDS

AND

SUPERSTITIONS

OF THE

SEA AND OF SAILORS

In all·Lands and at all Times.

BY

FLETCHER S. BASSETT,

/

LIEUTENANT U. S. NAVY.

CHICAGO AND NEW YORK:
BELFORD, CLARKE & CO.
1885.

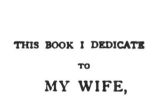

THIS BOOK I DEDICATE

TO

MY WIFE,

HELEN MAR

PREFACE.

THE present volume is an attempt at collecting the folk-lore of the sea and its belongings. Many of the myths here recorded are as old as history itself, and far older, and some of the most interesting legends have been frequently published; but, so far as I am aware, no comprehensive collection of the legends relating to the sea has heretofore been made. It is not claimed that the present work is exhaustive, for much has been written concerning the mysterious sea, and much remains for some future folk-lore collector, but the greater part of the legends of the sea are here assembled.

These legends are derived from various and widely-different sources. Comparative mythology has taught us not to despise the most frivolous tale, if we may, by comparison, illustrate more sober myths or legends by its use. I have adopted, as a safe guide for the interpretation of the nature-myths of the sea and the air, the teachings of Cox, whose writings have generally received the sanction of scholars. The standard works of Smith, Anthon, Murray, Gladstone, Keary, Fiske and Kelly have also been freely consulted and quoted. These mythological ideas of early nations often serve as a key to the interpretation of more recent superstitions. "The religious myths of antiquity, and the fireside legends of ancient and modern times, have their common root in the mental habits of primitive humanity. They are the earliest recorded utterances of men concerning the visible phenomena of the world into which they were born."[*]

Many writers on folk-lore have been consulted, and especially, as relating to the sea, "Melusine," a Parisian folk-lore journal, the publications of the Folk-lore Society, the works of Jal, of Jones, of Bottrell, Hunt, Gregor,

[*] Fiske—Myths and Myth-makers.

Sébillot, Grimm, Thorpe, Kuhn and Campbell. Illustrations of our subject also come from the legends devised by monks and priests during the middle ages, who often availed themselves of the myths of antiquity and the superstitions of pagan people, to serve their purposes, and thus there grew up many legends of saints and demons, and many usages, observances, and ceremonies among sea-faring men. The writings of Maury, Collin de Plancy, Schindler, and many others furnish us with a host of these legends.

The traditions, beliefs and customs of modern sailors have been culled from the various collections of folk-lore, and from the pages of nautical writers, such as Jal, Marryat, Basil Hall, Melville, Cheever, Cooper, and others, mentioned in this work, and from the collections of voyages and travels of Pinkerton, Navarrete, Pigafetta, and others. Personal notes and observation made during a service of fourteen years in the navy have supplemented these observations.

Th poets and ballad writers have, again, furnished much valuable material. Their words are but the crystallized expression of popular ideas — the reflex of public opinion, clothed in elegant or musical form. "The old folk songs, as they are aptly termed, remain to us now a vast store-house of historical evidence of the manners and customs, of the thoughts and beliefs, of bygone times." There is a surprising amount of legend and folk-lore stored away in Shakespeare, Moore, Longfellow and other poets, not to speak of the ancient classics, which overflow with legends and traditions of popular origin.

In attempting to solve the many problems presented in the various parts of this volume, I have endeavored to avoid a bias toward any theories. In general these superstitions are the results of widely different causes, and it will be found that while originating, as did most myths of antiquity, from speculations upon natural phenomena, other influences have had an equal effect in elaborating the modern superstition. In fact there is often a rational basis underlying these traditions, which, if it has not given rise to the legends, has often perpetuated them. The uneducated sailor could know little of the ancient

sea-gods, nereides, sirens, etc., but he could recognize in
the seal, the manatee, or the dugong, the face and figure
of a fish-tailed woman. He could know but little of the
classical and biblical traditions concerning aquatic monsters, but he could see in the huge forms that sported
about him the terrible kraken or the monstrous sea-
serpent, or he could imagine the form of the latter in
the floating sea weed.

These natural causes have also been aided, in the
perpetuation of these superstitions, by the conservatism
of the sailor, who clings to his beliefs with great tenacity.
Grimm illustrates this point when he says: " The early
Christian Norseman believed in Christ, and yet he called
upon Thor in voyages and difficulties." The sailor, as
has often been remarked, is a credulous infant in many
things. He often fears less a murderous volley than a
corpse or coffin, and is less alarmed by the howling
tempest than by fancied signs of wreck or disaster in
the air or sea. Gibbons best expresses these facts:

" There is but a plank between a sailor and eternity;
and perhaps the occasional realization of that fact may
have had something to do with the broad grain of superstition at one time undoubtedly lurking in his nature.
But whatever the cause, certainly the legendary lore of
the sea is as diversified and interesting as the myths and
traditions which haunt the imagination of landsmen, and
it is not surprising that sailors, who observe the phenomena of nature under such varied and impressive aspects,
should be found to cling with tenacious obstinacy to
their superstitious fancies. The winds, clouds, waves,
sun, moon, and stars have ever been invested with propitious or unlucky signs; and within a score of years we
have met seamen who had perfect faith in the weather-
lore and traditions acquired during their ocean wanderings."

Buckle gives an excellent reason for the sailors' belief in many of these superstitions: " The credulity of
sailors is notorious, and every literature contains evidence
of the multiplicity of these superstitions, and of the
tenacity with which they cling to them. This is perfectly
explicable. Meteorology has not yet been raised to a

science, and the laws which regulate winds and storms being in consequence still unknown, it naturally follows that the class of men most exposed to these dangers should be precisely the class which is most superstitious."

Cooper also says: "There is a majesty in the might of the great deep, that has a tendency to keep open the avenues of that dependent credulity which more or less besets the mind of every man. The confusion between things which are explicable and things which are not, gradually brings the mind of the mariner to a state in which any exciting and unnatural sentiment is welcome.

While it is true that the sailor is conservative in his beliefs, I do not believe that he is more superstitious than those of his class who dwell on the land. A comparison of his credulities with the superstitions of the same day and age of the world will not, I believe, result to his disadvantage. Superstition and credulity were rife everywhere when most of the sailor traditions were born, and many of them, as will be shown, are but adaptations of similar beliefs on land — many were first imagined far inland, by people who never saw the sea.

The old type of sailor, who believed in the mermaid, the sea-snake, and the phantom ship, is fast disappearing, and, with the gradual substitution of the steamship for the sailing-vessel, he is being replaced by the mechanical seaman, who sees no spectre in the fog, nor sign of disaster in the air, or beneath the wave.

Scientific progress has demonstrated the non-existence of imaginary creatures beneath the waves; better meteorological knowledge has banished the spectres of the air, and shown the unreliability of weather-indicators, and the decay of priestly influence has caused the abandonment of sacrifices and offerings to the sea, its deities or its saints.   F. S. B.

CHICAGO, March 10, 1884.

CONTENTS.

CHAPTER I.

THE SEA, THE WINDS AND THE WEATHER.

" The tales of that awful, pitiless sea,
  With all its terror and mystery,
The dim, dark sea, so like unto death,
  That divides and yet unites mankind."
               Longfellow.—Golden Legend.

" Winds that like a demon
  Howl with horrid note,
Round the toiling seaman
  In his bonny boat."

MONG the many wonderful changes wrought in the various conditions of life by the progress of scientific investigation and modern achievement, there are none so complete as those affecting the man of the sea. The swift journey to Europe has become an affair of so little moment to many that it is hardly thought of until land fades from sight, and the modern traveler sets out on his voyage around the world with less trepidation than the Roman poet felt and described, when he left his native city for the short journey that carried him across a narrow sea into temporary banishment. It is difficult, then, for us to realize the terrors which the ocean possessed for the ancient mariner—almost impossible for us to understand the implicit belief which he evidently held in the many monsters, fiends, physical dangers and curious phenomena that would now only serve to provoke laughter or astonishment.

Not only was the sailor in ancient times exposed to greater sea peril by deficiencies in the construction of his vessel, but, in addition, his imagination created a host of

11

fancied dangers to terrify him. The dangers of the sea voyage are often portrayed by classical writers. Horace, in his third ode, in lamenting the departure of Virgil for Athens, paints these terrors in vivid colors; speaking of horrid sea-monsters and terrific waves, Andocides, accused before the courts at Athens, said, "The dangers of accusation and trial are human, but the dangers encountered at sea are divine."

"Sea voyages among the Egyptians were looked upon as sacrilegious." *

Nor did these imaginary terrors disappear with antiquity. The first charts had portrayed on them numbers of huge monsters, horrible dragons, and terrific giants, scattered here and there like the ships marked on charts of more recent date.

The land-locked ocean known to the ancients had been filled with unknown terrors, and the distant lands bordering on it, with wonders and strange inhabitants. Monsters abode in the waters, gods of monstrous shapes ruled them, enchanting sirens, horrid giants, and terrible dragons inhabited the islets and rocks, and on the dry land beyond, there dwelt strange enchantresses, fire-breathing bulls, dwarfish pigmies, and man-eaters. The crude ideas concerning geography, making the earth now a disk, now a drum, a boat or a flat surface surrounded by water, aided in perpetuating to later ages these curious beliefs.

Thus sailors as well as landsmen, in all ages, have been prone to indulge in fancies of all kinds concerning the winds and waves. Such notions are naturally directed to the weather, the object of so much care and solicitude to the mariner.

In antiquity, the Great Ocean was thought to be unnavigable. Flowing around the world like a river, it became, as we shall see, a river, then a sea of death.

This circumambient ocean was not peculiar to the Greeks. We find it in other cosmogonies, as the Norse and Arab geographers, about 1300, revived the idea.

As men became more and more acquainted with distant waters, their ideas concerning this unknown ocean expanded. At first it was the Central Mediterranean in which were located all the Homeric dangers of the ocean. This was gradually extended to the westward, and finally into the Great Western Sea, after the French discovery of the Canaries (1330).

* Mure.—Hist. Gr. Lit. 1, p. 17.

offer sacrifices to the spirit of whirlpools in rivers. An eddy in the upper falls of the Mississippi was thought to be haunted by a demon, to whom sacrifices were made. Canadian Indians thought the spirit of a drowned man haunted an eddy, and that it drew down sticks that were thrown in.

In Mexico, children were offered to Tlaloc in a whirlpool.[*]

The bore, that sometimes is found in tidal rivers, has been the subject of many fancies.

[†]A bore on the southwest coast of Ireland is called the avenging wave. A man killed a mermaid here, and the wave suddenly rushed to engulf him (the next time he ventured out); and so each time until he was drowned; and it even chases his descendants, the story tells us.

The bore that occurs in the mouths of some rivers has been thought a demon or dragon. Its name, *Eagre*, is thought by some to be a corruption of *Eagle*.[‡] The Egyptians had a tradition that that bird caused whirlpools in the Nile, and the Phœnix was fabled to appear with the inundation. [§] Chinese fire cannon-balls at the bore in Canton river, while some shoot arrows. A certain governor, not succeeding in these methods, threw himself in, and exists as a water-spirit. The bore at Hangchow is thought to be caused by a spirit.

The bore is called Hygra in Gloucester and in the Humber.[‖] Blind [**] thinks this a corruption of Ægre, from Œgir, the Norse sea-god. Carlyle says: "Now to this day, on the river Trent, the Nottingham bargemen call it Ægre. They say, 'Have a care; the Æger is coming.' The older Nottingham bargemen had believed in the god Œgir." It is so named by Drayton in "Polyolbion."

A legend of St. Patrick says the waves are caused by serpents, which that redoubtable saint inclosed in a box, when he cast them out of Ireland.

If we are to believe modern mythologists, breakers are often personified in Greek tales as wild bulls, and the exploits of heroes, from Perseus to St. George, are, most of them, traditions of the defeat of waves beating on the coast.

---

[*] Bancroft.—Native Races, vol. iii.
[†] Jones.—Credulities, 3.
[‡] G. Massey.—Book of the Beginnings.
[§] Dennys.—Folk-lore of China.
[‖] Brewer.—Reader's Handbook.—Hygra.
[**] Contemporary Review, 1881.

*A Norse tradition reports that the noise of waves on a certain beach is the whisper of an old king and his queen, buried in mounds near there. The "moan of the sea" at Elsinore, in Denmark, is said to portend death, or to "want some one."

In "The Fisherman," Phœbe Cary says:

> "And I hear the long waves wash the beach,
> With the moan of a drowning man in each."

In Moray Firth, the fishermen call the noise of the waves "the song of the sea."† The sighing noise of a wave on the coast of Cork is believed to portend the death of some great man.

So,‡ not more than thirty years ago, the hollow, mournful sound of the waves on the coast of Cornwall was said to be a spirit, *Bucca* (Puck), and foretold a tempest.

The sound of the Nåsjoir, or death wave, of Icelandic legend, was said to resemble the struggles of a dying man.

The waves are still called in French "Moutons" (sheep), when whitened by the coming breeze. §So in Ariosto,—

> "And Neptune's white herds low above the waves."

So, in Scotland, the waves preceding a storm are "dogs afore the maister"; those following, "dogs ahin' the maister."

El Masudi‖ tells us the Arab sailors believed that the "blind waves," or high seas of the Abyssinian coast were enchanted, and they said verses to charm them, as they were lifted up on them.

Cambry ** says the inhabitants of Finisterre divined events by the movements of the waves.

Fishermen on our own coasts call the swell sometimes seen during a fog, the fog-swell, and believe it is caused by the fog. It is really the swell caused by the incoming tide.

An idea long existed that the ninth or tenth wave was greater and more powerful than others. This belief existed in Ovid's time, who says,†† "The wave that is now coming

---

* Dasent.—Popular Tales from the Norse.
† Kennedy.—Fireside Stories of Ireland.
‡ Hunt.—Romances and Drolls of the west of England.
§ Hoole's Translation.
‖ Golden Meadows, 954 A.D.
** Voyage Dans la Finisterre.
†† Fasti.

o'ertops all the others; 'tis the one that comes after the ninth and before the tenth." The *fluctus decumannus*, or tenth wave, was then preferred.

THE NINTH WAVE.

Allatius[*] writes thus, during a voyage from Messina to Malta, "I saw the captain, who was accounted an experienced and skillful mariner, standing at the bow, while he muttered and pointed at something with his finger. I approached, and inquired what he was doing. The old man, with a cheerful countenance, answered, 'I am breaking the force of a fatal wave, and am making the sign of the cross, and saying the prayers proper for the occasion.' I said 'Do you, then, know, amongst all these waves, which is the fatal

[*] Allatius.—De Græcorum Hodie quandorum opinationibus (1645).

one?' 'Yes,' he said, 'by so many waves by which the ship is tossed, none but the ninth can sink it.' And as the ship was immediately driven more violently, and the water suddenly beat high over it, 'This,' said he, 'is the ninth, take the number count on.' Strange it is that every ninth wave was much greater than any of the others, and threatened the ship with immediate destruction. This wave, however, whenever it approached, the captain, by his muttering and signing of the cross, seemed to break, and the danger was averted."

Forbes* says the ninth is thought the greatest wave by the Hindoo boatmen. The Welsh bard, Taliesin,† refers to it as greatest. An old Welsh sea-poem says the dead are buried "where the ninth wave breaks." In a Bardic story, "a fleet is destroyed by the ninth wave." Welsh‡ fishermen called the ninth wave the "ram of Gwenhidwy," the other waves her sheep.

Sir Thomas Browne§ refutes the tenth wave superstition. ‖ Tennyson thus speaks:—

> "And watched the great sea fall
> Wave after wave, each mightier than the last,
> 'Till last, a ninth one, gathering half the deep,
> And full of voices, slowly rose, and plunged,
> Roaring, and all the wave was in a flame."

Hone** says: "A common affimation is that the tenth wave is the greatest, and always the most dangerous." In an account of the loss of the ship "Fanny," in this century, the tenth wave is said to have risen above the rest. A modern novelist †† says, "Our fishermen (in England) call it the death wave, not always the ninth." In a late tale, a sailor says: "I made de sign of de holy cross, an' de wave broke before it reached us." ‡‡

In Scotland a distempered cow could be cured by being washed by nine surfs. In the trial of Margaret Ritchart, witch of the eighteenth century, we read of the further efficacy of the water from the ninth wave.§§ "Go thy way to the sea-syd, and tell nyne heave of the sea cum in, that is to

* Oriental Memoirs.
† G. Massey.—Book of the Beginnings.
‡ Brewer.—Readers' Hand Book.
§ Vulgar Errors, 1644.
‖ Holy Grail
** Gregor.—Folk-lore of Scotland.
†† Mary C. Hay.
‡‡ Capt. Hall.—Adrift in the Ice Fields.
§§ The Lancashire Witches.

say, nyne waves of the sea, and let the hind-most go of the nyne back again, and the nixt theraifter, take three looffuls (spoonsful) of the water, and put within the stoupe, and quhen thou comes hame, put it in thy kime, and there will get thy profit back again."

*There is a belief among Shetland fishermen, that water out of the "third die," if gathered up, had great medicinal and mischief-working power. So old fishermen believed they could find their way in a fog by their knowledge of "da moder-die," or wave tending toward land.

Icelandic† fishermen say there are three great waves that follow in succession, in which boats should not be launched. These waves are called Olág, and boats should put to sea in the lág, immediately following them. Should a boat's crew be wrecked in the operation, they say a great calm comes over the sea, called *Dauthaldg* (death's calm), during which other boats are safe. Breakers called *Ndoldur* (death's breakers) are often seen at sea, redder or bluer than the surrounding waves. When two of these waves clash together, they make a sound called "death's clash," and portend wreck.

These curious beliefs have no foundation in fact. It was doubtless noticed that there were waves greater than those preceding and following, but no regularity can be observed in these. The mystic numbers three, nine (3 x 3), and ten, were not unusually chosen when any doubt existed. Massey thinks the idea is connected with the nine months or ten moons of gestation, and the new birth or resurrection thus typified. We need not, however, go so far as this in our imagery.

The tides, those mysterious pulsations of the ocean, have been the theme of many curious speculations.

‡Aristotle and Heraclitus say they are caused by the sun, which moves and whirls the winds about, so that they fall with violence on the Atlantic, which thus swells and causes the tides.

Pliny§ believed in tides of extraordinary height. Pytheas said they were caused by the increase of the moon, and ‖Plato accounted for them as caused by an animal living in a cavern, which, by the means of a mouth or orifice

---

* K. Blind.—Contemp. Review, September, 1882.
† Maurer.—Islandische Sagen.
‡ Plutarch.—Morals. Goodwin's Trans., Vol. III.
§ Bk. II., Ch. 99.
‖ Plutarch.—Morals. Goodwin, Vol. III.

causes the alternations of ebb and flow. He also says the winds, falling from the mountains of Celtic Gaul into the Atlantic, causes a tide.   * Seleucus said that the motion of the earth and moon produce a wind, which, pressing on the Atlantic, causes a tide. † Vegetius says they are a natural movement of respiration of the sea.

‡ El Masudi records the Mediæval beliefs among the Arabs. He says some think them caused by the moon's heating the waters so that it swells and rises higher; others, that they are caused by vapors generated in the bowels of the earth; others, that its movements were like the temperaments of men, without rule and reason. Others said they were caused by the alternate decomposition of the sea by the air, and of the air by the sea, thus causing the ebb and flow.

§ Brunetti Latini, in the 13th century, said the tides are caused by the efforts of the earth to breathe. This had been asserted in antiquity, and refuted by Pytheas. St. Jerome says they come from caves by a law of Nature. ‖ Bede (the false) says they are caused by a great serpent which swallows and vomits the water.

** Another old author says they are caused by the ice melting at the poles.

†† Blind says Shetlanders believed they were caused by a monster living in the sea, or in the words of an old fisherman, "a monstrous sea-serpent that took about six hours to draw in his breath, and about six to let it out again."

‡‡ The Chinese believe that supernatural beings cause the tides, and Japanese legends of the " ruler of the tides," still exist.

§§ The Malay Nias say they are caused by the movements of a huge crab.

‖ Respect to the god Somnath causes the tides, say modern Hindoos.

*** Michael Scott, the great wizard, was popularly said to have controlled the tides. He sent a man to run on the

* Plutarch.—Morals. Goodwin, Vol. III.
† Inst. R. Milit, Vol. XII.
‡ Golden Meadows, 954 A.D.
§ Tresor.
‖ De Mundi Constitutione in Theo. Martin Notices des Anciens, sur la marée, 1863.
** B. de St. Pierre, Etudes de la nature.
†† Contemporary Review, September, 1881.
‡‡ Dennys.—Folk-lore of China.
§§ Rosenberg.—Q. in Mélusine, November, 1884.
‖ Tarikh Mahmud in Panjab Notes and Queries.
*** Conway.—Demonology and Devil-lore, I., 118.

banks of the Wambeck, the tide following up, so long as he did not look behind. Terrified by the noise of the advancing waves, he disobeyed the injunction, and the tide stopped.

In Russia the tides are popularly said to be controlled by the water king's daughter.

There is a superstition in many places that people die on the ebb of the tide. This is as old as Pliny, who says, *"Aristotle says that no animal dies except at the ebb of the tide." He further says it has been proven true only as regards man. Dickens alludes to this notion in "David Copperfield." So, in another part of England, it is believed that a child born at the rising of the tide will be a male, and in Scotland,† good wives set eggs for cocks at flood, for hens at ebb.

‡ At Hull, in Cornwall and in Northumberland, it is believed that people wait for the tide. So Shakspeare makes the hostess say of Falstaff,—

§ "'A parted even just between twelve and one, even at the turning o' the tide."

║ Marryat thus chronicles the belief. "Dr. Mead has observed, that of those who are at the point of death, nine out of twelve quit this world at the turn of the tide."

** "In Brittany death usually claims his victims at ebb."

†† On Cape Cod, and in many other districts along the New England coast, it is firmly believed that a sick man can not die until the ebb tide begins to run. Watchers by beds of sickness anxiously note the change of the tides, and if the patient lives until the flood begins to set in again he will live until the next ebb. The most intelligent and best educated people born and brought up on the New England coast are not entirely free from this superstition, and to them there is a weird meaning in the words of Dickens in describing the death of Barkis: "And it being high water, he went out with the tide."

Water spouts, destructive to the smaller vessels formerly used, have always been objects of dread to the mariner.

They were called Prester §§ by the Greeks, whence probably the name *prister*, used by Olaus Magnus for the whirlpool. Lucretius says:

*Bk. II., Ch. 47.
† Gregor.—Folk-lore of Scotland.
‡ Choice Notes, p. 164.
║ King Henry V. Act ii, scene 3.
║ King's Own.
** L. de Sauvu in Mélusine, September, 1884.
†† Boston Transcript, 1885.
‡‡ Jones.—Credulities, p. 77.

> " Hence with much ease, the meteor we may trace,
> Termed from its essence, Prester by the Greeks."

* Pliny says of it, calling it Typhoon, " It may be counteracted by sprinkling it with vinegar when it comes near us—
this substance being of a very cold nature."

El Masudi† thus reports beliefs current in his day:
"There are *Timmins* (dragons) in the Atlantic seas.   Some
believe this is a wind arising in a whirling column from the
bottom of the sea.   Some say it is a black serpent rising in
the air, and succeeded by a terrible wind; some that it is a
terrible animal living in the bottom of the sea; some say
they are black serpents, passing from the desert into the
sea, and living five hundred years.   Abbu Abbas says they
are killed in the clouds by cold and rain."

‡Especially were they objects of superstition in the Middle Ages, as is manifest from their popular title, " dragons
de mer," or *sea dragons*.   Various ways were adopted of getting rid of these troublesome visitors.   Cannon-shot were
fired into the solid column.   P. Dan, in his "History of
Barbary " (1649), says that custom was even then followed,
and it has been continued to much later times.   He also says
it was conjured away by presenting a black-handled knife
placed at the extremity of a mast or spar, repeating prayers,
signing the cross, etc., meanwhile.   John of Brompton tells
us,§ "Another very extraordinary thing happens once in
every month of the year, in the gulf of Salato; a great black
dragon is seen to come from the clouds, and puts its head
into the water, and its tail seems as though it were fixed in
the sky; and this dragon drinks up the waters so greedily,
that it swallows up along with them any ships that may
come in the way, along with their crews and cargo, be they
ever so heavy.   And those that would escape the dragon,
must, as soon as they see the dragon, make a great noise,
with loud shouting, and beating on the deck; and when the
dragon hears the tumult and the shouting, he will move off
to a distance."

∥ Pere Rêné François also tells us: " Dragons of the sea
are very great whirlwinds that will sink a ship, which they
pass over.   The sailors, when they see them coming afar

---

* Nat. Hist.—Bk. II., Ch. 41.
† Golden Meadows, 954 A.D.
‡ Aubin.—Dictionnaire de Marine, 1702.
§ Chronicle in Angl. Scriptorium.   Tylor P. C., I., 326.
∥ Merveilles de La Nature, in Jal. Glossaire Nautique, " Dragons."

PRAYER IN THE HOUR OF PERIL.

81

off, raise their swords, and beat them against each other in the shape of a cross, holding that this causes the monster to flee from alongside. *The weather was thick and we went spooning towards Gardafu, when suddenly we saw a shape like a black and thick cloud, falling at some distance from us into the sea. One of our Greeks from Chios took his sword and said several prayers with the sign of the cross, and commenced to hack at the deck, from which he cut two or three pieces. . . . There were some Indian gentlemen who took their alfanges or scimiters, to defend themselves from this restless demon."

† So B. Crescentio: "This column, pillar or water spout, the sailors, credulous in infidel things, and firm in their faith, hold that it will disappear by taking a knife with a black handle, and saying the evangelist of St. John, and the Pater Noster, without saying "et in terra," etc., and by making three crosses in the air, and at every cross sticking the point of the knife in the side of the ship."

‡ Purchas chronicles similar beliefs: "Often they see come afar off, great whirlwinds, which the mariners call dragons; if this passeth over their ship, it breaketh them and overwhelmeth them in the waves. When the mariners see them come, they take new swords and beat one against the other in a cross, upon the prow or toward the coast from whence the storm comes; and hold that this hinders it from coming over their ship, and turneth it aside."

§A little later Thévenot is an eye witness of such a scene. "One of the ship's company kneels down by the mainmast, and, holding in his hands a knife with a *black* handle (without which sailors never go on board for that reason), he reads the gospel of St. John, and when he comes to the words, 'Et verbum carne factum est et habitant in nobis,' the man turns toward the waterspout, and with the knife cuts the air toward that spirit, as if he would cut it; and they say then, it is really cut, and lets all the water fall with a great noise."

‖ Père Dan is also a witness. After hearing an account of the terrors of the approaching monster: "This account gave us very great alarm, and sent us to our prayers, and insomuch as we were told by the sailors that in such

* Les Voyages du Sieur Vincent le Blanc, 1509, in Mélusine.
† Nautica Mediterranea, 1637, in Jal. (Gloss.) Nautique, " Dragons."
‡ Pilgrims, 1646.
§ Travels.—1687.
‖ History Barbary, 1649, in Jones' Credulities, p. 77.

extremity they were accustomed to recite the evangelist of St. John, that commences 'In Principio,' etc., I said them very loud, and we perceived, a little after, that the meteor melted away."

*When this failed, two men fought with black-edged swords, making them cross. In one of Columbus' voyages, passages from the "Evangelist" were read to dissipate a waterspout.

†Aubin says Catholic mariners say the "Evangelist," and others pray to dissipate them. He says some think them water drawn up by the sun, and sailors think they presage great storms.

These curious ideas with regard to the waterspout were not confined to sailors, nor to the middle ages.

‡We read in the Arabian Nights: "The sea became troubled before them, and there arose from it a black pillar, ascending toward the sky, and approaching the meadows; and, behold! it was a *jinnee* of gigantic stature."

§Greeks of the middle ages called these phenomena *Prester*, and thought them a fiery fluid, because lightning and sulphurous smells sometimes accompany them.

‖Wainaku Africans told Dr. Krapf of a great serpent that arose like a column from the sea, bringing rain. In mythology** and folk-lore, the rain is often figured as a serpent.

A Finnish legend says the waterspout is Vidar, a water-god.

††Chinese and Japanese say these phenomena are caused by dragons, and affirm that they have been seen going up and down in them. Drums and gongs are beaten to dissipate them. Japanese call them *tatsmaki* (spouting-dragon).‡‡

Falconer in the "Shipwreck," and Camoens in the "Lusiad," allude to firing cannon at them. Russian peasants pretend to dispel whirlwinds by cutting the air with crossed knives.

The twisted column was readily imagined a serpent or dragon, and the name endured after the conception of the animal nature of the meteor was lost. Doubtless can-

---

*Jones.—Credulities, p. 78.
†Dictionnaire de Marine, 1702.
‡Lane.—Arabian Nights, Vol. I, 30-7.
§Jones.—Credulities, p. 77.
‖Krapf.—Travels in Africa, p. 198.
**Goldhizer.—Mythology Among the Hebrews.
††Doolittle.—The Chinese. II. 306.
‡‡Kaempfer.—Japan in Pinkerton, VII, 634.

non were at first fired at them, for the same reason that
gongs were beaten, and swords clashed together to terrify
them — and not with the modern idea of breaking the
column.

There were various other things imagined of the sea.
From it came all the universe, according to the writer of
Genesis, where we are told the earth was without form, but
"darkness moved upon the face of the waters." Geology
has proven that the sea at one time covered much of what
is now dry land; and bones of extinct sea-monsters, alluded
to in another chapter, have been found on inland plains,
and even on high table-lands. Not only the Hebrews, but
other nations held these same ideas.* "The theory of a
wet origin is traceable in Vedic, Assyrian, Hebrew, Greek,
German, and other cosmogonies," says Blind. According
to Pherecydes and Thales, the sea was the first of all
elements. A Frenchman† wrote a book to prove that not
only the earth, but the entire animal and vegetable kingdoms, came out of the ocean, in which existed the egg of
all creation. ‡Shakspeare hints that the sea is the origin
of dew.

From the ocean came many of the gods, and in the
ocean was their abode, as we shall see in another chapter.
So in it was, in many beliefs, the heaven or the hell.
Esquimaux placed there the better of their two heavens;
there Typhon and many demons abode, and there, as we
shall also see, in middle-age belief, lay purgatory and paradise. Nåstrand, the Norse shore of the dead was there, and
there the Taouist placed his sixth court of hell.

So from the sea came riches and knowledge, as well as
living beings.§ From it arose Oannes, Hea, Quealzcoatl,
Viracocha, Manco Capac, Bochica, and other primitive
heroes, who brought the arts and sciences with them.
Lakshmi, the Hindoo Venus; Kama, the Cupid; Aphrodite, and Viracocha sprang from the foam of the sea In
Greek mythology, semi-divine heroes are the offspring often
of a sea-steer, a river-god, or a stream, and many heroes are
descendants of the Oceanids.

There is a Buddhist legend that living beings were
created out of sea-foam. Pierre de San Cloud‖ says Adam

* Scottish and Shetlandic Water-gods, Contemporary Review, August, 1882.
† M. Maillet.—Telramund.
‡ Antony and Cleopatra. Act iii.; scene 2.
§ See Ch. II.
‖ Baring Gould.—Legends of Old Testament Characters.

and Eve created animals from the sea by striking it with rods—the former bringing forth beneficent animals, the latter evil ones.

In Norse legend, the sons of Borsford, a primeval giant, find two pieces of wood floating, and from them form man and woman.

The sea-animals and its fabled inhabitants are wise and beneficent, powerful and malignant, and the marvelous rich hoard of the Niflungs was robbed to furnish the wonderful quantities of gold brought to man by the mermaids and water-sprites of story and song.

Perhaps in this Niflung hoard is typified the close con-nection of the water and fire cult, and at the same time the antagonism between the lunar and solar worships often observed in antiquity. Blind * shows many things in sup-port of the first: "This hoard is probably but the phos-phorescent color of the sea-foam. Poseidon and Amphi-trite dwell in golden palaces beneath the seas; and the sea-hall of the mer-lady's offspring, Grendel, glowed with fiery glimmer. From the lakes and marshes comes the fire-drakes, or the will-o'-the wisp, and the wonderful St. Elmo light, and fiery dragons; Loki and Apollo, both sun-gods changed to fish. Aphrodite weds Hephaistus, fire-worker; Indus is fire and water-god; Varuna also. Fire controls water," etc. To these hints we may add that the sun in antiquity was supposed to rest at night in the ocean, and here, doubtless, is the cause of the splendor of these sea-palaces, and the hoard is stolen splendor from the lord of day.

These ideas also illustrate the fabled regenerative powers of the sea. The animals of the sea were also fabled to possess great regenerative powers, and the fish early became a phallical animal in folk-lore. The efficacy of sea-water in the rites of baptism has been stoutly main-tained, and its medicinal character and virtues often cele-brated.

This worship of water and this belief in it as the origin of all things is a natural one, and is very ancient. The early Aryans saw no difference between the waters of the air and the streams of the earth, and from adoring the sky and its many gods it became easy and natural for their descendants to worship the sea and its fancied gods, and to

* Contemporary Review, September, 1882.

fear it in its anger and propitiate its demons. From the primitive conception of the sea itself as a god, it was but a step to the notion that it was ruled by its resident deities, who must be worshiped and propitiated.

Water containing all the   of development, in it the future must be hidden; and thus we find its gods and its residents empowered to know the future. Thence arose a belief in the indications of waves and other natural phenomena, instances of which we shall often encounter in these pages.

But the mariner was more nearly concerned in the winds that raised these mighty waves and meteors, and the resources of his arts and prayers were expended to obtain favorable breezes, to allay the storm, or dissipate the calm. His principal deities had most to do with the winds that either brought him good fortune, or wreck and disaster.

Gods of the wind have ever been powerful divinities.

* " In the polytheism of the lower as of the higher races, the wind-gods are no unknown figures. The winds themselves, and especially the four winds in their four regions, take name and shape as personal divinities, while some deity of wider range, a wind-god, storm-god, air-god, or the mighty heaven-god himself, may stand as compeller or controller of breeze and gale and tempest." Neither time nor space can here be allotted to an extended study of the mythology of the winds, a subject ably treated by Cox, Brinton, Tylor and others, but it is pertinent to our purpose to give some brief account of the wind-gods, their powers and attributes.

Legends of the winds are so numerous, that a volume would scarcely contain them. We shall see the appearance of the spectre-ship and of the St. Elmo light connected with premonitions of wind and storm. These were only two of the many apparitions, that, like those of the moon and planets, were deemed indications of coming tempests, or prognostications of fair weather.

Doubtless the very name of wind, *animos* or *spiritus*, meaning also breath and soul, animal and spirit, favored the formation of legends concerning the winds, as we still see the outcome of these in the similarity between gust and ghost, the spirit in the breath being the spirit of the air. This has been observed of many languages.† The same

---

* Tylor.—Primitive Culture, II., 266.
† Brinton.—Myths of the New World.

words express wind, spirit, life and breath in Hebrew, Greek, Latin and other European tonges, as well as in Dacota, Choc-taw, Netela and Esquimaux. This resemblance of the air to the breath, of the wind to the soul, accounts for many legends connected with these subjects, and partly for the prominence given to the winds in mythology.

The ancients attributed to many of their gods power over the elements. Jupiter or Zeus, above all, brought tempests. As, says Homer,—

"Sudden the Thunderer blackens all the skies."

And Sophocles,—
"But Jove denies
A favorable wind."

As chief god and storm god, he controlled all other wind gods, and navigators sacrificed to him.

As Jupiter Pluvius, rains were sent by him. Poseidon or Neptune, Oceanus, Nereus, Pontus and other sea-gods raised storms, and sacrifices were made to them, and to the winds themselves, which were personified, and depicted according to their several characters.

*Eurus, the southeast, was a gay young man; Auster, the south wind, bringer of rain, a gloomy old man (whence our word *austere*); Zephyus, southwest, was figured as a young and gentle youth, and Boreas, the rugged north wind, as a rough and wild old man. Boreas was the principal storm wind, and to him numerous altars were erected.

The Greeks sacrificed to him when about to encounter the Persian fleet at Magnesium, and accounted its destruction as an answer to their prayers. Hesiod says Boreas, Zephyrus, and Notus were sent from heaven; the other winds were Typhonic.

These winds were controlled by Æolus in his wind cavern in the island of Æolia, and Æneas finds him,—

†"Where, in a spacious cave of living stone,
The tyrant Æolus, from his airy throne,
With power imperial curbs the struggling winds,
And sounding tempests in dark prison binds."

Æolus could confine the winds in a bag, and so for Æneas,—

"The adverse winds in leathern bags he braced,
Compressed their force and lock'd each struggling blast.'

* Murray.—Hand-book of Mythology.
† Dryden.—Æneid, Bk. I.

(So Abbuto, the ipanese wind-god, is depicted with a bag between his shoulders.)

He gave them to Ulysses, liberating the one fair wind, but the curious crew freed the others, and the ship was driven back again.

This abode of the winds changed from time to time. Diodorus Siculus says the priests of Boreas lived in Buto (Great Britain). There is a French tale of a Russian prince who entered a cave in a forest during a storm. He met an old woman, who informed him that this was the cave of the winds, and these soon after entered. With Zephyr, a handsome youth, the prince traveled to Felicity.

Virgil locates the cave of the winds at Lipari islands. Diodorus makes Æolus a real monarch of Sorrento, who invented sails and storm signals—ancient prototype of "Old Probabilities." His island,* Æolia, with its triple wall of brass and   t   delights, was a sort of terrestrial paradise; the first of many in Homer's poems.

Other Greek divinities were fabled to possess power over the winds. Poseidon, Amphitrite, and even inferior deities, as Triton, were said to possess this power to a limited extent. Minerva gave to Iphigenia a fair wind, from Tauris, and Vulcan sent a storm against the Argonauts, until the more powerful Juno interfered, when †

> " His bellows heave their windy sides no more,
> Nor his shrill anvils shake the distant shore."

So others possessed these magic powers. Calypso could control the winds, the Sirens invoke them, and Circe gave to Ulysses a fair wind ‡

> " A freshening breeze her magic power supplied,
> While the winged vessel flew along the tide."

The winds were doubtless anciently represented under other forms. For such is Orpheus, with his lyre, who charms fish, moves the Argo, and fixes the Symplegades. This wind-lyre is represented in folk-lore by numerous harps that have lured mermaids from their caves, or

> § " Harpit a fish out o' saut water."

* Keary.—Outlines, etc., p. 308.
† Ap. Rhodius, Argonautica.—Fawkes' Trans.
‡ Pope.—Odyssey. Bk. X.
§ Jamieson.—Scottish Ballads, 1-98.

* "Orpheus, who charms by his lyre, the Sirens with their alluring lay, and the piper, with his baneful tune, are but the wind."

Mercury or Hermes, the winged messenger, was doubtless the wind. The harpies were storm gusts, that with the two sons of Boreas, fight for the mastery. " This,"† says Ruskin, "in its literal form, means only the battle between the fair north wind and the foul south one." They were represented as foul birds. Amphion, Pan and Zethios represented the winds.‡

Storms and tempests came from Typhon. Hesiod says:§

"Lo! from Typhœus is the strength of winds."

‖ The Hermean zodiac from Egyptian temples shows us Typhon causing winds and lightning. He was the demon of the lower world, or night.

** Rimmon or Mirmir, was a Chaldean wind-god.

†† In Hindoo lore, the Ribhus were storm-demons, as also the Maruts, offspring of Rudrae, and attendants of Indra. Hamamunt is son of the winds, and travels on the storm-clouds. Another Vedaic storm-deity is Rudra or *Briga*, a word from the same root as brew. So the phrase " brewing a storm " has been referred to the soma, nectar, and ambrosia distilled at godlike banquets. In Germany, mists are yet said to be brewed by witches, elves, or dwarfs.

Vayu,‡‡ or Indra was, however, chief god of the winds and atmosphere. The winds, in Vedaic legends were twenty-one, each guarded by an elephant. The Pitris were wind-gods, and the Rakshasas, wolf-shaped storm demons.

§§ In Semitic lore, Samaël was a known storm-demon, and from his name we have the samiel or simoom. Zoroaster believed in a wind-causing spirit, Vato or Vad, a Dev, or evil one.

Semkail was also an oriental wind-god. We read in Mottalib,‖‖ "I keep the winds in awe with the hand which you see in the air, and prevent the wind Haidje from coming forth. With my other hand, I prevent the sea from overflowing."

* Fiske.—Myths and Myth-makers.
† Queen of the Air.
‡ Cox.—Aryan Mythology, II., 251.
§ Theogony.
‖ G. Massey.—Book of the Beginnings.
** Brewer.—Reader's Hand Book.
†† Kelly.—Indo-European Folk-lore.
‡‡ Keary.—Outlines of Primitive Beliefs, 142.
§§ Brewer.—Reader's Hand Book.
‖‖ History of Abd-el-Mottalib.—Trans. by Compte de Caylus, 1742.

Eight angels, subject to Solomon's will, rule the winds in Talmudic and Koranic legends.

Rabbinical* legends also tell of the Simorgue, a great bird that causes the wind by moving its wings. Béchard is a wind-causing demon in the "Clavicle of Solomon." †El Kazwini says: "The winds come from the bottom of the sea," as Pliny likewise asserts concerning Auster.

In Arab legend, Sakina, an angel, presides over the winds.

The Norse Sagas represent Odin as the great wind-god, who swept along the sky with a retinue of souls. The gusts preceding a storm were said to be the souls of women hunted by Odin and his gang.

From this legend doubtless descended the many tales of the wild huntsman, still heard in storms by the German peasant. ‡Carinthian and Swabian peasants still set out a bowl of meal for the wind-god in gales, saying, " There, meal thou hast for thy child, but thou must be off." These attendant demons of the winds are, like the Greek Harpies, gusts of the coming storm. Husi was the Finnish storm-demon, especially of the north wind, and was attended by a retinue of cats, dogs, etc. §In Russian peasant-tales, Vikhar is the whirlwind, flying as a bird in the gale, and stealing people away. The wind-demon was said to be attended by the souls of unbaptized children, and English peasants say they hear their wails.

The Wildhunt receives various names, and is known all over Europe. It is connected with Herodias, being " La Chasse Herode," and " Chasse Maccabei," with the Frei-schütz, being " Häckelbarend," or "Grand Veneur," and with the Wandering Jew, who is said to have appeared in it in Brittany, and caused tempests, etc., in 1604. ‖In Swabian folk-lore, the wind-demon is called Neck, and rides a stall-ion from the sea. They are the dogs** of Annwyn in Wales, and the Heath-hounds in ††Devonshire. Many other legends exist concerning the Wildhunt, but these need not detain us longer.

‡‡Odin rode his gray steed Sleipnir, the wind, only in bad weather, and on it passed over the ocean. Wodin's

* Brewer.—Reader's Hand Book.
† Marvels of Creation.
‡ Wuttke.—Deutsche-Volksaber glauben.
§ Ralston.—Russian Folk-lore.
‖ Blind.—In Cont. Rev., October, 1882.
** Sikes.—British Goblins and Welsh Folk-lore.
†† Mrs. Bray.—Legends and Traditions of Devonshire.
‡‡ Thorpe.—Northern Mythology.

day, or Wednesday, was long an unlucky one in the sea-man's calendar. He was also named Nikar, as we shall find. Often appearing as a favorable wind-giver, he was named *Oskabyrr*, or wish-wind. *Ogauban, the Norse Æolus, had the winds in a leathern bag.

†Odin's third son, Niörd, sails the waves and raises sea-storms. He was especially the mariner's god. To him was consecrated the *Spongia marina*, or "Neptune's goblets." Œgir (whence our ogre) was another Norse storm-god. I shall speak again of the goddess Helgi, who attacked Eric the pirate in a northerly storm of hail.

‡Kasi was also a Norse wind-god.

Norse legends represent the north wind as Hraesvelg, or "Corpse Devourer," in the guise of an eagle, and Scott says Shetlanders thought the north wind came from the movements of its wings, and made offerings to it.

§ " Where the heavens' remotest bound
With darkness is encompassed round,
There Hrasvelger sits and wrings
The tempest from its eagle wings."

This conception of the wind as a bird, or as caused by a bird, will often be met with in these pages. So Aquilo and Aquila, north wind and eagle, have the same derivation in Latin, as Vultur and Vulturnus also. ‖In the Hindoo Somadeva, Garuda's wings cause a storm. These birds are doubtless of angelic origin, and embody the idea of good spirits in the air in opposition to evil ones.

The winds are often personified in Norse folk-tales.

Tuulen-ty-bät ** is a Finnish wind-god, and sends good winds. Uiro-tadi and Ukko, the supreme god, also con-trolled the winds. The Circassian Seoseres was a wind-god as well as a water-god.†† Kamskatdales say Billukai, the supreme god, controls the winds.

‡‡ Esthonians called the wind-god Tuule-Ema (wind's mother). They say. "Wind's mother wails; who knows what mother will wail next?"

Poznisky was a Sclavonian wind-deity; Poswijd, Stryba,

*Grimm.—Teut. Mythology. p. 690.
†Sæmundic Edda, 18.
‡Grimm.—Teut. Mythology, 531.
§Sæmundr Edda Vafthrudnir mal, 37.
‖Grimm.—Teut. Mythology, 633.
** Castren.—Finnish Mythology, 37-68.
†† Steller.—Kamskatka, 266.
‡‡ Tylor.—Primitive Culture, 1-368.

and Vichera, Polish storm-deities, Okka Peernis was a Letton god of wind and sky.

*Stribog was an old Russian god of winds. Baba Yaga, a witch, moves in storms.

†In Cornish legends, the moaning of the wind is "the calling of the northern deep," and is said to be a certain Tregeagle, who sold himself to the devil, and is condemned to clean out Dosmary Pool. In carrying away sand, he is said to have dropped it and caused a bar in the harbor, and so the winds are called Tregeagle's roar. Penzance boatmen say the devil himself was carrying sand and broke his apron-string, thus causing the bar.

‡The winds were personified in Indian lore, and names given to represent their character. The great bear-slayer, Mudjeekeewis (west wind), was chief of all. Wabun, the east wind, young and beautiful, and Kabibonnokka, the north wind, fierce and terrible, with Shawondasee, the south wind, fat and lazy, were his children.

§Gaöh was Iroquois "father of the winds." The Utes say the winds are caused by the breathing of monstrous beasts in the south and north.

‖The Creeks called the Supreme Ruler the "master of breath"; Cherokees, the "eldest of winds." Huchtoli was the Choctaw storm-god. All Indian tribes regarded the winds as in the power of the spirits of the four cardinal points, and many represent them in bird form. Navajos say there are white swans at each point.

In the Palenque cross, the wind, as a bird, dominates over the north point. Dacotahs called the west the home of the spirit of the storm-breezes. The owl was the Chippeway spirit of the north wind, the butterfly, of the south. Algonquins said the thunder-spirit used one of the four winds as a drumstick to cause thunder. Iroquois Indians said the winds were caused by a water-lizard, and by the thunder-bird, Hahnes; and the Northern Piutes, by a water-god shaking his tail.

Dr. Brinton tells us that many tribes, from Algonquins to Peruvians, believed storms were caused by the struggles of four giants, who ruled the winds. Many of the legends of their origin and descent are connected with the winds,

* Ralston.—Russian Folk-lore.
† Hunt.—Romances and Drolls of the North of England.
‡ Brinton.—Myths of the New World.
§ Morgan.—Iroquois, 137.
‖ Brinton.

and in many instances their ancestors are identified directly with the winds. In Yucatan myths, four gods, identical with the winds, stood at the corners of the earth, like giant Atlantes. In Mandan legend, the four winds are as many gigantic tortoises; in Quiché, they are four maize-bring-ing animals. Kukalkan was a Maya lord of the four winds.

Mixcohuatl was a Mexican storm-god, the tropical whirl-wind, and *Quetzalcoatl also, "Lord of the four winds." Our word hurricane comes from the name of the Quiché god of storms, Hurakan,† and Incas believed the winds abode in a cave, the "House of Subsistence," as did the Iroquois.

Caribs say Maboyo, a demon, causes hurricanes, and Saracon is a bird, once a man, who raises storms.

The four Peruvian wind-gods were Manco, Cacha, Anca, and Uchao, and they arose from a lake.

Brazilian Tupi Indians said the winds were caused by Tupan, the Thunder-bird.

Greenland Esquimaux‡ say storms at sea are caused by a certain giant kayaker, who paddles on the water in his kayak, and raises tempests at will.

Sillam § Innua, owner of winds, Sillagiksartok, weather-spirit, and Sillam Aiparive, lord of winds, were also pos-sessed of power over the elements.

Polynesians had various wind-gods to whom fishermen and sailors sacrificed. ‖ Veromatantoru and Tairibu were worshiped in one group, and Ta-whiri-ma-tea in another. Maui, the chief Polynesian deity, was also a wind-god. ** Alo Alo was a Tongan storm deity. Sowaki was a New Zealand god of the elements, and Tokalam has a grove dedi-cated to his service in one of the Fiji islands, he being a great wind-god. Sacrifices were made to these gods, and the Fijians invoked their aid to destroy invading fleets.

The Chinese said dragons brought clouds, and tigers winds, and they believed the gusts in a typhoon to be caused by a dragon (Tin-mi-loong), "bob-tail dragon,"†† and say it is seen in them. The Japanese wind-god was

* Bancroft.—Native Races, p. 259, vol. iii.
† Bancroft.—Native Races, p. 475.
‡ Rink.—Tales and Traditions of the Esquimaux.
§ Cranz.—Grönland.
‖ Ellis's Polynesian Researches.
** Mariner.—Tonga, II, 15.
†† Grant.—Mysteries of all Nations, 56.

Abbuto, who had steel claws and tigerish countenance. The devil of King James's witches had an eagle's beak and steel claws, and cold blasts came from his wings.

*Futen, another Japanese storm deity, often figured in engravings and in temple statues, has the face and claws of a cat. Kama-Itachi, a kind of weasel, is represented as the whirlwind.

In the whirlwind the influence of the storm deities and demons was particularly recognized. In early German,† it was Zio (god). To-day it is swine-tail (Schweinazahl) a nick-name for the devil, or, as in Saalfield, Saxony and Markland, it is called, with the devil, Stöpke. Or it is Herodias whirling through the air, or " wind's bride " (winds-braut), or Freya chased by Odin and his gang. In Russia it is Vikhar, a sort of demon. It is also caused by lesser powers than these. In Russia witches are credited with originating it. Sorcerers also caused them, and in Celtic belief, fairies had a hand in them. In Scotland they were "a furl o' fairies ween." So in Poland it is a dance of evil fairies. By sticking a knife in one you get rich at your soul's expense,‡ and in Russia, Lyesby, a demon sometimes traveling in the whirlwind, was thus controlled.

Pau Puk-Keewis,§ the Algonquin magician, was the creator of the whirlwind.

The storm raising demon is particularly apparent in a Cornish legend, related by Bottrell.‖ A smuggler captain, unable to enter port, swears and tears his hair out, throwing it to the winds, as an offering to his fellow-demons, when the storm ceases. Popular belief on this subject is illustrated by the saying of **Burton: "The air is not so full of flies in summer as it is at all times of fiery devils, that stir up storms, cause tempests, etc." "Aeriall spirits or devils are such as keep quarter for the most part in the aire; (they) cause many tempests, thunder, lightning, tear oakes, etc."

We see by these examples of popular belief in wind-gods and storm demons that the sailor originated no new ideas, but adopted common beliefs concerning these wind-causers. His fighting off the water spout with black knives, finds its

*Greey.—The Wonderful City of Tokio.
†Grimm.—Teut. Mythology.
‡Ralston.—Songs of the Russian People, p. 3, 88.
§Schoolcraft.—Indian Tribes.
‖Traditions and Fireside Stories of West Cornwall.
**Anatomy of Melancholy.

analogy in the Russian ideas concerning the whirlwind. Did he sacrifice to his wind-gods, either by offerings or by ceremonies and prayers, what more was he doing than the mountaineer of the Alps or the French peasant, who prays for rain? In Normandy it was formerly a custom to fire silver bullets at a rain cloud to disperse it, and a Tyrolese mountaineer is recorded as firing his small cannon at the winds to calm them. Savages go still further, and threaten the wind. * Paraguayan Indians rush against them with fire-brands and clenched fists, Kalmucks fire guns at the storm demons. Namaguas and Aleuts shoot arrows into the storm cloud, and Zulu rain doctors whistle to the lightning to leave the skies.

Many notions existed concerning the influence of the planets on the weather. Among them is one, not yet by any means extinct, that the moon controls the weather. Says the Padrone in the " Golden Legend,"—

" For the weather changes with the moon,"

and Longfellow has thus preserved one of the most precious beliefs of sailor-lore.

Here, again, we are only in the current of popular ideas on the subject. Doctor Lardner † tells us: " many, it is true, may discard predictions which affect to define, from day to day, the state of the weather. There are few, however, who do not look for a change of the weather with a change of the moon. It is a belief nearly universal that the epochs of a new and a full moon are, in the great majority of instances, attended by a change of weather, and that the quarters, although not so certain, are still epochs when a change may be probably expected. No navigator, from the captain or master, to the commonest seaman, ever doubts for a single moment the influence of a new and full moon over fair weather and foul."

These and similar beliefs existed in antiquity.

‡ Varro, quoted by Pliny, says that a new moon with erect horns on the fourth day presages great storms at sea. " If a darkness comes over the moon's face, in whatever quarter it breaks, from that quarter wind may be expected." This latter is not far from true. He further says that if the new moon, on rising, has the upper horn obscured, rainy

* Farrar.—Primitive Customs. p. 2.
† Cabinet Cyclopædia.
‡ Nat. History, Bk. II, Ch. 39.

weather is presaged when the moon wanes; but if it is the lower horn, rain at full moon; if the middle of her crescent, at once will it rain. He also declares that obtuse horns at rising of the new moon presage frightful tempests. If the moon, while winds prevail, does not appear before the fourth day, stormy weather will continue. If it appear bright and flaming on the sixteenth day, violent tempests will result.

Virgil thus epitomizes these ancient beliefs,— .

> *"When first the moon appears, if then she shrouds
> Her silver crescent tipp'd with sable clouds,
> Conclude she bodes a tempest on the main,
> And brews for fields impetuous floods of rain;
> Or if her face with fiery flushing glow,
> Expect the rattling winds aloft to blow.
> But four nights old (for that the surest sign),
> With sharpened horns, if glorious then she shine,
> Next day, not only that, but all the moon,
> Till her revolving race be wholly run,
> Are void of tempests, both by land and sea,
> And sailors in the port their promis'd vows shall pay."

> "And that by certain signs we may presage
> Of heats and rains, and winds' impetuous rage,
> The Sovereign of the heavens has set on high
> The moon, to mark the changes of the sky."

The moon in her first or last quarter in the horizon is thought to betoken fair weather. This superstition existed also among the Indians. †Pliny says the fourth or fifth day of the new moon was particularly watched for indications of the weather, both in Rome and in Egypt. If the horns were then obtuse, it was considered a sign of rain; if sharp and erect, of wind from the direction of the highest horn; or high wind at night, if both were equal.

This reverence for the moon is without known beginning, extending back into antiquity. Isis, patron of navigation, is the moon also, and the influence of the moon on the tides, half guessed at, led observing men to attribute to it a great power in indicating weather.

Aratus asserts that the appearance of the moon affects the weather. Lucullus goes further in his ideas of the in-fluence of the moon, and asserts that oysters and shell-fish become larger during the increase than during the wane of the moon.

These ideas are perpetuated in more modern times.

*Georgic I, Dryden's Trans.
†Lib. II. Bk. 39.

*Bartholomeus says: "The moon is the mother of all humours, minister and lady of the sea."

†Newton calls her "Ladye of Moisture," and ‡Lydgate sings,—

> "Of Lucina, the moon, moist and pale,
> That many showers fro' heaven made availe."

Another old English author says: "The moone gathereth deawe in the aire, for she printeth the vertue of her moysture in the aire, and chaungeth the ayre in a manner that is unseene, and breadeth and gendereth deawe in the utter parts thereof."

§Bede intimates similar beliefs: "If she looks like gold in her last quarter, there will be wind; if on the top of the crescent black spots appear, it will be a rainy month; if in the middle, her full moon will be serene."

Alcuin calls the moon "the prophetess of the weather."

Shakspeare records the common beliefs in various places. In "Hamlet," ‖ she is

> "The moist star,
> Upon whose influence Neptune's empire stands."

In "Timon of Athens,"—

> "The sea's a thief, whose liquid surge resolves
> The moon into salt tears."

And again,—

> ** "Therefore the moon, the governess of floods,
> Pale in her anger, washes all the air."

In France, the moon on the fourth day indicates the weather for the month, and also in Belgium, while in Germany it is the third, fourth or fifth day. In France, "If the horns of the moon are turned toward the sea, there will be eruptions of the sea during the year." In Belgium, a flame-colored moon on the sixth day indicates a tempest. Many beliefs concerning the influence of the moon on plants and animals exist in most European countries, and need not be repeated here. The influence of the moon on the tides, and other natural phenomena connected with her appearance,

---

* De Proprietatis Rerum.
† Directions for the health of Magistrates and Scholars, 1574, in Douce, 1-167.
‡ Stories of Thebes, in Douce, l. c.
§ De Rerum Natura.
‖ Hamlet, Act I, Sc. 1.
** Midsummer Night's Dream, Act II, Sc. 2. See also Winter's Tale, I, 2.

~~doubtless~~ gave rise to many of these beliefs.   Marryatt says
~~fishermen~~ in England still think that fish spawned at full
moon, rot soon after being taken out of the water, and that
fish hung up in the moon soon decay.

Thomas[*] tells us that the Indians in New Jersey thought
the moon prognosticated the weather.   Many other savage
tribes have beliefs connected with the moon and the
weather.   Peruvians and Mexicans had their feast of water-
gods at full moon.

A circle about the moon has long been thought portentous.   Wet weather will follow, say the wise, the sooner the
smaller the circle.   This circle is in Cornwall a "burre," or,
"buiger."

[†]Falconer, in the "Shipwreck," says:

> "The waning moon, behind a wat'ry shroud,
> Pale glimmer'd o'er the long-protracted cloud;
> A mighty halo 'round her silver throne,
> Where parting meteors crossed, portentous shone:
> This in the troubled sky full oft prevails,—
> Oft deem'd a signal of tempestuous gales."

Varro says if the full moon have such a circle, it foretells
wind from the brightest quarter of the circle; if the circle
is double, the storm will be the more violent; and if there
are three, it will be a terrific gale.

In Scotland, this circle is called a "broch," or "brugh."

> [‡]"About the moon there is a brogh,
> The weather will be cold and rough."

And an English proverb reads, "The moon with a circle
brings water in her beak."

[§]In the dictionary of Dr. Jamieson we find this: "A
brugh or hazy circle around the moon is accounted a certain
prognostic of rain."

[‖]In the Shetland Islands, the lunar halo is called Van-
gar-for, interpreted, "rain-go-before."   A small bright circle is a "cockseye," and indicates unsettled weather.

Milanese and French proverbs assert that such a ring
around the moon announces rain; and a Calais saying runs:

> [**]"Circle round the moon,
> Sailors go aloft full soon."

* History of West New Jersey.
† Canto I.
‡ Swainson.—Weather-lore.
§ Jamieson.—Etymological Dictionary of the Scottish Language.—"Mone."
‖ Blend.—Contemporary Review, May-September, 1882.
** Swainson.—Weather-lore.

But a Breton proverb qualifies its effects:

> *" Never a circle to the moon
> Should send your topmasts down,
> But when it is around the sun,
> With all the masts it must be done."

A Spanish proverb runs thus: "The moon with her circle brings water in her beak." The same is believed in Pomcrania.†

Longfellow again interprets the sailor belief in this respect.

> ‡" I pray thee put into yonder port,
> For I fear a hurricane."
> "Last night, the moon had a golden ring,
> And to-night, no moon we see."

Lunar rainbows were equally portentous, not without some foundation. Moon-dogs indicate a change of weather in Whitby, England.

In the "Ancient Mariner," the moon gives omens unfortunate when

> "The rain poured down from one black cloud,
> The moon was at its edge."

Another superstition is embodied in the verse,—

> "Clomb above the eastern bar,
> The horned moon, with one bright star
> Within the nether tip."

And also Alan Cunningham,—

> "There's tempest in yon horned moon."

This "star-dogged moon" was long thought to be an ill omen, portending storms, and is still so regarded in Lancashire and at Torquay, England.

In a Scotch ballad, we read,—

> §"An ominous star sits above the bright moon."

And again, in a scene of wreck,—

> ‖"And the moon looked out
> With one large star by her side."

* Sebillot Litt. Orale de H. Bretagne.
† Tenne-Volkssagen aus. Pom.
‡ Golden Legend.
§ Cunningham.—Folk-lore of Scottish and English Peasants, p. 294.
‖ Cunningham.—Folk-lore of Scottish and English Peasants, p. 273.

4

call **this** dogging-star "Hurlbassy," and
tempests. "One star ahead of the moon
er, and one star chasing her, are signs of storm."[*]
an old ballad, "Sir Patrick Spence" (1281), we read:

> [†] " I saw the new moon late yestreen
> Wi' the auld moon in her arms,
> And if we gang to sea, maister,
> I fear we'll come to harm."

This appearance of the moon was long thought to portend tempests, and is still thought to do so in Scotland.

We have elsewhere alluded to the moon in her quarters
as a boat and as a sign of dry weather. If it is upset—that
is, the horns point downward—it will be rainy. In an old
English play, by Dekker,[‡] we find this:

> " My love, do you see this change i' the moon ?
> Sharpe hornes do threaten windy weather."

And a Scotch rhyme has it,—

> [§] " The horny moon is on her back,
> Mend your shoon and sort your thack."

Dr. Jamieson again says: "It is considered as an almost
infallible presage of bad weather, if the moon lies sair on
her back, or when her horns are pointed toward the zenith.
It is a similar prognostic when the new moon appears with
the auld moon in her arms."

[‖] English fishermen say you may hang your hat upon it
then. In Liverpool, it will rain when the horns are up, as
it is a boat full of water. We read in "Adam Bede": "Aye,
the moon lies sair on her back there. That's a sure sign of
fair weather!"

French and Italian proverbs say, "The moon eats the
clouds"; and modern seamen firmly believe that the moon,
when she rises in a storm, will soon eat up the clouds.
Many an old seaman has assured me of this during anxious
watches.

These beliefs concerning the influence of the moon are
still widespread. As Dr. Brinton[**] says: "As the moon is
associated with the dampness and dew of night, an ancient

---

[*] History of Carrickfergus, 1827.
[†] Chambers.—Scottish Ballads.
[‡] Match Me in London, Act I, Sc. 3, 145.
[§] Brand.
[‖] Dyer.—English Folk-lore, 39-40.
[**] Myths of the New World.

and widespread myth identifies her with the goddess of water. Moreover, in spite of the expostulation of the learned, the common people the world over persist in attributing to her a marked influence on the rain."

Science has nevertheless fully disproved many of these beliefs still current among landsmen as well as seamen.

Abbé Marcel, of Geneva, carefully investigated the changes of the moon in relation to the weather. In 742 lunar months, there were 2,630 changes of weather, 93 at new moon, 90 at full moon, 109 the day after full, 107 the day after new moon, so that the proportion of change of weather at new moon was 0.125, at full moon 0.12.

Toaldo collated the weather observations made at Padua for forty-five years. He called the changes three days before and after. He found the proportion of change of weather at change of moon, 6.7 at new moon, 5.6 at full, and 2.3 at the quarters. But his interval is too long to be of any value, and his conclusions are rejected by Dr. Lardner, who fully investigated the subject, and disproved the supposed influence of the moon.

With regard to halos, a paper published in the *Quarterly Journal of Meteorology*, by two distinguished English meteorologists, analyzes extended observations of these, amounting to 155 solar and 61 lunar halos, during the six years ending June, 1881. Of the 155 solar observations, rain fell 81 times on the same day, 31 the day after and not at all 26 times. Of the 61 lunar observations, rain fell 34 times on the first day, 6 on the second day, and not at all 8 times. Rain fell within 48 hours, with the wind at south or west, in 80 per cent. of the solar halos, and within 3 days in nearly all of the observations of lunar halos. But this was in England, in a wet climate, where rain was nearly sure to fall within these periods, and near London, where the atmosphere was damp, and halos more common.

With regard to the moon's effect in clearing up the clouds, we must be credulous, notwithstanding the assurances of Mr. Park Harrison, who, in 1868, assured the British Association of Sciences, that the moon at full did help to clear up the clouds, the difference of reflected heat between full and new moon being two degrees, sufficient to clear up the clouds.

Many other beliefs with regard to the moon's power over the waters are alluded to in these pages, testifying to the universality of these legends. In astrology she was the

sign for sailors and nautical folk.   She is found hereafter
connected with the cat, the dolphin, and with mermaids,
and other weather-prophets.   These analogies lead, doubtless, to many of the beliefs concerning the moon.   *" To the
ancients the moon was not a lifeless ball of stones and
clods; it was the horned huntress Artemis, coursing
through the upper ether, or bathing herself in the clear
lake; or it was Aphrodite, protectress of lovers, born of the
sea-foam in the east near Cyprus."

The sailor but reflected, and perhaps, as in most of his
beliefs, perpetuated, ancient ideas on this subject.

Clouds were also closely studied by early navigators; but
their indications being more real, we may expect to find
fewer traditions and legends connected with them in sailor-
lore.   The long, striated clouds that appear in fine weather,
extending nearly across the sky, are called " Noah's ark,"
and if they extend from east to west, they portend a dry
spell; if from north to south, wet weather.

Shooting-stars are thought, in parts of England, to foretell tempests.

So Virgil, in the " Georgics,"—

> "And oft, before tempestuous winds arise,
> The seeming stars fall headlong from the skies."

Pliny and Aristotle both say comets cause winds and
great storms, and a prejudice against these harmless wanderers yet exists in many quarters.

Homer says:

> "As the red comet, from Saturnius sent,
> To fright the nations, with a dire portent
> (A fatal sign to armies in the plain,
> Or trembling sailors on the wintry main.)"

And again,—

> " The blazing star
> Threatening the world with famine, plague and wars
> To sailors storms."

Proctor says no comet is here meant, the words being
mistranslated.   It is only,—

> "A bright star sent by the crafty son of Kronos."

Diodorus says of Timoleus' expedition to Sicily, B.C. 344:
" The gods announced by a remarkable portent his success

*Gubernatis.—Zoölogical Mythology.

and future greatness. A blazing star appeared in the heavens at night, and went before the fleet of Timoleus until he arrived in Sicily."

Bede says that they portend bad weather, but they have, in modern times, no influence at all over the weather, and their appearance has long ago lost its terrors along with that of the eclipse, long an auspicious omen to landsmen and sailor alike.

CHAPTER II.

THE DEITIES, SAINTS AND DEMONS OF THE DEEP.

Have sight of Proteus rising from the sea,
Or hear old Triton blow his wreathèd horn."
Wordsworth.

' The timber that frames his faithful boat,
Was dandled in storms on the mountain peaks,
And in storms with a bounding keel will float,
And laugh when the sea-fiend shrieks."
John Sterling—" The Mariner."

THE sea, no less than the land or the air, has been peopled with many imaginary beings, some inhabitants simply, others ruling or controlling spirits for good or evil. Not only in antiquity have these beliefs prevailed, but traces still linger in maritime language and tradition, of these wide-spread ideas of good and evil spirits,—of thinking and sentient beings, having a home beneath the wave.

In the present chapter appear the Deities and Demons who ruled or controlled the waves, and to whom the prayers, fears, and hopes of the mariner have been specially directed. It is not possible to treat fully of the subject in the limits of a single chapter, so little more will be done than to mention these deities and relate their principal attributes.

It is among the nations of antiquity, as also among the less cultivated peoples that now inhabit the globe, that we find the greater part of these legends.

The first of these beings, is found in the meagre accounts of the nations that first inhabited the plains between the Euphrates and Tigris rivers. *Prominent among Babylonian deities was Hea, or Hoa, called " Deity of the Abyss," who had temples in *Ur* and other maritime cities. He was also lord of arts, and taught them to men. Sennacherib, when about to undertake a maritime expedition down the Tigris, offered to this god a golden boat, a golden fish, and a golden coffer. Akkad inscriptions call him *Nukim-nut*, "great inventor," " Lord," "Great Master," etc. He was also ruler of Hades and the lower world. Daokina, his spouse, was goddess of the deep. Lenormant says *Hea* means fish.

Nor is this the only tradition of this semi-divine sea-monster.

Assyrian records tell of a similar deity, On, or Oannes, who possessed like attributes. Alexander Polyhistor,† quoting from earlier writers, says, " In the first year there made its appearance from a part of the Erythræan Sea an animal endowed with reason, who was called Oannes (according to the account of Apollodorus). The whole body of the animal was like that of a fish, and had under its fish head another head, and also feet below similar to that of a man, subjoined to the fish's tail." Six such monsters are said to have afterward arisen from the Persian Gulf, and Berosus tells that a semi-demon, Annedotes, very like Oannes, arose from the sea during the historical period.

‡ " In his time (King Amnemus) a monster named Idotia again issued from the Erythræan Sea, with a form which was a mingling of man and fish."

" During his reign (Daronos) there again issued forth from the Erythræan Sea four monsters."

"And under him (Edoranchos) appeared one more, rising from the Erythræan Sea, and being a mixture of man and fish, whose name was Odala."

Abydenus also tells of them, but calls them by different names. We also hear of them through Pindar, Hyginus and Helladius.

Photius Byblius says: " He (Helladius) relates the fable of a man named Oes, who came out of the Erythræan Sea, having the perfect body of a fish, with the head, arms and feet of a man, and who taught astronomy and letters. Some say that he had come out of the primeval egg, whence his

* Lenormant.—Ancient History of the East. Eng. Trans.
† Lenormant.—The Beginnings of History, 1883.
‡ Berosus, in Lenormant.—The Beginnings of History.

name, and that he was altogether a man, but resembled a fish, having dressed himself in the skin of a whale."

* Berosus again says, "This being (Oannes), in the day-time, used to converse with men, but took no food at that season, and he gave them an insight into letters and sciences and every kind of art. He taught them to construct houses, etc. In short, he instructed them in everything which could tend to soften manners and humanize mankind. When the sun set, it was the custom of this being to plunge again into the sea, and abide all night in the deep, for he was amphibious.'

The account of Helladius probably hints at a solution of the whole mystery, which is important, as here is doubtless the birth of the whole generation of mermen and tritons. † Gesenius thinks the story typifies the arrival of a more cultured race through the Red Sea; Neibuhr, that the description is of a man clothed in a fish-skin.

In a succeeding chapter,‡ we shall find an analogous case, where the arrival of a conquering race is concealed under a tradition of sea-men or sea-monsters. Here, doubtless, the same thing is meant. These traditions preserve the memory of invasions of superior races, probably coming through the Persian Gulf. Portions of their dress might consist of the skin of the shark or other fish.

§ Layard and Botta found, among the remains of Nineveh and Babylon, huge statues of divinities very like these just described. They represented a man with a fish-skin covering his back, the head forming a kind of mitre above his head, and the tail protruding below.

Nin, the chief Nineven deity, was a sort of Hercules, Saturn and Neptune.

‖ A hymn also exists to *Kho-tum-ku-ku*, daughter of the Ocean.

**Another marine deity of the Babylonians was Derceto, or Atergatis. The moon was her emblem, and she plunged into the sea to escape the god of evil. Semiramis was traditionally her daughter.

Derceto became a Syrian deity, and Damascus and Hieropolis were chief seats of her worship.

---

* Blind.—Scottish, Shetland and other Water-gods. Cont. Rev., Sept., 1881.
† Cary.—Ancient Fragments.
‡ See Chap. iii.
§ See Layard's Nineveh.
‖ Records of the Past.
** Cox.—Aryan Mythology, Bk. II., Ch. 2.

* Berosus tells us that a goddess, Homoroka, reigned over the fish in the sea, and she was called in Chaldaic Thalath, or in Greek Thallassa (the sea).

The Assyrian fish-god became the Phœnician and Syrian Dagon, which Milton thus characterizes,—

> "Dagon his name; sea monster, upward man,
> And downward fish."

Dagon, philologists tells us, is from a word meaning fish (*Dag*).

The ancient Egyptians were not sea-faring, so we find few water deities among them.

Isis, the Egyptian Moon-goddess, spouse of the Sun, closely resembled Derceto. Although not strictly a sea-goddess — for the ancient Egyptians feared and detested that element—she was patroness of navigation; her cult was borrowed by the Romans, and her feast, on the 5th of March, was made the chief festival of navigators.

Num was the Egyptian lord of the water, god of the Nile, their ocean, and to him were dedicated the sacred barks, and festivals were held in his honor by the boatmen of the Nile.† It was believed that he appeared in the river as late as the sixth century.

The Phœnicians, the chief mariners of early antiquity, had numerous gods of the sea. Derceto has been spoken of, and also Dagon, whose worship among the Philistines is often alluded to in Holy Writ. Astarte was the chief Sidonian goddess. She was the Venus of Semitic lands, also called Ishtar, or Ashtaroth, and was venerated by mariners. The Cabiri, famous gods of learning and arts, were, in Syrian legend, inventors of navigation. Some writers affirmed them direct descendants of Noah, hence naturally protectors of navigators. There were several of them, and figure-heads, called *pataikoi*, were placed on the prows of Phœnician vessels to represent them. Many of the attributes of the Cabiri were transferred to the Dioscuri, or twin sons of Leda.

On the coins of Ascalon, Derceto was figured with the moon above her head, and at her feet a woman with fish-tail.

Diodorus says, "The goddess, which by the Syrians is called Dercetus, has the face of a man, but the rest of the image is the figure of a fish." Lucian says, "The upper

* Cory.—Ancient Fragments.
† Simocatta, VI, 16, in Maury.—"Magie."

half was the perfect figure of a man; the lower part, from the thighs downward, terminated in the tail of a fish."

The Greeks were, of all antiquity, chiefest nation at sea, so we may readily expect to find among their pantheon of gods, a great number of deities of the watery element.

*Coming, then, to the better Greek sea-gods, we have Poseidon first of all, god of the sea and master of the watery element. He was fabled son of time, (Kronos), and flood (Rhea). Herodotus says he came from Libya, but some philologists say his name is connected with Si-don (Ship of On); others with potamos (river). He was god of the sea (Mediterranean) and ruler of the water, whether of cloud or of earth streams. He gathered clouds, raised and calmed the waves, sent storms, but granted safe voyages, and all other divinities of the sea were subject to him. He was inventor of the ship, and, curiously enough, created the horse and bull—carriers on land. Arion, Scyphios, Pegasus and the golden-fleeced ram of Phryxus were his offspring. He dwelt with the other gods on Olympus, but had a palace at Ægea under the waves. Numerous temples were dedicated to him, but chief among them were those on the capes of Sunium, Tænaria and at Corinth. He was represented as a severe old man, bearing in his hand a long trident, and riding in his car, drawn by horses or dolphins, and attended by Tritons, Nereids, and other marine monsters. Black and white bulls were favorite sacrifices to him, as says Virgil,—

> "There hecatombs of bulls—to Neptune slain,
> High flaming, please the monarch of the main.'

for to Neptune, the Latin god of the sea, were transferred in later times most of the attributes of Poseidon.

Virgil gives us this picture of the marine monarch,—

> † " Where'er he glides
> His finny coursers, and in triumph rides,
> The waves unruffle, and the sea subsides.
> His finny team Saturnian Neptune join'd,
> Then adds the foamy bridle to their jaws,
> And to the loosen'd rein permits the laws.
> High on the waves his azure car he guides;
> Its axles thunder and the sea subsides,
> And the smooth ocean rolls her silent tides;
> The tempests fly before their father's face,
> Trains of inferior gods his triumphs grace,
> And monster whales before their master play,
> And choirs of Tritons crowd the wat'ry way."

*Cox.—Aryan Mythology, II., 282.   Dryden.—Æneid, Bk. V

Prayers and sacrifices were made by Greek, Roman and Phœnician mariners to him, not only before setting out on a voyage, but also in case of calms, and after safely returning from a voyage.

Menelaus, in "Iphigenia in Tauris," says:

> "O Neptune,
> Who in the ocean dwell'st, and ye, chaste daughter
> Of Nereus, to the Nauplian coast convey
> Me and my consort, from this hostile land!"

He is represented as occasionally warring with deities of the shore, thus typifying the changes wrought by the waves of the sea; and from his realm come those marine monsters, the Bellerophon, the Andromeda monster, and others, certainly representing the incursions of breakers and waves. Amphitrite is his consort, and Triton, one of his sons, always attended upon him. Many legends were, in course of time, gathered together concerning him by the later poets and mythographers.

When Æolus wrecked the Trojan fleet, Neptune thus rebuked him:

> *"Hence to your lord my royal mandate bear,
> The realms of ocean and the fields of air
> Are mine, not his. By fatal lot to me
> The liquid empire fell, and trident of the sea."

†Amphitrite, Poseidon's fair consort, was also powerful at sea. She was figured as a beautiful woman, with a net on her hair, and crabs' claws on her forehead. She generally appeared in Neptune's car, but sometimes rode a marine animal. Her statue was in Corinth.

‡Oceanus resided in the ocean-stream that was fabled everywhere to encompass the known world, and his palace was far to the westward, toward the setting sun. From him proceeded all the watery element—rivers, lakes and seas. He was the ocean personified. He was rather a powerful monarch than a god, but to him mariners sacrificed with great care on going on long voyages. He is represented as an old man, seated on the sea, and dwelt in its depths.

> "Where aged Ocean holds his watery reign."

* Dryden.—Æneid.
† Cox.—Aryan Mythology, II, 6.
‡ Iliad, XIV, 346; XXI, 195.

*Tethys was his consort, and the Oceanids, three thousand ocean nymphs, his daughters. Libations and sacrifices were made to them.

†Oceanus is the personification of the sea itself, first imagined to surround the earth like a river, never ending.

‡Proteus und Nereus were two divinities residing in the deep sea, only inferior to Neptune. Both were gifted with wisdom, but Proteus could change his shape at will. (Apollodorus asserts this of Nereus, also.)

> " Proteus, a name tremendous o'er the main,
>   The delegate of Neptune's watery reign "

says Homer; and Virgil further tells us:

> § " In the Carpathian bottom makes abode
>   The shepherd of the sea, a prophet and a god;
>   High o'er the main in watery pomp he rides,
>   His azure car and finny coursers guides,
>   Proteus his name. "

He traditionally kept the seals belonging to his father (Neptune's) herds. To him Telemachus resorted for advice.

Camoens speaks of

> | " The consecrated waters of the deep
>   Where Proteus' cattle all their gambols keep."

Proteus possessed this power of changing his shape at will (a characteristic of all the water-people) to the greatest extent; hence our word *protean*.

**Nereus, son of Pontus, was a prophetic sea-god, and father of the Nereids, the nymphs of the wave, fifty in number. Amphitrite and Thetis, both ocean queens, were among the number. Nereus is represented as an old man. with long flowing hair, and he dwelt in the Ægean Sea, in a beautiful palace.

††The Nereids were ocean-naiads. The names are from the same root, and are connected with naval, nix, Niobe, and other maritime words. The Nereids represent the qualities and properties of the sea, and are represented as half woman, half fish. They are, therefore, the ancestors of

* Cox.—Aryan Mythology, II, 6.
† Keary.—Outlines of Primitive Belief.
‡ Cox.—Aryan Mythology, II, 256.
§ Georgics IV.—Dryden's Translation.
| Lusiad, I, 19.
** Cox.—Aryan Mythology, Bk. II, p. 256.
†† Cox.—Aryan Mythology, Bk. II, Ch. 6.

a tribe of mermaids, such as we shall meet farther on. They attended the superior gods, and had altars on the sea-shore, where sacrifices were made to them. They came out of their dwellings when the waves arose. Anciently they were represented as very beautiful. Polybius first gave them the fish-tail.

They assisted the Argonauts, when sent by Juno.

> *"Here o'er the sailing pine the nymphs preside,
> While Thetis' forceful hands the rudder guide,
> As oft in shoals the sportive dolphins throng,
> Circling the vessel as she sails along."

Panope and Thetis were especially invoked by sailors.

†Aphrodite possessed limited powers over the waves. Her name is derived from *Aphros*, foam, and, like Derceto and Atergatis, she sprang from the sea. Hesiod says:‡

> "Her gods and men
> Name Aphrodite, goddess of the foam,
> Since in the sea-foam nourish'd."

> "Thy imperial sway extends
> O'er the wide seas."

§She represents the dawn, and, in her car, is attended by the Hours and Graces. She first landed at Cythera, and Cyprus was the chief seat of her worship. She became the goddess of love, and, as Venus in Rome, lost many of her maritime attributes. Temples were numerous to her, especially at Athens, Sparta, and among the islands of the Grecian Archipelago. A rude stone first represented her, but later artists carved those beautiful representations, a few of which still exist. She had various surnames as goddess of the sea, all connected with it, as Pontia, Epipontia, Eualia, Marina, Pelagia, Thalassia, and Pontogenia. Living sacrifices were seldom offered to her.

Phorcus was another sea-divinity. He represents the whitening sea-foam. He was keeper of marine monsters, and his consort was Keto (whale).

Zeus, or Jupiter, as great god of the heavens and air, was powerful above all other gods on land or at sea. Storms were sent by him, and mariners sacrificed to him. At the Bosphorus was an altar to Zeus Quirnos, sender of favorable winds.

* Appolonius Rhodius.—Argonautics. Fawkes' Trans.
† Cox.—Mythology Aryan Nations, Bk. II, Ch. 2.
‡ Hesiod.—Theogony.
§ Cox.—Aryan Mythology, Bk. II.

*Sophocles says:

> " Jove desires a favoring breeze."

Juno, nurtured by Oceanus, was also a favorite of mariners.   Homer says:

> † " By Juno's guardian aid, the watery vast
> Secure of storms, your royal brother passed."

She is said to have driven Hercules out of his course by raising a storm.

To the Argonauts:

> ‡ " Juno, propitious to her favorite crew,
> Inspir'd the breezes that serenely blew."

Alcyone, when her husband was in danger, prays to her for aid:

> §"All pow'rs implored, but far above the rest,
> To Juno she her pious vows address'd,
> Her much-lov'd lord from perils to protect,
> And safe o'er seas his voyage to direct."

‖ Minerva, or Athene, reputed author of navigation, and builder of the ship "Argo," was especially reverenced by Attic mariners.   As a warlike goddess, she was especial patroness of military seamen.

When incensed against the Greeks,—

> ** " Hence on the guilty race her vengeance hurl'd,
> With storms pursued them through the liquid world."

And she assures Telemachus,—

> †† " My power shall guard thee, and my hand convey;
> The winged vessel studious I prepare,
> Through seas and realms, companion of thy care."

She was reputed daughter of Jupiter, and was also called Pallas.   Hence when Ulysses is beset by storms, we read,—

> ‡‡ " Jove's daughter, Pallas, watched the favoring hour;
> Back to their caves she bade the winds to fly,
> And hushed the blustering brethren of the sky."

* Iphigenia in Tauris.
† Odyssey, Bk. IV. Pope's Trans.
‡ Appolonius Rhodius.—Argonautica.
§ Ovid.—Metamorphoses.
‖ Cox.—Aryan Mythology, Bk. II, Ch. 2.
** Pope's Odyssey, Bk. V.
†† Pope's Odyssey, Bk. IV.
‡‡ Pope's Odyssey, Bk. V.

In the later Greek period, her worship increased, and she finally usurped the place of Poseidon, as chief Mariner's deity.

Æolus, as lord of the winds, had power over the deep, and

> *"His word alone the listening storms obey
> To smooth the deep, or swell the foamy sea,"

although he was subject to Jupiter, and responsible to Neptune and other superior deities.

Greek mariners also venerated the other winds, and sacrificed to them, to Boreas especially, as we saw in the last chapter.

†Artemis, or Diana, possessed limited power at sea, and, as goddess of the chase, was especially adored by fishermen. Says Virgil,—

> "As Helenus enjoin'd, we next adore
> Diana's name, protectress of the shore."

She was a moon-goddess, supposed to be the same as Isis, whom we have seen as an especial patron of navigation. The Tauri, in the Crimean peninsula, worshiped a goddess corresponding to her, and sacrificed shipwrecked strangers to her. The Greek fleet, sailing for Troy, were wind-bound, and were commanded by a soothsayer to sacrifice Iphigenia to Diana, but a goat was eventually substituted. Fish were sacred to Diana.

Apollo, the great god of the Delphic temple, was especially venerated by mariners, and had numerous seaside temples. Upon Mount Actium stood his statue, visible far at sea, at once a guide and a safeguard to mariners. Augustus sacrificed to it before the great battle fought there. A celebrated temple to him stood on Mount Leucas, alike also visible far at sea. As Apollo Delphinius, in the guise of a dolphin, he conducted a ship-load of sailors to his sanctuary, where they became his priests.‡

Priapus, god of fertility, was also venerated by fishermen.

Glaucus was also a fisherman's deity, and was a son of Poseidon. Camoens tells us he was

> "The god who once the human form did know,
> And by the power of poisonous herb was made
> To take the shape of fish."

* Pope's Odyssey, Bk. V.
† Cox.—Aryan Mythology, Bk. II, Ch. 6.
‡ Cox.—Aryan Mythology, Vol. II, p. 25.

* He was fabled a fisherman, and observing that half-dead fish bit the grass and were revived, he attempted it and became a fish. It was a belief in Greece that once a year he visited all the coasts and islands, prophesying. He is represented as an old man, dripping with water from his hair and beard, his breast covered with sea-weed, and the lower part of his body fish-shaped. He represented the play of fantastic waves. He had a hand in building the mystic ship "Argo."

† Ino, or Leucothea, and her son Melicertes, or Palæmon, were also dcities of the sea, being made such by Poseidon. Ino threw herself into the sea with her son, to escape one of the Furies. As Leucothea she appeared to Odysseus when wrecked, and saved him. She was invoked to save from wreck, and so was Palæmon, who is figured riding on a dolphin. Ino was granddaughter to Poseidon.

Portumnus was the Roman god of harbors, and a grand temple was raised to him at Ostia, and a festival annually held there on the 7th of August.

The Dioscuri, or twin sons of Leda, and brothers of Helen, were universally revered by mariners. We shall see them appearing to the Argonauts as stars, and another legend says they took part in the expedition. They were able to avert shipwreck and to save wrecked people. The legends concerning their agency in the St. Elmo light will be related. In Sophocles' "Electra," Castor says,—

> "But we with speed to the Sicilian deep,
> To guard the adventurous barks of those who stem
> The ocean, must repair."

And Horace:

> ‡ "Thus the twin stars indulgent save
> The shatter'd vessel from the wave."

Likewise, from Appolonius Rhodius:

> § "Ye guardian twins, who aid our great designs,
> By humble prayer the heavenly powers incline,
> To steer me safe to each Ausonian bay."

> "Safeguards of sailors, who the twins implore
> When on the deep the thundering tempests roar."

* Cox.—Aryan Mythology, Vol. II, 257.
† Cox.—Aryan Mythology, Vol. II, 205.
‡ Carmina Bk. IV, ode 8.
§ Appolonius Rhodius.—Argonautics.   Fawkes' Trans.

* And Theocritus:

> "Still you the wreck can save, the storm dispel,
> And snatch the sailors from the jaws of hell,
> The winds disperse, the roaring waves subside,
> And smooth to stillness, sleeps the lunar tide."

Hyginns says Neptune conferred upon them the power of aiding mariners, and Pausanius calls them *Anactes* (chiefs). They were made constellations, as Gemini.

Triton was also an inferior sea-deity. He was a son of Poseidon, and dwelt in the sea. Was powerful at sea, and could calm the waves. He is generally shown blowing a shell, and is figured man above, and fish below, the waist. He often attends upon Poseidon's car. There were in later times a crowd of Tritons, half man and half fish, and the name was afterwards used to indicate the merman.

Triton says to the Argonauts:

> † "Hear, from my sire, the monarch of the main;
> I boast my science; o'er these scenes I reign."

Triton is thus described by Appolonius.

> ‡ "His every limb, down to his swelling loin,
> Proclaim'd his likeness to the powers divine;
> Below his loins, his tapering tail extends,
> Arched like a whale's, on either side it bends."

Pliny represented him with a single tail, like a dolphin, with hands like shells, and head covered with them, and with green eyes. Pausanius says: " I have seen another Triton among the curiosities of the Romans, but it is not so large as this of the Tanagrians. The form of the Triton is this: the hair of the head resembles the parsley that grows in marshes; the rest of their body is rough with small scales; they have fish-gills under their ears; their nostrils are those of a man, but their teeth are broader and like those of a wild beast; their eyes seem to me azure, and their hands, fingers and nails are of the form of the shells of shell-fish; they have, instead of feet, fins under their breast and belly, like those of the porpoise."

Sometimes they are figured with the forefeet of a horse.

Cybele was also a maritime deity. Mopsus says:

* Idyllica.—Fawkes' Trans.
† Appolonius Rhodius.—Argonautics. Fawkes' Trans.
‡ Appolonius Rhodius.—Argonautics. Fawkes' Trans.

5

* " Haste, to the fane of Dyndimus repair,
There Cybele with sacrifices implore,
So will the winds tempestuous cease to roar."

Doris, wife of Nereus, and mother of the Nereids, was a divinity of note among mariners, who also venerated the gods of their particular district. Rivers were deified, and many had priests dedicated to their service.

Among the ancestors of the Greeks, we also find maritime deities; not, however, so abundant, nor so universally worshiped. The early Aryans were acquainted with the Caspian Sea, but most of their maritime deities are gods of the atmospheric sea. In fact, we find that they, like their descendants, confounded the aerial and the aqueous seas. As Kelly says, † " The origin of most water-gods and nymphs of the European Aryans may be traced back to the storm and rain deities of the parent stock, and the greater part of the myths relating to the sea are to be understood as primarily applying, not to the earthly, but the cloud-sea, for no other great collection of waters was known to the first Aryans in their inland home."

‡So we find Indra, god of the firmament, and chief deity of the atmosphere, governing the weather and dispensing thunder, lightning and rain. He was the ruler of the storm. Rudra, " howler," or " terrible," was, however, directly god of storms, the father of the Maruts, and sender of numerous ills. He controlled the winds, his children.

But Varuna, " coverer," was god of the seas and rivers, the Indian Neptune. §A fish was his sign, the wind his breath. He was rather god of the heavenly sea, but soon became lord of all waters. Like Neptune, he provided a home for man. He has other names, meaning lord of the waters (Kesa), watery hair (Vari-lowa), and king of aquatic animals (Yadah-pati). His wife Varuni sprang from the ocean, and is also goddess of wine.

Varuna is represented as an old man, with a club and a noose.

‖Vayu is the Hindoo Zephyr. His name means wind. He is closely associated with Indra, and often rides in his chariot. He is also called Marut.

* Appolonius Rhodius.—Argonautica. Fawkes' Trans.
† Curiosities of Indo-European Traditions.
‡ Cox.—Aryan Mythology, Vol. I, p. 386.
§ Cox.—Aryan Mythology, Vol. I p. 330.
‖ Keary.—Outlines of Primitive Belief, 142.

* The Maruts are sons of Rudra, or of Indra, and are storm-gods, variously stated as from twenty-seven to one hundred and eighty in number. They are armed with thunderbolts, and are feared as storm-bringers.

† The Apsaras are nymphs of the heavenly sea. Their name signifies "moving in the waters." Originally personifications of the vapors and cloud-mists, they became the houris of the Hindoo heaven. They are also called Nâvyah, or celestial navigators. The Ramayana says (Wilson),—

> "Then from the agitated deep upsprung
> The legion of Apsarases, so named
> That to the watery element they owed
> Their being."

‡ Lakshmi, like Aphrodite, sprang from the sea-foam and floated ashore on the lotus at creation. She was the fisherman's goddess, and had four arms.

The Scandinavian gods of the sea may next claim our attention. So maritime a people could not but have many deities of the watery element.

§ Odin, the all-father, and most powerful god, sent storms and controlled the waves. As such a powerful god, storm and rain bringer, he became Hnickar, and we shall find him again when we consider the demons of the sea. Odin visited Sigurd's ship in this guise, boarding it from an island at sea, and the storm ceased on his landing.

He is the Psychopomp, or Soul-carrier, of Norse Mythology, and, granting safe voyages to the soul, naturally became a maritime god.

∥ Thor, Odin's son, ruled the tempest and clouds, sent thunder, and dashed the waves against the coast. He raised a storm and sank the great sea-serpent Jormungandr to the bottom of the ocean.

But Niörd (the Nereus of the North) was chief god of the ocean. He was also called Vanagir and Mördur. He dwelt in Noätun, "place of ships," ruled the ocean and wind, had fishing and maritime pursuits under his care, was invoked by sailors and fishermen, and sacrifices were made to him by sea-coast people. He represents the mild sea of the coast. His wives were Nerthus and Skadi (hurtful), and

* Keary.—Outlines of Primitive Belief, 149.
† Kelly.—Curiosities of Indo-European Traditions, 31.
‡ Cox.—Aryan Mythology, Bk. II, Ch. 8.
§ Thorpe.—Northern Mythology, Vol. I, p. 96.
∥ Thorpe.—Northern Mythology, Vol. I, pp. 94 and 195; Saemundr Edda, 20.

the latter came from Thrymheim, home of the winds. Their children, Freyr and Freya, were powerful at sea, and were worshiped by sailors.

*Freya was in Shetland *Vana-dis*, or water-goddess, and her day, Friday, has been sacred to sailors for centuries, and hence an unlucky one for voyages.

†The representative of Oceanus, the dweller in the deep sea, was Œgir (*ogre*, terrible), or Hler, the god of the raging sea, whose waves boil with his kettle. His wife was Ran (plunder, robbery), and his nine daughters, the waves. Ran is the northern Amphitrite. She takes in her net all persons drowned at sea, and even lurks beneath the ice for them. "Fara til Râna" (go to Ran) meant to drown.

Thus we find, in Tegnér's "Frithjof's Saga,"—

‡"Let none go empty-handed
Down to azure Ran.
Icy are her kisses,
Fickle her embraces.
But we'll charm the sea-bride
With our ruddy gold."

"For us, in bed of ocean
Azure pillows Ran prepares."

§"May Rana keep
Them in the deep,
As is her wont."

Œgir's name is from the same root as that from which Ocean is derived, and the ogre of the nursery becomes the *orca* or sea-monster of the middle agès, and possibly the *roc*, that bird of terror to middle-age travelers.|

Other European peoples have had their divinities of the sea. Holda, an old German goddess, could ride on sea and waves, and was feared by sailors.** Fasolt is invoked as god of storms in an old formula, his brother Ecke ruled over waves and floods, and Merment was also a storm-deity.

Ecke, says Grimm,†† was the same as Œgir. So Niörd became Nerthus, the Germanic Neptune.

Neptune was worshiped in Roman Gaul, and a large mosaic picture of him was found at Pau, and has, as one of his symbols, the cross.

*Blind.—Contemporary Review, Aug., 1880.
†Thorpe.—Northern Mythology, Vol. I, pp. 27, 196, 200.
‡Taylor's Trans.
§Simrock.—Deutsche Mythologie, Vol. I, p. 807.
|Simrock.—Deutsche Mythologie, 807.
**Thorpe.—Northern Mythology, Vol. I, p. 234.
††Teutonic Mythology. Eng. Trans., Vol. I, p. 298.

Nav was an old British god of the waters,* Neith a Celtic water-goddess, Man-a-nan an Irish sea-deity, and Avaron, Welsh lord of the deep.

† Hu Gadarn, the Welsh Noah, became the Celtic Neptune, and Nev was also a water deity.

Albion, patronymic deity of Britain, and son of Neptune, was reputed a sea-deity, and introduced ship-building into Great Britain.

‡ Geofon was, says Grimm, an old Anglo-Saxon sea-god.

Shony was a water-divinity to whom Shetland fishermen poured out a libation, as we shall see in a subsequent chapter.

§ Lir was a Celtic Neptune.

Ostyak sailors venerated spirits in the river Obi. Num‖ is a Samoyed water-god. Storjunkove is a Lapp deity, appearing to fishermen and bringing them luck.** Seoseres was a Circassian wind and water god. In the Finnish Kalevala, Ahto is the lord of the waves;†† Tuoletan chief deity of the sea; Ween Kummingus, king of the sea, and Weenemäuta, queen of the sea, while Akka, queen of straits and passes, is often seen on the rocks combing her long hair.‡‡ Poznisky was a Slavonian water-god, causing storms and tempests.

In Eastern story, Alrinach is a divinity powerful at sea, appearing in the guise and dress of woman. In Mohammedan legend, Æger is a sort of god of the sea. Muthiam, king of evil spirits, is feared and reverenced by East Indian sailors.

§§ Kidir or Chidder was Arab god of voyages and brother of Elias, who ruled the wind.

‖‖ In Whydah, Africa, Hu is sea-god, and the king annually sends a young man as a sacrifice, to be thrown into the sea. In Dahomey, it is Abue. Du Chaillu says a spirit, Mbuiri, is supposed to exist in a stream at Ngounyai Falls. Wanika and Akra tribes have water-deities, and Kaffirs sacrifice oxen or millet to river-gods.

Dale says some tribes gave a fetich to the waves for

* G. Massey.—Book of the Beginnings.
† Davies.—British Mythology.
‡ Teut. Mythology, I, 239.
§ Gen'l Vallery.
‖ Conway.—Demonology. I, 213.
** Thorpe.—Northern Mythology, Vol. II, from Castren, Finn Mythology.
†† Fraser's-Mag. Vol. V, p. 390, from Castren.
‡‡ Kalevala.—Le Duc's Translation to French.
§§ D. Ohsson.—Hist. Ottoman Empire, 1821. Brewer, R.H.B.
‖‖ Burton.—Dahomey, Vol. II, p. 166.

Numba, ocean spirit. In Loango the king is a god, *Santo*, and has power over the winds and waves. A Basuto god, dwelling on the bottom of the sea, is Ramochasoa.*

Crossing the Atlantic, we find an almost universal belief in water-gods among tribes near large bodies of water. Greenland Esquimaux, believed in a huge god, the giant Kayaker; Kamtchatkans think storms are raised by Mitgh,† a spirit of the water, with fish-like extremities. Tongarsuk is also a storm deity in Greenland, as well as a goddess, his mother, Arnar Kuasak, who lives in a palace beneath the waves guarded by seals, and from it sends forth the animals of the sea. Storms are also raised by Kayarissat (*Basking-fisher*).

‡ Pampagussit was a sea-god of New England Indians.

§ Dacotah Indians believed in Unktahee, first god of the water, and the Ojibway water-god was a toad. Long-fellow says,—

> ‖ " Broke the treacherous ice beneath him,
> Dragged him downward to the bottom,
> Buried in the sand his body.
> Unktahee, the god of water,
> He the god of the Dacotahs,
> Drowned him in the deep abysses
> Of the lake of Gitchee Gumee."

** J. A. Jones gives a tradition of the Indian tribes of an ancestral fish-god who conducted them from Asia to America.

The Kaïbâlit tribe of Arizona Indians believed in a watter-goddess, Tilcompa Masoits (grandmother goddess of the sea), who brought mankind and speech out of the sea.

†† Mexican tribes regarded Coxcox or Cipactli as lord of the waters, and ‡‡ Tlaloc also as water-god. Opochtli was their god of fishing and fishermen. Nets were consecrated to him. Chalcihuitlicue §§ was goddess of the water in Tlascalla, and could raise storms and sink canoes.

‖ A Mexican proverb says: "We are all of us children of *Chal*," water-goddess.

* African Folk-Lore Journal, Vol. I.
† Steller—Kamtchatka.
‡ Maine Historical Coll., Vol. II, p. 110.
§ Eastman.—Dakota, p. 118, 126.
‖ Hiawatha, Ch. 16.
** B. Gould, Myths of Middle Ages, 502.
†† Clavigero—Mejico, Vol. VI, p. 1-4.
‡‡ Bancroft.—Native Races, Vol. VII, p. 396.
§§ Bancroft.—Vol. II, p. 361.
‖ Tylor.—Primitive Culture, Vol I, p. 258.

* The Chiachas, a Peruvian tribe, regarded Marua-cocha as the water-god. They scooped up a handful of water at each river, drank it, and begged the deity to allow them to cross. Manco Capac and Mama Oello, who arose from lake Titicaca, were Quichua gods, and mythical ancestors of their royal line.†

‡ But "Viracocha" (white seafoam-god) was chief Peruvian deity of the sea. He also arose from Lake Titicaca, bringing the arts and sciences with him. A temple long existed near Callao, dedicated to him. Peruvians had also a sea-god with a lobster's head and claws, and a man's body. The Muyscas said *Chia*, the moon, was goddess of the water. In the ancient Zac empire, a goddess was thought to live at the bottom of Lake Guatavita. Wichaana was Zapatecan god of fish.

The Botocudos of Venezuela believed in a water-god— *Taru*.

§ Polynesian sea-gods were numerous. Tawhiri-matea and Taaruatai were the Neptunes of one tribe in the Society Islands, and Ruhahatu of another. Another deity is Akaenga, the master of the lower waters, who catches souls in a net, and washes them about in it.

‖ A Maori sea-god is Tangaroa. Fish and reptiles are his children.

** Ika-tere, his son, was also "father of fish."

†† In Australian myths, Nguk Wonga is the spirit of the waters.

‡‡ In the Hervey Group, Vatea is lord of the ocean, and became a whirlpool. He is figured one side man, the other shark, having one human eye, hand, foot, and ear, and the other organs those of a shark. He was great lord of the ocean, and father of gods and men. He invented nets and fishing.

In a prayer of great antiquity,—

§§ " Vatea is the guardian of the ocean,
By him is it ruffled,
By him it is calmed."

* G. de la Vega.—Commentarios Reales, VoL VI, p. 17, in Tylor (5).
† Herrera.—Los Indios, 4-285.
‡ Prescott.—Peru, I, p. 7.
‖ Grey.—Polynesian Mythology, p. 3.
‖ Gill.—Myths and Songs of the South Pacific (12).
** Tylor.—Primitive Culture, Vol. I, p. 259.
†† Eyre.—Australia.
‡‡ Gill.—Myths and Songs of the South Pacific (3).
§§ Gill.—Myths and Songs of the South Pacific (39).

In a song,—

> "Oh! let the storm be restrained,
> Vatea, god of winds."

He lived in a mysterious land. His brother, Tirniran, is lord of fish,* and half sprat. He lives in the sacred isle. Tikokura is the storm-wave. His home is in the ocean. Raka (trouble), the god of winds, lives there also. The winds and storms are his children, each one blowing through a hole in the horizon, and he controls them.

†The Fijian fishermen's god is Roko Vona; another is Vosavakandua, and they have many minor   d , called Luve-ni-mai (children of the water). Little flags are set up when they are about to land, to prevent them from taking to the woods.

The fisherman's god in Ranatonga is a cocoanut-leaf, bound up with sennit, called Iku-ko-kua. At Mangaia, it was the frond of a cocoanut, bound with sennit. This is supposed to be powerful in allaying storms, and is called a Mokoiro, and is affixed to the prows of the boats. A certain priestly family perform this ceremony, and no one thinks of going to sea without these attachments. In Ranai, one of the Sandwich Islands, two large stone images, seen by Ellis, represented Raeapua and Kaneapua, sea-deities worshiped by fishermen. Another sea-god was Mooarii, a shark. On each point of land, temples were erected to him, and the first fish of the catch were given to him. They had other sea and weather-gods, and during a storm at sea they offered up a *pule kurana*, a kind of prayer.

A shell-fish called *Uva* was also a Fijian deity.

A Hawaiian god was Kunra, and Hina, a goddess, who were supposed to drive the annual shoals of fish to the island, and hence were adored by fishermen.

‡Hiro was a Tahitian sea-god. While asleep in the ocean, the wind-god raised a storm, but he was aroused, and lulled the waves to rest.

Kahai Khani is a Tartar "Prince of the Sea." Maui-Megala is a Pegu divinity, daughter of the lord of the sea.

Burmese sailors and fishermen dedicate fruits, rice, etc., to Nat, or the spirit of the waters, who would otherwise destroy the fish.

Riu-to is Japanese god of the bottom of the sea, and is

---

*Gill.—Myths and Songs of the South Pacific (5).
†Gill.—Myths and Songs of the South Pacific.
‡Grey.—Polynesian Mytho'ogy.

SANDWICH ISLANDERS EQUIPPED FOR HEAVY WEATHER.

73

shown as a dwarfish figure, bearing a lantern on his head. He, as well as Midsumo-Kami,* a water-god, and Jebisu, a sea-god, is adored by fishermen. Tusannoo-no-Mikato, brother of the sun-god, is also god of the sea.

In Japanese legendary history, the gods of the sea and air assembled to assist a great queen against Corea. Kai-Ku-O, dragon-king of the sea, sent his messenger Isora, with jewels that controlled the tides.

†The Chinese god of the sea, Tsuikvan, was one of the three spirits attendant on Fo or Cang-Y, god of the lower heaven. Navigators sacrificed to him. Kemung is a god of storms in China.

Ma Chua is a great sailor-goddess. She is figured as a grotesque idol, and has numerous temples. One at Ningpo is very large. Her image is also kept in exchanges. She was the daughter of a seafaring man. She dreamed she saw her father in a storm and in danger, and exerted herself to save him. She is called queen of heaven. holy mother, and other titles. Sailors take ashes from incense-lamps in front of her shrines, and carry them in a red bag, or hang them about the junk. ‡When storms occur, they kneel at the bow (the sacred part of their junks), and burn incense before her image, imploring her to save them. They make offerings to her on arriving safely from sea. Among her attributes are Favorable-mind ear, and Thousand-mile eye, seeing and hearing danger afar off.

§Tien-how is another tutelary goddess of sailors. In every large junk her shrine is placed, having her image in a glass case, and inscriptions to her. Homage was paid her, and especial honors in sailing and landing.

Staunton says, "Foong-ah-Vanny is a sailor's god." Sailors in Canton junks worship a goddess with the formidable name of *Chao-Chao-Laong-Koo*, who saved many junks from wreck.

A recent writer says: ‖"Kwun-ing (Kemung? or Marehu?) is their chief divinity, seemingly amalgamated with the 'queen of heaven,' and as a goddess her peculiar delight is to save those that are in danger by sea. She can assume thirty-two different shapes, and proceed to different parts of the world on her missions of mercy. In Buddhism, she holds the highest place as a savior of mankind."

*Siebold.—Nippon, Part V., p. 9.
†Grant.—Mysteries of All Nations, p. 54.
‡Doolittle.—Manner and Custom of the Chinese, 1-263.
§Jones.—Credulities, p. 44.   ‖Gibbons.—Boxing the Compass.

*River sailors are devotees of Loong Moo, the dragon-mother. Shrines are placed along the banks, and ceremonies and sacrifices of fowls made in the boats before sailing.

The origin and development of these ideas with regard to the gods of the watery element are plainly apparent. The primitive mind deals not in abstract ideas of a deity, but requires some typical representative constantly before it. Thus nature worship was prevalent among our ancestors, as it still is among savages and half-civilized people. So the sky, the air, the earth and the sea are at first themselves deities, and the names of many primitive gods discover their identity with the objects they represent: Dyaus (the sky), Varuna (the coverer), Thor (the thunderer), are examples of this.† At first the gods of the elements are the gods of the watery sea. So among the early Aryans, Varuna is lord of atmospheric and ocean seas. But as the Greeks especially became acquainted more and more with the sea in all its aspects, these gods were multiplied, and a chief god of the sea was created or borrowed from some other maritime nation. Every characteristic of the ocean depths was reproduced in some god, and so the Greek Pantheon abounded in maritime deities. In the Norse theogony, parallels to these are found. The chief difference is one of climate. There in the North, the terrible sea had a greater impression on the mariner than the mild, sunny wave of the south, and thus the gods are more fierce and terrible, and Œgir and Ran had perhaps more worshipers than Niörd and Frey.

The first effects of christianity upon these heathen ideas were two-fold. For, while the vows and oblations paid to Neptune, Œgir, or some inferior deity were by the teachings of the church transferred to the virgins and saints, not immediately was the memory of these heathen gods lost. So, not being able to suppress them, the church set to work to degrade them. We consequently find many of the gods are become demonized, and Odin, the beneficent wind-giver, is Nick, the demon of the sea, and the Devil himself, who is in fact a degraded god (the Indian Deva) has his representative in the ocean depths, under the name of Davy Jones.

* Jones.—Credulities, p. 47.
† See Max Müller.—Essay on mythology in " Chips from a German Workshop."

To the many gods of antiquity, then, succeeded the one god of Mohammedan and Christian religions. But the conservative mariner still retained memories of the once powerful gods of the sea. Not only did the Catholic mariner believe that Christ stilled the waves, and still possesses power to save from peril, but he also attributed to the Virgin and saints unusual powers over the winds and waves. To this day he trusts in their aid in time of peril and to them he makes his vows, and dedicates his memorial tablets or votive offerings. The Virgin is patroness of innumerable sea-side temples and chapels, and "Our Lady of the Waves," and of Blachernes, are only ready examples of a class.

*As early as 200 A.D., we find her aid efficacious. The Varangians, under Askold and Dir, attacked Constantinople about that time, with a Russian fleet, and the good Bishop Photius was able to raise a storm and destroy this fleet with the mantle of Our Lady of Blachernes, by spreading it on the waves.

† A legend of Boulogne, in 663, relates that while the inhabitants were at prayers, a ship without guide or pilot came sailing in with the Virgin on board, and she indicated to the people a site for her chapel.

‡ The Virgin, as related in the account of spectral lights and apparitions, saved from shipwreck Æthelsiga (in the 11th century), the Earl of Salisbury (1220), Edward III., and Edward IV. of England. The former monarch, overtaken in the English channel by a storm, exclaimed, "Oh! blessed Mary, holy Lady! why is it, and what does it portend, that in going to France I enjoyed a favorable wind, a calm sea, and all things prospered with me; but on returning to England, all kinds of misfortunes befall me?" The storm, the account says, immediately subsided.

The latter sovereign "prayed to God, our Lady, and Saint George, and amonges other saynts he specially prayed Seint Anne to help him."

§ Joinville says a sailor who fell overboard during the voyage of St. Louis to France, was asked why he did not swim. He replied that it was only necessary to exclaim, "Our Lady of Valbert!", and that she supported him by the shoulders until he was picked up.

* Jones —Broad, Broad Ocean, p. 233.
✦ Collin de Plancy.—Légendes Pieuses du Moyen Age.
‡ Jones.—Credulities, p. 34.
§ Jones.—Credulities, p. 35.

There was a statue at Venice, according to Fynes Moryson, that performed great miracles. A merchant vowed
perpetual gifts of wax candles, in gratitude for being saved
by the light of a candle on a dark night. This statue and
that of St. Mark were saluted by ships.

Erasmus says of the people in the shipwreck, "The
mariners they were singing their Salva Regina, imploring
the Virgin Mother, calling her the Star of the Sea, the
Queen of Heaven," etc. "In ancient times Venus took care
of mariners, because she was supposed to be born of the
sea, and because she left off taking care of them, the Virgin
Mother was put in her place." He says one sailor tried to
float ashore on a rotten and worm-eaten image of the Virgin.

The Virgin sent a wind to aid the wind-bound fleet of
Orendel in the Kleber Meer, according to Middle-age legend.

* De Plancy says a tradition at Havswyck, in Holland,
is that a boat laden with fragments of a church, in 1188, was
mysteriously stopped at a certain spot, and could not be
forced farther on until a chapel to the Virgin was commenced on the spot.

A tradition existed in Belgium that an image of the Virgin was found on the beach by sailors, and became at Lom-
buzyde an especial mariner's shrine.

Benecke says a statue of the Virgin was of old placed in
a niche in Hamburg wall, near a certain landing. Sailors
and fishermen particularly addressed their vows to her, and
made offerings in return for successful ventures. In 1470, a
chapel was built there, and the statue transferred to it.

† The shrine of Notre Dame de la Garde, at Marseilles,
whose apparition to boatmen in peril is related in another
chapter, is the object of great veneration to the Provençal
sailor. The image of the Virgin was formerly ablaze with
diamonds, and a silver statue now adorns the altar.

‡ Norman sailors, in 1700, particularly believed in the
saving power of Notre-Dame de Déliverance, whose chapel
stood between Caen and Bayeux. A legend is told of a ship
coming into the port of Havre, in 1700, whose crew, in great
peril, vowed their penances to her, but these were of no avail,
until they were joined by those of the Protestant captain
and his heretical crew.

* Collin de Plancy.—Legendes Pleuses du Moyen Age
† Collin de Plancy.—Legendes Pleuses du Moyen Age.
‡ Collin de Plancy.—Legendes Pleuses du Moyen Age.

Another Norman legend relates that Notre Dame des Neiges, in Havre, obligingly sent a concealing snow storm **to prevent** blockaded ships from falling into the enemy's **hands.**

*Kingston says: "I am assured that formerly, before the days of insurance offices and political economy, merchants frequently insured their ships at the highly esteemed shrine of Matozimbo, by presenting a sum equal to the pay of captain or mate, and that, too, without stipulating for any equivalent should the vessel be wrecked."

Nor were the saints accounted far inferior to the Virgin in their wonder-working powers at sea.

Of these saints, St. Anthony was accounted one of the most powerful. He was a priest of Padua, and is said to have preached a sermon to the fishes, hence is especially a fisherman's saint. Accordingly, we find the padrone, in Longfellow's " Golden Legend," appealing to him,—

> "Now all is ready, high and low,
> Blow, blow, good Saint Antonio."

And

> "With the breeze behind us, on we go,
> Not too much, good Saint Antonio! "

† Pietro delle Valle, a sixteenth-century traveler in the East Indies, tells us that the Portuguese kept an image of Saint Anthony in their ships and made it responsible for the winds. They prayed to it, then, if this were not effectual, resorted to lashing the image to the mast, as detailed in another chapter.

St. Nicholas was, however, pre-eminently the sailor's guardian. He was a saint of Myra, in Italy, and is said to have restored a sailor to life, and to have allayed a storm while on his way to the Holy Land.‡

§ A company of pilgrims was sailing along on its way to Jerusalem, in 900, one of whom had engaged to carry to the sacred spot a cruse of oil, given him by an old woman just before leaving port. A great storm arose, and St. Nicholas appeared, saying: "Fear not, but throw the cruse of oil which you carry with you into the sea, for the 'woman' who gave it to you was the devil." They did as

* Lusitanian Sketches.
† Jal. Gloss. Nautique.—"St. Antoine."
‡ Lappeloo and Gras.—Vita Sanctorum. Q. by Brand, I, 418
§ Liber Dictus Paradisus. — Malaphrastes. — Brewer in Notes and Queries, August, 1881.

commanded, and the oil swelled and blazed like sulphur, while the storm ceased.

* In the Norman French life of this saint, sailors in a storm cry out, "Help, O Lord Saint Nicholas, if thou beest such as men say!" and he appeared and saved them. The same life also records these lines:

> " Hear you who go by sea
> Of this Baron we speak,
> Who is in all so kindly
> And at sea so mighty."

Peter of Langtoft calls him,

> "The Bishop of St. Nicholas, whos help is ey redie,
> To shipmen, in alle seas, whan thei on him crie."

Mariners in the Ægean are also said to have called on him when in danger of wreck, and he aided them to port. The St. Elmo fire was called by Italians, Fires of St. Nicholas. Bishop Hall says a Grecian sailor prayed to St. Nicholas not to press too hard with his wings on the sails. Greek sailors in the seventeenth century took to sea thirty loaves of bread, consecrated and named St. Nicholas' loaves. In case of a storm, they were thrown into the sea, one by one, until they were efficacious in calming the waves. There were some three hundred and seventy chapels in England alone to this saint. His church at Liverpool was the most celebrated, and was consecrated in 1361. A local author says, †"In the vicinity there formerly stood a statue of St. Nicholas, and when the faith in the intercession of saints was more operative than at present, the mariners were wont to present a peace-offering for a prosperous voyage on their going out to sea, and a wave-offering on their return; but the saint, having lost his votaries, has long since disappeared."

‡ A mariner in the "Absurda" of Erasmus says he is going to dedicate a piece of sail-cloth to St. Nicholas, in gratitude at having escaped shipwreck.

§ St. Nicholas' Chapel, near Hythe, England, is thus alluded to by an old Kentish author; "This is one of the places

> ' Where such as had escapt the sea
> Were wont to leave their guifts.'

* In Hampton.—Medii Ævi Kalendarium.
† Lambarde.—Perambulations of Kent, in Jones' Broad, Broad Ocean, p. 35.
‡ Jones.—Credulities, p. 40.
§ Lambarde.—Perambulations of Kent,

Inasmuch as if any of the fishermen on this coast had hardly escaped the storme, then should Sainct Nicholas not have only the thanks of that deliverance, but also one or more of the best fishes for an offering."

* There is a legend of a certain altar-screen in the church at Arboja, in Sweden, that testifies the great power of St. Nicholas. It had been sunk during a siege by the people of a foreign town to escape capture. The Swedes found it, however, but found it too heavy to raise. Some one suggested to name over all the saints, but all failed to assist until St. Nicholas was invoked, when the screen came up. It was sent to Arboja, and St. Nicholas became the patron of that church.

✝ Armstrong in 1756, writes: "Near the entrance to the harbor (of Ciudadella) stands a chapel dedicated to St. Nicholas, to which the sailors report that had suffered shipwreck, to return thanks for their preservation, and to hang up votive pictures representing the dangers they had escaped, in gratitude to the Saint for the protection he vouchsafed them."

‡ Kanaris, the Greek hero of the fire-ships in Chios harbor in 1828, went immediately to St. Nicholas' Church, after the success of his undertaking, and presented two wax tapers to his shrine.

St. Nicholas is shown in paintings as patron of sailors, with an anchor by his side, and a fleet in the background. In other representations, he is seen on board a sinking ship in a storm at sea, and sometimes has a light on his head.

Hospinian (1531) says the invocation of St. Nicholas by mariners took place from the accounts of Vincentius and Mantuanus (B. xii. ch. 1).

> " Cum turbine nautae
> Deprensi Cilices clamore vocavant
> Nicolai, viventes opera, descendere quidam,
> Coeli tuum visus sancti sub imagine patris:—
> Qui freta depulso fecit placidissimus vento."

§ In the Salisbury Missal (1540) he is shown resuscitating two children who had been cut to pieces and put into a tub. Hampton thinks this tub was taken for a boat, and the children for sailors, and in this way, he became a maritime saint.   But we do not need to go so far for the origin of

* Jones.—Broad, Broad Ocean, p. 235.
✝ Armstrong.—History of Minorca.
‡ Jones.—Credulities, p. 42.
   ⁀pton.—Medii Ævi Kalendarium.

his power. The legend doubtless owed its origin to the degradation of semi-deities alluded to above, by the church. As Farrar * says: "The Scandinavian water-spirit Niken, inhabitant of lakes and rivers, and raiser of storms, whose favor could only be won by sacrifices, became in the middle ages St. Nicholas, the patron of sailors and sole refuge in danger."

St. Peter, as the fisher-apostle, became a maritime saint, and was often invoked in storms. The St. Elmo light was called St. Peter's fire, as we shall see.

† Cortez chose him as patron saint; "and heying at sea, Cortez willed all his navie to have St. Peter for their patron."

St. Peter is said to have entered a fisherman's boat on the Thames, which at once carried him without oars or sail, to the spot which he chose as a site for Westminster Abbey.

‡ The patron saint of gunners was Santa Barbara, who once saved a dwelling from lightning, and the gun room in Mediterranean ships as well as the powder-room is still called " La Sainte Barbe."

St. Anne was also powerful to aid in great danger. Edward IV. called on her for aid, and we shall see the St. Elmo light called St. Anne.

Some of her miraculous deeds were performed on this side of the Atlantic.§ There are in the church of Beaupré, in Canada, votive pictures showing ships in distress, with this saint hovering over them, to rescue them. She was the especial patron saint of Canadian mariners.

St. Bartholomew is invoked by boatmen on the turbulent little Kœnig sea in Bavaria, and they cry before embarking: " Holy Bartholomew! shall I return? Say yes." The echo responds affirmatively in fine weather, but if it is thick and misty, no echo is heard.

‖ Brand says St. Hermes was of old a mariner's saint in England. He, as well as St. Erasmus, and St. Gonzales de Tuy, was connected with the legends concerning the St. Elmo light.

** Fournier says: "It is a custom to invoke St. Telme, and to recite an orison. This saint was, during his life, greatly devoted to instructing sea-faring men of things pertaining to their safety, and likewise in assisting them in

* Primitive Customs.
† Jones.—Credulities, p. 109.
‡ Brewer.—Readers' Hand Book.
§ Harper's Magazine, 1881.
‖ Popular Antiquities.
** Hydrographie, 1643.

their necessities, and since he died at Tuy, a city of Gallicia, and showed himself so favorable and benign to those who have invoked him, sailors have taken him as their protector."

* Victor Hugo says sailors in Guernsey formerly believed that St. Maclou lived in a square rock called Ortach, near Les Casquets, and they were accustomed to kneel there in passing.

† St Ronald was a favorite maritime saint in the North. Scott says sailors paid their vows to him, to St. Ninian and to St. Ringar.

St. Cyric was invoked by Welsh mariners. ‡ Southey says:

> " The weary mariners
> Called on St. Cyric's aid."

§ Lambarde writes: "For within memory there were standing in Winchelsea, three parish churches, St. Leonard, St. Giles and St. Thomas, and in that of St. Leonard there was erected the picture of St. Leonard, the patron of the place, holding a fane (or Æolus sceptre) in his hand, which was movable at the pleasure of any that would turne it to such pointe of the compass as best fitted the return of the husband or other friend, whom they expected."

| St. James the Greater came to Spain from Palestine in a mysterious marble bark without sail or helm. He was a patron saint of Spanish sailors.

St. Genevieve is said to have destroyed a tree in a Spanish harbor that, with two attendant demons, wrecked many ships. She was tutelary saint of the harbor.

** St. Mark calmed the sea when his own dead body was conveyed from Egypt, says Leo Antonio More, in the "Description of Africa" (1600). He is patron of Venetian fishermen.

†† St. George was appealed to by Sardinian fishermen to drive away enemies of the tunny, as being general dragon-slayer. They also appeal to St. Michael, who was with Peter fishing.

St. Michael, as god of the wind, has been alluded to in another chapter. ‡‡ A Slavonic legend relates that this

---

* Les Travailleurs de la Mer.
† Scott.—Notes to Pirate.
‡ " Madoc."
| Perambulations of Kent, in Jones' Credulities, p. 30.
| Baring Gould.—Legends of the Saints.
** Jones.—Credulities, p. 36.
†† Jones.—Credulities, p. 70.
# Conway,—Demonology and Devil-lore,

saint had a contest with the devil as to which could dive
the deepest in the sea.   When it came Satan's turn to dive,
the saint caused the sea to freeze over him by making the
sign of the cross.

Many saints have had power over the sea, or have caused
miracles at sea, who were not regarded as maritime saints.

*St. Clement was reverenced by some mariners.   The
anchor is his emblem.   He suffered martyrdom, and was
cast into the sea with an anchor about his neck.   The waters
were driven back, and a chapel appeared over the spot.

†St. Vincent was also cast into the sea with a millstone
about his neck, but returned his own body to the shore.
While on the way to Spain, the body sunk near the cape
named after him, in the wreck of the ship.   In 1147,
Alonzo I. returned it, and a crow is said to have perched
on the prow, and one on the stern of the ship, and guided
it safely into port.   Hence the crow is figured as his emblem.

St. Benedict made iron float, embarked on a mat, and
saved drowning men.   He was invoked in shipwrecks.   St.
Christina floated with a millstone about her neck.   This is
shown in a picture at Venice.

So St. Kea,‡ surprised at rising tide while at his prayers,
sailed to shore on the rock on which he was kneeling.

St. Marculf, in France, in 1558, is said to have destroyed
a pirate fleet, raising a storm by prayer, and St. Hilarion,
attacked by pirates at sea, stopped their ship while in full
headway, so was invoked against pirates in the Mediterranean.

St. Leonore is said to have saved a sinking ship by waving a bishop's letter at it.

At Etretat, in Normandy, is a chapel to St. Sauveur, the
Holy Savior, who is the fisherman's patron there, as well as
in many other places.

§ St. Helena, who allayed a storm by throwing a piece of
the holy cross overboard; St. Asclas, who stopped a boat in
the Nile by his prayers; St. Loman, who sailed on the Boyne
against wind and tide,‖ St. Germanus, who is said, in 429, to
have allayed a storm at sea by pouring a few drops of oil
on it, and St. Rosalia, who was a Sicilian saint, were vener-

* Jones.—Credulities, p. 56.
† Mrs. Clement.—Legends of the Madonna and Saints.
‡ Dunn.—Legends of Saxon Saints.
‖ Jones.—Credulities, p. 72.
¶ Grant.—Mysteries of all Nations, p. 175.

ated by mariners, and some of them had numerous chapels dedicated to them.

*St. Columba was a favorite marine saint with Northern nations. His image, stolen in 1355, caused a storm, and it was in his chapel in the Hebrides that a moist stone was kept, to raise a gale.

St. Cesarea was exposed to drown in a cave on the Italian coast. Mariners still say a light is seen there at times, supposed to be her luminous body.

†St. Patrick is said to have had great power over the sea. He cast a stone altar, consecrated by the pope, into the sea, seated thereon a leper who had been refused passage in a ship, and made the chair sail in company with the ship. He also caused a ship carrying his nephew, St. Lumanus, to sail against the wind.

Legends of Sainte Adresse, in Normandy, relate that sailors in danger, after an invocation of the Virgin had failed, succeeded when they invoked the saint's aid.

St. Thomas of Canterbury, St. Edmund, and St. Nicholas were united in saving one of the fleet of Richard, in 1190.

Sailors generally, in the Mediterranean, venerate the saints of their own town or district, and pay their vows at their shrine.

‡Cetti says Italian fishermen chose by lot a saint for each day, and fish were dedicated to him,—an impartial method, to say the least.

§Klemm says Neapolitan fishermen, if their saints did not respond to their appeals, threw their images overboard.

A giant statue of St. Christopher stood on a promontory in Granada, so that sailors, seeing it from afar, would make their vows to it. He was a ferryman who rowed Christ across a river. So there stood a colossal statue of this saint at Monte Pellegrino, in Sicily.

St. Francis Xavier was long esteemed a powerful maritime saint, and St. Phocas was a patron of Greek sailors, St. Elias of Slavonic mariners.

‖Flemish fishermen caught a whale that was too large for the small bay into which they towed it. They finally

*Jones.—Credulities, p. 37.
†Jones.—Credulities, p. 42.
‡Jones.—Credulities, p. 36.
§Kulturgeschichte.
‖Translations and Miracles of St. Vaast.

appealed to St. Arnould for help, and, by his assistance, landed the monster.

*Quallee Walce Sahib, a great Mahometan saint, was invoked by a captain to stop a leak in his ship. The saint was under the barber's hands, but sent the mirror which he was holding. It flew to the ship, and stopped the leak by sticking to the ship's side. When the captain came to thank the saint, he bade him bring the glass, and showed the astonished man where it had adhered to the ship's side.

†A favorite maritime saint in Japan is Jakushi Niurai, whose emblem was the cuttlefish, often seen cut on his statues in seaside temples. In a great storm at sea, a huge fish attacked a junk, and mast and rudder were broken. A priest on board prayed to the saint, who appeared and bade him throw overboard his image, which the priest possessed. He did so, and the storm ceased. The image was afterwards restored to the priest by a cuttlefish.

Saints not only sailed the seas in curious crafts, but many walked on its surface. So St. Peter of Alcantara, St. Hyacinth, St. Marinus, St. Columba, St. Blaise, St. Peter Telme and St. Francis de Paul are asserted to have quietly walked the waters. As St. Scothinus ‡ walked on the Irish sea he met St. Barras, his brother, sailing in a boat. To an inquiry of the latter, he answered that he walked in a beautiful meadow, and to prove it, stooped, and gathered a handful of flowers. Not to be outdone, the other saint immediately scooped up a handful of fish, to prove that they traversed the sea.

The captain of a Venetian ship said to Loyola: "Why do you sail with me? A saint has no need of such vulgar means. He walks the waters and imitates Christ."

The good offices of the Virgin and saints were necessary to overcome the evil machinations of the devil and his subject demons, who were thought to dwell in ocean, lake, sea, and river.

> "Spirits, that have over water gouvernement,
> Are to mankind malevolent;
> They trouble seas, floods, brooks, and wels,
> Meres, lakes, and love to inhabit wat'ry cells;
> Hence noisome and pestiferous vapours raise.
> Besides they men encounter divers ways.
> At wrecke's some present are; another sort
> Ready to cramp their joints that swim for sport."

* Jones.—Credulities, p. 42.
† Mitford.—Tales of Old Japan.
‡ Jones.—Credulities, p. 56.

Among the sun-worshiping nations of antiquity, it was thought that his splendor was obscured at night by the machinations of evil demons, who opposed his passage in the waters of the lower world. This demon in Egyptian representations * is Typhon, or Apophis, the "lord of the deep," etc. Thence grew up a host of legends concerning a demon who had his abode in the sea, unclean to these people, and Typhonic influence was thought to cause the storms and tempests of the deep. Typhœus in Greek legends was a dragon-monster, who warred against Jupiter, and was imprisoned under Mount Ætna. The name indicated the whirlwind in Greece and Rome. "Ty-foon" in China still designates the revolving sea-storm; "to-fan" the hurricane in Hindoostan, and "tuphon" the whirlwind in Arabia. •

"Typhœus was father of the winds that bring ruin and havoc," says Hesiod; and he was also parent of the Hydra, Cerberus, Nemæan Lion, and other monsters fabled to have come out of the deep. Captain St. John says the Chinese consider Tyfoon "the mother of winds." The name is perpetuated in the appellation for a circular storm, current in nautical language.

| Satan, in early ages, figured as Leviathan, and in an old gem is so shown, with the church, in the guise of the ship of St. Peter, triumphant over it.

† In Hindoo legend, Panchayana is a demon living in the sea in the shape of a conch-shell, and the Maruts were veritable storm-fiends.

Argunas saved his brother from a marine demon.

‡ In an old Persian manuscript, the devil appears in the guise of a fish, and an old middle-age Inferno picture figures him as a cat—the malevolent animal at sea.

Bad was a Persian demon of winds and storms. In Arabian belief, §*Jinns* or giants caused disaster at sea. In one story in the Arabian Nights, a *Jinnee* wrecks ships. | Béchard, according to the "Clavicle of Solomon," was a storm-demon.

In an old Jewish legend, the devil is angered because God gave man dominion over the things of the sea, deeming that his region; but he was allowed to possess a certain

* Wilkinson.—Ancient Egypt.
† Mahâbrârata.
‡ Collin de Plancy.—Dict. Infernale.
§ Lane.—Arabian Nights.
| Collin de Plancy.—Dict. Inf.

power over the winds and waves. This is much like Pluto in the "Iliad," when Neptune was made lord of the seas,—

> * " Pluto, the infernal, heard alarmed,
>   And, springing from his throne, cried out in fear,
>   Lest Neptune, breaking through the solid earth,
>   To mortals and immortals should lay bare
>   His dark and drear abode of gods abhorred."

When the devils were cast out and entered the swine, they entered the sea; Micah says, "Thou wilt cast all their sins into the sea."

†Marcus, the Eremite, in recounting the six classes of demons, says the fourth class is the water-demons, drowning men, raising storms, etc.

Alvinach was a middle-age demon of the western sea, causing shipwreck and disaster, and appearing in female guise.

‡Wierus says a demon, *Forneius*, in the shape of a marine monster, existed in the middle ages, and another, Ganygya, sought the souls of drowned persons.

Luther thought the devil raised storms, and said he laid some twenty caused by him. St. Thomas Aquinas says the same. St. Nicholas saw him at sea, sword in hand. He figures as storm-raiser in numerous other saintly legends, and Dante and Tasso testify to his power.

§Du Cange says the devil is called *Hydros* in a Latin manuscript, and that Neptunus, under the name of Aquatiquur, became a personification of the devil. Remegius and St. Augustine say the devil was evolved from water.

‖Duchesne says: "In the year 1148, a frightful whirlwind arose, overthrowing houses and rooting up trees, when it was asserted that fiends were seen fighting, in the shape of wild animals." William of Malmesbury says of fiends: "Sometimes they seize the sailor."

Various legendary demons are encountered in northern lore. Grendel's ** mother was an aquatic demon; and Beowulf slew another one. The wives of the northern Neptunes, Ran and Skade, were, as we saw in the last chapter, regarded as evil deities of the sea.

* Pope.—Iliad.
† Jones.—Credulities, p. 72.
‡ De Præstigiis Demonium.
§ Dictionary.
‖ Norman Chronicles.
** Ludlow.—Popular Epics of the Middle Ages, Vol. I.

In the story of Frithjof, Helgi, the northern Pluto, sends the storm-spirits, the witches Heyd and Ham, against the hero's ship.

So Tegner,—

* "Now two storm-fiends came
Against Ellide's side;
One was ice-cold Ham,
One was snowy Heyd."

"Loose they set the tempests' pinions,
Down-diving in ocean deep;
Billows from unseen dominions
To the gods' abode they sweep."

And these demons are thus more minutely described,—

"A whale before Ellide gliding
Like a loose island seeth he,
And two base ocean-demons riding
Upon his back, the stormy sea.
Heyd, in snow-garb, shining brightly
In semblance of an icy bear,
Ham, his loud wings flapping widely,
Like a storm-bird, high in air."

†Certain demons called Landvættir were believed, in Denmark, to threaten ships from the shore, and a law of Ulfliote, in the thirteenth century, required that the figure-heads then carried at the prow must be taken off on approaching shore, so as not to frighten these malevolent spirits. In the Issefiord (a part of Cattegat Strait) a sea-demon formerly dwelt, who stopped each ship and demanded a man from it. But it was found, by consulting the priests, that he could be exorcised, and this was done by procuring the head of Pope Lucius (beheaded at Rome) and showing it to the demon.

Three winged fiends attacked the crew of one of Gorm's‡ ships, in his voyage to the Isle of the West, and were only appeased by the sacrifice of three men.

§In the romantic legends of William of Orange, Des-rame's head is thrown into the sea, and demons so haunt the spot that sailors dare not approach it.‖ There is an old legend that Satan got into the ark, and tried to sink it by cutting a hole.

* B. Taylor.—Tegner's Frithjof Saga.
† Formanna Saga, 106; Thorpe.—Northern Myth., II, 117; Grimm.—Teut. Myth., 877.
‡ Keary.—Outlines of Primitive Belief, 444.
§ Cox and Jones.—Romances of the Middle Ages.
‖ Conway.—Demonology and Devil-lore, I, 122.

*It was asserted that a demon of the flood was wont to be seen, on the breaking up of the Rhone glaciers, sword in hand, riding on the swollen stream. Sometimes, in female shape, he came to make the river overflow the land. Du Cange says a demon lived in the Rhone, called *Dracus.*

†Anton says a sailor on board the French brig Duc de Grammont, at Zante, while blaspheming and calling on the devil, was borne off by Satan in the shape of a horrible monster.

To these accounts of maritime demons in the middle ages, we may add a story of a more tangible shape, believed to be demoniacal in character. The Abbe de Choisy tells the tale:‡ "Great noise among the sailors; some one suddenly cried, 'There is the devil! we must have him!' Soon all is in motion; everyone took arms: naught is seen but pikes, harpoons, and muskets. I ran myself to see the devil, and I saw a large fish, which resembled a ray, except it had two horns, as a bull. It made several bounds, always accompanied by a white fish, which from time to time came to attack it, and then went under it. Between its two horns it carried a little gray fish, which one calls the pilot of the devil, because it conducts it, and it sticks it when it sees fish, and then the devil goes like an arrow."

We may find legends of maritime demons among modern sailors. §In Icelandic belief, if an oarsman leaves a little of the handle of the oar uncovered, the devil will use it.

The devil, according to a story from Schleswig-Holstein,‖ still ferries people across Cuxhaven bay. He does this to liberate himself from the consequences of a certain compact. He had procured a ship for a certain captain, the latter to yield himself up with the ship, which was to be kept busy so long as there was a cargo. This Satan tried to find, so as to keep the vessel cruising until the compact expired, but he was outwitted at the end of the first cruise by the captain's son, who crowded sail on and let the anchor go. The fiend tried to hold the anchor, but went overboard with it.

A Dutch captain, proverbially lucky, was thought to have sold himself to the devil, who one day appeared, in a coach-and-four, and carried away his victim.

*Conway.—Demonology and Devil-lore, 1-117.
†Life of Louis XIII.
‡Relation of an Embassy to India.—Collin de Plancy.
§Folk-lore Record, 1879.
‖Schmidt.—Seeman's Sagen.

*In a German story, a demon pilot boards a doomed ship, whose crew have given themselves up to a desperate carouse. He conducts them through a cleft in the rocks into the mouth of hell, himself escaping in a phantom boat.

Demons haunt many lakes in Bohemia, Austria, Hungary, and the Tyrol.† One, in the guise of a frog, decoyed a maiden to his palace below the water, where she found jars filled with the souls of drowned persons. She was able to liberate them. Water-demons are, in Bohemia, believed to float on the waves in the shape of a red flower. They walk on earth nine times a year, clad in a green coat, and claim a victim each time.

Balarnu ‡ is a Wallachian water-demon, living in marshes and water-falls. The devil, in a folk-tale, changes himself into a fish, to pursue a young man.

In a Russian tale, the devil's imp drags down men boating,§ and in Lake Kerikoff is fabled to live a demon, who upsets boats and seizes victims.

A sort of marine demon appears in several ‖ Breton tales, related by old sailors. In one he is distrusted and set ashore from his ship, returns in a pirate, and captures his late captain. In another, as a common sailor, he performs prodigies of valor, and enriches his captain.

In another, the devil enlists as a common sailor, is discovered and tormented by the crew, and finally disappears. Red Beard is a demon who stirs up storms at St. Pol de Leon.

**Jochinus, a dwarf goblin, is seen by Guernsey mariners on Ortach Rock, and such a vision portends drowning. He is a sea-green monster, with finny feet and claws for hands. He knows the names of the drowned, and the spots where they lie.

Kühleborn is a demon of the waves, in Fouque's Undine. In an old woodcut in Lacroix,†† the devil with horns and hoofs holds the stern of a merchant ship that is just starting from the shore.

Satan is said to have raised a storm at Bongay in England, in 1597, coming out of the waves in the shape of a dog.

*Schmidt.—Seeman's Sagen und Schiffer Märchen.
†Gubernatis.—Zool. Mythology.
‡Schott.—Wallachische Märchen.
§Collin de Plancy.—Dict. Infernale.
‖Sébillot.—Contes des Marins.
** Victor Hugo.—Trav. de la Mer.
†† Military and Religious Life in Middle Ages.

English children in Lancashire* were formerly told that if they went near the water, Jenny Greenteeth would get them. The water demon is also "Greenteeth" in Bohemia.

Satan at sea is encountered in many early ballads. In one,

> "The ship roll'd in the heavy deep,
> The wind no longer blew,
> And over them, greedy to sink them all
> The fierce wild raven flew."

For satan had assumed this garb.

†In Scotch legend, the devil and his demons infest deep pools and streams, and it is dangerous to bathe there. A diver going down to get some plate, water-demons told him to go up and not come back. He went down a second time, and never re-appeared.

The witches alleged that they were aided by the devil, as recorded in another chapter.

In an old Scotch legend, the devil appears in seaman's dress. Norwegian sailors still fear an evil spirit, Drang, and say his spittle is the froth of the sea.

‡Davis tells a sailor legend of a Captain Folgerus, a daring seaman, whose luck was proverbial. In a gale off Cape Horn, he bargains with the devil to assist him. Satan holds on to his masts until a clear spot is seen in the sky, when he begs the captain to release him from his bargain. This being done, he lets go, and the masts are lost. "The De'ill himself can't hold to a bargain if he has a Cape Horn gale against him."

A story is told by Thatcher,§ originally from German sources. In this, a certain sailor binds himself to serve Satan after fifty years, on condition of certain services. When his Satanic Majesty comes to claim his own, the shrewd mariner gets rid of him by engaging him to pump the sea dry, and by so placing the pump that the water all ran back.

Sailors in the sixteenth century∥ firmly believed in the appearance of Satan at sea, in the Western part of the Atlantic. Denis says a demon was fabled to rise from the waters in the neighborhood of St. Brandan's Isle. Sailors testify their regard for Satan's power by the frequency

* Henderson.—Folk-lore of the North Counties.
† Gregor.—Folk-lore of Scotland.
‡ The American Nimrod.
§ Superstitions (1821).
∥ Goodrich.—Man Upon the Sea. See Frontispiece.

aming geographical locali-
ties, as well as familiar objects on shipboard. Hell Gate
on our own coast, and the Devil's Current in the Bosphorus,
are examples of the first kind.

"Busy as the Devil in a gale of wind" is a well-known
adage. The devil-fish is the *Lophis*, or fishing-frog, as also
the *Rana*, or cuttle. "Devil's smiles" are the deceptive
gleams of fair weather, or the scowl on an angry captain's
face. The "Devil's table-cloth," reminiscence of the Cape-
spectre, is still seen spread in threatening weather. Devil-
bolt, Devil's-claw, and other names are met with, and the
difficult seam at the margin of the deck is a devil, giving
rise to the adage, "The Devil's to pay and no pitch hot,"
among calkers.

The Devil as a water-fiend is also encountered among
uncivilized people.

Rock demons appear in numerous legends of the African
tribes, as well as in the beliefs of the Indians of our
Northern lakes and rivers. In *Australia, demons are said
to haunt pools, and afflict bathers at times.

They particularly desire females. The native doctors
are believed to control them. Nguk-wonga is a demon who
causes erysipelas in the limbs of boy-bathers, and a stone
amulet is carried, to counteract his evil influence.

† In Van Diemen's Land, Burryup is a water-demon that
is said to carry away native women to his palace.

Nauganauga‡ is a Fijian water-demon, who dashes into
pieces celibates who try to steal around the rocks at low
tide. Another marine-demon, Adrum-bu-Sambo, steals fish
from nets. In Polynesian belief, a still-born child, when
thrown into the sea, becomes an evil spirit.

Phillippine Islanders believe in a water-demon, Nonos,
who raises storms and wrecks boats. A vampire water-
demon is encountered in Malacca. Muibura has a dog's
head and alligator's body.

A Japanese water-demon is § Kappa, who swallows boys
who go down to swim without leave.

Chinese believe in the devil's influence in causing storms.
A sudden squail is called by Chinese sailors Tin-Foo-Foung,
Devil's head-wind.

* Eyre.—Australia, Vol. VI, p. 342.
† Taylor.—New Zealand, p. 48.
‡ Tylor.—Primitive Culture.
§ Conway.—Demonology and Devil-lore, I, 112.

Numerous water-devils are found in Ceylon. Cinghalese "Devil-plays," constantly allude to them. "Oh thou black devil, thou livest constantly in streams and drains. Come, thou black devil, out of the lake." Offerings are also made to a black female devil, said to linger among the rocks at the bottom of the sea. *Pnük is a Siamese water-demon.

Nyang is a Madagascar demon, who is prayed to keep the sea from upsetting the boats. Abue is a Dahomey "King of the Sea."

Dacotah Indians thought demons lurked beneath the waters.

† We find these lines in "Hiawatha,"—

> " Give our bodies to be eaten
> By the wicked Nee-ban-aw-baigs,
> By the spirits of the water."

And when the Indian hero sailed across the lake,—

> ‡ " But beneath, the evil spirits
> Lay in ambush, waiting for him."

Algonquins and Winnebagoes believed in the existence of water-demons in lakes and rivers.

§ Greenlanders think water-demons exist, and say the oldest man must drink first so as to avoid them. Gigantic demons, in the shape of gulls, seals, bears, etc., are found among their beliefs. ‖The Atalit are certain evil spirits, that have their homes beneath the waves, and drag people down. The Tornit are certain other demons, seen at sea in bad weather, gliding over the surface of the water, without a boat.

** Carib legends say souls of the wicked go to the sea shore and capsize boats. Curumon is a Carib water-demon. ††Shoshones believe in water-demons (pahonahs).

Brazilian Indians believe a water-fiend catches children who are sent to draw water.

‡‡ Ovalle says there are bad angels who infest the seas and wreck boats. Mosquito §§Indians said Wihwin a demon in the shape of a horse, came out of the sea to devour men.

* Bastian.—Œstlich Asien, p. 24.
† Longfellow.—Hiawatha.
‡ Longfellow.—Hiawatha.
§ Tylor.—Primitive Culture, I, 216.
‖ Rink.—Tales and Traditions of the Esquimaux
** De la Borde.—Cariba, 532.
†† Bancroft.—Native Races, Vol. III, p. 157.
‡‡ History of Peru.
§§ Bancroft.—Native Races, p. 497.

The name Devil suffered some strange transformations in the seaman's mouth. It was an adaptation from Div, Divus, Jove, Deva, etc. The God of antiquity, became in the course of time deva, a Satan, and afterward Devil, *the* Satan. It finally became, in sailor phrase, Davy. *Dyved is a fabulous Welshman of *Taffy*, the thief of evil spirit, and Duffy is a West India spirit. So "Davy Jones' locker" is became the ocean, the deep, the sea-bottom, the place to which the body was committed, and to which the souls of the wicked fled. Jones is for Jonah, whose locker was the whale's belly, and who, in view of his sacrifice to the storm-fiend, is the embodiment of malevolence at sea. "He is a Jonah," marks the un-lucky wight for figurative sacrifice, and "gone to Davy Jones's locker," is synonymous with lost at sea. Smollett says in his day Davy Jones was "the fiend who presides over all the evil spirits of the deep, and is seen in various shapes, warning the devoted wretches of death and woe."

†Collin de Plancy says he sometimes appeared, a giant breathing flames from his wide nostrils, and having big eyes and three rows of teeth.

Another name for the maritime devil, perhaps more widely known than the last, was that of Nick, or Old Nick. The name, in the north of England, is used to denote Satan, especially among seafaring people. He is so named in a Devonshire proverb of a remote date. We may‡ safely trace the name for this evil spirit of the waters through the Anglo-Saxon Nicor, Danish Nökke, Old Norwegian Nikr, Swedish Neck, Icelandic Nyek, German Necker, Nocca, Beigo-Gallic Neccer, Old Norse Nikar, Old High German Nickus, to the Norse Hnickar, the seizer, the robber, one of the twelve names given to Odin, Norse god of all, who was the Jupiter Pluvius, or rain-god, of the North, and whose offspring are the Nixies, Northern naiads of the deep sea.

Various other etymologies of the name occur, but need not detain us. Various origins of the name are also pro-posed. Lenormant suggests, with great reason, that Nix and Nick are from the same root as Naiad, Nymph, Neptune, etc., the Greek word *Naein*, to flow, being the primitive origin of them all. Hampton § would trace the words farther back to the *Anak* or *Anactes*, or Castor and Pollux, whom we

* Gerald Massey.—Book of the Beginnings.
† Dictionnaire Infernale.
‡ Grimm.—Teut. Myth. Vol. II, p. 488,
      § Evi Kalendarium.

have encountered as maritime deities. But this is a doubtful conjecture.

* Morley says Odin under the name of Nikarr, gets his title from a word signifying violence, as it appears in the Greek *Niké*, victory, and in the Latin *necare*, to kill. So "Nuecen, to kill, English, knock, having been cut up to Nicken, has become the Old Nick of more recent times."

† A recent writer carries the name Nickar back to the Egyptian Nika, or Naker,—a name of the Apophis serpent of the lower world, the Typhonic enemy of the sun in his night journey. In Goa, Africa, Neck is a devil.

‡ Grimm says the Life of St. Matthew, written in German in the thirteenth century, translates Necken—Neptune. Lenormant's derivation of the word is perhaps the nearest to the truth. But as to Odin's connection with the name. "He only appears as Nikar once," says Grimm, in the Snorra or Younger Edda, 3. He there visits Sigurd's ship at sea as Hnickar. § Norse legends say he often appears in this guise, in the shape of a sea-monster (German Nikhus is crocodile), presaging shipwreck and drowning to seamen. Scott, in "Demonology," says, "Nixas, or Nicksa, a river or ocean-god, worshiped on the shores of the Baltic, seems to have taken uncontested possession of the attributes of Neptune. The Nixa of the Germans is one of those facinating and lovely fays whom the ancients termed Naiads. The Old Nick known in England is an equally known descendant of the Northern sea-god, and possessed a large portion of his powers and terrors. British sailors fear him, and believe him the author of various calamities of their precarious life."

| Odin was called as Fisherman's deity Hvael, or whale, and as the whale and walrus were caught with great danger, so Odin, as maritime spirit, became diabolic.

| The Danish Nökke is seen and heard often on the coasts. He is represented as an old monster, or as a young or old man. A knife is carried, or a nail, in a boat when going to sea, as he fears steel. In the song, "The Power of the Harp,"—

" The foul, ugly Nick sat and laughed on the wave."

* English Writers.
† Massey.—Book of the Beginnings.
‡ Teut. Myth., II, 447.
§ Thorpe.—Northern Mythology. II. 20.
| Thorpe.—Northern Mythology. Vol. II.

Olaus Wormsius says he was said often to appear to sailors on the deep sea, presaging immediate storms and disaster. He says the redness of drowned people is owing to this demon's having sucked their blood through the nostrils.

*In Norway the Nökke are said to abound in rivers, firths and lakes, and require an annual human sacrifice. One was commonly reported to rise in a certain river when any one was drowned, and cry "Saet over!" (cross over!) They are said to be able to transform themselves into various shapes, sometimes appearing with half the body like that of a fish, or of a horse, or a boat. If any one touches them he is in the Evil One's power. Particularly were they greedy after children, catching them and dragging them beneath the water, but they were only dangerous after sunset. †On appearing, it was deemed best to say, "Nyck! Nyck! needle in water! The Virgin Mary cast steel into the water! Thou sink! I float!" for the appearance of steel in the water was thought to control them. They also were called Söetrold (sea-trolls). When they appear at sea they are considered very powerful, and if one in danger of shipwreck would promise a son or daughter, he would escape the calamity. Frequently the Nök changed his form or abode.

‡He may be bridled when he comes as a horse, and he is known by his hoofs being turned backward.

At one place in Norway he is fabled to appear as the water-horse when stormy or threatening weather is impending. At another place he is called the Vigtrold (harbortroll), who shouts to warn mariners when danger is near. A Nök in Svend waterfall is fabled to have caused the death of many persons. A priest tried twice to cross the river, but only succeeded the third time, by catching the spirit, in the shape of a dog, and drowning it.

§In Swedish, Neckan is the musical sprite of the water. Rudbechius says Neckar assumed various shapes and governed the sea. In Sweden, when you bathe, you should carry a piece of steel or iron into the water, for they say that sometimes Nick appears as a young man on the surface of the sea, and he is said to be especially severe on young maidens who have not treated their lovers well.

* Faye.—Norsk Sagen. p. 57.
† Thorpe.—Northern Mythology, II, 20.
‡ Grimm.—Teut. Myth.
§ Thorpe.—Northern Mythology, II, 39.

In all these countries he is thought to be very anxious about his soul. So his children, when told "You have no soul, and will never be saved," ran shrieking into the sea.

*German legends of Nick and the nixies are abundant. In old works, Necca, Necco, Nickar, or Neckar, is governor of the sea, assuming the name and form of some animal, or of a man in a boat. Nixen, or Nickers, are water-fairies of the sea, streams and lakes. Males are called Nix, females Nixie. Some say their ears are slit, others say they have fish-like backs. Some are represented clothed, others covered with moss and sea-weed. Nickelman or Häckelman, sits on the water with a long hook, to drag children down below.

He often appears in the evening calling for help, and dragging down the person who comes to assist him. Stories of Nick are told, with variations, of nearly every lake, river and stream in Germany, Austria and Bohemia. Nick appears as a serpent, in a story from the Black Forest, dragging a maiden down with him below the water.

†A water-fiend in Bode required an animal sacrifice, so a black hen was thrown in as a substitute for a mortal. When the water is disturbed, Nick frequently clasps his hands and laughs, for some will drown. The metal nickel is said to have been named after Old Nick, who stole silver and substituted the baser metal. Neckar, or Nick, kills the maidens who disobey his orders, or who marry mortals. So with Undine, after her return to the Rhine depths, and a similar story is told by Grimm. Another Rhine story is told of a Nick carrying off a woman who was washing linen on the bank. He always devoured his children. The services of midwives were said to be frequently required in the Rhine depths.‡ The messenger of Nix is Nixcobb, who communicates with mortals. He is a short, deformed dwarf, covered with shells, sea-weed and moss. In a German story, "Nix of the Mill-Pond," a man is carried away by the Nix. An old witch bids his wife comb her hair by the pond. Her husband's head appeared. The next day she played a flute when half his body arose from the water. The third day she turned a golden spinning-wheel, when he reappeared and emerged from the lake. This tale is believed by Cox to symbolize the sun breaking up the winter-sleep of nature.

* Wuttke.—Deutsche Aberglauhen.
† Wolf.—Deutsche Mährohen und Sagen.
‡ Legends of the Rhine.

7

Stones thrown in the Nick-haunted lakes raise a storm.

At Blankenburg, a ship ran ashore, and the crew could not get her afloat, until a Nix came and assisted, with a long hook.

In Hesse, children are told to keep away from the water, or " Nöcken will get you."

* A nick is said to have carried a fisherman's boat from a lake on Rügen to the top of a tall tree. Another was said to have been seen near Marburg, in 1615, and they were frequently seen, according to old chronicles, in the Elbe near Magdeburg, where they were fabled to have prevented the construction of an acqueduct. At Leipsig, they were fabled to require a victim each year, and were thought especially to desire children.

An old legend of 1664, told by Prätorius, says a maiden served a Nix for three years. Sailors and fishermen at Neumark say that the Nix requires a sacrifice every three years. One in the Rhine requires a midwife's services, and repays her with a lot of ashes, which turn to gold.

† In Austria, Donaufürst asks all who came to the river what they wish most, and then ducks them in the river, where is all, and everything.

The rivers, springs, and lakes in Belgium and Holland are haunted by the Necken. Near Ghent, it is said that he has been seen on the banks of the Scheldt. In Brabant, it is thought that he cries like a child to attract people, and that he sucks the breath and blood of drowning persons. A story is told of nixies dancing on the strand, and a young man got possession of the glove of one of them, and she plunged into the water, but it was soon stained red, for Nick had slain her for conversing with a mortal.

‡ The " Water-king of Wangerong " came to Dort to claim a bride. Not being able to get her, he buried in sand a part of the coast.

In the Faröe Islands, Nikar drags people down occasionally.

Scotch seamen formerly believed in " Nigg of the Sea." Storms gathered while he slept. The Celtic water-god Neithe is conjectured a Nick.

Nyck, in Iceland, is a water-kelpie who carries off a maiden who foolishly mounts on his back.

* Kuhn and Schwartz.—Deutsche Sagen.
† Simrock.—Deutsche Mythologie, p. 150.
‡ Schmidt.—Seaman's Sagen und Schiffer Mährchen.

* Nöck is said by some to have fish extremities.   The
nixies, his children and subjects, are sometimes naked, hung
about with shells and sea-weed, and when clothed, betray
their presence by dripping garments.   They love to dance
in the moonlight, and, like mermaids, foretell the future,
and are possessed of protean wisdom.

The Anglo-Saxon knew him.   † Turner says: " Neccus, a
malign deity, who frequented the waters, was feared in the
North.   If any perished in whirlpools, or by cramp, or by
bad swimming, he was thought to be seized by Neccus.
Steel was supposed to expel him, and therefore all who
bathed threw some little pieces of steel in the water for
that purpose."   Beowulf says the Nicor were supernatual
elves in lakes, rivers and seas, ever ready to injure, and able
to raise storms.   He says they were fiendish and savage
enemies of the sailor.

"Brother Fabian's Manuscript," quoted by Hardwick,‡
says,—

> " Where by the marishes bloometh the bittern,
> Neckar the soulless one sits with his ghittern,
> Sits inconsolable, friendless and foeless,
> Waiting his destiny,—Neckar the soulless."

And so in Matthew Arnold's poem,—

> " In summer on the headlands,
> The Baltic sea along,
> Sits Neckar, with his harp of gold,
> And sings his plaintive song."

Thus we have seen the devil borrowed by the sailor from
his terrestrial abode, and made to do duty in ocean depths.
During the middle ages, a belief in Satan's power was universal, and this was fostered by the priests; he, sometimes,
as in the case of Nick, being a degraded heathen god.
"Amphibia," says a German writer, "appear as bad and
demonical animals," and thus the water-king is malevolent.
But Satan, as prince of the air and sea, had, in popular lore,
a bad character.   The mediæval conception of the maritime
devil, transmitted to more modern times, is thus aptly
summed up by Fiske: " Like those other wind-gods, the
psycopomp Hermes, and the wild huntsman, Odin, he is
prince of the powers of the air. . . .   Finally he takes a

* Thorpe.—N. Mythology, Bk. III. p. 87.
† Anglo-Saxon History.
‡ Lancashire Traditions.

hint from Poseidon, and from the Seven Maidens, and appears as a water-nymph or nixy, and as the Davy (Deva) whose 'locker' is situated at the bottom of the sea." There he now remains, no longer terrifying the practical modern mariner.

CHAPTER III.

THE STORM-RAISERS.

"I think I'd like to be a witch.
  I'd churn the sea, I'd tether the winds,
  As suited my fancy best.
  I'd wreck great ships, if they crossed my path,
  With all the souls on board."

Old Cornish Song.

"Oh! sing and wake the dawning!
  Oh! whistle for the wind!
  The night is long, the current strong,
  Thy boat it lags behind!"

Kingsley—A Myth.

THE Deities, Demons and Saints were not the only powers capable of controlling the elements. Although they were believed to exercise chief dominion over winds and storms, it was also believed that many human agents possessed the power of controlling winds and waves, generally through an invocation or conjuration of these superior spirits.

This belief in the storm-raising power of certain persons existed early in the history of man. Homeric Telchians were a tribe of dwarfish wind-makers, allied to the four dwarfs, Northri, Austri, Vestri and Suthri, placed by the Sagas at the four corners of the world. *According to the Edda, Giants and Giantesses caused storms.

The phrase still in use, "a capful of wind," reminds us of Eric VI., of Norway, "Windy-Cap," as he was called, just as the sailor phrase, †a "bagful," in a heavier blow, carries us back to Æolus and his windbags. Eric, who lived 907

* Grimm.—Teut. Myth. II. 637.
† Jones.—Credulities, p. 66.

101

A.D., was believed to be able to control the winds, turning his cap in the direction sought.

*Grimm tells a German tradition of a man who could conjure the wind by shifting his cap from one side to the other.

†Olaus says of Eric: "Eric was in his time held second to none in the magical art, and he was so familiar with the evil spirits whom he worshiped, that what way so ever he turned his cap, the wind would presently blow that way. For this, he was called "Windy-Cap."

In the "Khorda Avesta," Vahista conjures the North wind, as an evil spirit.

Seneca says there were in antiquity those who, by their incantations, raised storms. Tibullus tells of a magician who could control the elements, and the same is affirmed by the Codex Theodosius.

‡Plutarch, speaking of a visit of Demetrius, a grammarian, to Great Britian, says: "Very soon after his arrival, there was great turbulence in the air, and many portentous storms; the winds became tempestuous, and fiery whirlwinds rushed forth. When they ceased, the islanders said the departure of some one of the superior genii had taken place."

§It was likewise alleged that a storm arose in the fifth century, when Diagoras went to sea, in consequence of his atheistical opinions.

In the middle ages, a belief in these weather-makers became nearly universal. A ninth century writer, ‖Agobard, tells us: "In these districts, almost all persons, noble and plebeian, townsmen and rustics, believe that hail and thunder may be produced at the will of man, that is, by the incantations of certain men who are called *tempestarii*." "It was generally believed that these sent hail stones from their ships in the upper air, to pelt off the fruit." He says, that when people were asked, what they meant by "the storm being raised," some, with little hesitation, as is usual with the ignorant, declare that it is from the incantations of these persons, called *tempestarii*, and utter execrations against them.

In Germany, about 1000, A.D., certain "Defensores" were

* Grimm.—Teut. Myth. II. 71.
† Olaus Magnus.—History Goths, 1658, III. 13.
‡ Morals.—Goodwin's Trans.
‖ Jones.—Credulities, p. 45.
‖ De Tonitru et Grandini—in Works.

credited with these weather-raising powers. *In a middle-age confessional, a question as to belief in weather-makers was inserted, and penances imposed for such beliefs. Laws were also passed against such persons. †Mallet says there are such laws in the statutes of Charlemagne, and in ancient statutes of Norway. Later, French and Italian laws declared it a penal offense to become a weather-maker. The pope joined in the crusade against such persons, and declared against them in two bulls, issued in 1317 and 1327.

Marco Polo tells us many wonderful stories of weather-makers.‡ Mongol weather-makers in his time used a certain stone called "Yadah," repeating certain incantations over a basin in which it was suspended. A Tartar chief, Nogodan, was said to have raised clouds, and enveloped in them an opposing army, thus defeating it. Of Cashmere sorcerers found in his day he says they "can by their sorceries bring on changes of weather and produce thunder." Modern travelers repeat similar traditions concerning them. § Polo says of Sorcerers in the Isle of Socotra: "Thus, if a ship be sailing past with a fair wind and a strong, they will raise a contrary wind and compel her to turn back. . . . In fact, they make the weather as they list, and produce great tempests and disasters."

Later traditions affirmed these beliefs of certain persons.

Remigius says a certain sorcerer caused a storm on a clear day, nearly killing a peasant. |Arnanson says sorcerers in Iceland used as a storm-bringing charm a *ling's head.* This has in its open mouth a cylinder of wood with a magic charm, called *Vedur-gapi*, engraved on it. When this was stuck up on a pole over a cliff, it would bring a wind. De Plancy says this power of controlling the winds was obtained by an amulet made of a fish's jaw, with ten magic characters engraved on it, so arranged that initiated persons only could see the words " Thor hafot '" between them.

Thorgrim, Thorlefr and Thorgard, in the Icelandic Gisli Saga, raise storms. In the Finnish epic,** a sorcerer not only causes a storm, but also freezes the ocean. Among the evil things ascribed to rope-makers in France during the middle ages, storm-raising was included.

* Dobeneck.—In Schieble, Das Kloster.
† Northern Antiquities.
‡ Yule.—Marco Polo, Vol. II.
§ Yule.—Marco Polo, Vol. II. p. 341.
| Icelandic Legends.
** Kalevala.—Le Duc's Translation.

* Cassas says that hurricanes in the Gulf of Carnero were caused, according to common report, by sorcerers, who, when offended, kindled great fires in caverns, causing the enraged earth to send forth their storms.

† In an unpublished Harleian MSS. it is asserted that Sir Roger Wallysborn allayed a storm at sea, by showing a fragment of the true cross.

Toledo sorcerers were reported to have endowed a Salamancan professor with the power to raise storms. The Polish physician, Twardowski, was, in common opinion, able to raise storms.

Pirates and smugglers were generally accredited with these storm-raising powers, and numerous folk-lore tales supply instances of this belief.

‡ Sprengel says sorcerers used the Evangelists to appease the demons of the storm. Godelmann thus recapitulates the beliefs concerning them: " When God allows the Devil to send down hail, he directs the Sorcerer to cast small pebbles behind him, while he scatters sand taken from the water in a ditch, into the air; makes a little hole, casting wine therein, or stirs about water with the fingers."

§ Reginald Scot says: " These, I say, take upon themselves also the raising of tempests."

Bras de Fer, a sorcerer condemned to the galleys, raised a breeze, to avoid being thrown overboard as a Jonah, by turning a stone with his toe.‖

Sorcerers of the Isle of Orleans, in the St. Lawrence river, could raise storms. Jean Lavallée wrecked many vessels of Sir Hovenden Walker's fleet in 1711, by raising a storm and pursued them at sea with fogs and storms.

** In Cornwall, a certain Lord and Lady of Pengerswick were said to have called up storms when they would, and are believed to have been unpopular landlords, thus execrated.

Tregeagle was another Cornish storm-fiend. He is heard at many places on the coast wailing during the storm, at the failure of his efforts to accomplish certain difficult tasks. †† At Ipswich, Harry Main howls every time his rope of sand breaks.

* Jones.—Credulities, p. 72.
✦ Hazlitt.—Popular Antiquities.
‡ Malleus' Maleficarium, 1490.
§ Discovery of Witchcraft.
‖ Abbe Lecuire, Hist. de Satan, p. 358.
** Bottrell.—Traditions of West Cornwall.
†† Drake.—Legends of New England.

Mrs. Cookson repeats a Manx legend of a certain Mac-Lear, who controlled the winds,—

> "From New Year's tide round by the ides of yule,
> Nature submitted to his wizard rule,
> Her secret force he could with charms compel,
> To brew a storm, or raging tempests quell."

* Baxter tells us of "an old *reading* parson named Lowis, not far from Framingham, that was hanged, who confessed that he had two imps, and that one of them was always putting him on doing mischief, and (being near the sea) as he saw a ship under sail, it moved him to send him to sink the ship, and he consented, and saw the ship sink before him."

† There was a tradition among French sailors that certain shipmates had the power to control the winds through the possession of a ring, worn on the little finger of the right hand. The possessor must, however, be careful to spend no more than three months on a single voyage, nor must he remain on shore more than three days, or his life would be forfeited.

Indian and savage sorcerers and medicine-men are fancied to control the winds and clouds. A sorcerer at Freshwater Bay ‡ kept the winds in bags, like Æolus, and used certain incantations to control them. A Cree sorcerer sold winds, giving three kinds for a pound of tobacco.

Khoi-Khoi Hottentots pretend to control the winds and raise storms. New Zealanders say their priests cause winds to blow at will, and can also make canoes lighter, to sail more easily. "The crew were in great strait because they had no priest to charm their canoe, to make it sail bravely," says a recent traveler.

§ Tylor says, "Raising the wind had its origin in all seriousness, describing one of the results of the sorcerers' art, practiced especially by Finn wizards, of whose uncanny power over the weather our sailors have not to this day forgotten their old terror."

And perhaps no one could, in the opinion of the seaman of a century ago, raise a wind so effectually as a Finn. ‖ Olaus Magnus alludes to their trade in winds, and we shall

* World of Spirits.
† Collin de Plancy.—Dictionnaire Infernale.
‡ Brinton.—Myths of the New World.
§ Primitive Culture.
‖ History of the Goths, 1658.

speak of it in its place. This led sailors to consider them as unlucky. * Dana, in his charming book, says the black cook of his first ship long feared a certain seaman, thinking him a Finn. He said Finns were wizards, and he had known a Finnish sailmaker who could do what uncanny things he would. He had a rum-bottle always mysteriously half full, although never replenished, and often consulted. He talked to the bottle and finally cut his throat in an unseamanlike way. The cook had heard of a ship in the Gulf of Finland which was beating against a head wind, when another hove in sight, passed her with a fine breeze aft and all sails set, proving to be a Finnish vessel. Dana doubted his tales, whereupon the oldest seaman in the ship was appealed to. He remembered that a certain Finn was accused by the captain of a ship, with whom he had quarreled, of giving him a head wind, and even shut up in the fore-peak a day and a half, which summary proceeding brought the wind fair. † Only a very few years ago (1857) a sailor was tried in England for killing a mulatto at sea, on the " Ruby Castle." His defense was that he thought the man a Finn, and so put him out of the way of doing harm.

‡ Schmidt has a story of a Finn mate who goes to a certain stone on the seashore, and by incantations raises a storm, but declares that his life will be a forfeit for this power of controlling the elements. § Le Duc says that Finn sorcerers still pretend to control the winds, and inclose them in bags.

‖ Hereby it is not intended to deny but spirits can raise or bestow winds or tempests. It may be by arbitrary means, though I see some are willing to excuse Lapland from such "indictment."

** Finn wizards are celebrated in Shetland lore. They were certain mythical creatures, at·times men, at others, when they had donned a seal-skin, they became seals. They wrought many magical spells at sea, chasing boats and raising storms. In such cases, silver thrown overboard would save the boat.

Blind ingeniously conjectures these mysterious creatures to have been old Norse sea-pirates, who, coming as a con-

* Two Years Before the Mast, p. 46.
† Jones.—Credulities, p. 16.
‡ Seeman's Sagen und Schiffer Mährchen.
§ Kalevala.
‖ J. Goad.—Astro-Meteorologica, 1686.
** Blind, in Contemporary Review, September, 1882.

quering race, were doubtless wonder-workers, in the eyes of the simple islanders. In an old charm for sprains, "A Finn came ow'r from Norway," and hence was wonder-working. The tales of their casting off their seal garb and coming ashore, alluded to the throwing aside the Norse armor (often made of seal skins), to join in the social dance on the rocky beach. As many Norse heroes are traditionally charm-

THE CREW ACCUSE HOLCROFT OF BEING A JONAH.

workers and weather-makers, these conjectures appear probable.

*Holcroft tells us that sailors, in a voyage to Scotland, thought him a Jonah, because he was an actor. On Easter Sunday, as he was walking the quarter-deck, reading aloud, several approached him, and one asked him what he was

* Memoirs.

reading, advising him to read a prayer-book instead of a book of plays. "By the holy father, I know you are the Jonas, and, by Jasus, the ship will never see land till you are tossed overboard, you and your plays with them!"

* Being becalmed at sea in a Spanish vessel, the sailors thought the heretic, Stevens,   ed it.

† Melville says the sailors in a packet-ship believed that incantations, muttered over the Bible by a steerage passenger, raised head-winds, and they even threatened to throw her overboard.

A Cornish tradition informs us that Sir Cloudesly Shovel's fleet was wrecked on the Scilly Islands, by a storm raised by a condemned criminal reading the CIX Psa

‡ Thatcher tells this story: "In the ship President, bound out from Charleston, a sailor declared a storm was brought on by his wickedness, and finally jump
the fore-rigging. When the ship returned, a storm again
se, and the sailors declared that Sam's chest must go, too. A Scotchman got it, and when he threw it overboard, the storm ceased. When near New York, a squall came up, and the crew declared there still remained some of the dead man's effects. His shoe was finally found, and when it was flung overboard, the men were assured of their safety."

§ A lawyer or a priest was also viewed askant when embarking on shipboard; "kittle cargo," they were called. Priests were unlucky, probably because of their black gowns and their principal office—that of consoling the dying and burying the dead; and lawyers, from a general antipathy of sailors to that craft—"sea-lawyer" being a term of reproach to an argumentative or wordy sailor, and "'and-shark," a synonymical appellation of the gowned men.

Another reason urged against priests, was that the devil, the great storm-raiser, was their especial enemy, and sends tempests to destroy them. ‖ Brewer says Jonah's and St. Paul's voyages probably gave rise to these ideas of clerical ill-luck.

The superstition is widespread. ** Japanese fishermen deem it an ill-omen to meet a *bonze* or priest on their way

* Stephens.—Cent. America, II, p. 464.
† Moby Dick.
‡ Superstitions, 1827.
§ Folk-lore Record.—Henderson, Gregor, etc.
‖ Readers' Hand-book.
** Miss Bird.—Japan.

to their boats. *Scotch fishermen do not allow you to say "minister" or "kirk" in their boats. The former is called "the man wi' the black quyte (coat)"; the latter "the bell-hoose." The presence of a minister in the boats is seen with misgivings, as he may be a Jonah.

Priests were thought able to control the elements in France in the middle ages. Martin de Arles says they threw stones in the air, to raise a storm.

Arab religious men, or Marabouts, were supposed to be influential in raising storms. The voyages of Teonge, a chaplain in the English navy, on the Barbary coast, in 1679, attest this. He says: "It hath been very tempestuous all night and so continueth. Wee may suppose their Mara-botts are at work to drive us from their coast, but Good is above the Devill." †A letter in *Galignani*, of Paris, in May, 1856, from Constantine, Africa, says that when these Marabouts did not raise a wind to the satisfaction of customers, they were ducked, to insure a breeze.

‡A caste of priests in Egypt are still thought to be able to control the winds, and board Nile boats for that purpose. Villiers says: "He (our boat captain) said that this caste of Santons were subject to a king in the mountains of Cossara, and had such powers, that, if caught in a storm at sea, a calm was restored; and if a cannon-ball made a hole in the ship, a Santon could stop it."

§We are told in a Norse Saga: "Bishop Sigurd took all his robes, and went forward to the bow of the king's ship; ordered tapers to be lighted, and incense to be brought out. Then he set the crucifix upon the stern of the vessel, read the Evangelist and many prayers, besprinkled the whole ship with holy water, and then ordered the ship-tent to be stowed away, and to row into the fjord. Now, when all was ready on board the Crane to row, she went into the fjord without the rowers finding any wind; and the sea was curled about the keel-track like as in a calm, so quiet and still was the water; yet on each side of them the waves were lashing up so high that they had the sight of the mountains."

‖A conjuration still exists, employed by priests in the middle ages to allay storms, after using which the cross was

* Gregor.—Folk-lore of Scotland.
† Jones.—Credulities, 71, *note.*
‡ Villiers.—Egypt.
§ Olaf Tryggvason's Saga.
‖ Schieble.—Das Kloster.

shown to the four points of the compass, and holy water sprinkled about.

*According to Provençal legends, a monk embarked in a galley, when a great storm arose. The crew were about to sacrifice him, but he begged a respite, and allayed the storm, within the hour granted him.

† So women were thought unlucky at sea, although ‡Pliny says the ancients thought a storm at sea would subside on a woman's showing herself *nuda corpore* to the winds. Children, on the contrary, were usually lucky.

The sea near St. Jean du Doight (Finisterre) enrages itself at sight of a woman.§

| Holcroft says, however, "Hearing a child cry in a woman's arms," a sailor exclaimed, "So, we have a squall, we shall soon have a breeze."

But none of these wind-raisers were so universally known as the witches, once thought supreme over the winds. This was an early belief. **Pomponius Mela, writing 45 A.D., says there were in the island of Sena (Isle au Sein), on the coast of Gaul, certain Druidesses who controlled the winds: "It contained some of these venerable virgins, who pretended that they could raise storms and tempests by their incantations." "They are called gallicenæ, supposed to be of great genius and rare endowments, capable of raising storms by their incantations, of transposing themselves into what animals they please, and occasionally able to fortell what is to come."

The "Pœnitentiale" of Theodore avers that the Anglo-Saxons believed witches could raise storms, and asserts that among the evil practices of communicants, were to be reprehended those practiced by the *emissores tempestorum*. In the old tale,†† "The Lambton Worm," a "witch wife" is sent by a wicked queen to wreck the hero's ship, but has no power over the sacred "rowan-wood" of which it is built.

Early legends exist of Scandinavian witches. Olaus Magnus tells us of their storm-raising powers. We also read in the old saga of Olof Tryggvason: "When he came north to Sullen fjord, he intended to sail in it to look for Rand, but a dreadful tempest and storm was raging in the fjord.

* Jal.—Glossaire Nautique.
† Grant.—Mysteries, 395.
‡ Natural History, Vol. XXVIII, p. 23.
§ M. G. Lescal in Melusine, 1884.
| Memoirs.
** Jones.—Credulities, 64.
†† Ludlow.—Popular Epics of the Middle

This was repeated by Rand's wizard arts, whenever Olof approached the fjord.

*A witch in the Grettir Saga allays a storm. She says "How shall it be said that it is past hope that I may deal with the gale that has been veering about the while." Odde, a celebrated wizard, boiled *seid* to raise a storm (Seid is "a boiling," and is but the magic hell-broth of the witches).

The Bernese chronicle avers that a woman raised a storm for a certain Count of Kyburg, to clear his enemy from his castle. Remigius says that more than two hundred witch weather-makers were burned; that "they beat the water so long with switches and rushes given them by the devil, that a thick mist and fog came up." These weather-making witches are said also to have rolled a cask about, until a storm was produced.

Lapland witches were especially noted for their wind-raising powers. They, too, were said to cause storms by throwing sand in the air, with incantations and charms. Congreve, in "Love for Love" (1695), says,—

"O'ons, I'll marry a Lapland witch as soon, and live upon selling contrary winds and wrecked vessels."

English witches were still further celebrated.

†Reginald Scot thus combats popular ideas: "No one endued with common sense but will deny that the elements are obedient to witches, and at their commandment or that they may, at their pleasure, send rain, hail, tempests, thunder and lightning, when she, being but an old doting woman, casteth a flint-stone over her left shoulder toward the west, or hurleth a little sea sand up into the element, or wetteth a brown sprig in water and sprinkleth the same in the air; or layeth a stick across a bank where never was a drop of water, or burieth sage until it shall be *rotten ;* or diggeth a pit in the earth, and, putting water therein, stirreth it about with his finger, or boileth hog's bristles; all which things are confidently asserted by witches and affirmed by writers."

‡ Another old work thus alludes to these witches: "The imagination of women persuadeth them that they are capable of disturbing the air, of exciting tempests, and of inducing maladies. But Satan's prescience, enabling him to discover what shall take place in the heavens, he puts this in

their head, when they wish to be avenged of their neighbor, it is that they hope to succeed by casting flint-stones behind their backs, toward the West, by throwing the sand of a torrent in the air, by placing beams across a river, by boiling hog's bristles and other absurdities."

* Again we are told, " The broom dipped in the water by the witch does not bring rain, but the demon having power over the elements, by God's permission, can do so immediately."

King James VI, who wrote shortly after Scot, affirmed that witches could and did do all these things, and added to their wind-raising repute the royal authority. King James had himself been a victim of their machinations. In 1590, while on his way from Denmark, to bring his bride to Scotland, his ship was assailed by a storm, but missed a greater tempest, sent against him, it was said, by a number of witches. The chief actors were a Dr. Fian and Agnes Sampson, a celebrated witch. They were tortured, and made various confessions. Dr. Fian said Satan was the chief agent, and he sent a mist, to cause the king's ships to go ashore. Both he and the women testified that all, two hundred witches and warlocks in number, sailed in sieves on Hallowmas-eve, and were met by the devil (one said he rolled along like a huge wave), and were given by him a black cat. This was drowned in the sea, with cries of "Hola!" raising a great tempest.

† Satan raised the mist by casting something like a football into the sea. They also chased a cat, to raise a storm. "The devil promised John Fian to rais ane mist, and cast the King's Majesty in England, and for performing thairof he tuik ane thing lyk to ane futt-ball, qu' hilk apperit to the same Johnni (an eyewitness) lyk to a wisp, and cast the same in the see, qu' hilk causit ane vapour and ane reik to rys."

Agnes Sampson, with four other witches, raised a tempest by throwing in the sea a cat, with portions of a dead man tied to it; and on another occasion, feasted on the wines of a foreign ship, and then sank her, with the devil's aid.

‡ The old chronicle of these events further tells us: "Thairefter, at Bergie Todis' house, they knitt to the foure feit of the catt foure jointis of men; quhilk being done, the

---

* Martin de Aries.
† Wright.—Sorcery and Witchcraft, 120.
‡ The Damnable Life of Dr. Fian.—Gents' Magazine, 1779, p. 449

said Janit fetched it to Leith, and about midnight she and twa Luike hop and twa wijfis, callit Slobeis, came to the peir-head, and saying their wordis, 'See that thair be na desait amang us,' and they cast the catt in the see, sa far as they mycht, quhilk swam owre and cam again; and they that war in the pains, cast in ane other catt in the sea at XI houris, after quhilk, be their sorcerie and inchantments, the boit perished betwixt Leith and Kinghorne."

Other Scotch witches raised storms at sea. Janet Irving, with Satan's aid, sank a boat with five persons, in Westray Firth. Alison Dick said to her husband, in 1663: "Mony ill turns have I hindered thee from doing this thretty years; mony ships and boats hast thou put down, and when I would have holden the string to have saved one man, thou would not." One of the charges against Elizabeth Bath-cart, was casting away and sinking George Hulde's ship, with several persons in it. She met with Satan on the sea-shore, and, by his aid, "maist cruelly sank and destroyed the schip." She was acquitted because they were not seen, "fleeing like crawis, ravens, or other foulis" about the ship, as was thought usual with witches.

*On Solway Firth, Maggie Forsythe was accounted a great storm-raiser. A sailor said: "I'll tell thee what, Margery Forsythe has mair forecast in the concerns o' the great deep than a wise mariner ought to despise."

Isobel Gowdie confessed that she raised a storm in 1662, by wetting a cloth, beating it upon a stone, and calling upon Satan. Similar means were employed by other witches.

Margaret Barclay caused the wreck of a ship by molding a figure of it in wax and casting it into the sea. She sank her husband's brother's ship, in sight of land.

Violet Leys, because of her husband's discharge from a ship, so haunted it with storms that it was near being lost, and much cargo was thrown overboard.

†A Dunrosses witch, becoming vexed at a boat's crew, put a wooden cup into a bowl of water, and sang to the devil. The water became agitated, the cup overturned, and the boat never came in.

‡Mary Lamont, eighteen years old, raised storms and allayed them by casting stones into the Clyde. She wrecked ships on Kintyre Mull.

* Cunningham.—Traditional Tales of the Scottish and English Peasantry.
† Gregor.—Folk-lore of Scotland.
‡ Grant.—Mysteries, &c.

8

Some witches knew the fate of boats at sea. Jona Dyneis prophesied evil to her husband's boat. Bessie Skebister predicted that the crew of a stranded boat were saved; and so great was her repute that boatmen and sailors, far and near, consulted her, and relied on her prognostications. Macbeth says to the witches,—

> *"Answer me,
> Though you untie the winds, and let them fight
> Against the churches; though the yesty waves
> Confound and swallow navigation up."

And the witches themselves relate their power over the wind and waves,—

> "*2d Witch.* I'll give thee a wind.
> *3d Witch.* And I another.
> *1st Witch.* I myself have all the other;
> And the very ports they blow,
> All the quarters that they know,
> I' the shipman's card."

And she further relates her means of controling them,—

> "Here have I a pilot's thumb,
> Wrecked as homeward he did come."

† Norna, in the "Pirate," says,—

> "Ye who taught weak woman's hand
> How to wield the magic wand,
> And wake the gates on Foulah's steep,
> Or lull wild Sumburgh's waves to sleep."

Again she says,—

> "The billows know my runic lay,
> The gulf grows smooth, the stream is still'd."

‡ Other witches tell us,—

> "We lay the wind in the devil's name,
> It shall not rise qu' hill we lyk to raise it again,
> If it does not, we may say, 'Theiffe! Theiffe!'
> Conjure the wind, and cause it to lie."

A belief in the storm-raising powers of witches was long-
§ est held in the Shetland and Orkney Islands. Marian Peebles,§ in the former isles, in 1642, assumed the shape of a

---

* Act IV, scene 1.
† Sir Walter Scott.—Pirate.
‡ Wright.—Witchcraft and Sorcery in the Middle Ages, p. 358.
§ Scott.—Demonology and Witchcraft.

porpoise, and wrecked a boat with five men. Another witch used a bowl in water, thus causing storms, and a third employed this means to wreck boats in the bay of Furzie.

These notions concerning witches prevailed also in England, during the sixteenth and seventeenth centuries.

The following extract from a state paper refers to the witches of the time of Charles I. *"The greatest news from the country is of a huge pack of witches, which are lately discovered in Lancashire, whereof it is said nineteen are condemned, and that there are at least sixty already discovered, and yet daily there are more reveal'd; there are divers of them of good ability, and they have done much harm. I hear it is suspected that they had a hand in raising the great storm wherein his Majesty was in so great danger at Sea in Scotland."

† In 1716, a Mrs. Hicks and her daughter were tried as witches in England. Among other things, they were said to have raised storms and wrecked ships by pulling off their shoes, and making with them a lather of soapsuds. Another old witch in Devonshire was popularly reported to raise storms. A visit to her cabin brought to light several implements of her incantations. A mop-handle had the head ornamented with a miniature sail, and a dried fish.

Another Devonshire tradition relates that three witches boarded a vessel at sea, feasted on rich food, and sank the vessel.

At Borrowstone, a witch was accused of sending a storm to wreck her son, who had been washed overboard by one wave and back by the next.

‡ An old woman named Leckie, living in Somersetshire, was said to have caused storms. She would come to the pier and call for a boat. If it came, all in it would be wrecked. If it did not come, the same fate awaited them. She appeared in her own shape in her son's vessel, and raised a storm by blowing a tin whistle, when the ship was wrecked, but the men saved. Seamen affirmed they often heard the old lady's whistle in a gale. A witch on the Isle of Man was said to have caused a storm and the loss of all of the herring fleet. She was put in a spiked barrel and rolled down a hill.

§ The witch of Fraddam, alluded to in the " Legends of

* " The Lancashire Witches."
† Scott.—Demonology and Witchcraft.
‡ Scott.—Notes to Rokeby, p. 16.
§ Bottrell.—Traditions of West Cornwall.

the Spectre Ship," cruises still off the coast of England in her coffin, and raises storms. At St. Leven, Cornwall, is a cubical pile of stones called Madge Figge's chair. A witch so named was fabled to sit there and conjure up storms.

Another witch is still to be seen, at times, on the Logan rock, on the same coast, gloating over wrecks.

* We read in Sandy's Ovid, "I have heard of sea-faring men, and some of Bristol, how a quartermaster in a Bristol ship, then trading in the streights, going down into the hold, saw a sort of women, his own neighbors, making merry together, and taking their cups liberally; who having espied him, and threatening that he should report their discovery, vanished suddenly out of sight; who thereupon was lame forever after. The ship having made her voyage, nowe homeward bound, and neere her harbour, stuck fast in the deep sea, before a fresh gaile, to their no small amazement, nor for all they could doe, together with the helpe that came from the shore, could they get her loose, until one (as Cynothea, the Trojan ship), shoved her off with his shoulder." This was alleged against the witches as a piece of revenge, and they were convicted and executed.

The witch of Hayle received money so late as the eighteenth century for keeping storms from sailor's vessels. One of the last storm-raising witches was Annie Bodenham. But says Grant: † "It is but a few years since a pretended wizard professed to remove an evil spell from a sea captain, by making him throw a stone in the sea, and by uttering certain gibberish."

‡ Middleton reproduces these popular ideas concerning witches,—

> "She raises all your sudden num'rous storms
> That shipwreck barks."

Storm-making witches were known all over Europe. In the Norse Gisli Saga, a witch, Andbroga, raised a storm by going around "against the sun," and wrecked ships. In § "Grettir the Strong," a witch, makes the sea smooth before a boat. According to a Schleswick-Holstein legend, three witches are overheard by a lad to declare their purpose of following and wrecking their husbands' ships. They declare that a clean-handed person, with a virgin sword, could

* Jones.—Credulities.
† Mysteries of all Nations.
‡ "The Witch."
§ Magnusson and Morris.

repel them. When they came, in the shape of three waves, the youth struck them with his new sword, and the waves were red with blood. When the sea-faring men returned home, all their wives were dead.

Mannhardt tells a story of a German girl, who, when asked what she was doing at a fountain, replied: "I am doing what mother does. She takes a stick and turns it round in the fountain, and then there comes a storm." *

We hear of the deeds of storm-raising witches in New England. Margaret Jones, of Charlestown, was executed for witchcraft.† Soon afterward a ship, on which the witch's husband was to have sailed for the Barbadoes, commenced to roll violently at anchor in smooth water, continuing the motion for twelve hours. Finally the husband of the executed witch was arrested, and while on his way over to Boston, when asked by the sheriff if he could not stop the ship's rolling, did so on being shown the warrant for his arrest.

A ship going from London to Virginia, in 1674, is said to have encountered storms and other disasters from the machinations of witches.

Polly Twichell, who lived in Casco Bay in the seventeenth century, was said to raise storms, wreck ships and put to sea in severe gales.

‡ Goody Cole, in the " Wreck of Rivermouth," prophesies disaster. The skipper says,—

> " I'm scary always to see her shake
> Her wicked head."

The ballad recounts that she was jeered at by the pleasure party, prophesied the boat's loss, which occurred soon after.

§ Moll Pitcher, at Lynn, was also reputed a storm-raiser, and there are other legends of witches on our coast, who raised storms and wrecked ships.

We have seen how potent were the Finns and Laplanders in the sailors' imagination, in raising storms and in smoothing the waves. But they were also particularly famed for a traffic in winds, selling them to sailors for a stated price.

This selling of winds, as we have before said, is chron-

---

* See also Nicolai Remigii, Cologne, 1596, in Figuer, Hist. du Merveilleux, 1870.
† Mass. Hist. Collection.
‡ Whittier's Poems.
§ Drake.—Legends and Folk-lore of New England.

icled of these same Laplanders and Finns by Olaus Magnus.*
They gave a cord with three knots in it. If one were
loosed, a fair wind would blow; if two, a storm, and three,
a gale.   Olaus says, " The Finlanders were wont formerly,
among their other errors of gentilism, to sell winds to merchants that were stopped on their coast by contrary winds,
and when they had their price, they knit three magical
knots, not like the laws of Cassius, bound up with a thong,
and they gave them to the merchants, observing this rule,
that when they unloosed the first, they should have a good
gale of wind; when the second, a stronger wind; but when
they untied the third, they should have such cruel tempests that they should not be able to look out of the
forecastle to avoid the rocks, nor move a foot to pull down
the sails, nor stand at the helm to govern the ship; and they
made an unhappy trial of the truth of it, who denied that
there was any such power in the knots.

  † An earlier chronicler writes thus concerning this trade:
" In that Ilonde is sortilege and witchcraft, for women there
sell the shipmen wynde, as it were closed vnder thre knotes
of threde, so that the more wynde he would have, the more
knotes he mvst vndo."

  ‡ Two later authors speak of the selling of wind-knots
" practiced by the Norwegian Finnlapps."

  § Cotton Mather says: "A Laplander, the successors of
old Biarni, who can with looks or words bewitch other
people, or sell winds to mariners."

  Drayton, in the " Moon Calf," sings (865),—

  "She could sell winds to anyone that would
  Buy them for money, forcing them to hold
  What time she listed, tie them in a thread.
  Whichever way the seafarer wended
  They rose or scanted, as his sails would drive
  To the same port, whereas he would arrive."

  ‖ Thorpe tells a legend of a skipper of Aarhus, who was
given by a " Finlap," a bag containing the winds, whereby
he might have any wind he wished, by hanging it outside
his cabin door.

  The Finns did not, however, possess a monopoly in this

* History of the Goths.
† Higden —Polychronicon, 1484.
‡ Scheffer.—Lapponia and Ziegler.
§ Magnalia Christi Americana.—" More Wonders," etc.
‖ Northern Mythology, Bk. II, p. 198.

profitable wind-trade ; others were early in the field. Glan-
vill tells us concerning the inhabitants of Vinland:* "They
often sell winds to navigators cast or detained on their
shores. They make a ball of thread by tying in it several
knots. They loose as many as three or more, according to
the strength of the wind desired."

† At Siseby, on the Schlei, lived a witch imp, some fifty
years ago, who sold winds to fishermen, giving them a cloth
with three knots tied in it.

‡ Winds were sold at one time at Mount St. Michael, in
Normandy, by a Druidess. Three arrows were given the
purchaser, but they must be shot by a young man under
twenty-five.

§ Scott tells us: "At the village of Stromness, on the
Orkney main island, called Pomona, lived, in 1814, an aged
dame called Bessie Millie, who helped out her subsistence by
selling winds to mariners. He was a venturesome master of a
vessel, who left the roadstead of Stromness without paying his
offering to propitiate Bessie Millie. Her fee was extremely
moderate, being exactly sixpence, for which, as she explained
herself, she boiled her kettle, and gave the bark the advan-
tage of her prayers, for she disclaimed all unlawful arts."

They were sold in the Isle of Man during the present
century.‖ Old John McTaggart was a trader between Kintyre and Ireland. Wishing to get a fair wind to waft his
bark across to the Emerald Isle, he applied to an old woman,
who was said to be able to give this. He received from her
two strings, each bearing three knots. He undid the first
knot, and there blew a fine breeze. On opening the second,
the breeze became a gale. On nearing the Irish shore, he
loosed the third, and such a hurricane arose that some of
the houses on shore were destroyed. On coming back to
Kintyre, he was careful to loose only two knots on the remaining string."

** Sumner thus chronicles the common belief,—

"In Ireland and in Denmark both,
 Witches for gold will sell a man a wind,
 Which, if in the corner of a napkin wrapp'd,
 Shall blow him safe unto what coast he will."

* De Proprietatibus Rerum, Bk. 60, p. 172.
† Thorpe.—Northern Mythology, Bk. III, p. 23.
‡ Brewer.—Reader's Hand Book. " St. Michael."
§ Notes to Pirate.
‖ P. McIntosh.—History of Kintyre, 1870.
** Last Will and Testament, 1660. Brewer.—Readers' Hand Book.

And we read in " Rokeby,"—

" What gales are sold on Lapland's shore."

*Chinese mendicants pretend to sell winds, and so late as 1861, John Suttern, in Cornwall, claimed that he could buy a wind, but the trade has grown unprofitable in this age of steam, and we hear of it seldom.† Two persons, George and Eppie Foreman, were reputed a few years since, in a village in England, to deal in winds. No boat sailed without their being consulted.

These weather-makers all derive their power from the same source—Satanic intervention in the control of the elements. They are represented as having their power only through invocations of the Prince of Darkness, who had succeeded to the degraded gods of heathendom in his control of the weather. Sorcerers and witches were popularly supposed to derive all their powers from Satan, and hence the powers of the law and of the church were invoked against them. Women, being regarded as cruel and crafty, were especially his agents, hence were deemed unlucky on board ship, and as witches, possessed of great power over the storm and the wave. Although they derived their power from an opposite source, it was really a step in the same direction that led to the transferrence of this control from the saints to more accessible, and more venal agents.

We must regard the sale of the winds as a survival of an earlier stage of fetichism. The knots are a charm, serving precisely as the charm of the African, to work out the desires of the possessor. The transition from the bag of Æolus, that must be loosed to free the winds, to the knotted string was a natural one. The loosing of these knots corresponded to the shooting of arrows by the Namaquas, firing of muskets into storms by the Kalmucks, and other measures to charm or frighten the storm-demon.

Having thus considered the agents engaged in weather-making, there still remains a large class of weather-makers —passive instruments for the most part, in the hands of these agents—the secret of whose connection with the winds and weather is often past discovery. Not only were these animate beings imagined, for various reasons, to have some mysterious dealings with the storm-powers, but we also find

*Grant.—Mysteries of all Nations, p. 55.
† Fraser.—V, p. 46.

BESSIE MILLIE SELLING FAIR WINDS.

inanimate objects and obscure actions classed in the same category.

Certain animals were once thought to provoke storms at sea, and were thus regarded as unlucky by seamen. A dead hare on board ship has long been thought a storm-bringer. The hare is unlucky in many folk-lore stories. Many people, as Lapps, Finns, Chinese, Arabs and Hottentots, will not eat it. As an animal supposed to see at night, it was connected with the moon, shining by night, and we have Eastern traditions of the hare in the moon. Hence it is, with the moon, a weather-maker.

In Hottentot lore, it was the servant of the moon. Gubernatis says: * "The mythical hare is undoubtedly the moon. Spots in the moon suggest it, and the same name is used in Sanskrit for them and for the hare. In a Buddhist legend, it is transfigured into the moon."

It is connected with many superstitions in Germany, and English witches are said to have become hares. Camden says a day was set apart in Ireland for killing hares, found among the cattle, as witches. A writer in the *Athenæum*, in 1846, speaks of a witch in Scotland "who has been seen a hundred times milking the cows in the shape of a hare." Traditionally, it is greatly affected by the weather, and is especially frisky about the vernal equinox, and hence the proverb, "As mad as a March hare," or as it was in the seventeenth century, "Staring madde like March hares." †

In Cornish belief, a white hare appears before a storm, on the docks and wharves.

"Fishermen in Berkshire," says an old chap book, "look on all hares to be devils and witches, and if they but see a sign of a dead hare, it sets them all trembling."

An English ship got into a gale not many years since, and a dead hare found on board was immediately thrown into the sea, as the bringer of the storm.

‡ In Scotland, you must not say to a fisherman, "you have a hare (kink) in your creel," or name the animal in his boat, or bring any portion of it there, for it is sure to provoke a storm.

It is also unlucky on board of French ships.

§ The cat was still more widely feared as a storm-bringer,

* Zoological Mythology, Vol. I.
† Bokke of Knowledge.
‡ Grant.—Mysteries, p. 502.
§ Hazlitt.—Pop. Antiq. of Great Britain.

and is always unlucky on board ship. She "carries a gale in her tail," and is *thought particularly to provoke a storm by playing with a gown or apron, rubbing her face, licking her fur the wrong way, etc.

† In Sicilian belief, the mewing of a cat while telling a rosary for sailors, presages a tedious voyage. Provoking a cat will certainly bring a gale, in sailor belief, and drowning one will surely raise a tempest. ‡ Fielding says, "The kitten at last recovered, to the great joy of the good captain, but to the great disappointment of some of the sailors, who asserted that the drowning of a cat was the very surest way of raising a favorable wind."

§ Cheever says: "We took on board at Gibraltar a large and beautiful cat. We were bound to ———, and, as it happened, had a tedious succession of light head winds and dead calms. The sailors at last began to look on our new comer as a sort of Jonas on board. The next morning, the black cat was missing, and suspicion fell very justly on an old sailor who had been heard to threaten her life. I asked this old sailor what could induce him to commit such an act of cruelty. He acknowedged that he sank her to get a breeze."

‖ Brand says: "Sailors, I am informed on the authority of a naval officer, have a great dislike to see the cat on board ship, unusually playful or frolicsome; such an event they consider prognosticates a storm, and they have a saying on these occasions that 'a cat has a gale of wind in her tail.'"

** In Newcastle, England, throwing a cat overboard provoked a storm, and sailors' wives in Scarborough, some years since, kept a black cat in the house to insure their husband's safety at sea.

Marryat tells a sailor-story of the murder of a cat, where great disasters followed. The captain and first lieutenant, in opposition to the wishes of a crew, shot a cat, and are killed shortly afterward in a boat expedition.

†† In "The Honest Penny," a cat causes a storm at sea.
‡‡ There is a story told on Block Island, of a man who

* Grant.—Mysteries, p. 394.
† Gubernatis.—Zoological Mythology, Vol. II, p. 64.
‡ Journal of a Voyage to Lisbon. 1775.
§ Sea and Shore.
‖ Popular Antiquites.
** Folk-lore Record.
†† Dasent.—Tales from the Norse.
‡‡ Livermore.—History of Block Island.

shut a cat up in a barrel to prevent a skipper from sailing, against whom he had a grudge, and no wind came until the cat was released.

*In a Chinese tale, an *iron cat*, General Mao, appears floating on the water, sent by the water-king to raise a storm.

Flaws on the surface of the water are in sailor-lore "cat's-paws." †There is a Hungarian proverb that a cat does not die in water, hence its paws disturb the surface. A larger flurry on the water is a "cat-skin." So it rains "cats and dogs," and the stormy northwest wind in some parts of England is the "cat's-nose." In Chinese-lore, tigers cause storms, and the Japanese wind-god has steel claws and a tigerish countenance.

In Germany, there is a proverb that any one making a cat his enemy, will be attended at his funeral by rats and rain.

‡In Lancashire belief, stormy and wet weather is coming when the cat frisks about the house. §It is said in Iceland if she stretches so that her paws touch each other, bad weather will ensue.

‖Scotch fishermen declare that if the cat sneeze or licks her paws, rain will surely come. **In Shetland, the cat "gaanin in da luft," foretells wind, and "sleepin' upon her harns," (with the back of her head down) indicates calms.

†† "If the cat washes her face over the ear
'Tis a sign the weather'll be fine and clear,"

says an old proverb. But if she only washed it over one ear, it was a sign of bad weather.

‡‡Melton, an old writer, says: "When the cat washes her face over the eare, we shall have great store of rain."

Cats were, as we have seen, used by witches in raising a gale, and are said to smell a wind, while pigs see it. On shipboard, the malevolent character of the cat is shown in nautical nomenclature, and the song lately popular,—

"It was the cat,"

* Giles.
† Gubernatis.—Zoological Mythology, Vol. II, p. 64.
‡ Notes and Queries.
§ Powell and Magnusson.—Icelandic Legends.
‖ Gregor.—Folk-lore of Scotland.
** Blind.—Contemporary Review, September, 1882.
†† Swainson.—Weather-lore.
‡‡ Astrologaster.

is liable to more than a double interpretation. The cat-o'-nine-tails is not a desirable acquaintance, nor do sailors have a love for the miscellaneous gear connected with raising the anchor, such as the cat-head, cat-fall, cat-tail, cat-hook, cat-back, etc. The lubber's hole, through which it is thought derogatory to the able seaman to pass, is in French, "Trou de Chat." Weak tea is called by sailors "cat-lap," an unsatisfactory sleep, a "cat-nap."

* "The cat in folk-lore is commonly diabolical," says Gubernatis, "and in the bag of proverbs has probably a diabolical allusion. The popular idea that it has nine lives, expresses its mystic character."

Cats see better at night, are connected with the moon in many legends, are witches' familiars, and hence are eyed askant by many.

† The Egyptian goddess of evil, Pasht, was a cat-headed goddess.

‡ Hecate transformed herself into a cat to escape Typhon, and Diana became a cat. Hellenic cosmogony declared that the moon created the cat. Freya, the Norse goddess, was attended by cats, and thus Friday, her day, was thought unlucky.

§ In Hungary, every cat was thought to be a witch from its seventh to its twelfth year. The nightmare often comes as a cat in Germany, where also the sea was popularly called a *cat*.‖

** Blind thinks the cat's sensitiveness to meteorological changes may have helped the formation of these ideas in regard to her connection with the weather. This is doubtless true, but the chief cause of the superstition was, perhaps, her connection with the moon, and her supposed diabolical character; especially true, it was believed, of the black cat, the representative of the cloudy, moonless night.

†† A spectral dog "shony" is said to predict a storm when appearing on the Cornish beach

To mention the name of a dog will bring on a storm, say Scotch fishermen, and the dog when he howls fortells the tempest, in common belief. ‡‡ "The wind will come from

* Zoological Mythology, Vol. II, p. 65.
† Zoological Mythology, Vol. II, p. 66.
‡ Ovid.—Metamorphoses, V, 195, 52.
§ Gubernatis.—Zool. Mythology, Vol II, p. 67.
‖ Simrock.—Deutsche Mythology, 217.
** Contemporary Review, September, 1861.
†† Hunt.—Romances and Drolls of the North of England.
‡‡ Tenne.—Volkssagen aus Pommern.   p. 247.

the direction in which a dog points his nose when he howls." He is connected with the Wild Hunt in nearly all folk-lore—is a psychopomp, or soul-bearer, and is generally diabolical. On board ships, however, he is not usually disliked, probably by reason of his usefulness on watch, in port.

Many birds were thought to have dealings with the storm-spirits. Fishermen in the English Channel thought the east wind caused by the flight of curlew, or herring-spear, on dark nights. In an old ballad they are called "the seven whistlers," and portend storm. Seven is a number suspiciously mystical. *They were thought to announce great disasters, when passing over Yorkshire villages. In Lancashire they are called "Wandering Jews," and there is a tradition that they are the souls of Jews who assisted at the crucifixion, and hence are doomed ever to wander. We have seen that the Wandering Jew was a storm-bringer, in folk-legend.

† An old fisherman said to Buckland: "I think no good of them. There's always an accident when they come. I heard 'em once one dark night last winter. They come over our heads all of a sudden, singing 'Ewe, Ewe,' and the men in the boat wished to go back. It came on to rain and blow, and was an awful night, and sure enough, before morning, a boat was upset, and seven poor fellows drowned. I know what makes the noise, sir. It's them long-billed curlew, but I never likes to hear them."

‡ The cuckoo is, in England, a noted weather-bird, and fishermen listen for its first notes in the spring, as an indication of the weather and luck for the year. Cuckoos are thought in parts of England to appear before an equinoctial gale, and such a storm is a *gowk-storm*,—after that bird.

The swan floating in the waves is a harbinger of good weather, in many places.

Sea-fowl are regarded as furnishing indications of coming storm or sunshine in various localities.

> " When sea-birds fly to land,
>   A storm is at hand,"

is the general expression of this belief. .

§ In England, in 1790, it was said that rain and high winds

* Notes and Queries.
† Curiosities of Natural History.
‡ Dyer.—English Folk-lore.
§ Grant.—Mysteries of all Nations, p. 396.

from the south-southwest follow the appearance of sea-mews, within twenty-four hours. A Scotch rhyme says,—

> * "Sea-gull, sea-gull, sit on the sand,
> It's never good weather when you're on the land."

So the chattering and chuckling of sea-gulls, and fluttering of all sea-fowl in calms, cleaning their feathers, says Pliny, is a sign of bad weather, and later traditions report the same.

† "Sea-gulls in the field mean a southeast storm, when it is over, they go back on the beach," is a belief in Scotland, also alluded to by Scott,—

> "The sea-birds, with portentous shriek
> Flew fast to land."

We find the same ideas in three old English works. Wilsford ‡ says, when sea-mews make more than ordinary gurgling in the morning, wet weather will follow. This is corroborated in another old work, which also says that when fowls fly low over the sea, or high over the land, bad weather will follow. Again we read, "Some have observed evil weather to follow when watery fowls leave the sea, desiring lande; the fowles of the land flying hygher, the crying of fowles above water, making a great noyse with their wynges, also the seas swelling with unaccustomed waves."

These ideas may be traced back to antiquity. Virgil says,—

> § " When crying cormorants forsake the sea,
> And stretching to the coast, wend their way;
> When watchful herons leave their wat'ry stand,
> And mounting upward, with erected flight
> Gain on the skies and soar above the sight,"

wet weather will come.

The celebrated little bird, the Mother Cary's chicken, was also supposed to appear before a storm, as its name, the *Procellaria*, would indicate. It is also called alamottie and storm-fish. Its name Mother Cary's chicken means the bird of the Mater Cara, the Aves Sanctæ Mariæ, or the Oiseau de Notre Dame, of French sailors. Its name of petrel is from the Italian Petrello, or Little Peter, as it is

---

* Dyer.—English Folk-lore, p. 100.
† Sir J. Sinclair. Statistical account of Scotland, in Brand.—Bk. III, p. 218.
‡ "Nature's Secrets." Q. By Brand, III, 218.
§ Dryden.—Georgic, I.

supposed, like that saint, to walk the water. The tradition of its storm-foreboding character is shown in these lines from a modern poet,—

> *" The petrel telleth her tale in vain,
> For the mariner curseth the warning bird,
> Who bringeth him news of storms we heard."

And Mrs. Howitt says,—

> †" Oh, stormy, stormy peterel!
> Thou art a bird of woe,
> Yet would I thou couldst tell me half
> Of the misery thou dost know."

‡ Pennant thinks these birds gather from the water sea-animals, or their broken bodies, and hence find them in greater abundance before or after a storm, when the deep sea waves stir them up, and that thus mariners are warned of approaching storms.

The *goylir*, another sea-bird, is thought to appear before a storm, and was named by Spanish sailors "malafigo," or evil-bird.

It is thought by sailors a bad thing to kill a gull, and especially an albatross, and the "Ancient Mariner's" ill luck thus arose:

> § " At length did cross an albatross,
> Through the fog it came.
> As if it had been a Christian soul,
> We hailed it in God's name.
>
> * * * * * * *
>
> "And I had done a hellish thing,
> And it would work 'em woe,
> For all averred I had killed the bird
> That made the breeze to blow.
> 'Ah! wretch,' said they, ' the bird to slay,
> That made the breeze to blow!'"

But when the fog cleared away, they recant and say,—

> " Then all averred I had killed the bird
> That brought the fog and mist;
> ' 'Twas right,' said they, ' such birds to slay,
> That bring the fog and mist.'"

‖ De Quincey says Coleridge got the idea of the weather-

* Barry Cornwall.—Poems.
† The Stormy Petrel.
‡ Zoology.
§ Coleridge.—The Ancient Mariner.
‖ See Chap. VII.

bringing qualities of the slain albatross from a passage in Shelvocke's voyages, where the mate attributes a long spell of bad weather to the presence of an albatross.

A wide-spread tradition exists in many lands of the kingfisher. * This is, as Pliny tells us it was in Roman times, thus: " Halcyon days, days that are favorable to navigation. It is for this that the halcyon is more especially remarkable to the sea and those who sail on its surface. They hatch their young at the time of the winter solstice, from which circumstance these days are known as the 'halcyon days.' During this period the sea is calm and navigable, the Sicilian sea in particular. They make their nest during the seven days before the winter solstice, and sit the same number of days afterward." In another place the same author says, " For seven days before the winter solstice, and for the same length of time after it, the sea becomes calm, in order that the kingfishers may rear their young. From this circumstance they have obtained the name of halcyon days; the rest of the season is wintry."

Virgil says, in the " Georgics," among stormy weather prognostications,—

" Nor halcyons bask on the short sunny shore."

† Theocritus writes thus,—

' May halcyons smooth the waves and calm the seas,
And the rough southeast sink into a breeze."

‡ Simonides tells us: "When Zeus in the winter season creates twice seven mild days, mortals say, 'this tepid weather is nourishing the variously painted halcyons.'"

§ Plutarch bears testimony to the same tradition. He says, " But when the halcyon brings forth, about the winter solstice, the whole ocean remains calm and undisturbed, without the wrinkle of a wave. So that there is not any creature for which man has so great an affection, seeing that for her sake for seven days and seven nights together, in the depth of winter, they sail without fear of shipwreck, and may thus voyage on the sea with greater safety than they travel on the land." He also says she makes a floating nest of thorns, and sits on it.

* Nat. Hist., Bk. X, Ch. 47.
† Idylls.—Fawkes' Trans.
‡ In Plutarch's Morals, Goodwin's Trans.
§ Plutarch.—Morals.

9

* Ovid reports the ancient tradition,—

> "Alcyone comprest,
> Seven days sits brooding on her floating nest,
> A wintery queen.   Her sire at length is kind,
> Calms every storm and hushes every wind,
> Prepares his surface for his daughter's ease,
> And for his hatching nephews smooths the seas."

The Greeks gave the bird the name of Alcyon, saying that the daughter of Æolus, so named, drowned herself, and was changed into a bird, along with her lost husband, Ceyx. Later writers kept up the superstition.   Ariosto says,—

> ' Along the coast the mourning halcyon's heard
> Lamenting sore her spouse's fate."

And Camoens,—

> † " The halcyon birds their words of mourning told
> Along the roaring coast, sad scene of woe."

‡ Wilford tells us: " The halcyon, at the time of breeding, which is about fourteen days before the winter's solstice, foreshows a quiet and tranquil time, as it is observed about the coasts of Sicily, from whence the proverb is transported of *halcyon days*."

And Wild,—

> §" The peaceful kingfishers are met together
> About the decks, and prophesy calm weather."

Dryden says,—

> " Amidst our arms as quiet you shall be
> As halcyons breeding on a winter's sea."

And Southey,—

> |" The halcyons brood around the foamless isles,
> The treacherous ocean has foresworn its wiles."

And Shenstone, —

> ** " Why o'er the verdant banks of Ooze,
> Does yonder halcyon speed so fast?
> 'Tis all because she would not lose
> Her favorite calm that will not last."

* Metamorphoses.
† Os Lusiados.—Mickle's Trans.
‡ Nature's Secrets.
§ Iter Boreale, Vol. II.
| Epipsychcodrion.
** Ode to the Winds.

Milton also,—

> "The winds with wonder whist,
> Smoothly the waters kissed,
> Whispering new joys to the mild ocean,
> Who now hath quite forgot to rave,
> While birds of calm sit brooding on the charmed wave."

And Shakespeare,—

> † "Expect St. Martin's summer, halcyon days."

‡ Sir Thomas Browne is disposed to doubt the agency of the halcyons. "For at that time, which happeneth about the brumal solstice, it hath been observed, even unto a proverb, that the sea is calm and the winds do cease, till the young ones are excluded and forsake their nest, which floateth upon the sea, and by the roughness of the winds, might otherwise be overwhelmed." "But how fare hereby to magnify their prediction, we have no certain rule; for whether out of any particular provision they choose to set at this time, or whether it be their custom by concourse of care and providence of nature, is not yet determined."

This ancient tradition may perhaps be derived from one still more ancient. The Ribhus of Aryan mythology, storm-demons, slept for twelve nights about the winter solstice, as we know from translations from the Aryan writings; and one of Weber's texts reads, "The 12 nights are an image of the year." §

And another: "The Rhibhus sleep for 12 nights and days in the house of the sun-god *Savitar*."

Peasants of Lancashire say the weather for the year is foreshadowed by that of the twelve nights between Christmas and Epiphany.

‖ In Northern Germany, it is said that as the weather is during each of these twelve days, so it will be during each month of the year. ** Lloyd tells us it was so thought in England in his time. †† Forster says, "The fact, on which they (these beliefs) founded their existence, was the calm weather, which at that time of the year, on the shores of the Mediterranean, usually succeeds to the blustering winds of the early autumn."

* Christmas Hymn.
† King Henry VI, Act I, Scene 2.
‡ Pseudoxica Epidemica.
§ Kelly.—Curiosities of Indo-European Tradition.
‖ Kuhn.—Nord Deutsche Sagen, p. 411.
** Dial of Daies, 1590.
†† Natural History.

It was also believed in England, that if it blew on the fifth night of the twelve, there would be peril at sea for ships that year.

* The Ojibways had a tradition that the thunder-bird sat on her eggs during fair weather, and hatched out her brood in the storm.

Birds, as inhabitants of the air, and long supposed to commune with angels, were naturally chosen as oracles, and, as we shall see in another chapter, were chosen as augurs of future events. The extreme sensitiveness to atmospheric changes shown by many birds aided these ideas, and the real indications sometimes furnished by land and sea-birds of the coming storm or calm, were doubtless magnified by the anxious sailor. These indications, however, are not trustworthy, and seldom precede the changes more than a few hours, or sometimes even minutes. The killing of a sea-bird, as an albatross or a gull, would naturally, as a conse-quence of this regard for their supposed oracular character, be regarded as an ill omen, and as a presage of coming dis-aster.

Certain of the finny inhabitants of the deep were thought also to be able to portend storms.† Sailors yet say, when a shoal of porpoises or dolphins come along, diving and sport-ing in the waves, that a storm is impending, and that it will come from the direction taken by the fishes. This, also, is a very old superstition. Plutarch says, "When porpoises sport and chase one another about ships, expect then some stormy weather."

It was said that when dolphins carried Arion to the shore the winds ceased, or as Spenser has it,—

‡ "And all the raging seas forgot to roar."

Cæsar's pilot says,—

§ "In various turns the doubling dolphins play,
And thwart, and run across, and mix their way."

| Bede says he had often noticed the frequent leaping of the porpoise, and had connected it with the rise of the wind and the clearing of the sky.

** Stow tells us, "A Dolphin came forth of the sea, and

* Brinton.—Myths of the New World.
† Jones.—Credulities, p. 44.
‡ Marriage of the Thames and Medway.
§ Rowe.—Lucan's Pharsalia.
| De Rerum Natura.
** Chronicles.

played himself in the Thames at London to the Bridge; foreshewing happily, the tempests that were to follow within a week after. These, when they play in rivers with hasty springings and leapings, doe signifie tempests to follow."

* We read in an old play: "For the sky is overcast, and there was a porpoise even now seen at London Bridge, which is always the messenger of tempests, the watermen say."

† And Shakespeare again illustrates the subject: "Nay, master, said I not as much when I saw the porpus, how he bounced and tumbled? They say they are half-fish, half-flesh! a plague on them! They never come, but I look to be washed."

In Ravenscroft's "Canterbury Guests," we read,—

‡ "My heart begins to leap and play like a porpoise before a storm."

§ An old traveler tells us: "We saw several *Porpises*, playing with their heads above water, which I mention only because the seamen look upon them as forerunners of a storm."

‖ Wilsford writes: "Dolphins, in fair and calm weather, pursuing one another in one of their waterish pastimes, foreshow wind, and from that part *whence* they fetch their tricks; but if they play thus when the seas are high and tumbled, it is a sign of fair and calm weather."

And again, "Porpoises, or sea-hogs, when observed to sport and chase one another about ships, expect then some stormy weather."

** "Dolphins as well as porpoises," says Forster, "when they come about a ship and sport and gambol on the surface of the water, portend a storm." And Pennant remarks: "The appearance of the Dolphin and the Porpoise are far from being esteemed favorable omens by the seamen, for their boundings, springs and frolics in the water, are held to be sure signs of a gale." So we find in Crabbe,—

†† "The unwieldy porpoise thro' the day before,
    Had roll'd in view of boding men on shore,
    And sometimes hid, and sometimes showed his form,
    Dark as the cloud and flashing as the storm."

* Eastward Hoe.—Chapman, Johnston and Marstons.
† Pericles, Act II, scene 1.
‡ Jones.—Credulities, p. 14.
§ Smith's Voyage to Constantinople.
‖ Nature's Secrets.
** Natural History.
†† Poems.

Modern sailors do not, however, give these animals so malevolent a character. * "Mellville says, " Their appearance is generally hailed with delight by the mariner. Full of fine spirits, they invariably come from the breezy billows to windward. They are the lads that always live before the wind. *They are always accounted a lucky omen.*"

This is still a doctrine of sailor belief, and modern seamen would seem to have revived the ancient idea that the dolphin is favorable to man. Perhaps the porpoise, whose name, sea-hog, would seem to indicate a diabolic character, gave its bad reputation to its gentler companion.

Sailors also think that it will storm when dolphins come into port. † Scotch fishermen call the porpoise " louper dog," and say when they tumble with a forward motion, a breeze is coming, and also assert that they swim *against* the wind.

Perhaps the mythical character of the dolphin aided in giving it its malevolent reputation. It is generally understood to typify the moon. ‡ Gubernatis says, " The lunar horn announces rain; thus the scythe-shaped fin of the dolphin, appearing on the waves of the sea, announces a tempest to navigators, and saves them from shipwreck." All the animals connected in folk-lore with the moon are diabolical, a relic probably of the antipathy of the sun-worshipers to the queen of the night.

§ Plutarch says the cuttle-fish, appearing on the surface, is a sign of the coming storm; that " when the polypus gets to shore and embraces the rocks, it is a sign the wind is rising; but the cuttle-fish jump up to show the cold and the trouble at the bottom of the sea."

| Wilsford says, " Cuttle-fish, with their many legs swimming on top of the water, and striving to be above the waves, do presage a storm." Also, " Fishes, both in salt water or fresh, are observed to sport most against a rain than at any other time." He further says, " Cockles and most shell-fish are observed against a tempest to have sand sticking unto their shells, as a provident nature to stay themselves." " Floating sea-pulmones," says Pliny, " are portents of stormy days to come."

* " Moby Dick,"
† Gregor.—Folk-lore of Scotland.
‡ Zoological Mythology, Vol. II.
§ Morals.—Goodwin's Trans.
| Brand.—Nature's Secrets, Vol. III, p. 135,

* Pliny says, concerning the sea-urchin, " It is said that these creatures foretell the approach of storms at sea, and that they take up little stones with which they cover themselves, and so provide a sort of ballast against their volubility. As soon as sea-faring men observe them, they at once moor their ships with several anchors."

† Forster also: " Urchins of the sea, when they thrust themselves in the sand, and try to cover their bodies with sand, foretell a storm."

‡ In Icelandic belief, the fledermaus, a fabulous sea-animal, would cause great tempests, etc., if not thrown into the sea before the death of its captor.

From these animated storm-signals and weather-indicators, the transition to inanimate forms that may furnish, by their presence or absence, indications or provocations of the tempest or the favoring breeze, is easy.

Many inanimate objects were long reputed wind-raisers. Dead bodies on board were regarded as certain to cause disaster, which might ensue from the presence of portions of the skeleton, or the dried mummy of the corpse.

§ We read in the travels of an early writer the following example of this belief: "Another miracle happened as I was going by sea with the bones (of four martyred friars) to Polumbrum, . . . when the wind totally failed us." After relating that prayers, etc., were said, he continues: " But as time passed on, and no wind came, I gave one of the bones to our servant, whom I ordered to go to the head of the ship, and cast the bone into the sea; which he had no sooner done, than a favorable gale sprang up, which never failed us until we had arrived at our destined port in safety, owing entirely to the merit of these holy martyrs."

‖ Shakspeare illustrates this superstition,—

" *First Sailor.*—Sir, your queen must overboard; the sea works high, the wind is loud, and will not lie till the ship be cleared of the dead.
Pericles.—That's your superstition.
First Sailor.—Pardon us, sir; with us at sea it hath been still observed, and we are strong in custom. Therefore, briefly, yield her; for she must overboard straight."

** Fuller thus speaks of St. Louis: " His body was carried into France, there to be buried, and was most miserably

* Natural History.
† Natural History.
‡ Powell and Magnusson.—Icelandic Legends.
§ Travels of Oderic, 1318-50.
‖ Pericles. Act III, scene 2.
** " Holy War." Jones.--Credulities, p. 91,

tossed, it being observed that the sea cannot digest the cru-
dity of a dead corpse, being a due debt to be interred where
it dieth, and a ship cannot abide to be made a bier of."

St. Louis, then, was not so powerful as St. Mark, who
calmed the storm in his passage from Africa. * A quaint
old work, "A Helpe to Memory and Discourse" (1639), asks
whether " doth a dead body in a shippe cause the shippe to
sail slower, and if it doe, what is thought to be the reason
thereof?" Answer: "The shippe is as insensible of the living as of the dead, and as the living make it goe the faster,
so the dead make it not goe the slower, for the dead are no
Rhemoras to alter the course of her passage, tho' some there
be that thinke so, and that by a kind of mournful sympathy."

† Radzovillius relates that he brought two mummies from
Egypt, in a ship that was attacked by a fearful storm. The
pri   said masses and prayers, but asserted that they were
haunted by two spectres. The storm not subsiding, the
mummies were thrown overboard by the servant of Radzovillius, who alone was in the secret of their presence on
board.

‡ Another old traveler tells us, "I had, among my bag-
gage, the hand of a syren or fisherman, which I threw, on
the sly, into the sea, because the captain, seeing that we
could not make way, asked me if I had not got some mummy
or other in my bags, which hindered our progress, in which
case we must return to Egypt, to carry it back." "Most of
the Provençals have the opinion that vessels which transport the mummies from Egypt have great difficulty in arriving safe at port; so that I feared, lest, coming to search
among my goods, they might take the hand of the fish for
a mummy's hand, and insult me on account of it."

We also read, in the chronicle of the monastery at
Durham: "And so the bushop, the abbotte, and the reste,
being weirye of travellynge, thought to have stoulne away
and carried Sancte Cuthbert's body into Ireland, for his
better saifftie. And being upon the sea in a shippe, by
myricle marveillous, iij waves of water were turned into
blood. The shippe that they were in was dreven back by
tempeste, and by the mightie powre of God, as it should
seemé, vpon the shore or land."

* Jones.—Credulities, p. 92.
† Hierosolymæ Perigrinatio.
‡ Bouillaye le Gous.—Travels, 1657.

*Captain Warren, of an English merchant ship, found a derelict vessel, in August, 1775, that had long been ice-bound, with her cabins filled with the bodies of the frozen crew. His own sailors, however, would not suffer him to search the vessel thoroughly, through superstition, and wished to leave her immediately.

†Captain Basil Hall tells us: "This is a superstition easily accounted for amongst men whose entire lives are passed, as it were, on the very edge of the grave, and who have quite enough, as they suppose, to remind them of their mortality, without the actual presence of its effects." "The loss of a mast, the long duration of a foul wind, or any other inconvenience, is sure to be ascribed to the same influence."

‡Chaplain Rockwell says that his ship was driven unexpectedly to sea, with the coffined body of a man ready for burial on board. The man was buried at sea, but the crew insisted that the coffin should be cut into fragments, and thrown likewise into the sea, as it was deemed a bad omen to keep it. § Nelson was presented with a coffin made from the mainmast of the French ship Orient, his antagonist at the Nile, and, at first kept in the cabin, but the superstitious feelings of his crew caused him to stow it away out of sight.

❘Du Chaillu says he brought a box of negro bones on board ship with him in Africa. The sailors found it out, and were very reluctant to allow him to keep them on board, imagining that storm, wreck, and disaster were thus courted.

Collin de Plancy says that French fishermen and sailors, but a few years since, thought the presence of a dead body on board ship would bring a storm.

Canadian legends relate that the body of Father Labrosse, a priest who died on one of the islands of the St. Lawrence, protected the fisherman who conveyed it to the shore, safely leading his boat amid perils of storm and floating ice.

**There is a German tradition that suicides by hanging raise a storm. This is doubtless from a Norse legend that Vikarr, a pirate chief, was wind-bound on a cruise, and cast

* Westminster Review, q. by Jones—Broad, Broad Ocean, p. 27.
† Voyages (1811).
‡ Sketches of Foreign Travel (1847).
§ Jones.—Credulities, 92.
❘ My Apingi Kingdom.
** Kuhn and Schwartz.—Deutsche Sagen.

lots to see who was to be sacrificed. The lot fell on the chief himself, and he attempted to evade it by hanging himself symbolically, but Odin caused it to be real. So Odin comes in the storm to claim his suicides, and he hanged himself for nine days on Yggdrasil, the famous ash-tree. [*] In Markland, when a storm arises, it is said that some one has hanged himself in the forest.

The traditional appearance of a mermaid, or of any such apparition, was thought enough to insure a gale.

> [†] " The fishers have heard the water-sprite
> Whose screams forbode that wreck is nigh."

> [‡] " 'Tis a mermaid
> Has toll'd my son to shipwreck."

And this brings us naturally to bells.

The ringing of bells was long thought to conjure up storms. Bells, on the contrary, are rung in some parts of Europe to calm the winds. Bacon says "the sound of bells will disperse lightning and thunder; in winds it has not been observed." [§]In the "Golden Legend" we read: " It is said that evil spirytes that ben in the region of th' ayre doute moche when they here the belles ringen, when it thondreth, and when grete tempeste and rages of wether happen, to the end that the feinds and wycked spirytes should be abashed and flee, and cease of the movynge of tempests, and this is the cause why the belles ben rongen."

[|] A legend related by Jones runs thus: "Several sets of bells belonging to the churches in Guernsey, sank on their passage to France, where they were going to help pay the cost of war. Fishermen of St. Ouen's Bay still say they ring before a storm, and when they pretend to hear them, will not venture out."

[**] The legend of Tintagel bells in Cornwall, is that when a rival set of bells was being conveyed into the harbor, and vespers sounded, the pilot thanked God for the speedy voyage, but the captain scoffed, when his ship was wrecked, and still the bells sound in storms,—

> " Still when the storm of Bottreaux' waves
> Is waking in his weedy caves,
> Those bells that sullen surges hide
> Peal their deep tones beneath the tide."

[*] Kuhn.—Märkische Sagen.   [§] In Jones' Credulities, p. 104.
[†] Scott.—Lay of the Last Minstrel, xxiii.   [|] See Ch. xiv.
[‡] Middleton.—" The Roaring Girl."   [**] See Ch. xiv.

Christened bells were particularly efficacious, and many are still found in Europe, bearing inscriptions testifying to their power.

* Googe says,—

"For in these christened belles they thinke, doth lie such powere and might,
As able is the tempest great, and storme to vanquish quight."

Many seamen believe that the ships' bell will toll just as she is sinking, even if it be securely lashed in place.

†A legend of Helgoland tells us that a bell came to the island mysteriously floating on a crucifix, during an east wind-storm. When an east wind was thereafter desired, it was only necessary to go to the church, pray before the crucifix, and drink out of the cup, when the wind would come, within three days.

Stones were also endowed with wind-raising qualities. ‡ In one of the Hebrides was a chapel dedicated to St. Columba. A blue stone in it was always moist. When fishermen wanted a fair wind, they wet this stone. A similar stone existed in a chapel on Fladda Chuan,§ in the Western Islands. Stones in a well in Gigha Island are believed to raise a tempest if removed.

‖ Collin de Plancy says it was believed in ancient times that the Getæ had certain stones, Gedi, that would cause storms when plunged into water. This is like the stone "Yadah" of Polo's Mongol weather-makers.

A certain fog-bank across a cove in Cornwall is called the Hooper, or Hoola, and is thought to portend a storm. Norfolk fishermen believe that when any one is drowned, a voice is heard from the water, and portends a squall.

It was formerly believed in England that storms arose on the death of a great man, and did not subside until he was buried.

**"Chinese sailors observe various customs for producing a fair wind. On leaving port, they attract the attention of their divinity by the loud beating of a gong, and burning of fire crackers and incense sticks, and casting food offerings in the water."

Northmen had resort to runes, or magical verses, en-

* Naogeorgus.
† Noblook, 1643.
‡ Jones.—Credulities, p. 70.
§ Grant.—Mysteries, p. 422.
‖ Dictionnaire Infernale.
** Gibbons.—Boxing the Compass.

graved on bow, stern, rudder, etc., to propitiate the gods of
wind and waves.   One of these is alluded to in one of the
Sagas:

> "Sea runes thou must know,
> If thou wilt have secure
> Thy floating steed.
> On the prow they must be carved,
> And on the helm blade,
> And with fire to the oar applied.
> Nor surges shall be so lowering,
> Nor waves so dark
> But from the Ocean thou safe shalt come."

* And the ancient Edda thus speaks of them: " I know a
song of such virtue that were I caught in a storm, I can
hush the winds, and render the air perfectly calm."

† Blind gives us a Shetland charm, doubtless a degraded
tradition of some old rune,—

> "Robbin cam over da *vaua* (water), wi' a shū nū
> Twabbie, Toobie, Keelikin Kallikin
> Palk trick alanks ta robin,
> Guid! sober da wind!

‡ We also read of charms to raise storms or allay the
winds, used in Greenland by the Esquimaux.

§ The Italian traveler, Nicolo da Conto (1419–44), tells us
how Arab mariners then controlled winds.   A table was
placed near the mainmast, with a brazier of coals on it, the
crew assembled near by.   Incantations, addressed particularly to Muthian, king of wicked spirits, were repeated by
the captain, while the crew stood tremblingly by.   Suddenly, a sailor was seized with a frenzy, rushed to the table,
seized a live coal, and swallowed it.   He then said he must
have the blood of a cock, to quench his thirst.   One of these,
kept for the purpose, was given him, and he sucked the
blood and threw the body into the sea; then declaring to the
crew that he was able to promise them the desired wind,
he indicated its probable direction, and fell on the deck
exhausted.

∥ Before Barbary corsairs sailed, a Marabout, or holy man,
was visited and prayers sought, and a sheep purchased for
sacrifice.   When a storm arose, this was cut, and the entrails

* Sæmundr Edda, Havamal, p. 157.
† Contemporary Review, September, 1881.
‡ Rink.— Tales and Traditions of the Esquimau
§ Renard.—Les Merveilles del'Art Naval, 282.
∥ P. Dan.—History of Barbary, p. 321.

nearest the head thrown to the right to propitiate good spirits, and the others to the left to appease evil ones, these being accompanied with groans, cries, and incantations. Oil was also poured on the water, all the candles lighted, etc. If these all failed, the Christian captives in row-galleys were beaten, and made to pray to the Virgin and saints. At other times, they blew the breath to the right and left, lit no pipes nor performed necessary acts until the weather changed, repeating the sacrifices.

Sacrifices were made universally in antiquity, to obtain a wind. We shall recur to the subject of sacrifices in a later chapter; but we may say here that Virgil's picture is often repeated:

* " The shouting crew their ships with garlands bind,
Invoke the sea-gods and invite the wind."

† Hebertstein, a sixteenth century traveler, says that Russian sailors in the Baltic averred that a certain deity at a rocky promontory, the " Holy Nose," must be propitiated in order to get a wind. They were ridiculed by others, but one did get on shore, and poured on the cliff a libation of oatmeal and butter.

Savages, too, sacrificed to obtain a breeze. In Lake Superior, Indians sacrificed two dogs and some tobacco to the spirit of the waters, for a good wind. ‡ A traveler in the Indian packet " Lahore," in 1853, relates that the Indian crew and passengers gathered a sum of money and placed it at the disposal of the wind-spirit, for a good breeze. So a recent traveler in Japan says coins were thrown into the sea to obtain a breeze, and again, to propitiate the god of storms.

Instead of sacrifices, prayers were thought efficacious.

An old woman named Scott, living in the Orkneys half a century ago, prayed for winds for sailors' wives.

§ " About evening, the wind arose, after much invocating, whistling, many prayers and curses."

In Hassan's story, in the Arabian Nights, prayer allays a storm. It would perhaps be rash to say that a belief in the efficacy of prayer to obtain a favoring breeze, or allay a storm, is entirely extinct. The subject will be treated more fully in a subsequent chapter.

* Dryden's Æneid, IV.
† Jones.—Credulities, 68. See Chapter XII.
‡ Jones.—Credulities, 65.
§ Thornbury.—The Buccaneers, p. 77.

* A he-goat's skin suspended to the mast-head was thought by Hebrides Islanders to secure a good breeze.

† On board French ships, a game of cards was, a few years ago, thought to provoke a storm, and we can only imagine this to have influenced the late naval edict against playing on shipboard, except in the sacred precincts of the cabin.   Playing on a musical instrument was long thought provocative of a storm, and a seaman's prejudice against a "wind-jammer" is not yet extinct.   Chinese, when desiring a favorable breeze, woo the winds to the din of tom-toms and cymbals.

‡ French sailors once thought it only necessary to flog a boy at the mast, in order to obtain a fine breeze.

§ For a punishment, the boy received fifteen lashes of the whip.   They took care to turn the negro's posterior from the side in which they desire the breeze.   A mulatto called the married man, rubbed his head against the tiller, the stern of a boy, and the head of a cuckold being the best means to raise the wind.

| Italian sailors believe they can change the wind, by showing it their posteriors.

** A Hamburg tradition says that if you have long had a contrary wind, and meet a ship bound in the opposite direction, throw a broom before her, and you will get a fair wind.   In Altmark, if you want a wind, you must burn an old broom, in †† Pomerania, cast the broom in the fire, with the handle pointing toward the desired wind.   The winds are represented in popular ideas as sweeping the sky, as the witches' broom, which, long their favorite courser, on which they ride the wind, now represents it.

Thus Van Tromp's broom, which typified his ability to sweep the English fleet from the channel, may, in the opinion of his sailors, have brought to him fair winds to aid him in reaching Cromwell's fleet.   A northwest gale on our coast, that clears the sky of clouds, was called "sweeper of the sky," and the French name such winds "balai du ciel."

‡‡ Dr. Kuhn says the light scudding clouds, which are

* Grant.—Mysteries, 432.
† Jones.—Broad Broad Ocean, p. 239.
‡ Choice Notes, N. and Q., p. 60.
§ E. Corbiere.—Le Négrier in Mélusine, 1884.
| O. Jahn.—Q. in Mélusine, 1884.
** Thorpe.—Northern Mythology, Vol. III, p. 188.
†† Tenne.—V. Sag. v. Pom., 342.
‡‡ Märkische Sagen.

represented by the witches' broom, are talismans "in Germany and Lancashire."

These, in sailor lore, are the "mare's tails," where,—

> "Mackerel skies and mare's tails
> Make tall ships carry low sails."

*At Roscoff, in Brittany, fishermen obtained the dust swept out of the church De la Sainte Union, so as to obtain a favorable breeze by blowing it seaward; †and a Danish fleet on the Scotch coast is said to have been wrecked by a witch, who emptied a holy well, and swept out the church.

Sardinian sailors obtained a good breeze by sweeping a chapel after mass, and blowing the dust from it after departing ships.

Old sailors have not yet forgotten to scratch the mast for a breeze,—some say the foremast, others the mizzen; others say, stick a knife in the mizzen-mast, pointing the handle in the desired quarter. ‡"Scratch the foremast with a nail; you will get a good breeze."

Frazer says water from a well in West Scotland was scattered in the air, with invocations, to raise a storm, the cover being put on the well to prevent hurricanes from ensuing.

Benjamin of Tudela says the planet Orion caused storms in the China Seas, and wrecked junks.

A Russian story declares that a storm arose because a captain put to sea without paying a debt, contracted on a relic of the cross. He finally calmed it by throwing overboard a chest with the money, which, we are assured, floated safely to the claimant.

§In a Norman tale, the violation of an oath causes a storm. A young man promised his mother not to go to sea, but afterwards shipped in a man-of-war. A storm arose, destroying all on board.

∥In a Russian tale, a sin planned causes a storm, which is only allayed by repentance and prayer.**

††So the Fuegian taken on board ship by Fitzroy thought any wrong thing done or said would provoke a storm.

A Fiji mode of getting a wind, was to wish aloud for it, after taking a drink.

* Grant.—Mysteries, 346.
† Jones.—Credulities, 70.
‡ Kuhn and Schwartz.—N. Deutsche Sagen, 454.
§ Schmidt —Seeman's Sagen und Schiffer Märchen.
∥ Afanasieff-In Ralston—Russian Folk-tales, p. 43.
** See also Froude.—Short Studies, 158.
†† Fitzroy.—Voyage, p. 183.

*Natives of Vancouver's Island, in passing a certain mountain, would not name it, lest their boats be wrecked.

† To cut the hair and nails during a calm was formerly thought to provoke a gale. This belief is very old. Hesiod says the nails must not be pared before the gods. Petronius Arbiter says, however, that hair and nails should only be cut in a storm. ‡ He also says that forty blows were thought necessary to remove the evil effects of cutting off the hair and beard, when done at night by two fugitives in a Roman ship, who wished to escape detection.

§ Propertius says it is a bad omen to cut them at sea. Juvenal says that, as they are only given as a final offering to the gods, it will offend them to yield up such offerings at other times. Kirchman says, to dream of cutting off the hair, portended shipwreck to the ancient Roman.

‖ In Scotland, it was formerly said that if you combed your hair by candlelight or at night at all, your friends at sea would be lost. Many superstitions are recorded in folklore legends concerning the nails

** But none of these means were thought so effectual as whistling—a superstition not yet extinct, that

> " Whistles rash bid tempests roar."

†† Longfellow makes the Padrone in the "Golden Legend" say,—

> " Only a little while ago
> I was whistling to Saint Antonio
> For a capful of wind to fill our sail,
> And instead of a breeze he has sent a gale."

‡‡ Basil Hall, speaking of the sailors during a calm, says: "One might have thought that the ship was planted in a grove of trees, in the height of springtime, so numerous were the whistlers. This practice of whistling for a wind is one of our nautical superstitions, which, however groundless and absurd, fastens insensibly on the strongest-minded sailors at such times."

§§ Dr. Pegge, writing in 1763, says: "Our sailors, I am

---

*Sproat.—Farrar.
†Jal. Dict. Nautique.—Cheveux.
‡In Jal.—Glossaire Nautique.
§Brand.—III. 221.
‖Gregor.—Folk-lore of Scotland.
**Hazlitt.—Popular Antiquities of Great Britain.
††Part VI.
‡‡Voyages, 1811.
§§Gent. Mag., q. by Jones.—Broad, Broad Ocean, p. 239.

told, at this very day (I mean the vulgar sort), have a strange opinion of the devil's power and agency in stirring up winds, and that is the reason they so seldom whistle on shipboard, esteeming it to be a mockery, and consequently an enraging of the devil." *Dr. Andrews, an 18th century writer, says: "Superstition and profaneness, those extremes of human conduct, are often found united in the sailor, and the man who dreads the stormy effect of drowning a cat, or of whistling a country dance, while he leans over the gun-wale, will often be most profane."

In the "Ancient Mariner," the phantom woman, after ruining the souls of the crew, whistles thrice, and

"Off shot the spectre bark."

Yorkshire fishermen do not like whistling at sea; they say it brings both bad winds and poor luck. Scarbro' fish-ermen allow no whistling in their boats. †Fishermen of St. Ives do not like whistling at night. You may whistle for a breeze, but do not do so in a storm.

‡Holcroft says, during his voyage on the English coast: "I believe it was here I first remarked one of those many superstitious habits of seamen—that of whistling for the wind. I find it is common to them all, from the captain to the cabin boy.

Irish fishermen think whistling bad at sea. They say you should not even whistle for a wind in a dangerous place, for fear of a storm. A man traveling in a boat on the Irish coast some years since, came near getting a severe beating for whistling.

§Filey boatmen say: "We only whistle while the wind is asleep, and then the breeze comes," and they do not allow passengers to whistle in their boats.

In Swedish belief, whistling at sea brings storms and whirlwinds on shore. French sailors have similar beliefs, and ‖Germans say a storm comes, when you whistle at sea; a fresh breeze only, if you hug the mast at the same time.

In a Greenland story, a man raises a storm by blowing a whistle to the four points of the horizon, thus invoking the four winds.

* Brand.—Antiquities, Vol. III, p. 239.
† Bottrell.
‡ Memoirs, Vol. I, p. 281.
§ Jones.—Credulities.
‖ Liebrecht, Volkskunde, 332.

Williams says Fijian fishermen, when not whistling for a wind, entice it with playful words.

*"Whistling in bad weather makes it worse, for it attracts wind. Whistle a lively tune in good weather, and, to insure a wind, say flattering words, such as, 'Come, brother wind,' 'Come, old boy.'" "Some old sailors can even get a wind by saying, 'Come, come, arouse thee, old boy!' but they must flatter it well."

† Bishop Heber also tells us, of the boatmen in the Ganges: "I was amused to find that these boatmen have the same fancies with our English sailors, about whistling for the wind."

‡ A Yorkshire fisherman forbade a young lady from entering his boat, saying, "Not that young lady; she whis-tles."

§ In "Notes and Queries" is an anecdote of a Catholic, who said to a lady, "Don't whistle, ma'am; every time a woman whistles the Virgin's heart bleeds."

This notion is closely connected with the adage,—

║ "A whistling girl and a crowing hen
  Will surely come to a bad end."

The possession of a pilot's thumb by witches and others would seem to indicate their power of controlling storms, as we have seen by the witches in "Macbeth."

Eric's thumb, stolen by pirates, raised such a breeze that they were glad to return it.

** In China, a southerly (or favorable) breeze can be obtained by holding a cap high up against the wind; and the lives of a boat's crew would be endangered by repeating the word *feng*, or wind.

So Esthonians, to get a favorable breeze, hang up a hat, turned in the direction a wind is desired, and whistle in that direction also. †† A snake's skin hung up in the same manner was thought to procure a breeze.

‡‡ Kamtchatdales would not cast sand out of their huts, nor sharpen an axe or knife while on a journey, for fear of raising a storm.

* Tenne.—Volkssagen aus Pommern.
† Journey Thro' India, p 428.
‡ Henderson.—Folk-lore of Northern Counties of England (44).
§ August 2, 1879.
║ Choice Notes, Notes and Queries, p. 13.
** Dennys.—Folk-lore of China.
†† Grimm.—Teutonic Mythology
‡‡ Tylor.—Primitive Culture.

A colonial writer says that certain passengers in a ship, incited by a sermon by Cotton Mather against a petition to the crown, firmly believed that a storm overtook the ship carrying the document, and demanded that it be thrown overboard.

In Icelandic belief, says Armanson, to obtain a favorable breeze, it is only necessary to pull out your shirt, pick the insects off it, and put them on the foresail. We may imagine this remedy would not, in some ships, want for material for its application.

CHAPTER IV.

WATER-SPRITES AND MERMAIDS.

"Thus on life's lonely sea,
Heareth the marinere
Voices sad, from far and near,
Ever singing, full of fear,
Ever singing, drearfully."

J. R. Lowell

" The Mermaid on the rocks she sat
With glass and comb in hand,
"Clear off, ye livery lads!' she said,
" ' Ye be not far from land.'"

Old Ballad.

THE powerful deities and malignant demons described in a former chapter were not deemed the only inhabitants of the deep. In the traditions of many peoples, there existed below the waves races of mortals, some resembling the human dwellers on earth, others possessing varied forms and attributes. In the sea also abode huge giants, diminutive dwarfs, cunning fairies and wonderful goblins —beings analogous to those believed formerly to exist on land, and forming a link between the powerful deities and the ordinary inhabitants of the sea depths.

* Norse tradition says that when giants and trolls were driven from the earth by Christian priests, they took refuge in the sea, and are seen by mariners on distant strands.

Such an one is described in the old Norse "Book of Kings." † "It is tall and bulky, and stands right up out of

* Thorpe.—Northern Mythology.
† In Jones' Broad, Brond Ocean.

the water. From the shoulder upward, it is like a man, while on the brows there is, as it were, a pointed helmet. It has no arms, and from the shoulders down it seems light and more slender. Nobody has ever been able to see whether its extremities end in a tail like that of a fish, or only in a point." This monster was called Hafstraub. "Its color was ice-blue color. Nor could any one discern whether it had scales or a skin like a man. When the monster appeared, the sailors knew it to be the presage of a storm. If it looked at a ship and then dived, a loss of life was certain, but if it looked away and then dived, people had a good hope that although they might encounter heavy storms, their lives would be saved."

*According to the Eddas, Hymir, a fabled giant, boiled his kettle when the storms raged. His name is from *humr*, the sea, and is connected with our word *humid*.

In the ancient Finnish Kalevala, a dwarf arises from the sea, and becomes a giant as high as the clouds.

These are like the giants (Jinns) in the Arabian nights, which are imprisoned in bottles, and which, says Lane,† were called in Arab-lore *El Ghowasah*, "divers in the sea."

Other giants, although not always abiding in the sea, were fabled to have more or less power therein.

‡Ligur is a giant fabled in Helgoland as having separated the island from the mainland. Many stones strewn about the coast were dropped by him.

Walcheren, a Dutch giant, when pirates stole his flocks, waded out into the sea, sank the ships with his little finger, and recovered his sheep.

§ A giant formerly lived in a cave near Portreath, England, who waded out and seized boats, dragging them in, and who seized drowning people sucked in by currents.

∥ More wonderful stories are told of Gargantua, whose deeds are renowned on many parts of the French coast. Many huge rocks and boulders on the coast, as at St. Just, St. Jacob, Plevenen, etc., were fabled to have been placed there by him. Others are said to be his tooth, his cradle, his bed, or the tombs of his limbs. Legends of his exploits are numerous. He drank of the sea, stepped over to Great Britain, and at numerous times swallowed ships,

* Thorpe.—Northern Mythology.
† Notes to Arabian Nights.
‡ Grimm.—Teut. Mythology, Vol. II, p. 586.
§ Bottrell.—Traditions of West Cornwall.
∥ Sébillot.—Gargantua dans les Traditions Populaires, 1883.

and even fleets. In some of these tales ships are blown up in his capacious stomach, and in others, whole fleets continue their combats, after he has swallowed them. An English fleet, thus absorbed, so disagreed with his gallic taste that he went in disgust to India, and threw them up.

* Mausthorpe, a famous Indian giant, was equally celebrated about Vineyard Sound. The rocks at Seaconnet are the remains of his wife, whom he threw into the sea there. He turned his children into fishes, and emptying out his pipe one day, formed Nantucket out of its ashes.

Dwarfs also went to sea. † St. Brandan met a dwarf a thumb long, floating in a bowl, during his wonderful voyage. ‡ El Masudi tells us of the China Sea: "When a great storm comes on, black figures arise from the waters, about four or five spans long, and they look like little Abyssinians. They mount in the vessels; but, however numerous, they do no harm. When sailors observe them, they are sure that a storm is near, for their appearance is a certain sign of a gale."

Fairies figure in many tales of the sea and of seamen. Fishermen in the Tweed believe they affect their fishing. Nets are salted, and salt thrown into the water to blind the sea-fairies. Perthshire seamen believe in them.

§ A Cornish tale says a fisherman found "piskies" playing, and watched them, but they detected him, and he was near being taken and destroyed. Another tale, that of John Taprail, is that he was awakened by a voice telling him that his boat, moored alongside another, was in danger. He arose to see to it, but found that a trick had been played on him, and his boat was all right. While on his way back he found a group of piskies distributing money in their hats. Slyly introducing his own, he obtained a share, was discovered, and barely had time to reach home, leaving the tails of his coat in the hands of the fairies.

According to the Irish Bardic legends, the King of Ulster was almost carried away by sea-fairies.

∥ Among Welsh fairies are the Gwragedd Annwn, or fairies of lakes and streams. These are not mermaids, nor are they sea-maidens. Some are said to inhabit Crumlyn Lake, and live in a fabled submerged town. They are said

* Drake.—Legends and Folk-lore of New England, p. 444.
† Grimm.—Teut. Mythology, Vol. II, p. 451.
‡ Golden Meadows.
§ Jones.—Credulities, p. 30.
∥ Sikes.—British Goblins and Welsh Folk-lore, 35.

to be descendants of villagers condemned to sink below the waters for reviling St. Patrick on one of his visits. *Other localities are haunted by these subaqueous fairies, and a young farmer obtained one of them, who was in the habit of rowing about in a magic boat with golden oars, by droping bread and cheese in the water. She left him on his striking her three times. Another lake-bride disappears when struck with iron. In another locality, lake-fairies inhabit beautiful gardens under the water.

In the Hebrides, sea-beans are supposed by some to be fairies' eggs.

In Holland it is said that elves are in the bubbles, seen on the surface of water, or that they will use eggshells thrown into the water, for boats.

†A French (Breton) story is told of a fairy who presented a sailor a rod that saved him from shipwreck, gave him a good breeze, and brought him a fortune.

‡Dieppe fishermen say they hold an annual bazaar on the cliffs, and attempt to decoy men there. If one went, and listened to their music, he would be drowned from the cliffs.

Breton stories are told of fairies who dwell in the *Houles*, or grottoes in the cliffs. A fisherman once saw them rub their eyes with a salve, and then take the shape of mortals. Obtaining the ointment, he used it, and was thereafter able to distinguish these people, even when, in the shape of fish, they were robbing the nets.

The fairies sometimes married men. They have flocks and herds, sometimes obtaining those of mortals by theft. They are generally beneficent, bringing riches in return for favors, and possess supernatural powers. They are generally beautiful, but are invisible by day, except to those whose eyes are anointed with the magic salve. Some are clothed like human beings, others covered with barnacles or shells. In some tales, they are endowed with the powers of Circe, metamorphosing men into animals.

It was formerly said, in Ile et Vilaine, that a fairy inhabited a certain grotto, and was seen sailing on the river in a nautilus shell, accompanied by other fairies.

In Polynesian mythology, fairies taught them how to net fish, and make reels.

* Sikes.—British Goblins and Welsh Folk-lore, 68.
† Sébillot.—Contes des Paysauset des Pécheuns.
‡ Sébillot.—Contes Pop. de la Haute Bretagne.

We also find at sea one of these familiar mischievous goblins, such as in German lore, under the name of Kobold, annoy the housewife and hostler.   He is a beneficent demon, taking his turn at the capstan and grog-tub.   *To French sailors, under the name of Gobelin, he is well known, and Norwegian sailors believe in his existence.   He singes their hair in sleep, raises the anchor in a calm, tears carelessly-furled sails, knots ropes, etc.

†In the fifteenth and sixteenth centuries, he was called Kobalos, in Germany.   Now he is known as Klabauter-mann, or Klabautermännchen, as he is a small man, with large, fiery red head, and green teeth.   He is dressed in yellow breeches, horseman's boots, and a steeple-crowned hat.   He is a beneficent visitor, and is on good terms with the crew, as long as he is treated well, often assisting in their tasks.

These characteristics are aptly illustrated in the following lines:

‡ "About Klaboterman
That Kobold of the sea, a sprite
Invisible to mortal sight,
Who o'er the rigging ran;
Sometime he hammered in the hold,
Sometimes upon the mast;
Sometimes abeam, sometimes abaft,
Or at the bows, he sang and laughed.
He helped the sailors at their work,
And toil'd with jovial din,
He helped them stow the casks and bales,
And heave the anchor in;
But woe unto the lazy louts,
The idlers of the crew,
Them to torment was his delight,
And worry them by day and night,
And pinch them black and blue.
And woe to him whose mortal eyes
Klaboterman beheld,
It is a certain sign of death!"

§ In North Germany, it is said that his favor must be care-fully courted.   His favorite position is on the capstan, and he will occasionally take a glass of wine with the Captain, whose interests require him to be on favorable terms with this sprite.   He is given food, but must not be offered old

* Jal.—Glossaire Nautique, "Gobelin."
† Grimm.—Teut. Mythology.
‡ Longfellow.—Tales of a Wayside Inn.
§ Thorpe.—Northern Mythology.

clothing. *Schmidt says Plymouth fishermen aver a belief in him, and say he was not always visible until the time of danger. Should a fisherman lose his luck, he saw Klabauterman go over the bows. On account of the noise he sometimes raised on board, he was called Klütermann (clatterman).

† In French accounts of him, he originally appeared on board of a ship in the Somme. He is there called Goguelin.

‡ Brewer says he is seen sitting on the bowsprit of the spectre ship, dressed in yellow, and smoking a short pipe.

In many places water-spirits assumed the shape of a horse, of a cow, or a bull. § " Mythic water-horses, water-bulls, or cows are to be found in the religious systems of many nations of old. And they still haunt the imagination of living men, in the shape of Scotch water-kelpies, or of dapple-gray stallions and brown steers, that still rise from some German lake."

In Iceland, Hnickur appears thus, but with hoofs turned backward. He tempts people to mount him, and is then off. ‖ He was also called Vatua-hestur, Nennir and Kumber. Gray was the usual color seen, and sometimes other shapes were assumed. One came through the ice, and had eight feet and ten heads. When the ice splits in the winter, it is said to be the sea-horse coming up.

He somtimes induces persons, especially young girls, to mount his back, when he rushes into the water. He can be caught and tamed, and the horses reared from him are stronger than others, but more mischievous. When tamed, his bridle must not be taken off, or he will rush into the river. **Arnanson tells a story of a water-horse who was caught and bridled by a young girl. Just as she was about to mount him she said, "I feel afraid; I'm half inclined not to mount him." He rushed forthwith into the water, not liking to be called Nennir, or "I'm not inclined," nor can he bear to be called by the Devil's name.

In the Orkneys, the water-sprite appears as a handsome little horse, with his mane covered with weeds; and one is

* Seeman's Sagen und Schiffer Märchen.
† Jal.—Glossaire Nautique. " Gobelin."
‡ Readers' Hand Book. Klaboterman.
§ Blind.—Contemporary Review, August, 1881.
‖ Blind.—Contemporary Review, August, 1881.
** Icelandic Legends.

described in Bevis's "Orkney." In Shetland, the handsome little horse is named Shoopiltree or Shoopultie. He aided Graham of Morphil to build his castle.

When overloaded he said,—

> * " Sair back and sair hanes
> Duven the Laird o' Morphil's stanes,
> The Laird o' Morphil 'll never thrive
> So long's the kelpy is alive."

† Blind says an instance of a water-horse, yoked and worked during the day, is reported in the Landnama bok.

In Shetland, says Blind, he is also called Njuggle, Nyogle Neogle, or Niagle, all words of the same sort as Nöckel (Ger.), and derived from Nick, chief water demon. He is defined as "a horse, somewhat akin to the water kelpie." But in popular accounts, he differs from a horse in having a tail like a wheel. He is generally mischievous, stopping mills, etc. Stories are told in Shetland lore, of men mounting these water-horses, who were nearly being carried into the sea, only escaping by killing the horse.

‡ In Norway, when a thunder storm is brewing, the water-sprite comes in the shape of a horse.

§ Numerous tales are told of the Scotch kelpie, who was usually black. He would, if possible, decoy travelers to mount him, then rush into the water with them. He could be caught by slipping over his head a bridle on which the sign of the cross had been made, and then would work. A horseman saw one, attended by an old man. A blacksmith killed one with hot irons, by thrusting them in his side, when he became a heap of starch.

Burns says,—

> ‖ " When thowes dissolve the snawy hoord,
> An' float the ginglin' icy-boord,
> Then water-kelpies haunt the foord."

Nearly every Scottish lake has its water-horse. ** Gregor tells a story of a Scotchman who caught a kelpie, mounted his back, and nearly lost his life thereby, the water-horse rushing at once toward the lake. His rider escaped by

* Scotch and Irish Legendary Ballads.
† Contemporary Review, August, 1881.
‡ Faye.—Norsk Sagen, p. 55.
§ Gregor.—Folk-lore of Scotland.
‖ Tam O'Shanter.
** Folk-lore of Scotland.

OF THE SEA AND OF SAILORS.

striking the bridle from his head. * Another writer says of the water-sprite: "Sometimes it is described as wholly or partly human, as merman or mermaid, but more commonly the shape assigned to it, is that of a horse or a bull. The sounds of the kelpie, when heard during a storm, whether wild neighing, or hoarse bellowing, is reckoned a sure presage of misfortune."

Every lake in Perthshire has its kelpie, swelling the torrent to drown the traveler, and decoying women and children into the water.

† In Irish legend, water-horses are called Phookie and Aughisky, and are said to come up out of the lakes to graze; but some are carnivorous, one in Lough Mask destroying cattle when he came out. Another, that had been tamed, ran into the lake when he saw the water. Another in Loch Corub had a serpent's body, with a horse's head.

It is usually said of these water-horses, that their hoofs turn backward. Blind has pointed out that the wheel-shaped tail indicates the sun, or that here in these legends we have another phase of sun-worship, closely connected with water worship in many particulars. Bryant further argues that their backward-turned hoofs mean the *crab*, or the sun in the southern or Tartaric constellation; hence the water-horse is malicious and diabolic. His name, derived from Nick, indicates this character.

In the Isle of Man, we find the water-horse called Glashlan, Glashan, or Enach-I-Kibb, fairy stallion

‡ In North Germany, Jagow is the water-horse, who, in a story, came out of the water, harnessed himself to a harrow, and worried the other horses nearly to death. It is generally said there that the water-sprites possess herds of cattle.

Near New Schlemnin, in Mecklenburg, is a lake called the Devil's lake, whence issue on St. John's day the cries of a man. He is a peasant, who called on the devil, when his horses were exhausted in traveling. A black horse came out of the lake, jumped to the harrow, and assisted in the task, but when the peasant mounted him, he rushed at once into the lake.

§ The nixies that dwell in the waves are, in the Illyrian tales, of surpassing beauty. Often it happens that a youth

<hr />

* Lt.-Col. Leslie.—Early Races of Scotland and Their Monuments.
† Blind.—Scottish and Shetland Water Tales, Cont. Review, August, 1882.
‡ Kuhn.—Nord Deutsche Sagen.
§ Prof. Griesdorfer.—Letter to K. Blind., Cont. Review, August, 1891.

inspires them with love, and then they change themselves into water-horses, in order to carry him on their backs into their crystal realm.

*Stories of sea-horses are found in eastern lore. King Mihraj's mares are visited by one producing a superior breed. El Kazwini says sea-horses are larger than those of the land, have cloven hoofs, and smaller mane and tail. Their colts are spotted, he says.

In the historical legends of the Indian Archipelago, Parar-al-Bahrri is a sea-horse who carries the hero over the waves.

The horse is connected with the sea in many legends. † Neptune created the horse, and Centaur, sprang from the sea. Perseus' horse, Pegasus, is supposed by many to have been a ship. Caxton, in the "Book of Troy," and Boccaccio, in the "Genealogia Deorum," say the same. ‡ So Shakspeare likens a ship to Perseus' horse. The mother of Dyonisius was Hippos. Many heroes travel over the waves on the horse. Odin's horse Sleipnir thus conveyed his master, and various folk-lore tales make the hero imitate him. The ship is usually, in the Eddas, likened to a horse, and two of a famous Welsh triad of vessels were the black horse of the seas, and the horned horse. Sailors evidently recognized the analogies between the steed of the land and the courser of the seas, since we find nearly every part of the horse's anatomy, and much of his harness and fittings represented in nautical nomenclature. So with the cow. In Aryan mythology, cows represent clouds, and clouds were, as we shall see, widely represented as ships. "Die Bunte Kuh" was a famous German flag-ship in the middle ages. Certain marine mammals, as the walrus, sea-lion, etc., resembling cattle and horses in form, would aid the legend in its progress.

Water-cattle are also found in the folk-lore of many people. The Merovignan kings of France traced their descent from a water-bull, the direct ancestor of Merovæus.

A shepherd, in a French story of the eleventh century, finds beautiful herds of cattle at the bottom of the sea, and drives them out.

An old Icelandic natural history reports that the bellowing of sea-cows and bulls makes people mad.

* Lane.—Arabian Nights.
† Cox.—Aryan Mythology, II, 283.
‡ Troilus and Cressida, Act I, scene 3.

*Breton tales of the flocks and herds of the sea-fairies are numerous.

†In Scotch belief, water-bulls are friendly, and are inimical to the diabolic water-horses. In an old tale, a water-calf, who has grown into a young bull on shore, attacks a water-bull who has deluded a young girl into his power by assuming the shape of a young man, and kills him. ‡There are many Welsh tales of water-cattle, issuing from the lakes, etc.

Kaffirs say the sea-people have cattle beneath the waves.

Clouds reflected in the waves were often thought to be sheep and cattle. So in the Norse story, "Big Peter and Little Peter,"§ in the Gælic tale, "The Three Widows," and in the German legend of the "Little Farmer." These are the Cattle of Helios, and Herds of Neptune; and such fancies doubtless aided in spreading these myths of water-horses and cattle.

But the water-sprites usually appeared in human form.

From the naiads, nereids, and nixies sprang a crowd of fabulous inhabitants of the ocean, lake, river, and stream.

We have seen that the ocean, the streams and lakes, and even the fountains were fabled, in ancient Greece, to be peopled by these semi-deities—the Oceanids, the Nereids, the Naiads, and the Nymphs. ‖These, with the sirens, the harpies, the centaurs, and other demi-gods and demons, were the undoubted ancestors of the host of forms, angelic and demoniac, that have been fabled to haunt the streams of the ocean and the air. The ancestry of many of these have been traced back to older Aryan days, and the nymphs found to be none other than the Apsaras, the centaurs but the Gaudharvas, and the harpies, or sirens, representatives of the Maruts. But the effects of the Greek conceptions of these inhabitants of sea and air were more marked than of the older primitive ideas.

**As Tylor says: "Through the ages of the classic world the river-gods and the water-nymphs held their places, till, within the bounds of Christendom, they came to be classed with ideal beings like them in the mythology of the Northern nations, the kindly sprites to whom offerings were given

*Sébillot.—Litt. Orale de Haute Bretagne.
†Gregor.—Folk-lore of Scotland.
‡Sikes.—British Goblins and Welsh Folk-lore, p. 86.
§Dasent.—Norse Tales. Grimm Campbell.
‖Kelly.—Curiosities of Indo-European Folk-lore.
**Primitive Culture.

at springs and lakes, and the treacherous nixies who entice men to a watery death."

In spite of the opposition to water worship, made by the Christian priests, these beliefs prevailed, just as the belief in the more powerful sea-divinities endured, so that all the priests could do, was to degrade or maintain in their degraded position, the nymphs of the waves and the spirits of the deep.

The Sirens, at first bird-shaped, were afterwards, as we have seen, imagined beautiful maidens.* There finally grew up in mediæval conception, two classes of sea-beings. The first, the water-sprite, appeared in human shape, but was endowed with the faculty of assuming other forms at will. The second, the mermaid, had always the fish tail which ancient legends gave to many goddesses and water-beings.

Water-sprites were usually endowed with wisdom, often brought gifts or good luck, but were sometimes malicious, and even diabolic. All these qualities were inherited from their ancestors. Nick was diabolic, the nymphs often benefited mankind, and the Sirens were malicious and hurtful.

† According to the Eddas, Urda, who knew the past, Verande, skilled in present affairs, and Skulda, who prophesied the future, were all water-nymphs. Egeria of the fountain, who taught wisdom to Numa, had her representatives and followers in nearly every land.

Water-sprites appear in all countries, in ocean lake, river and fountain.

‡ Wilkina, the Viking, found one in a forest, and carried her away. She afterwards appeared, climbing upon the poop of his ship at sea, and stopped it, by putting the helm hard over.

The sagas have other stories of water-sprites, and one sings,—

> 'Cold water to the eyes,
> Flesh raw to the teeth,
> A shroud to the dead,
> Flit me back to the sea
> Henceforward never
> Men in ships sailing,
> Draw me to dry land
> From the depths of the sea."

The Drowning-Stol; a rock on the Norwegian coast, is

*Chapter I.
†Thorpe.—Northern Mythology, Vol. II, p. 13.
‡Wilkina Saga.

fabled to have been the seat of a "Queen of the Sea," who used to sit there, combing her locks, and bringing luck to fishermen.

* In Norwegian story the Grim, or Fossegrim, is a mysterious water-fairy, a musical genius, who plays to every one, and requires a white kid every Thursday. In Norway, also, was the Roretrold, or Rorevand, sometimes appearing as a horse, at others as a human water-sprite. † When people drown at sea, a water-sprite appears, in the shape of a headless old man.

‡ The Swedish Strömkarl sits under bridges, playing wonderful melodies on the violin, which cause everybody hearing them to dance. He will teach his tunes to anyone, for a consideration.

He greatly desires salvation, an idea emanating undoubtedly from the priests.

§ The "Lady of the Boundless Sea" figures in an old Norse fairy tale, bringing benefits with her.

In Icelandic legend, water-sprites make holes in the ice, called elf-holes. ‖ Arnanson tells an Icelandic story of a fisherman, who is always granted good luck by a "sea-troll," whom he has benefited, so long as he waited to set out on his day's journey, until the troll had passed his hut. Other legends say these elves go out fishing, and their boats are seen.

** The Danish water-sprite has a long beard, green hat, green teeth, shaggy hair, and yellow curls and cap. He was often malicious.

†† "They launched the ship into the deep,
　　The sea growled like a bear,
　　The White Goose to the bottom sank,
　　Some trold was surely there,"

says an old ballad. In another,—

　　" The good King of Loffer had launched his ship,
　　And sail'd the billowy main,
　　There came a trold and his daughter seiz'd,
　　And bitter his grief and pain."

In Holland, it is believed that water-sprites or elves float

* Thorpe.—Northern Mythology, Vol. II, p. 22.
† Grimm.—Teutonic Mythology, Vol. I, p. 491.
‡ Afzelius.—Swedish Folk-Tales.
§ Dasent.—Popular Tales from the Norse.
‖ Icelandic Legends.
** Grimm.—Teutonic Mythology, Vol. I, p. 491.
†† " Rosmer Hafmand."—Northern Ballads.

in bubbles, or in egg-shells that are thoughtlessly thrown into the water.

*A Dutch legend of 1305, reports that a knight who found a water-sprite, but afterwards killed it, died himself in consequence.

† In Germany, a crowd of various water-sprites is found. Frau Hulde, or Holde, is the spirit of fountains, and when the sun shines, she is combing her hair, and when it snows, she is making her bed. She is frequently seen bathing at noon. She is thought to take all drowned persons. During the twelve days near Christmas, she joins the Wild Hunt with Odin and his gang. At Ilsensten, Ilse is seen often in long white robe and black hat, and she is also called Jung-fern (maiden). In many places these water-sprites inhabited lakes, and raised storms, if stones were thrown in. These water-sprites inhabit every lake, river and pond in Germany, and innumerable stories are told of them. Some bring fort-une, others ill luck. Many come on shore to dance with the peasants, and are known by the wet *hem* of their gar-ments. Others are bloodthirsty and covetous. Should a water-maiden dally too long with the shore mortals, she is sure to suffer death on her return, and the waves appear red, above her abode. In Markland, children are told that the water-man will drag them in.

A party of fishermen found a lump of ice in the sea, and gave it to St. Theobald, their bishop, to cool his gouty feet. He heard a voice inside, and succeeded, by saying thirty masses, in saving and liberating the sprite within.

‡Bohemian fishermen believe in a water-sprite, who sits on shore with a club, and destroys children. They fear to aid a drowning man, for fear of offending the water-sprite, who, in revenge, will draw the fish from their nets. These sprites are shaped like a fish, with human heads.

The folk tales of Austria, Bohemia and South Germany, are full of tales of these water-sprites, that inhabit every lake, river and stream. One comes out of the Teufel sea, in the shape of a white lady. The services of a midwife are often required beneath the waves, and such services are usually well rewarded. A young girl lost in the woods was found by a water-man from the Teufel sea. Water-men are sometimes beneficial, women always malicious.

* Hagen.—Deutsche Gedichte des Mittelalters.
† Grimm.—Teut. Myth. Kuhn and Schwartz.—Deutsche Sagen.
‡ Wuttke—Deutsches Aberglauben.

* Boatmen say a water-sprite lives in the Traumsee, who requires a yearly sacrifice. A young miller, in love with a nun in a convent near by, was wont to swim the lake, to see his lady, but was claimed as a victim, along with the recreant nun. The deep and rock-bound lakes of the Tyrol are inhabited by maiden-sprites, whose songs are often heard. Offerings are frequently left on the banks of streams for them. They requite favors with benefits, and one struck dead the person who attempted to harm her. Water-sprites abound in the Danube and Vienna rivers, and old clothes are given to propitiate them.

† Bohemians will pray on the river-bank where a man has been drowned, and offer bread and wax candles to the spirit of the water. Duke Bresislaw forbade sacrifices, in Hungary, to water-spirits.

‡ The Donaufürst (Danube prince) is a malicious sprite, dragging people below the waves. Eddies and whirlpools are caused by him.

§ Bulgarians and Wallachians always throw a little water from each pail, as they believe that will spill out the water-spirit. In dipping water from a running stream, they are careful to hold the bucket down stream, to avoid catching the water-sprite, who dashes water in their faces.

‖ Russian traditions concerning water-sprites are abundant. Rusalkas are female water-sprites, and Vodyannies male spirits. The Rusalkas appear as beautiful maidens with long hair, bathing and sporting in the water. They tickle bathers to death. In many places, offerings of linen clothing are made to them, as they are thought fond of washing it. They cause storms and wind, are thought to influence the luck of sailors and fishermen, sometimes tearing nets and driving fish away. If game were dropped to the left of a path, a water-sprite would come to seek it. They drowned people in the overflow of rivers, especially about Whit-Sunday, when no one must bathe, for fear of offending them. During one week, called Rusalka week, relatives of drowned or shipwrecked people pour eggs and spirits on their graves. Offerings were made directly to the spirits, and in some places, a ceremony of expelling them with a straw figure is performed. Some are thought ghosts

* Jones.—Credulities, p. 68.
† Tylor.—Primitive Culture. Vol. I.
‡ Blind.—Contemporary Review, 1881.
§ Tylor.—Primitive Culture.
‖ Ralston.—Songs of the Russian People, pp. 139-146.

11

of still-born or unbaptized children, or of drowned persons.
The wild-fire, or jack-o'-lantern, was thought to be lighted
by them. At Astrakan, marine Rusalkas are thought to
raise storms and destroy shipping. They can produce a
flood by combing their hair. They come out and dance on
St. Peter's day. Anyone treading on the linen which they
spread out to dry, will be lamed. Anyone bathing on Whit-
Sunday without praying first will be drowned, and these
sprites sometimes drag people under with a long hook.
They float in egg shells. They are desirous to save their
souls, and one at Astrakan asked, " Is the end of the world
come? "

A water-sprite came out of Lake Ladoga, and promised
a fisherman great riches if he would subdue the "sprite of
the third wave, by throwing his axe into it."

* The Vodyannies were rulers of fish, and influenced the
weather and luck of fishermen. Their wives were drowned
women. One of these wives is said in a popular story to
have returned to visit her people, but, as in the case of
Undine, her body floated up to the surface soon after her
return. Another story is that a fisherman caught a Vodyanny child and returned him to the water on condition that
he drive fish to the net, which he faithfully did. A fisherman once caught a dead body in his net, but hastily threw
it overboard, finding it to be a Vodyanny. One must not
bathe after sunset, nor without a cross about his neck. In
the Ukraine, when the sea is rough, these water-sprites are
seen on the surface, and their songs are heard. In some
places a horse, smeared with honey and decked with flowers,
is sacrificed, in others, oil is poured on the water to appease
them.

Other traditions assert that they are fallen angels. They
sit on the shore, or sport in the waters at night.

† They are also called Pharaohs, and are supposed to be
the ghosts of the host drowned in the Red Sea. The chief
water-sprite is Tsar Morskoi. A Russian folk-story is that
a certain Ivan caught a fish, but liberated it, and in gratitude
he was conveyed to the palace of the Tsar, where Ivan fell
in love with his daughter. Both were driven out, and the
fish guided them on shore. Another tale is told of Chudo
Yudo, a water-sprite, who seizes people by the heard when
they drink, and carries off a maiden to his palace and weds her.

* Ralston.—Songs of the Russian People, 106, 129, 146.
† Ralston.—Songs of the Russian People, p. 171.

The daughters of Tsar Morskoi appear as a pigeon, a duck, or a fish, and change into maidens, by shifting their coverings.

In one tale, a peasant chalks a cross on a water-sprite's back, preventing him from going into his natural element, until the cross is removed.

A story told of Sadko, relates that he charmed with his music the Tsar Morskoi from the waters of Lake Ilmen, and was thereupon promised a rich reward. He cast a net, and drew a rich treasure to land. He became rich, and went to sea with his fleet of thirty ships. They were mysteriously stopped at sea, when Sadko confessed he had not offered "bread and salt to the Caspian." He was thereupon flung overboard, his *gusli*, or harp, with him. Arriving at the palace of Tsar Morskoi, he plays for him, charms him, wrecks a fleet, and is finally saved by St. Nicholas.

* The Wends say water-sprites appear in the market in smock-frocks, with the bottom dripping.

Esthonian stories are told of water-sprites, and in one case one dwelt in a well, and a gun was fired down it to quell him. In another tale, the "Lady of the Water," goddess of winds and waves, figures.

Esthonians could see a churl with blue and yellow stockings in the sacred brook of Wöhaanda.

The "water-mother," or Wele-Ema, is the name given the water-maiden, and Aisstin Scheria, that applied to the water-man.

† Water-sprites, called Ahktaisset, are known in Finland, having their dwelling below the sea, and recognized by a dripping garment. One was accustomed to come to market, and indicate to a butcher the desired portion, but the butcher maliciously cut off his finger on one occasion, and was soon after found dead with a red cloth about his throat.

Allatius says water-sprites, called *Navagidæ*, abounded in Greek rivers and streams, in 1600.

Water-sprites are encountered in Italian folk-myths. Orlando and Rinaldo § are pursued by numerous emissaries of Fata Morgana, who lives in a beautiful palace below the sea. They escape all perils, and finally penetrate to her palace. Orlando also encounters a lake-siren, whom he kills. Tasso describes a water-sprite, seen in a fountain.

* Grimm.—Teutonic Mythology. Vol. I. p. 492.
† Fraser's Mag. Vol. LV. p. 528. Folk-lore of Finland.
‡ Ariosto.—Orlando Furioso.

In another tale, the "Siren of the Sea," enters a ship through a hole bored to sink it, and carries off a maiden, whom she secures by binding her to the bottom with a golden chain.

* Gervase of Tilbury, writing in the twelfth century, says there were certain water-sprites in the south of France called Dracæ, in human form, who inhabited caverns and recesses beneath the water, and inveigled persons into them. Men were devoured, and women taken as wives. They were thought to lure them by floating about in the shape of cups or rings of gold. A woman is said to have returned after living with them seven years.

† In Brittany, the water-women are called Korrigan. They are beautiful by night, but plain by daylight, with white hair, and red eyes. They are but two feet high, and wear only a veil, have beautiful voices, and are reputed the ghosts of Gallic princesses, who refused to become Christianized. They hate the priests, but are not otherwise harmful. Water-sprites and fountain maidens appear in many parts of France, and numerous tales are told of them.

‡ Walter Mapes tells a story of a Welshman who got a water-sprite for a wife, but one day she disappeared, having found, by accident, her sea-bridle in the market.

Taliesin, the Welsh bard, tells of a certain *Gwillion*, a water-sprite inhabiting lakes and ponds.

In a modern story, a cave near Pendine, Wales, is inhabited by two water-sprites, who lure ships to destruction, assuming various shapes, and even carrying ships on their backs.

A Celtic water-sprite brought stones to aid in building a certain church.

In Scotland, the most famous water-sprite is "Shelly-coat," who appears covered with seaweed and shells.

§ "Shelly-coat," says Scott, "a spirit who resides in the waters, and gives his name to many a rock and stone upon the Scottish coast."

Ramsay calls him "Spelly-coat," and mentions the belief that you must put running water between you and him.

Two men heard from a small stream a cry of "lost, lost!" apparently from some one in distress. On approach-

---

* Dobeneck in Thorpe.—N. Mythology, Vol. II, p. 13.
† Sébillot.—Litterature Orale de Haute Bretagne.
‡ Walter Mapes.—Nugæ Curialum (1180).
§ Minstrelsy of the Scottish Border.

ing, it went up the stream; then, as they followed, down again, laughing at them, and rattling its shelly coat.

*The Tees river has a water-sprite, Peg Porter, who lures people down below. Froth is "Peg Porter's suds," and foam "Peg Porter's cream." Children must not play near there, or the sprite will get them.

In another river it is Peg O'Nell. She requires a life every year; and if no dog, cat, or bird is thrown in, will have a human life. A certain traveler, bound to cross the river when it was high, was warned that she would get him, but persisted in crossing, and was drowned.

A man, riding on a brown horse with a black mane on the right side, caught a water-sprite. She was very restless in crossing a ford, and, on bringing her to the light, she dropped down, a mass of jelly. A shepherd caught another, but suddenly dropped her in the river, on observing her web-feet.

†In the Orkneys, the sprite is "Tangy," covered with seaweed, or *tang*. ‡In Sutherland, Scotland, the Fualb-a-Banshee is a water-maiden with web-feet, and long yellow hair. She is mortal, and steel controls her. She is evil-minded, and much the same as the "water-wraith" of the old song,—

> By this the storm grew loud apace,
> The water-wraith was shrieking."

A sprite, the *Daoine-Shi*, comes out of lakes in the Highlands, playing melodious music, and questioning the clergymen on the subject of her soul.

§In a Highland tale, "The Widow's Son," we meet with the "Princess of the realm beneath the sea," who conducts the son to her sub-marine home.

The kelpy has been described in Jamieson's ballad, and appears as half-man, half-fish.

> "The human schaip I sometimes aip,"

and says he rules the waves, to the salt sea.

Some years since, a boat's crew were drowned in Solway Firth, because their cries were thought to be those of kelpies, so no one would go to their assistance.

*Stewart.—Superstitions of the Highlands, q. by Thorpe, N. M., II, 18.
†Gregor.—Folk-lore of Scotland.
‡Campbell.—Tales of West Highlands.
§Campbell.—Tales of the West Highlands.

* Sometimes the water-sprite appeared in the shape of a bird. The aquatic bird called a "Bobbrie" is one of these.

But whatever shape the water-sprite assumed, its appearance boded disaster.

> † "The fishers have heard the water-sprite,
> Whose screams forbode that wreck is nigh."

We may remember that Ariel becomes a water-sprite. Prospero says,—

> ‡ "Go make thyself like a nymph of the sea; be subject
> To no sight but thine and mine; invisible
> To every eyeball else."

Such sprites are not unknown even in modern England. § "There is scarcely a stream of any magnitude in either Lancashire or Yorkshire, which does not possess its presiding spirit in same part of its course." At Clitheroe is one which requires a sacrifice every seven years. Nor is our own practical land without them. Negroes of South Carolina‖ believe that the springs and subterranean rivers are inhabited by water-spirits, called by them "Cymbees,"— beings like the sprites of European tradition.

** Water-sprites figure in other parts of the world. In the Japanese story, "The Lost Fish-hook," a boy has his hook carried off by a large fish. To him appeared the " ruler of the tides," who set him afloat in a basket, in which he sank to the palace of the sea-dragon, saw and loved his daughter. The fishes are bled to find the hook, which is in the red-fish's mouth.

- The rivers of India are haunted by these water-sprites, especially the Ganges,—the wife of Buddha.

Sea-sprites figure in stories in the "Arabian Nights." Gulnare is one of these, and Abdallah catches one in his net. Three daughters of the sea, beautiful and beneficent, appear in the tale of "Al Habib."

†† Fishermen of Poyang lake, in Hunan, often miss their boats, which are temporarily borrowed for submarine purposes by the sprites of the lake. Music is always heard as these boats disappear, and they are safely returned to their

* Gregor.—Polk-lore of Scotland.
† Scott.—Lay of the Last Minstrel.
‡ Tempest, Act I; scene 3.
§ Farrar.—Primitive Civilization, p. 306.
‖ Popular Science Monthly, 1875.
** Mitford.—Tales of Old Japan.
†† Chinese Tales. By Pu Sing Ling.—Giles' Translation.

anchorages after a time. Lin, a boatman, fell asleep in his boat, and on awakening, found his boat in the possession of these sprites. The Water King, who lives beneath the waves, appeared, and gave his subjects lists of people to be drowned, two hundred and twenty-eight in number. In the storm that ensued, Lin was saved by virtue of a crystal square, given him as a talisman. Lin afterwards married one of the sprites, and she was able to revisit her friends when desirous of it, always returning with rich presents.

* Esquimaux fear the spirits of the waters. A water-sprite haunted Pend d'Oreille lake, and in Lake Winnipeg, the Indians feared to speak for fear of offending them. Mexicans and Peruvians believed in water-beings, evil and beneficent. Algonquins believed in water-sprites, Nee-ban-aw-baigs.

† In Ottawa legend, the spirits of Lake Michigan caused great storms. An Ojibway tale relates the seizure of a woman by a water-sprite in Lake Superior, who appeared in the shape of a tiger, and carried her to his water wig-wam.

‡ Among Guiana tribes, Orehue is the water-spirit. He is like a merman, but not always malignant. Sometimes he has the head of a horse or other animal. He sometimes seizes bathers, and drags them beneath the waves. He is believed especially to frequent a cove washed in the banks of the Pomeroon river. Many Indians would noiselessly row on the opposite banks at night. A dance in his favor is called the water-mawa dance. They carefully distinguish between this imaginary being and the manatee. Among other South American tribes, Gamainha is a spirit of the water.

§ Mae d'Acqua is a lovely female on shore, a fish in the water.

‖ Leewa is the water-ghost of Musquito Indians. The Suaranos say Wahua appears, rising from the water, and seizing maidens.

** Kaffirs say people live beneath the waves, and have herds and dwellings. Zulus also believe in semi-human beings, who live in the ocean.

Theal says Xosa Kaffirs believe in a water-spirit in the

* Bancroft.—Native Races, Vol. III, pp. 144-5.
† Schoolcraft.—Algic Researches, Vol. I, p. 131.
‡ Jones.—Credulities, p. 26.
§ Verne.—Giant Raft, ch. XI.
‖ Bancroft.—Native Races, Vol. III, p. 497.
** Theal.—Kaffir Folk-lore.

shape of a crocodile. A water-sprite, in a Kaffir tale, calls a woman and pulls her down.

*Ashango people say a water-sprite existed in the river Ngouyou, who made the rapids. This spirit, Fougamon, is a worker in iron. Fanti negroes say people used to take iron and leave it near the river, for the spirits to work up into useful articles.

The water-sprite figures most in the guise of a sea-maiden, as her name, mermaid, literally signifies, whether we speak of the German Meerfrau, Danish Moremund, Icelandic Margyr, or Breton Marie Morgan, Welsh Morva or Morreth, Dutch Zee-wjf, Swedish Sjötrold, Anglo-Saxon Merewif, Cornish Morhuch, Irish Merrow, or by any of the special titles their class receives.

The idea of creatures beneath the wave, possessed of a human form with fish-like extremities, is not a modern one. Aside from the many fish-gods of antiquity, as Oannes, Dagon, and others, we are told by † Megasthenes that a creature like a woman inhabits the seas of Ceylon, and Ælian assures us there are whales formed like Satyrs. Tritons and Sirens were also figured half fish, in ancient representations. Demetrius says the Western islanders who died in hurricanes, were mermaids. Pliny says they came on board ships at night, and sunk them, and that Molos, making free with a sea-maiden, lost his head.

‡ That ancient naturalist gave more circumstantial accounts of them. "Nor are we," says he, "to disbelieve the stories told of Nereids, completely covered with rough scales, as one has actually been seen in the ——, and the inhabitants heard at a great distance her lamentations, whinings, and howlings, when she was dying, and his lieutenant wrote to Augustus that a number of Nereids had been found dead on the coast of Gaul. Several distinguished persons of Equestrian rank have assured me that they themselves have seen off the coast of Gades a merman, whose body was of a human form. He was accustomed to appear on board ships in the night time, and the part on which he stood gradually subsided, as if sunk down by his weight." He also asserts their existence in India, and Solinus and Aulus Gellius speak of them. These accounts of Pliny are the first of the appearance of the real mermaid, although he

* Du Chaillu.—Equatorial Africa.
† Jones.—Credulities, p. 25.
‡ Nat. Hist., Vol. IV, p. 4.

does not speak of the fish-tail. This idea, however, as we have seen, was not a new one.

* The Nereids, daughter of the Oceanid Doris, and of Nereus, and mothers of many heroes, were at first imagined beautiful maidens. A mural painting in Pompeii shows such a one. Later they were given the fish-tail, thus becoming mermaids.

Achelous, brother of Nereus, and Calliope, were parents of the Sirens, and as we have seen, they, too, were gradually transformed from human-faced birds to fish-tailed maidens.

So also with the Tritons, offspring of Neptune and Amphitrite, who, at first regarded as men in form, were afterwards given the fish-tail and monstrous form, usually seen in art.

In the middle ages, stories of mermaids increased, and their characteristics were definitely settled.

Arabian writers often speak of them. †El-Kazwini says the Arabs believed that certain fish-men lived in islands in the Indian Ocean, and ate drowned men. Abou Muzaine says a Siren named the Old Man of the Sea, often appeared, prognosticating the good harvests. It spoke an unknown tongue. A similar animal caught a woman and married her, and their son spoke the language of both. Another similar animal, the Old Jew,‡ came to the surface in the Mediterranean, on Friday night, and played about ships all the Jewish Sabbath. Ibnala Bialsaths says sailors in his time caught on foreign shores marine women, with brown skin and black eyes, speaking a strange tongue. Ibn-Batuta, an old Arab writer, says he saw fish in the Persian Gulf with a human head as large as that of a child.

§ Theodore de Gazà saw several Sirens on board ship, in the Peloponnessian sea, which were put back in the water, after being kept on board some time. They were beautiful maidens. George of Trebizonde saw one in the open sea. Gyllius says the skin of sea men taken in Dalmatia is so tough that it is used to make saddle covers.

‖ In the Nibelungen Lieb, Hagen steals a mermaid's garments, but she foretold him good luck if he would give them back again. Another story is that a mermaid told Hagen's fortune, but he, dissatisfied with it, cut off her

* Landrin.—Les Monstres Marins, 282.
† Landrin.—Les Monstres Marins, 282.
‡ Bochar.—Hierozoicon.
§ Landrin.—Les Monstres Marins, 285 et seq.
‖ Ludlow.—Popular Epics of Middle Ages.

head, which mysteriously joined the body again, and a storm thereupon ensued.

The old poets allude to them.   Tasso makes two knights walk by a lake in a pleasure garden where,—

> " Two blooming damsels on the water lave
> And laugh and plunge beneath the lucid wave.

The blood of a mermaid was then thought a prophylactic. Ariosto relates that Orlando smeared his casque with the blood of a Siren;—

> " Naught resists his touch of flame e iron
> Save what has drunk the life blood of a Siren."

* Gower thus sings,—

> " Sirenes of a wonder kind
> Ben monstres as the bokes telleth
> And in the gret sea they dwelleth,
> Of body both and of visage
> Lik vnto women of yonge age,
> Up fro' the navel on high they be,
> And down benethe as men may see
> They bene of fishes the figure."

† Spenser says they are,—

> "Transformed into fish for their bold surqueedry."

‡ And Guyon shows two maidens disporting in a fountain.   An old verse of " Sir Patrick Spens " speaks of them,—

> " Upstarted the mermaid by the ship,
>   Wi' a glass and a kame in her hand,
> Says, 'reek about, reek about, my merry men,
>   Ye are not very far from land.' "

§ Vincent de Beauvais says mermen were avoided by throwing a bottle overboard, when they will stop to play with them.

So learned a man as Joseph Scaliger believed in them. Two Epirote sailors told him they had seen a Siren. Valerio Tesio, a Valencian, told him one was taken in Spanish waters, but was restored to the sea soon after.

Many heroes, like the demi-gods of old, claimed descent from sea-maidens.

---

* Confessio Amantis, 1393.
† Faerie Queene.
‡ Bower of Bliss.
§ Landrin.—Les Monstres Marins, p. 366.

Wieland, or Waylund, a mythical Vulcan of the middle ages, is said to have descended from a mermaid.

So the French Counts of Lusignan, ancient kings of Cypress and Jerusalem, still claim as their ancestor and founder a water-maiden, Melusina, whom an ancestor saw bathing in a fountain, and whom he wedded.

The romances of the middle age often speak of them. Such are the maidens of the Rheingold, celebrated in Wagner's melodious strains.

*In the romantic legends of William of Orange, a mermaid is caught by a cavalier, but liberated. In gratitude therefore, she saves her captor, when his ship is wrecked. When mermaids appeared " then began they all to sing so high, so low, so sweet, and so clear, that the birds leave off flying, and the fish leave off swimming."

The ballads of Chivalry extolled their beauty. Doolin says, of a beautiful woman, " I thought she was an angel, or a sea-siren."

†In a Sicilian tale, a maiden treacherously thrown into the sea, is carried off by a merman, and chained to his tail. A similar story is told by Gubernatis, but the maiden is here liberated, her brother feeding the siren meat, while seven blacksmiths sever the chain.

These mermaids particularly desire a human soul—a thing denied to them by the churchmen. ‡Paracelsus says: " So it follows that they woo men, to make them industrious and homelike, in the same way as a heathen wants baptism, to save his soul; and thus they create so great a love for men, that they are with men in the same union." This of the maidens, but mermen were not so friendly, often dragging people down, like Nick.

§In "The Eastern Travels of John of Hesse " (1389), we read: "We came to a smoky and stony mountain, where we heard sirens singing, *proprie* mermaids, who draw ships into danger by their songs. We saw there many horrible monsters, and were in great fear."

‖In 1187, a merman is said to have been taken near Suffolk, England. It resembled a man, but could not speak. It escaped one day, fled into the sea, and was not again seen.

*Cox and Jones.—Romances of the Middle Ages.
† Gubernatis.—Zoological Mythology. II.
‡ Treatise of Elemental Spirits.
§ Jones.—Credulities, p. 21.
‖ Histoire D'Angleterre, in Jones' Credulities, p. 20.

But the accounts of the early appearances of the mermaid are more circumstantial in northern countries.   Here, where Nick dragged people down, where Ran sucked the breath of the drowned, and where the Strömkarl and the Kelpie flourished, the mermaid was often seen, sitting on the rocks, combing her hair, and predicting disaster to the mariner.

* Pontoppidan, Bishop of Norway, tells us much of the appearance of mermaids on the coasts of that country. Near Landscrona, on the Danish coast, three sailors in a boat saw something floating.   On approaching it, it sank, then arose, and swam waist-deep.   It appeared like an old man, with broad shoulders, small head, deep sunken eyes, thin face, black beard and hair, with fish-like extremities. A minister, Peter Angell, of Sundmœr parish, told the bishop that he saw a merman lying on the strand dead.   It was about six feet long, dark gray in color, with the lower part like a fish, and a tail like a porpoise, a man's face, and arms joined by membranes to the body.

† We have earlier notices of them in the "Royal Mirror," which speaks of mermen and maids, calling the latter *Margyra*, and ascribing to them the attribute of a fish-tail, but saying nothing about its possession by the merman, or *Hafstrambr*.

‡ A later writer says: "Seamen and fishers in very tranquil waters sometimes see mermen and mermaids rise to the quiet top of the sea."   These are described as fair maidens, with fish-tail, long yellow hair, etc.   Their children are called Marmaëler, "Sea-talkers."   "Sometimes the fishermen take them home, to get from them a knowledge of the future."   "Seamen are very sorry to see these creatures, thinking they portend a storm."

§ Norwegian stories are numerous.   When the sea is calm they say the mermen (Marmenill) and mermaids (Margyr) rise to the surface.   The mermen are described as being oldish men, with long beard and black hair, man from the waist upwards and fish downwards, and the mermaid is described as usual.   The appearance of these beings forebodes a storm, and it is thought dangerous to hurt them.   A sailor enticed one to his boat and cut off her hand as it lay on the gunwale.   He nearly perished in the storm

* Natural History of Norway. q. Baring Gould.—Curious Myths, p. 508.
† Konigs Skugg, 1170.
‡ Faye.—Norsk Sagen.
§ Thorpe.--N. Mythology.   Faye.—Norsk Sagen.

that arose in consequence. If in diving they turn toward a ship, it is a bad omen; if from the ship, no evil will result.

St. Olaf, on one of his piratical cruises, met one of these sirens, who was wont to lure sailors to destruction.

* Icelandic chronicles relate that three sea-monsters were seen near Greenland. The first, seen by Norwegian sailors in the water, had the body of a man, with broad shoulders, stumps of arms, and a pointed head. Heavy storms succeeded its appearance. The second was like a woman to the waist, with large breasts, disheveled hair, and large hands on the stumpy arms, webbed like a duck's foot. It held fish in its hand and ate them, and the usual signs with regard to the manner of its eating or using the fish are then told.

† The "Speculum Regali," an Icelandic work, tells us: "A monster is seen also near Greenland, which people call the Margyr. This creature appears like a woman as far down as her waist; long hands and soft hair, the neck and head in all respects like that of a human being. The hands seem to people to be long, and the fingers not to be parted, but united by a web, like that on the feet of water-birds. From the waist downward, this monster resembles a fish, with scales, tail, and fin. This prodigy is supposed to show itself more especially before heavy storms. The habit of this creature is to dive frequently, and rise again to the surface with fishes in its hands. When sailors see it playing with the fish, or throwing them toward the ship, they fear they are doomed to lose several of the crew; but when it casts the fish, or, turning from the vessel, flings them away from her, then the sailors take it as a good omen that they will not suffer loss, in an impending storm. The monster has a very horrible face, with broad brow and piercing eyes, a wide mouth, and double chin."

This excellent account embodies most of the traditions regarding the appearance and prognostications from the sight of the mermaid, current since that time. ‡ The "Landnama," or Icelandic records of land, tells us of Marmenill, or mermen, caught off the island of Grimsey, and other annals tell us of their appearance there in 1305 and 1309.

§ We also read in the Chronicle of Storlaformus, of the

* Iceland, Its Scenes and Sagas.—B. Gould, p. 340.
† Jones.—Browd. Broad Ocean, p. 268.
‡ Jones.—Credulities, p. 21.
§ Chronicle of Storlaformus (1315), q. by Landrin, " Les Monstres Marins."

Hafstrambr: "It resembles a man from the neck, in its head, its nose, and its throat, except that the head is extraordinarily high, and elongated in front. It had shoulders like a man, and attached to them two stumps of arms without hands. The body tapers below, but it has never been seen how it is formed below the waist." He also describes the *Marguguer*. "It is formed like a woman, as far as the waist. It has a large bosom, thick hair, large hands, with fingers webbed like the foot of a goose, attached to its stumpy arms."

* Modern Icelandic folk-lore divides these beings into two classes. First, there are the Margyr, Hafgyr (Sea and Harbor-troll) or Haf-fru (Sea-maid), the seductive maidens of the sea, who have long yellow hair, often sleep in the boats, and occasionally drag them down, and who can be prevented from doing harm by the repetition of a sacred hymn. Then there are the Marmenill, or mermen, who never appear on the surface, but are occasionally caught in the nets, and who then become quite homesick, and earnestly beg to be put back into the water. †These make the *millepora*, coral, called in Iceland, Marmenill's Smi thi.

In a folk tale, a sea-troll appears in a stone boat, bringing luck to a ship, in good breezes and fine weather.

Mermaids are said still to be seen near Grimsey. They will pull men out of boats, but a *credo* will control them.

‡ Mermaids are seen on the Swedish coast, sitting on a rock combing their hair, with a glass in their hands, or spreading out linen to dry. They are said to be fatal and deceitful, and storms and tempests follow their appearance. If a fisherman sees one, he should not speak of it to his comrades. They are said to dwell at the bottom of the sea, and have castles, palaces, and herds of brindled cattle.

A certain knight, Gunnar, dwelt by a lake in Sweden (Anten). He fell in one day, was rescued by a mermaid, and used thereafter to meet her weekly. Failing to do so once, the water rose and drowned him out of his castle, and he sank to the water-maiden's abode while escaping in a boat. The stone near which his boat traditionally sank, is still called Gunnar's stone. Fishermen rowing by it, salute by raising their hats, else they would have no luck.

* Arnanson.—Icelandic Legends.
† Thorpe.—Northern Mythology, Vol. II, pp. 27-8.
‡ Thorpe.—Northern Mythology, Vol. II, pp. 27-8.

A fisherman of Unst saw a group dancing on the strand, picked up a seal-skin, and found a beautiful maiden in tears, who begged the skin, but perforce married him, when refused it. She often conversed with sea-people; one of her children found the seal-skin, showed it to her, and she was afterwards seen by her husband as a seal, diving from the rocks. They are thought to dwell in coral caves, resemble human beings, but are more beautiful. Wishing to come on earth, they cast off the hair garment. They are said particularly to love to revel about Ve Skerries (sacred rocks), are mortal, and are said to have been taken and killed by superstitious fishermen.

* The mermen were, as Blind shows, known by the name of *Finns*, and were said to possess great nautical skill, rowing boats nine miles an hour. Sometimes they pursued ships, when nothing should be said to them, but silver pieces thrown overboard would prevent them from doing harm. Another authority says these men alone doffed the seal-skins, and could only resume the seal form by retaining possession of the skin. One tale is told of a merman caught by a fisherman, who grew larger and larger, until the fisherman complied with his request to throw him overboard, when he promised him luck. The stories of sea-brides obtained by mortals are numerous, and the mermaids are always endowed with a fish-tail.

Fishermen in the Hebrides are said to have caught a mermaid during the present century.

Scotch stories of them are not wanting. An old tale, the "Master of Weemys," is of a ship encountering one at sea,—

† " She held a glass with her richt hande,
In the other she held a kame;
And she kembit her hair, and aye she sang,
As she flotterit on the faem.

Sayle on, sayle on, said she;
Sayle on, and ne'er bluine
The wind at will your sayles may fill
But the land ye shall nevir win."

In another legend a mermaid decoys a knight out to sea with her. In another, a fisherman catches a mermaid in a net. She ties two knots, and darkness comes; three, and a

* Blind. — Scottish and Shetlandish Water-tales. Contemporary Review, August, 1881.
†Scotch and English Legendary Ballads.

tempest. He shakes her off by a spell, and the storm ceases. Here we have the magic storm-causing witch-knots. We find in an old Scotch poem these lines,—

> "A mermaid from the water rose
> And spaed Sir Sinclair ill."

A sea-maiden promised luck to a Scotch fisherman if he would give up his son in three years. She got him, but his mother finally obtained him from the sea-depths by playing music to the mermaid.

*Sometimes the visits of mermaids were considered beneficial. A mermaid is said to have asked a Scotchman, who was reading the Bible, if there was comfort there for her. He said there was mercy for the sons and daughters of Adam, when she screamed and disappeared.

In the ballad, "Rosmer Hafmand," the merman carries a maiden to his sea-palaces, but she finally deceives him, and is carried back in a chest along with a young lover, whom she has passed off as a relative.

†A mermaid, who was accustomed to sing while seated on a stone in front of Knockdolin House, predicted disaster when the stone was removed, on account of her disturbing the young heir with her songs;—

> "Ye may think on your cradle, I'll think on my stane,
> And there'll never be an heir to Knockdolin again."

Mermaids were often dangerous. The young Laird of Lorntie was about to rush into the water, to save a young creature whom he saw struggling there, but was restrained by his servant, who said, "That wailing madam was nae other, God sauf us, than the mermaid." As they rode off, she exclaimed:

> "Lorntie, Lorntie,
> Were it na for your man
> I had gart your hairt's bluid
> Skirl in my pan!"

‡ Leyden's poem, "The Mermaid," is based on a tradition that a certain McPhail of Colonsay Isle, was carried off by a mermaid, and married her, but afterwards deserted her. She sang to him,—

* Gregor.—Folk-lore of Scotland.
† Folk-lore Record.
‡ Scott.—Minstrelsy of the Scottish Border.

> " The mermaids sweet sea-soothing lay
> That charmed the dancing waves to sleep,
> Before the Bark of Colonsay.
>
> And ever as the year returns
> The charm-bound sailors know the day
> For sadly still the mermaid mourns
> The lovely chief of Colonsay."

Many other ballads celebrate the adventures of these sea-maidens, who entice mariners into the sea, are sometimes caught in nets, can raise storms by singing, or by knotting their hair, and can be conquered by certain spells.

*In the Aberdeen Almanac of 1688, it was predicted, that if people should go to the mouth of the Dee on the 1st, 13th, or 29th of May, they would see "a pretty company of mermaids."

A school-master of Thurso, testified in 1797, that he saw a mermaid on the rocks, combing her long hair, and twelve years afterward, others were seen in the same place. In 1871, John McIsaac, of Kintyre, whose testimony was supported by others, averred he saw one on the coast of Scotland. They are often seen, by the islanders, sitting on the rocks between Jura and Scarba.

†A Dr. Hamilton wrote to the Edinburg magazine, some ears since, of the finding of a mermaid near the Shetland Islands, by two fishermen. They had it in the boat some two hours, but becoming superstitious, threw it overboard. It was gray in color, and had a fish tail, but neither scales nor hair on its body, nor webs nor fingers on its hands.

‡Waldron says: "Mermen and Mermaids have been frequently seen. Many surprising stories of these amphibious creatures have I been told."

§A young mermaid fell in love with a Manx shepherd, and in embracing him, held him so tight, that he feared she would do him harm. He accordingly repulsed her, when she flung a stone at him, and mortally wounded him.

‖Fishermen caught a sea maiden, but let her go, fearful of evil consequences. She was afterward asked what strange things she saw above the water, but the only thing she had particularly remarked, was that the water in which eggs were boiled was thrown away.

* Baring Gould.—Curious Myths.
† Gregor.—Folk-lore of Scotland.
‡ Waldron.—History and Description of the Isle of Man, 1744.
§ Scott.—Demonology and Witchcraft.
‖ Scott.—Minstrelsy of the Scottish Border.

A Manx diver reported that he found " below the fishes,"
palaces of mother-of-pearl, with floors of inlaid stones, and
inhabited by mermen and maids.

*Gervase of Tilbury reports the appearance of mermaids
in English seas: " They attract sailors by their sweet songs,
and lead them to wreck and destruction."

†Sir Thomas Browne says: " They are concieved to
answer the shape of the ancient syren that attempted upon
Ulysses, which, notwithstanding, were of another description, containing no fishy composition, but made up of man
and bird."

‡Coad says " The mermaid, I take it as I find it, whether
it were a reality or a spectre. I can promise spectres are
seen at sea some times, and I believe also that there are
such Mockyuga of Humane Nature seen, as an ape is on the
mountain."

The early English poets occasionally allude to them.
Shakspeare was well versed in the mermaid lore, as he
speaks of them in many plays.§

❘John Taylor, the " water-poet," thus sings of one,—

" Four miles from land, we almost were aground,
At last, unlook'd for, on our larboard side,
A thick turmoyling in the sea we spyed,
Like to a Merman, wading as he did,
All in the sea his nether parts were hid,
Whose brawny limbs and rough, neglected beard,
And grim aspect, made us half afraid."

He spoke to them in good Kentish, and finally guided
them out of danger.

Sabrina, goddess of the Severn river, was aided by them
when she took refuge in the river depths,—

** " The water-nymphs that in the bottom play'd,
Held up their pearlèd wrists, and took her in."

The fish-exhibition alluded to by Autolycus, in " Winter
Tale," " Here's another ballad of a fish that appeared upon
the coast of a Wednesday, the fourscore of April, forty
thousand fathoms above water, and sung this ballad against

*Schindler.—Aberglanben des Middelalters, 20.
† Pseudoxica Epidemica.
‡ Astro-Meteorologica (1886), p. 204.
§Midsummer Nights Dream, Act III, scene 2. Comedy of Errors, Act III,
scene 2. Winters' Tale. Antony and Cleopatra, Act II, scenes 2 and 3. Henry
VI, Act III, scene 2.
❘ " A New Discovery by Sea," 1623.
** Milton.—Poems.

the hard hearts of maids. It was thought she was a woman, and was turned into a cold fish, for she would not exchange flesh with one that loved her," is paralleled by one in the "City Match," *

> "Why, 'tis a man-fish,
> An ocean centaur, begot between a siren
> And a he stock-fish."

An old mariner's song runs thus,—

> "One Friday morning we set sail,
> And, when not far from land,
> We all espied a fair mermaid
> With a comb and a glass in her hand;
> The stormy winds they did blow."

Thus embodying the storm-raising omens of sailing on Friday, and of seeing a mermaid

† The Stationers' Company published, in 1684, an account of "a strange reporte of a monstrous fish that appeared in the form of a woman from the waist upward, scene in the sea."

Early navigators chronicle their appearance. Columbus, in his "journal," relates the appearance of three, raising themselves above the waves. He says he had previously seen them on the coast of Africa. He does not represent them as beautiful maidens, and they were probably manatee or dugongs. Hudson tells us: "This morning, one of our company looking overboard saw a mermaid, and calling up some of the company to see her, one more came up, and by that time she was come closely to the ship's side, looking earnestly at the men. A little after, a sea came and overturned her. From the navel up, her back and breasts were like a woman's, as they say that saw her, her body as big as one of us, her skin very white, and long hair hanging down behind, of color black. Seeing her go down, they saw her tail, which was like that of a porpoise, speckled like a mackerel."

In 1812, a gentleman of Exmouth saw a creature like a mermaid sporting in the water. One was seen on the Argleshire coast, on June 4, 1857, rising three or four times out of the water. Other appearances of them in 1817 and in 1863, near the Suffolk coast, are recorded. The skeleton of a so-called mermaid found on one of the islands, was ascertained to be that of a dugong.

* Mayne.—City Match, 1639.
† Jones.—Credulities.

*A story is told among seafaring men that a diver once saw a beautiful mermaid outside of his glass diving-bell. She told him she would protect him, if he would always recognize her in any shape. He promised, but, some days afterwards, he crushed a polypus with his foot. The next time he went down, the mermaid told him it was her whom he had injured, and he soon after met his death in consequence.

† Cornish fishermen call them merrymaids, or Morgan (sea-women). At a place on the coast, a sudden lifting of the fog disclosed seals on a rock, and these were said to be mermaids. Another rock on the Cornish coast, called Mermaid's Rock, is said to be a haunt of these maidens just before a wreck. Certain young men visited these rocks at such a time, but never reappeared. Senten Harbor was traditionally choked up by a mermaid. One is said to have been caught by an old man, and, in return for carrying her to sea, she gave him the power of dispelling witches, and also bestowed on him her comb. A family in Cornwall still display this comb (really a piece of a shark's jaw) in proof of this visit. A story entitled "The Mermaid's Revenge" tells us that a certain poor couple bathed their child daily

in the sea. One day it slipped from their hands, was exchanged for a mermaid, which grew up in their family. She was afterwards betrayed by a lover, and he was dragged into the water, while walking on the strand, some time afterwards, as a punishment for his crime.

So-called mermaids have been exhibited several times in England. ‡In 1755, a carefully made imposture representing a mermaid, said to have been captured in the Grecian seas, was exhibited in London. Another, said to have been captured at sea by a Captain Forster, was shown at Covent Garden at the same time, and there is an account of the exhibition of one in Chamber's "Book of Days," in 1809. In 1822, a figure made in the East Indies, and brought to London, consisting of a fish-tail joined to an

BARNUM'S MERMAID.

* Bottrell.—Traditions of West Cornwa'l.
† Hunt.—Romance and Drolls of the West of England.
‡ Gould.—Myths of the Middle Ages.

ape's body, was exhibited in London, purchased at a high figure by Barnum, and brought to America. I believe it is now in the Boston Museum. * Schele de Vere says a living mermaid was advertised in England, but was found to be a woman with a fish's tail sewn to her body.

Welsh tales of mermaids are told by Sikes, and by other writers.

† The story of the surgeons of Myddvai, relates that one of their ancestors, while sitting on the banks of the dark Lake Lyn y Van Vach, saw three maidens in the water, and courted them. They, however, called him "eater of baked bread," and refused to have anything to do with him. One day, however, he saw unbaked bread floating on the lake, ate it, and was thereby possessed of one of the mermaids. She declared that she would leave him, should he strike her thrice. He did so, in angry moments, and she left him. It is related that she visited her sons, and taught them medicine, in which their descendants are yet skilled. Welsh mermaids, however, are scarce, all the water-sprites and water-fairies of their stories being without the fishy tail that characterizes the mermaid proper.

A mermaid, looking like a maiden of seventeen years, was seen at Ren-y-hold in 1782.

‡Gwenhidwy, whose sheep are the waves and who,

' Drives her white flocks afield, and warns in time
  The wary fisherman,"

was fabled a mermaid. "Take the mermaid's advice, and save thyself; take shelter when you see the mermaid driving her flocks ashore," says an old Welsh poem.

§ The Irish mermaid is called Merrow, or Moruach (sea-maid). Mermen have green hair, red eyes and nose, and are fond of brandy. A man obtained a sea-wife, but on returning home one night, he saw two seals on the beach, and found that one was his wife, who had obtained her seal-skin.

An old Celtic legend says Liban and her family were drowned in Lough Neagh, but she became a mermaid, married a knight, whom she fascinated, and was baptized.

| The first merman was Fintan, who came to Ireland

* Wonders of the Deep. p. 29.
† Choice Notes, Notes and Queries, p. 33 and 34.
‡ See Chapter I.
§ Croker.—Fairy Legends of the South of Ireland.
| Popular Folk-lore of Ireland, Eclectic Mag., 1874.

before the deluge, was saved in the form of a fish, after-wards lived on shore, and was converted by St. Patrick, and became a saint himself. Old sculptures show him, like the Assyrian Dagon. In the cathedral of Omfert County, Ireland, a sculptured mermaid is seen, carrying a book in her hand.

A story of the Lady of Gollerus, given by Croker, relates that a mermaid was caught by getting possession of her enchanted cap (cohuleen druith). She says she is daughter of the king of the waves, marries her captor, but, as usual, finds the cap and disappears. The tale of the " Last of the Cantillons " relates that deceased members of that family were left on the sea-side to be carried away by sea-men, but that a curious fellow watched these people, and they de-clared no more should be thus carried away. In the story of the Lord of Dunkerron, he encounters a mermaid,—

" For a beautiful spirit of ocean, 'tis said,
The Lord of Dunkerron would win to his bed;
When by moonlight the waters were hush'd to repose
That beautiful spirit of ocean arose,
Her hair, full of lustre, just floated and fell
O'er her bosom that heav'd with a billowy swell."

He follows her to sea-caverns, but, after a time, on visit-ing the earth and returning, he finds that she is dead, killed by the enraged mermen.

* John Reid, of Cromarty, caught a mermaid, who begged to be put in the water, promising to fulfill three wishes. He did this, and obtained what he wished.

Rathlin Island is haunted by a mermaid:

" 'Tis said, at eve, when rude winds sleep,
And hush'd is every turbid swell,
A mermaid rises from the deep
And sweetly tunes her magic shell."

† In another legend, the daughter of the king of the land of youth appears to a young hunter, and he follows her to her courts beneath the waves.

A mermaid is said to have been found in a shark's belly in Ireland, and is minutely described as being of the size of a nine-year-old boy, with long hair, olive skin, one thumb, webbed fingers, etc. It was thrown into the sea.

‡ The Irish feared to kill seals, saying that they were the

* Hugh Miller.—Scenes and Legends, p. 263.
† Croker.—Fairy Legends of the So' th of Ireland.
‡ See Froude.—" Short Stories," p. 187.

souls of those drowned at the flood, and that they can put aside their skin and appear in the guise of mortals, but cannot return to their watery element, if the skin is stolen.

Among the many legends of the famous piper, is that version in the tale of Maurice Connor, the Irish harper, who

ARION

pipes a mermaid from the waters, but is in time charmed by her and accompanies her. So Arion, in danger of sacrifice by the Greek crew, plays first and charms the fish, until he is borne ashore to Corinth. The romantic historians of Ireland assert that Tuire, or sea-maidens, played about the Milesian ships on their way to Ireland.

*Breton stories of mermaids are abundant, and fishermen say they often see them on the coast. One (a "Siren") caught by a peasant, brought bread, clothing, silver and gold, to purchase her freedom. † Brantôme says, "Nereids were abundant in French waters during the middle ages." The most celebrated one was Melusina, whose marriage to Raymond of Toulouse, was related above.

She was said afterwards to haunt the castle on the death of any one, becoming thus a *banshee*.

From the middle-age treatise of Paracelsus‡ comes the legend of Undine, whose story is so charmingly told by Fouqué. She is really a water-sprite, who visits her foster-parents, and on one occasion sees and loves a wandering knight, who marries her, when she becomes the possessor of a soul, and various vicissitudes common to mortals await her. She once revisits the water-depths, and strange enough, returns unharmed, but the knight soon after dies.

There is a French legend of Poul Dahut, a rock on the Breton coast, where the daughter of a sea-king, Dahut, is said to sit in rough weather.

§ A Breton tale is told of a lady, who found a mermaid on the beach, and put her into the water. The grateful sea-maiden brought her a shell, with a drink in it, telling her to give it to her son. Instead, she gave it to her cat, which became wise, but malicious, while her son was always half-witted.

In Provence, a gold ring is thrown into the water, and verses repeated, to charm the water king.

A *negro* mermaid was exhibited at St. Germain Fair in Paris, in 1758, and a shop in Ostend contained, in 1881, a figure said to be a mermaid, a cut of which was shown in Harper's Magazine.

‖ In an old "History of the Netherlands," we find this account of the appearance of one in 1493, at Haarlem: "At that time there was a great tempest at sea, with exceeding high tides, the which did drown many cities in Friseland and Holland; by which tempest there came a sea-woman swimming in the Zuyder-Zee, betwixt the towns of Campen and Edam, the which, passing by the Purmeric, entered into the strait of a broken dyke in the Purmermer, where she

* Sébillot.—Litterature Orale de Haute Bretagne.
† Dictionnaire Historique.
‡ Treatise on Elementary Spirits.
‖ Gubernatis —Zoological Mythology.
⁑ Baring Gould.—Curious Myths, p. 509.

remained a long time, and could not find the hole by which she entered, for that the breach had been stopped after that the tempest had ceased. Some country women and their servants who did daily pass the Purmeric, to milk their kine in the next pastures, did often see this woman swimming on the water, whereof at the first they were much afraid; but in the end being accustomed to see it very often, they viewed it nearer, and at last they resolved to take it if they could. Having discovered it, they rowed toward it, and drew it out of the water by force, carrying it in one of their barks unto the town of Edam. When she had been well washed and cleansed from the sea-moss which was grown about her, she was alike unto another woman; she was apparalled, and began to accustom herself to ordinary meats like unto other mortals; yet she sought still means to escape, and to get into the water, but she was straightly guarded. They came from fare to see her. Those of Harlem made great sute to them of Edam to have this woman by reason of the strangenesse thereof. In the end they obtained her, where she did learn to spin, and lived many years (some say fifteen), and for the reverence which she bare unto the signe of the crosse whereupon she had been accustomed, she was buried in the churchyarde. Many persons worthy of credit have justified in their writings that they had seene her in the said towne of Harlem."

There is no fish-maiden here. If we are to believe the story at all, we may reasonably suspect this to be some outcast like Caspar Hauser, a human being trained to the shallow water of the pond, and placed to live there and be adopted by her finder, or we may account it the designed fraud of some sharp Hollander. In fact, more careful study has demonstrated that the earliest accounts of her only described her as a water-woman, and the mermaid myth was afterward invented.

A mermaid is said to have appeared to Antwerp whalers and said,—

> * "Sailors, throw out a cask
> So soon you whales shall have."

† A mermaid prophesied the destruction of Zevenbergen, a wicked city of Holland, in 1721, and also of Minden,—

> " Zevenbergen must perish
> And Lobbeken's seven towers still remain.'

* Landrin.—Les Monstres Marins.
†Schele de Vere.—Wonders of the Deep, p. 25.

*Gaspar Schott gives a curious sketch of a Triton with human body, arms and head, and fish tail.

† Ludovicus Vivus relates that in his time a mermaid was taken in Holland, and carefully kept for two years; that she began to speak, or at least to make a very disagreeable noise in imitation of speech; that she found an opportunity, and got into the sea.   The same writer says that Lieutenant Transmale saw at the time he was sent with some men on an expedition in the Bay of Hodudela, as did all the people that were with him, in clear daytime, two mermaids, the one greater, the other smaller, which they took to be

TRITON, FROM SCHOTT.

man and wife, swimming together, and the hair of their heads hung over their neck, and that it appeared between a green and grayish color; and that they could see that they had breasts.   They were all above the waists shaped exactly as a human creature, but from thence downward they seemed to go off tapering to a point.   About six weeks afterward, near the same place, a like appearance was seen by upward of fifty people.

Holland afterward became celebrated for its mermaids, so much so that in that country, and its colonies, the mermaid was deemed a native production.

* Physica Curiosa, 1662.
Ruysch.—Natural History.

* Valentin, a curate of Amboyna, published in the Dutch tongue a large collection of facts, in support of the existence of the mermaid. Many certificates accompanied his description, and the beautifully colored figures, in the curious work referred to.

† In 1611 it is said a mermaid or sea-woman was taken alive near the island of Boro, which was fifty-nine inches long. She lived four days and seven hours and then died, as she would not eat anything. She was never heard to articulate any noise. One Samuel Falvers, in Amboyna, preserved the body for some time, and made out an exact

THE MOLUCCA SIREN.

description of it, by which it appears that her head was like a woman's, properly proportioned, with eyes, nose and mouth, only the eyes, which were light blue, seemed to differ a little from the human species. The hair, that just reached over the neck, appeared of sea-green and grayish color. She had breasts, long arms, hands, and all the upper parts of the body almost as white as a woman's, but leaning somewhat to the sea-gray. The lower part of her body appeared like the hinder part of a fish.

* Poissons, Ecrivisses et Crabes de divers couleurs et figures extraordinaires, q'on a trouvé dans les Iles Moluques, Amsterdam, 1717.
† B. Gould.—Curious Myths.

Dr. Kerschur, in one of his scientific reports, relates that another mermaid was caught in the Zuyder Zee, and dissected at Leyden by Professor Peter Pau, and in the same learned report, he makes mention of still another, who was found in Denmark, and who was taught to knit, and foretell future events. This mermaid had a pretty face, mild, sparkling eyes, a small, tiny nose; long, drooping arms; the fingers of her hands joined by a cartilage like a goose's foot; the breasts round and hard, and the skin covered with white shells. He asserted that the mermaids and mermen constitute a submarine population, which, partaking of the skill of the ape and the beaver, build their grottoes of stone in places inaccessible to all divers, and where they spread out their beds of sand, in which they lie, sleep and enjoy their loves.

The mermaid of the Royal Museum at the Hague was seen by Alexandre Dumas, during a visit there. He describes it as quite dried and withered, and in color very like the head of a Caribbee. Her eyes were shut, her nose flattened, her lips sticking to the teeth, of which only a few remained; her bosom was consyicuous, though sunk; a few short hairs stood out upon the head; finally, the lower part of the body terminated in a fish's tail. There was no opening for dispute. It was really and trully a siren, a mermaid, a sea-nymph. "If, after all this, there shall be found those who disbelieve the existence of such creatures as mermaids, let them please themselves. I shall give myself no more trouble about them."

* Dimas Bosque, physician to the viceroy of the island of Manara, relates in a letter inserted in Bartholdi's "History of Asia," that walking one day on the sea-shore with a Jesuit father, a party of fishermen came running up to them to invite the father to enter their barge, if he wished to behold a prodigy. There were sixteen fishes with human faces in the barge—nine females and seven males—all of which the fishermen had just drawn up with a single cast of their net. Their teeth were square and closely set together. The chest was broad and covered with a skin, singularly white, which left visible the blood-vessels. Their ears were elevated like our own, cartilaginous, and covered with a fine skin. Their eyes were similar to ours in color, shape and positicn; they were inclored in their orbits,

Landrin.—Les Monstres Marins.

below the forehead, furnished with lids, and did not possess, like fishes, different axes of vision. Their nose only differed from the human nose, by its being rather flatter, like the negro's, and partially slit up, like a bulldog's. In all of them the mouth and lips were perfectly similar to ours.

The females had round, full and firm bosoms, and some of them appeared to be suckling their young, as when the breasts were pressed upon, a very white and delicate milk jetted out. Their arms, two cubits in length, and much fuller and plumper than the men's, had no joints; their hands were joined to the cubitus. Lastly, the lower portion, beginning with the haunches and thighs, was divided into a double tail, as we see in ordinary fishes.

* German tales of the mermaid proper are not numerous. Gœthe's "Waterman" is a pretty version of a Danish tale of a mermaid. A merman visits the church, and weds a maiden who falls in love with him. He brings a ship for her, and they embark,—

> " But when they were out in the midst of the sound,
> Down went they all in the deep profound."

In German legend, there is a queen of the sea, Merreimne (Norse Marmenille, mer-woman). She was fished up from the sea in a net, but the terrified fishermen hastily threw her overboard.

Three men are said to have caught a mermaid at Weningstede, in Schleswick-Holstein, but they put her back in the water, on hearing her cries. It is there believed that they foretell a storm, when seen about the bows of a ship. A "Waterman" is said to have stopped a ship at sea, and to have refused to let it go until the queen, a passenger thereon, should descend to his palace, where a midwife was needed.

Gœthe's ballad, "Sir Peter of Stauffen," depicts the power of the mermaid's song; and there is another old ballad, where a waterman

> " Drags her down to his ocean cave
> The gentle Amelie."

The Lorelei, who is fabled to sit on the rocks in the Rhine, and lure boats to destruction, is celebrated in song by Heine and Doenninger, and mermaids are represented in Wagner's Rheingold.

* Baring Gould.—Curious Myths, 510.

An old German legend is told of a certain countess, who was seized while bathing, by mermaids and men, and stripped of her jewels. She expressed a great desire to recover her wedding-ring, at least, and on the seventh day thereafter, it was found in the stomach of a fish, caught near the spot where she had bathed.

*A Hamburg skipper, Jan Schmidt, saw a mermaid in 1610, while at sea near Bayonne, just at daylight. He knew she would drag some one down, so had his men repulse her with long poles and pikes. When she found them prepared for her, she uttered a piercing cry, and dove down into the sea.

At Nidden, in West Prussia, a mermaid sits on the rocks and decoys persons to her, but they are drowned ere they reach her.

Frisians say there are but seven mermaids, and that a man devoting himself to one of them, will suffer death, should he ever abandon her.

In an Esthonian tale, a fisherman sees a daughter of the "Mother of the Seas," falls in love with her, and marries her. She leaves him on every Thursday, and, on watching her, he finds she has a fish-tail.

†In the Finnish Epic, the "Hostess of the Sea," rises at the sound of Waïnamoïnen's harp (the wind), and combs her long locks by the seaside. That hero catches a mermaid, but as he is about to cut her open and eat her, she disappears.

Wallachian, Wendic, and Russian stories of water-sprites are told, some of whom assume the shape of birds, and fly through the air. Many of these are a kind of a cross between mermaids and sirens.

Mermaids are said to have been seen near Portugal in 1531, and Spanish and Italian stories of them are recorded.

‡Lamia is a water-maiden in modern Greece, who is represented as malicious, greedy, and sensual, dragging people into the water. Mermaids are not, however, so abundant in southern waters, as in the colder seas of the north.

§Chinese say mermaids are of the shape of demons, and are ruled by a harpy, Nükira, who, when the heavens were torn, mended them, but left a hole in the northwest, whence

*Schmidt.—Seeman's Sagen und Schiffer Märchen.
†Kalevala.—Le Duc's Translation.
§Hahn.—Greichishe Märchen.
‡Dennys.—Folk-lore of China.

emerge the cold winds. They call mermaids sea-women (hai-nü), and numerous stories are told of them. One is said to have been captured at Nanchow in 1800, and many saw her; and another was found at Nüshan. A cabinet councillor is said to have found one on the beach in Corea, and carried her to sea, putting her in it.

*In the Loochoo Islands also, one is said to have lived with a native ten years, but finally she climbed a tree, and disappeared. Here we have a nymph of the sky-sea.

Japan is, however, the headquarters of these coy maidens of the sea. Here an old Dutch navigator obtained the first "veritable" mermaid, and they may still be procured of ingenious natives. Numbers have been shown in museums, etc., deftly made by uniting a child's head to a fish's body. At Bartholomew fair, in 1825, there was exhibited a mermaid, obtained by a Dutch ship from Japan, and the Ottoman minister to Paris, in 1840, related that he had seen a veritable sea-woman, brought from Eastern seas.

A Japanese legend relates that a mermaid prophesied an epidemic.

† Ottawa Indians believed in the existence of a mermaid with two fish-like extremities, and called her daughter of the flood. Pascagoula Indians had traditions of a race emerging from the sea, who worshiped a mermaid.

An Ottawa tale is told of a certain Wassaur conveyed by a spirit-maiden to the "Spirit of the Sand Dunes," in Lake Superior.

‡ B. Gould tells a tale of an Ottawa chieftain who saw a beautiful woman arise from the water. She wished to have a human soul, but could only have one by marrying a mortal.

The tribe drove her away, and the result was a war of extermination with another tribe (Adirondacks), and finally one was left, who was carried down by the water-maiden at St. Anthony's Falls.

These maidens have often been seen on our shores.

§ Captain John Smith saw, in 1614, off an island in the West Indies, a mermaid, with the upper part of the body perfectly resembling a woman. She was swimming about with all possible grace when he descried her near the shore. Her large eyes, rather too round, her finely-shaped nose, somewhat short, it is true, her well-formed ears, rather too long, however, made her a very agreeable person, and her long green hair imparted to her an original character by no means unattractive. Unfortunately the beautiful swimmer made a slip, and Captain Smith, who had already begun to experience the first effects of love, discovered that from below the waist the woman gave way to the fish.

* Jocelyn also tells of them: "One Mr. Miller, relates of a triton or mermaid, which he saw in Casco bay; the gentleman was a great forder, and used to go out with a small boat or canoe, and fetching a compass about a small island, there being many islands in the bay, he encountered with a triton, who, laying his hands upon the sides of the canoe, had one of them chopped off with a hatchet by Mr. Miller, which was in all respects like the hands of a man; the triton presently sunk, dyeing the water with his purple blood, and was no more seen."

The following account from a newspaper, of a similar occurrence, is given,—

" John Dilercy related a curious story of some American fishermen One night, it being a perfect calm, they observed a mermaid coming into their vessel, and fearing it to be some mischievous fish, in the fright of one of them, cut the creature's hand off with a hatchet, when it sank immediately, but soon came up again and gave a deep sigh as one feeling pain. The hand was found to have five fingers and nails like a woman's hand."

The Richmond *Dispatch*, of July, 1881, published an account of a negro woman who said that she, being pursued to death by some one in Cuba, jumped overboard, and was, after drifting for hours, rescued by a band of mermaids, who took her to their sea-caverns, and finally placed her on board a vessel bound for New Orleans.

In a daily (Boston) paper of October 31, 1881, is contained the following account of a mermaid captured in Aspinwall Bay and brought to New Orleans,—

" This wonder of the deep is in a fine state of preservation. The head and body of a woman are very plainly and distinctly marked. The features of the face, eyes, nose, mouth, teeth, arms, breasts and hair are those of a human being. The hair on its head is of a pale, silky blonde, several inches in length. The arms terminate in claws closely

*Jocelyn's Voyages, 1673, p. 23.

resembling an eagle's talons, instead of fingers with nails. From the waist up, the resemblance to a woman is perfect, and from the waist down, the body is exactly the same as the ordinary mullet of our waters, with its scales, fins and tail perfect. Many old fishermen and amateur anglers who have seen it pronounce it unlike any fish they have ever seen. Scientists and savants alike are 'all at sea' respecting it, and say that if the mermaid be indeed a fabulous creature, they cannot class this strange comer from the blue waters."

Torquemada says that Mexican legends of the mermaid related that she, the tortoise and the whale, formed a bridge of their bodies for a man to pass the House of the Sun.

* Herbert Smith says there are stories on the lower Amazon, of water-maidens with long black hair, who sing and entice young men into the water. Uangaia, King of the Fishes, assumes many shapes, and entices women into the waters.

† Moravian missionaries in South America brought from thence wonderful stories of mermen and mermaids, some having seen these beings, with brown skin and long hair, in the water. The natives feared them and would not harm them, fearing disaster.

Negroes of Surinam told English officers, in 1801, that they often saw mermaids playing in the river on moonlight nights.

The tradition of the mermaid will long survive in nautical nomenclature. English fishermen call the frog-fish Meermaid, although no reference to the mermaid is intended. The *Spongia palmata* is called the mermaid's glove, and the outer covering of shark's eggs, as well as the hollow root of the sea-weed *Fucus polyschides*, are named the mermaid's purse.

Having thus traced the history of the mermaid, and given an account of her in all corners of the earth, we are prepared to believe her origin not an unnatural one, but a development of ideas originating in antiquity, and fostered during an age of credulity and superstition. Her origin is undoubtedly mythical, but various causes natural and legendary have assisted the myth in its growth. As before said, these maidens are originally cloud-nymphs. This an-

* Brazil.
† Schele de Vere.—Wonders of the Deep, p. 22.

cestry has already been partially traced in the present chapter. Analogies between the mermaids and these ancient mythical beings have been given. Like Proteus, they may (at least the water-sprites can) change their forms at will. This is an attribute of their primitive form, that of the Apsaras, or "formless ones," whose cloud bodies arose from the vaporous deep. Like Nereus, they are possessed of great wisdom. This is also an attribute of all the primitive beings who arose from the deep, as Oannes, Hea, Viracocha, etc. Like the ancient sea-deities, they are benificent, since they possess great wealth. This latter characteristic is alleged of all the sea beings. The hoard of the Niflungs, the golden palace of Neptune, and of Œgir, the Rheingold, and other instances of this wealth, will be remembered If they are malicious, or diabolic, they derive such a temperament from Nick, or from Typhon, from their ancestors the Sirens, or their prototypes, the harpies. The bad omen derived from their appearance may be traced at least to Melusinar, who, after her death, becomes a *banshee* or evil apparition. Perhaps the Christian influence in the degradation of heathen deities may have aided in establishing a diabolic character. The song of the mermaid, by which she often lures to destruction listening mortals, is but the dangerous lay of the Sirens, or the sweet attractions of Circe. *The Myth is ancient, as Hylas was so charmed in the Argonautic voyages.

This lay is none other, as we have seen, than the sweet strains of Orpheus' harp, and here perhaps is the origin of the mermaid's comb, doubtless the ancient lyre. Being thus always malevolent, when seen at sea, and ominous in appearance, she would be naturally connected with the weather, a significant fact corroborating her cloud-parentage. The fish-tail peculiar to the mermaid is doubtless derived primarily from the Assyrian Oannes, and we have seen Tritons and Nereids thus represented. The Sirens, anciently birds, became, later, beauteous maidens, and were finally endowed with the scaly appendage.

† Price has thus embodied these ideas: " The Nereids of antiquity, the daughters of the sea, born seers, are evidently the same with the mermaids of the British and Northern shores; the habitations of both are fixed in crystal caves or coral palaces, beneath the waters of the ocean; and they

* Ap. Rhodius.—" Argonautica." I, 131.
† Introduction to Warton's History of Poetry.

are alike distinguished for their partiality to the human race, and their prophetic power in disclosing the events of futurity. The Naiads differ only in name from the Nixen of Germany and Scandinavian Nissen, or the water-elves of our countrymen Ælfric."

Philologists find, however, that even this difference does not exist, since from a Sanskrit word *Sna*, to flow, are derived the names for Naiad, Nereid, Nymph, Nick, etc.

These beings require some recompense for their services, which represents the ancient sacrifices to the water-deities. The priestly influence is again visible in the notion that this gift is baptism, or salvation. The myth of marriage to mortals is of more difficult interpretation, and is closely connected with the legends of their having the power of changing their form, and of the possession of some mysterious garment whereby the change is effected. This garment was originally a swan's plumage, but is sometimes a peculiar cap, a seal-skin, or even a girdle. The swan story is first told in the *Katha Sarit Sagatha*.

* Svidatta saw a swan in the Ganges, plunged in, and followed the maiden to her palace beneath the waves. The story is common to many lands, and is even known among the Mongols and Tartars. Æschylus savs the Phorkides were swan-shaped. In the Hymn to Apollo, the clouds are swan-nymphs, attendant on Phœbus, the sun. "Here, then, we have the groundwork of all those tales which speak of men as wedded to fairies, nymphs, nixies, mermaids, swan-maidens or other supernatural beings." "From the thought which regarded the cloud as an eagle or swan, it was easy to pass to the idea that the birds were beautiful maidens; and hence that they could at will, or on the ending of the enchantment, assume their human form." "Then would follow the myth that the only way to capture these beings was to seize their garments of swan's or eagle's plumes, without which they were powerless."

But while we may acknowledge the mythical origin of these beings, there are many natural causes whose influence aided in the formation and perpetuation of the mermaid myth. Much of the testimony recorded above is too circumstantial to be accounted a mere trick of the imagination, or morbid fancy of the writers.

Species of existing sea-animals have certainly aided in

* Gould.—Myths of the Middle Ages.

perpetuating these many stories of maidens of the sea. The dugong and manatee especially have a human look, having large breasts and short, arm-like fins. *Scoresby says the front view of a young walrus without tusks resembles a human face. Speaking of their habit of rearing the head above the water, he says, " I have myself seen a sea-horse in such a position, and under such circumstances, that it required very little stretch of the imagination to mistake it for a human being; so like, indeed, was it, that the surgeon of the ship actually reported to me his having seen a man with his head just appearing above the water." French and German heraldic signs represent mermaids with one or two tails.

The French call the manatee *femme marine*, and the Dutch name the dugong *mannetje* (little man) and Baardanetzee (little beard). Professor Owen thinks these animals are the mermaids of fable.

In Oriental legend, the dugong is the mermaid of the Indian ocean, and their tears are pearls, and attract persons to them. Stories of mermaids singing or talking may also have arisen from hearing the cries of the seal, said by navigators to resemble those of an infant. The well-known friendliness of that animal to man, and its gentleness, would favor the current ideas concerning mermaids. Thus, while the mythical idea grew up in a superstitious age, the reports of mariners of these strange animals to a people equally ignorant in science, would foster and preserve the growths of the myths.

† Schele de Vere, in alluding to the accounts given of mermaids by the Moravian missionaries, in South America, conjectures these mermaids to be the Canthoeirus, a race of savages who almost live in the waters of the great rivers of the Amazon valley, often attack boats, and are greatly feared by the natives. Here would be a natural element in the growth of the mermaid myth. ‡ Hone tells a story of a certain Vega, who, in 1674, leaped into the sea and was drawn ashore five years afterwards, covered with scales. He had forgotten his language, but was recognized by his family. He lived several years afterwards, but finally disappeared. § Tieck pronounces the story authentic.

* Voyages.
† Wonders of the Deep.
‡ Hone.— Table Book, Vol. II, p. 188.
§ Das Wasserman, 1881.

These, along with the other phantoms of the deep, no longer appear to the intelligent mariner of this scientific age. Yet in remote corners, and to skeptical vision, such apparitions still are recorded.

But in spite of the occasional reports of such visions, we may reasonably conclude with the Swedish poet, Stagneli, that,—

> "The Neck no more upon the river sings,
> And no mermaid to bleach her linen plays
> Upon the waves in the wild solar rays."

CHAPTER V.

SEA-MONSTERS AND SERPENTS.

"Canst thou draw out leviathan with a hook?"
Job, xxxvi.

"Of that sea-snake, tremendous curled,
Whose monstrous circle girds the world."
Scott.—Lay of the Last Minstrel, vi.

'God quickened in the seas and in the rivers,
So many fishes of so many features,
That in the waters we may see all creatures,
Even all that on the earth are to be found."

DU BARTAS but echoed the ideas of his own and of preceding ages. The strange catalogue of fishes which he proceeds to give, elsewhere repeated, by no means exhausted the fauna of the sea, according to the ideas of antiquity, and the beliefs of the middle ages. We have seen the waters of the globe peopled with deities, with demons, and with human or semi-human beings and sprites; with giants, dwarfs, elves, and trolls. It would have been strange, if the same fertile imaginations that figured these beings, to correspond with similar creations on the land, had not placed in the waters other wonders, the parallels of similar land-animals commonly supposed to exist.

Thus, then, as there had been imagined, throughout all antiquity, land-monsters, dragons, and serpents of prodigious size, we may expect to find in the ocean, the scene of so much mystery and dread, animals of a similar character, proofs of whose fancied existence is evidenced by the

Du Bartas.—Divine Weeks and Works.

names, sea-elephant (morse) *Macrorhinus proboscidens*, sea-horse (walrus), sea-swallow (flying-fish), sea-leopard (*Stenorhynchus Leopardus*), sea-bear (Otarie), sea-cow (Manatee) sea-dragon (*Cottus*), sea-lion (*Platorhynchus*), sea-wolf (*Anarhynchus lupus*), and sea-hog (porpoise), terms still existing in marine nomenclature.

 * I have already described the strange half-fish monsters that were said to have appeared from time to time from the Persian Gulf. There were other monsters in those seas at that time. † Berosus says there were seen in Chaldean waters, monsters with four-fold bodies of dogs, but with fish-tails, and men with fish-tails, horses with fish-tails, and serpents with fish-heads and fins. Omoroka, a monster-woman, presided over these.

Monsters of the deep are alluded to in many places in the Bible. ‡A whole chapter of Job is devoted to the Leviathan. Commentators have devoted much time to it, but have never agreed as to whether it is intended to describe the crocodile, the behemoth, the dragon, or the serpent. The subject will be alluded to again in the present chapter. Other monstrous sea-animals are spoken of, but are plainly fictitious.

§ A Talmudic tale assures us that a fish came ashore in the Mediterranean, so large that the people of sixty cities ate from, and those of sixty more salted down some of its flesh, and from one of its eyes, three hundred measures of oil were obtained.

Classical authority has bequeathed us many monsters. Such, according to the mythographers, were the aquatic demons who attacked Andromeda, sent by Neptune to devour her, in revenge for a boastful speech. This monster, the *Pistris*, was paralleled by that which attacked Hesione,‖ from which Hercules delivered her by jumping down the monster's throat, whence he emerged, after three days' confinement, by hacking his way out. But Perseus and Hercules were Sun-gods, and these monsters are therefore understood to be clouds sent from the sea, dispersed by the sun's power. Other monsters were known in antiquity.** The Chilon had a man's head, and lived on its own humors.

* See Chapter II.
† Cory.—Ancient Fragments.
‡ Job, Chapter XLI.
§ Jones.—Credulities, p. 53.
‖ Cox.—Aryan Mythology, p. 292.
** Schele de Vere.—Wonders of the Deep, p. 10.

The Balena was like a whale, but was cruel to its mate. The Dies was a fish with two wings and two legs, living only a day. The Hippocampus was half-horse, half-fish, and covered with scales.

*Aristotle tells of a gigantic squid, or calmar, ten feet four inches long. Trebius says one came ashore at Carteia, and ate salt meats. It climbed a high fence, was attacked by dogs, and only subdued with great difficulty. Its head was as big as a cask, its arms thirty feet long, and its body estimated at seven hundred pounds. Ælian says one destroyed warehouses in Spain, and was killed with difficulty. Pliny says a great mollusk, called Arbas, had such long arms that it could not enter Gibraltar Straits without grounding. Strange monsters attended Amphitrite and Poseidon.

In Hindoo legend, Krishna slew a monster that lived at the bottom of the sea. Pâli legend tells of a gigantic crab that lived there also.† Hanamaut slew a monster and was devoured by another, liberating himself by distending his body and bursting the monster open. Here is doubtless another cloud-myth, as Hanamaut is son of the winds. Varuna, god of the watery element was attended by animals having the heads of antelopes, and the tails of fish. Like Krishna and Apollo, Indus, Vishnu, Ahura Mazda, Feridun, Sigurd, and others slew monsters of the deep.

But the accounts of sea-monsters became more circumstantial and more numerous in the middle ages, as men became better acquainted with the great outer sea. Many of these fabulous creatures are borrowed from antiquity. ‡"The middle ages did not await the dream of Olaus to possess marine monsters. Antiquity had abundantly provided them, and in joining to these conscientiously those of the bible, they peopled the depths of the ocean with a thousand creatures. The Leviathan cleaved with his gigantic fins the eastern seas, the § Physeter, that Solin had borrowed from Pliny, rejecting so great an abundance of water that it could sink a ship easily, and, as a vast water-sprite, play with its débris," were among these.

Perhaps the earliest and most marvelous accounts of these aquatic giants came from the Arabs—the earliest mediæval navigators. ∥El Kazwini gives us several ac-

* Landrin.—Les Monstres Marins, p. 20.
† Ramayana.—Wilson's Trans.
‡ Denys de Montfort.—Mollusques, in Buffon's Natural History.
§ Pliny.—Natural History, Vol. IX, p. 3.
∥ Marvels of Creation, 956 A.D.

counts of these: "In the sea of China is a fish more than three hundred cubits long; fear is entertained for the ship on account of it; and when the people know of its passing by, they call out, and beat with wood, that it may flee at their noises; when it raiseth its fin, it is like an enormous sail." He says further, that an enormous fish in the same waters beats and sinks ships with its tail, and that another has an owl's face. "As to the sea-tortoise, it is very enormous, so that the people of the ship imagine it to be an island. One of the merchants relates as follows regarding it. 'We found in the sea an island, elevated above the water, having upon it green plants, and we went forth and dug holes for fire to cook. Whereupon the island moved, and the sailors said, 'Come ye, to your places, for it is a tortoise, and the heat of the fire hath burnt it, lest it carry you away.' 'By reason of its body,' said he, 'it was as though it were an island, and earth collected upon its back in the length of time, so that it became like land, and produced plants.'" Another chronicler, El Wardee, corroborates these statements of El Kazwini, and it is doubtless to their account that we owe the tales of monsters given in that veracious chronicle, the Arabian Nights Entertainments. Sinbad encountered the island-fish in his third voyage. He relates that they were becalmed near a little green island, and many landed on it, he among the number.* "We had not long landed, when, on a sudden, the island trembled, and shook us terribly. The people on board saw our situation, and called out to us to re-embark directly, as what we had taken for an island, was only the back of a prodigious fish."

Again he says: "I saw fishes of a hundred and two hundred cubits long; far from being dangerous, they fly from the least noise. I saw also other fishes, about a cubit long, which had heads like owls."

A monster, who has a human body with shark's head, while on shore, and is a shark in the sea, figures in the story Al Habib. Another monster fish opposed his progress, but was subdued by a magic charm.

† El Masudi says there are whales in the sea of Zeudi 44,500 cubits long. ‡ A Jewish work, the Bara Bathra, says a ship was three days in passing from the tail to the head of a whale.

---

* Lane's Arabian Nights.—Sinbad's Third Voyage.
† Golden Meadows.
‡ Landrin.—Les Monstres Marine, p. 180.

El Wardee, Sinbad and El Kazwini all tell of fish the shape of a cow, and of one the shape of a camel. *Ibn Batuta says that he saw a fish, whose head was as large as a mountain, and whose eyes were the size of two great doors. Arab cosmographers told of the island Kalken, where men lived, with the heads of marine monsters upon their shoulders.

Christian writers related marvels equally great. Many of them have described the Bishop-fish and Monk-fish,—

MONK-FISH.　　　　　　RONDELET'S BISHOP-FISH.

† "And which I most admire,
The mitred bishop and the cowlèd friar;
Of which examples, but a few years since
Were shown the Norway and Polonian prince."

‡ Rondelet gives a more explicit description of them, "In our time there has been caught in Norway, after a great tempest, an ocean monster, to which all who saw it incontinently affixed the name of the monk; for it had a man's

* "Voyages."
† Du Bartas.—Divine Weeks and Works.
‡ Universum Piscum Historia (1554), in Landrin, p. 288.

face, rude and ungraceful, with a bald, shining head; on the shoulders, something like a monk's hood; long winglets, instead of arms; the extremity of the body terminated in a tail."

Rondelet says it was caught and taken to the King of Poland, but made vehement signs to be put in the water, and when this was done, plunged in and disappeared.

*De Vere says Holland originated the stories of the bishop-fish and monk-fish. In 1305, a sea-knight was caught here, covered with a complete suit of armor. It died in three weeks. A tradition of this curious fish existed in later times. †Buchan says, "Among the prodigies of this time (874), they reckoned those sea-fishes then appearing, which are seldom seen, and after long intervals of time. But they never appear but in shoals, *nor without some unlucky presage.* The common people call them Monachi-marini, i.e., Sea-monks."

Probably a tradition of these notions remains in the name given the Squatina Angelus—of "Sea-monk," and the "Capuchin" (Stemmalopus Cristatus).

Scandinavia abounded in these monsters. ‡Gesner tells of the Island-fish on which mariners landed. Olaus Magnus, in his chapter on "Anchors Fastened on Whales' Backs," says, "The whale hath upon his skin a superficies like the gravel that is by the seaside, so that ofttimes, when he raiseth his back above the water, sailors take it to be nothing else than an island, and land upon it, and they strike piles into it, and fasten them to their ships; they kindle fires upon it to boil their meat, until at length the whale, feeling the fire, dives down suddenly into the depths, and draws both men and ship after him unless the anchor breaks."

§Another old work gives us curious monsters. The Physeter has head and neck like a horse, and ejects water from a tube in his head. The Alcetre had a head and snout like a boar, and spouted water from a tube.

Ariosto represents Astolfo as being carried on the back of an enormous whale, to the island of Fata Alcuna,—

‖"Among the rest, a mighty whale is view'd,
The greatest, sure, that ever swam the flood,
And as he lay unmov'd, by looks deceiv'd
We all the monster for an isle believ'd."

*Schele de Vere.—Wonders of the Deep.
†History of Scotland, in Mangin, p. 359.
‡De Piscum (1587) in Landrin, p. 148.
§Wolfhart.—Prodigiorum ac Ostentorum Chronica. Q. by Wood, "Atlantic," June, 1884.
‖Hoole's Ariosto, VI, p. 260.

* Francheval, in the "Bestiare d'Amour," tells us, "So there is had a kind of whale, which is so great that when it has its back above the water, the sailors who see it think it an island, because its skin is rough like sea-sand, so that the sailors land on it as if it were an isle, and lodge and dwell on it eight or fifteen days, cooking their meat on the whale's back. But when it at last feels the fire, it carries itself and the others beneath the waves."

† Père Fournier also tells us of a great monster, "In the reign of Philip II., king of Spain, there appeared one in the ocean, very different from others, for it appeared partly above the water, having two great wings, and sailing like a ship. Some vessel having seen it, and having broken one wing with a cannon-ball, this monster entered with great swiftuess the Strait of Gibraltar, with horrible cries, and ·finally came ashore at Valentia, where it was found dead. Its skull was so large that seven men could enter into it, and a man on horseback enter its throat; two dead men were found in its stomach. The jaw-bone, seventeen feet long, is still in the Escurial."

The island-fish, under the name of the Kraken, became celebrated in northern annals, and is the Leviathan of Milton.‡

> "Him haply slumbering on the Norway foam,
> The pilot of some small night-foundered skiff
> Deeming some island, oft, as seamen tell,
> With fixed anchor in his scaly rind,
> Moors by his side."

§ Pontoppidan tells us: "Norwegian fishermen, without the least contradiction in their accounts, say that when they sail several miles out to sea, particularly during the hottest days of the year, the sea suddenly seems to become shallower under the boats, and if they drop the lead, instead of finding eighty or one hundred fathoms' depth, it often happens that they only find thirty. It is a sea-serpent which thus interposes itself between the depths and the waves. Accustomed to this phenomenon, the fishermen cast their nets, assured that there will be in those parts an abundance of fish, especially of cod and ling, and draw them in richly loaded. But if the depth of the water

* Bestiare d'Amour. Q. by Landrin, p. 149.
† "Hydrographie." Q. by Landrin, p. 148.
‡ Paradise Lost.
§ Natural History of Norway. Q. in Jones' B. B. O., p. 254.

continues to decrease, and if this movable and accidental shoal rises higher, the fishermen have no time to lose; it is the serpent awakening and moving, rising up to respire the air and extend its huge folds in the sea. The fishermen ply their oars lustily, and when at a safe distance they see, in fact, the monster, which covers a mile and a half of ocean with the upper half of its body. . . . From the floating mass issue numerous spikes or shining horns, which rear themselves like masts covered by their yards; these are the arms of the Kraken."

* Eric Falkendorf, Bishop of Nidros, wrote to Pope Leo X. (in 1520), a letter on this subject, in which he alleged that he landed on one of these Krakens, and said mass, after which it sank into the sea.

We have the following account of it from the voyage of St. Brandan: "But at the last they went upon an ylonde, weaying (waving) to them they had been safe, and made thereon a fyre to dresse theyr dyner, but Saynt Brandan abode styll in the shyppe. And when the fyre was hote, and the meet nigh soden, then the ylonde began to move; whereof the monkes were aferde, and fledde anon to the shyppe, and left the fyre and meet behynde them, and mervayled sore of the movyving. And Saynt Brandan com-forted them and sayd that it was a grete fiss, he named Jasconye, whiche laboureth nyght and daye to put his tayle in his mouth, but for gretness he may not."

Saint Maclon is represented in legend as having performed a feat similar to that of the Bishop of Nidros, a whale obligingly coming up, and, after allowing him to perform mass on his back, sinking into the depths.

† Olaus Wormsius (1643) says the Kraken is "an island rather than a beast, and is immortal," in which latter statement he is supported by Olaus Magnus, Bartholin, and other writers of his own and succeeding times.

The Kraken was the subject of a mediæval Anglo-Saxon poem. ‡A "Kraken" is said to have stranded in the Gulf of Newangen, Norway, in 1680, and the odor of its decaying carcass tainted the air for miles around. Many government officers visited it, and deposed as to its presence. The sea at length washed away its remains.

* Schele de Vere.—Wonders of the Deep, p. 42. Landrin, p. 29.
† Landrin.—Les Monstres Marins, p. 29.
‡ Landrin.—Les Monstres Marins, p. 29.

*Denys Montfort gives a picture of a Kraken.   He says the Danes call them Âuker-trolls.

Bartholemeus says there are two Krakens, existing from the beginning of the world, and their number will not increase.

† Scott says the Kraken was believed to haunt the waters about the Shetland and Orkney Islands. "The Kraken, that hugest of living things, was still supposed to cumber the recesses of the Northern Ocean; and often, when some fog-bank covered the sea at a distance, the eye of the experienced boatman saw the horns of the monstrous leviathan, welking and waving amidst the wreath of mist, and bore away with all press of oar and sail, lest the sudden suction, occasioned by the sudden sinking of the monstrous mass to the bottom, should drag within the grasp of its multifarious feelers his own frail skiff."

"Some years since, a large object was seen in the beautiful bay of Scalloway, in Zetland, so much, in vulgar opinion, resembling the Kraken, that, though it might be distinguished for several days, yet the hardy boatmen shuddered to approach it, for fear of being drawn down by the suction supposed to attend its sinking."   Fishermen averred they often saw its horns protruding mast-high from the sea.   The bones of an animal stranded in 1800, supposed to be a Kraken, were found to be those of a shark.

‡ Many chapels on the coast of France have ex-voto pictures of contests of ships with the Kraken, and a large one exists at Notre Dame de la Garde, at Marseilles.

§ In 1834, Captain Neill, of the ship "Robertson," of Greenock, saw and took a sketch of a great monster, which appeared like a vessel on her beam-ends.   On approaching nearer, its head and snout were plainly seen, its eye looking like a large hole.   Its head above water was some twelve feet in length; its width some twenty five feet.   The snout was fifty feet long.

Many of these accounts of the appearance of the Island-fish, or the Kraken, seem to refer to the cuttle-fish, or polyp.   Curious stories are related of its appearance.

‖ Captain John Magnus Dens told De Montfort that an enormous polyp appeared in the ocean, and, stretching its

* Landrin. op. cit, p. 29.
† Notes to " Pirate."
‡ Landrin.—Les Monstres Marins, 29.
§ Jones.—Broad, Broad Ocean, p. 255.
‖ Mollusques in Buffon.—Hist. Nat.

arms above the bulwarks of the ship, took ten men off a stage on which (it being calm) they were working, outside the vessel. It then seized the shrouds, pinning to them two more men. It was harpooned several times, but finally escaped, with the loss of a limb nearly twenty-five feet long.

In the Chapel of St. Thomas at St. Malo, France, there is an ex-voto painting of a ship in the act of being dragged down by an enormous cuttle-fish. This ship, according to the legend, was attacked by this monster, on the African coast, and was only rid of its foe by using hatchets vigorously, and by calling on St. Thomas for aid.

Fishermen in the East Indies are said to have been so beset by these animals, and are obliged often to cut off their limbs to get rid of them.

* In 1861, the French corvette Alecto, Lieutenant Bouyer, encountered at sea, between Teneriffe and Madeira, a monstrous polyp, which was reported as being from sixteen to eighteen feet in length, not including its arms. A drawing was made, which was shown to the French Academy, representing the animal. Its posterior portion was secured, and brought to France.

† Holcroft says the sailors, in one of his voyages, told him many stories of appearances of the Kraken near Greenland and on the Scottish coast.

‡ Wood thinks De Montfort's picture not overdrawn, and says the Kraken is an acknowledged fact.

Other stories of sea-monsters were told. Olaus Magnus is responsible for many tales of these. § In his chapter "On Many Kinds of Whales," he tells us: "Some are hairy, and of four acres in bigness; the acre is two hundred and forty feet long and one hundred and twenty broad." Another kind "hath eyes so large that fifteen men may sit in the room of each of them, and sometimes twenty or more; his horns are six or seven feet long, and he hath two hundred and fifty on each eye, as hard as a horn, that he can stir stiff or gentle, either before or behind." He further tells of fish with horrible shape, some with square black heads, ten or twelve cubits long, with huge eyes, ten cubits in circumference, having a red flaming iris, looking like a lamp at night, and with a hairy head, the hair much

* Mangin.—Mysteries of the Ocean, 288.
† Memories.
‡ J. G. Wood, Atlantic Monthly, June, 1884.
§ In Jones' Broad, Broad Ocean.

like goose-feathers. They easily drag down the strongest ships. He likewise says: "Round the shores of the North Sea are many caverns of unfathomable depth, whence issue monsters out of the deep." *He tells a strange story of a monster like the sea-elephant, that came ashore on the beach, where fishermen caught it "by raising the fat along its tail, and attaching to it strong ropes, which they fastened to rocks and trees on the shore. Then they waked up the huge animal by throwing stones at it with a sling, and compelled it to retire to the water, leaving its skin behind."

Ariosto and Boiardo relate many tales of maidens bound and left on the sea-shore to be devoured by sea-monsters. *Orca* is the monster spoken of. This orca is certainly none other than our Ogre, the degraded sea-god Oegir, famous in Northern annals. †Angelina is thus exposed, and is delivered by Rinaldo, who jumps into the monster's mouth, and fixes his anchor in its terrible jaws. He then wounds it grievously, and anchors it to the shore, until it expires. Boiardo represents Lucina so bound, and rescued by two knights.

‡Pongo, a terrible monster, half tiger, and half shark, is said to have so completely devasted a part of Sicily, that all the inhabitants within a radius of twenty miles were devoured.

A mediæval French poem, by Philippe de Thaun, describes an attack of a monster which he calls *Cetus*.

Procopius says a gigantic sea monster destroyed many persons before he was killed.

§Geoffrey says Morvidun, a Welsh king, was swallowed by a monster who came out of the Irish sea.

Beowulf destroyed a sea monster by the aid of magic.

‖Lacroix gives a cut of a *sea dog*, covered with scales, having a dog's body and a fish's tail.

**Spalding says a sea monster appeared in the river Don, in 1635, with the head of a dog, arms, body and hands of a man, and tail of a fish.

Paul Egede says, "The 6th of July we saw a monster, which raised so high on the waves that its head reached to

* Landrin.—Les Monstres Marins, p. 240.
† Hoole's Ariosto. Bk. IX.
‡ Brewer.—Reader's Hand Book.
§ Conway.—Demonology. Vol. I. p. 368.
‖ Lacroix, from Dyalogue des Creatures, 1482.
** Nordhoff.—Harper's Mag., Vol. XIV.

the mainsail. Instead of fins, it had great ears hanging down like wings. It had scales on its body, which ended like a serpent."

* Icelandic legends tell of a monster called there Skrimsi, living in a fiord at Grimsey, who bit off the heads of seals, and wrecked ships.

† An account of one of these, seen by a farmer, gives it as thirty-six feet long, a succession of humps. An old account of one seen in 1345, says, "At some times it seemed like a great island, and at other times there appeared humps, several hundred fathoms apart, with water between them."

‡ Arnanson says one appeared in 1749, thirty feet to forty feet long, with a hump on its back. Grimsey fishermen say it came ashore in 1819, and left traces.

§ These animal-monsters have often the shapes of men, sometimes they are like a horse without a tail, and some have a shelly coat of mail. Leaden bullets will not hurt it. Sometimes it rolls in the dust, and people are often made mad by its screams.

We read in Smith's travels (1750), "On sailing along the coast of Corsica and Sardinia, June 9th, we saw a sea monster, which appeared several times the same day, spouting water from its nose to a great height. It is called Caldelion, and is said to appear frequently before a storm. A storm came on Monday, which lasted four days."

The traditions of sea monsters existed until after the great maritime discoveries. The early charts have monsters, huge whales, and serpents portrayed on them. | Camoens speaks of

> "The distant seas
> Where only monsters do abide."

Shakespeare speaks twice of sea monsters, but his meaning is very vague.** The hippopotamus is by some supposed to be meant, as it was represented as unnatural and ungrateful to its progenitors. Others think the whale is meant.

In the "Prayse and Reporte of Maister Martyne For-

* Maurer.—Islandische Sagen.
† Gould.—Scenes and Sagas of Iceland.
‡ Icelandic Legends.
§ Powell and Magnusson.—Icelandic Legends.
| Lusiad.—Mickles' Trans.
** King Lear.—Dyer Folk-lore of Shakespeare, 504.

bisher's Voyage to Meta Incognita " (1578), we read that the crew found "a strange fish dead, that had been cast from the sea on the shore, who had a boane in his head like an Unicorne." This is evidently a sword-fish.

Two notices of exhibitions of strange fish are given by Jones, one *" The Description of a Rare or Rather Most Monstrous Fishe, taken on the east coast of Holland the 17th of November, Anno, 1566," and the other, " A moste true and marvellous strange wonder, the lyke bathe seldom been seene, of XVII monstrous fishes taken in Suffolke, at Donnam Brydge, within a myle of Ipswiche, the XV daye of October, in the yeare of our Lorde God, 1568." These are described by Stow.

A reminiscence of such exhibitions are given in Shakspeare, in The Tempest,† and the same act alludes to sea monsters.

‡ Rondelet gives a curious figure of a sea-lion, with scaled body and four feet. He says he was told at Rome that one appeared after the death of Pope Paul III.

A monster was seen from the "Osborne" yacht in June, 1877, like a turtle, with a head six feet in diameter, long neck, and two fins, fifteen feet long on each side. § Wilson believes it to have been a tape fish, specimens of which, sixty feet long, have been captured.

As the further progress of maritime discovery displayed these unknown seas to the gaze of the world, it was found that these monsters did not exist there, or, as Addison puts it, ‖ "The sea is generally filled with monsters when there are no fleets upon it."

**A popular legend reports that a sort of Kraken lives on Portland shoals, dragging ships down with its long and spider-like arms.

††A monster was found periodically to come out of Lough Derg, the Irish Purgatory, and devastate the country, until Finn McCail, a legendary hero, killed it, when its blood reddened the lake, thus giving it its name (Red Lake). Another tradition gives St. Patrick the honor of subduing this monster, by chaining it to the bottom of the lake. Such

* Broad, Broad Ocean, 205.
† Act II, scene 5.
‡ Histoire des Poissons, 1554.
§ A. Wilson.—Sea Serpents of Science.
‖ Spectator, 27.
** Notes and Queries.
†† Kennedy.—Fireside Stories of Ireland.

monsters are common in legend, and such are the Wantley Dragon, the Lambton Worm, the Dragon subdued by St. George—doubtless nature myths—the hero being solar, and the monster aqueous.

*A monster is said to have appeared in the Elbe at Hamburg, in 1615, with a horse's body, and a pig's head, with four great tushes in his mouth. Another, with a stag's body and horns, appeared in 1638. An old harpooner went in search of it with his boat, but when he struck it, the electric fluid from its body passed through the harpoon line, paralyzing him, and killing him.

Depositions of the captain and surgeon of the British Steamship Nestor, set forth that a monster like a great turtle, with head twenty feet long, body forty-five feet and tail one hundred and fifty feet long, striped black and yellow, was seen in September, 1877, in Malacca Straits, in daylight.

According to a Russian tale, a prince killed a water monster, who lived in a river, agitating the water for seven versts by his motion. †A monster pike figures in Lithuanian and Finnish legends.

A monster shaped like a calf, is said to appear in Ostro Wittchen lake, West Prussia. It is said to be the embodiment of the souls of the drowned.

‡Tarascon gets its name from a Rhone monster, whose overthrow was, not many years since, celebrated by the " Fête de la Tarasque."

Legends of sea-monsters in other countries are related. Utah Lake and Bear Lake in Utah, are popularly said to be inhabited by monsters. A sea-monster is said to have been caught on our coast in 1869, thirty feet long, and being part beast and part fish. It was figured in Harper's Weekly. Another pretended sea-monster was exhibited at Wood's Museum, in New York, and the following account is the latest, of the appearance of these monsters: §"On the 16th of last October, when the vessel was forty-six miles south of Alaska, an object was perceived in the distance whose proportions and shape indicated it to be a monster sea-lion. A boat was immediately lowered. As the distance was decreased between the boat and the huge animal, they became convinced that it was the famed sea-serpent. When they came

* Simrock.—Deutsche Sagen.
† Ralston.—Russian Folk-lore, p. 267.
‡ Brewer.—Readers' Hand-Book.
§ Johnson.—Mate of Whaler Alaska in San Francisco Chronicle, 1884.

within a few hundred yards, the monster made a dash for the boat, striking out its immense tail against the craft. Several of the occupants were precipitated into the water, and were rescued with difficulty. A harpoon and lance were fired into the body of the beast, and it disappeared beneath the surface. Half an hour later it reappeared, floating on the water, dead. It was secured with ropes and towed to the vessel, and hoisted on the deck. There the capture was seen to be a villainous-looking thing. Its head closely resembled that of an alligator, while the body resembled that of a lizard. It measured thirty-three feet in length, the tail being nine feet long. The tail was cut off and stuffed and brought to this city, and is now on exhibition."

* Jourdan says a sea-monster in the shape of a man, was seen near the Bermudas during great tempests.

Indian tribes had legends of aquatic monsters. Dr. Brinton relates the following story of a monster in the Connecticut river.

"While Aba and Jona were thus drifting down the stream in their birch-bark canoe, and supposed they were safe from all jealous interference, Walo, the deadly enemy of all true lovers, was lurking under the alders which fringed Deep Hole. As the canoe approached, he dove into the depths, where he lay silent until the canoe came to a pause in the quiet waters of the pool, and the lovers, lost to all but their happiness, were indulging in mutual caresses; Walo then rose suddenly to the surface, and, opening his enormous jaws, swallowed the canoe and its occupants at a gulp, and disappeared in the blackness of the unfathomable pool."

† Marquette says a monster with a fish's tail was figured on the rocks at a certain point in the Mississippi. Hennepin says a number of men were drowned here (at St. Anthony's Falls), and Indians sacrificed in passing, to this figure.

‡ In Algic legend, Hiawatha caught a fish so large that its oil and fat filled a large lake, and fed all animals.

Swan tells a legend of Shoalwater Bay, of a certain man who was swallowed by a sea-monster, and who was cut out of him, but after he was dead, and a stone image on the rocks near the spot represents him.

* Discovery of the Bermudas.
† Brinton.—Myths of the New World.
‡ Schoolcraft.—Algic Legends.

INDIANS AND ROCK NEAR ST. ANTHONY'S FALLS.

217

*Indians of California have a tradition that a monster was caught in their seines, while fishing at sea, but was afterwards lost, while towing him through a whirlpool. Haidab Indians believe in a sea-monster, *Tchinnose.*

†Esquimaux believe in sea-monsters, that live at the bottom of the sea, and in great spiders, and monstrous gulls, which endanger the sailor's life. All priests of the higher order are supposed to serve a novitiate as a sea-monster.

‡Father Kircher tells of the following legend of a sea-cow: "There appears in the province of Kwangtung, a kind of fish which is called *Swimming Cow* (Vache qui Nage). This beast sometimes emerges from its element, and herds with the other cattle in order to fight them, and to give them blows with its horns, the same as if it had always abode with them, and had never done otherwise than they. But since it happens that this animal loses the hardness of its horns, some time after it has remained on the land, it is obliged to return to the water, to recover what it had lost, in refurnishing to these same horns the hardness which they had lost."

The Japanese represented that a monstrous cod-fish stretched its length under all their islands. This fish, *Jish-in-uno*, seven hundred miles long, was formerly thought to cause the tides, as well as convulsions of the land.

§A sea-monster was the traditional ancestor of the emperors of Japan. Kappa is a monster, with a monkey's head and body, and tortoise's claws. He seizes children and drags them into the water. He is fond of cucumbers, and these are often thrown into the water, to propitiate him when boys go in bathing. Griffis was warned not to bathe in a certain place in Fukin, as he would be dragged down by this monster. A woman was accidentally spilled out of a "jin-ricksha" into a pond, and drowned. It was said that Kappa got her. People in Tokio say they often see Kappa in the river, and one is said to have dragged a man down in the typhoon of July 6, 1874.

In Siamese belief, there are giant crabs and great scorpions in the sea, who drag ships down.

In New Zealand waters, Tipua, a great monster, lives at

* Bancroft.—Native Races, III, 377.
† Rink.—Tales and Traditions of the Esquimaux.
‡ La Chine Illustré, p. 271. In Landrin, p. 251.
§ Griffis.—The Mikado's Kingdom.

the bottom of the sea. *Taniwha is a river-monster, who drags people into the water. † Fijians say a monster clam and a huge octopus live in ocean depths.

‡ The Barotse, an African tribe, fear a monster in the Lecambi river, who is said to drag canoes down, and they feared to pass a spot, where he was said to lie, after dark. Prayers and exorcisms were used to control him.

§ Cata Wangol was an Australian aquatic monster, with long teeth and large eyes. Stones found on the beach were its eggs.

Of all the monsters of the deep, the sea-serpent has received the most attention, and accounts of its appearance are constantly appearing, while thousands implicitly believe in its existence.

Accounts of a serpent-like monster living in the deep were given very early in the history of mankind. | Akkad inscriptions allude to the "serpent that beats the sea." ** Typhon, the opponent of the sun, in his under-world journey at night, is shown in Egyptian sculptures as a serpent, Apophis.

Many commentators think a serpent is meant by the description of the Leviathan in the Scriptures.†† In Amos IX. we read, "And though they be hid from my sight at the bottom of the sea, thence will I command the serpent, and he shall bite them."

Pliny and Valerius Maximus tell us of monster serpents living in the sea. The former says serpents three hundred feet long came out of the Ganges. ‡‡ He also says a monstrous serpent, able to seize and draw down an elephant, was seen in the Indian ocean. Solinns says the sea-serpent inhabits the Eastern sea, and is twenty cubits long. §§ Palladius, speaking of the Odonto-tyrannus of the Ganges, says it "swallowed an elephant without chewing it."

Sea-serpents are spoken of in ancient Hindoo books. Vishnu and Nava Yama rides one, and, in later writings, Bhimas also.

Stories of them multiplied during the latter part of the middle ages. Du Cange quotes a Latin MSS., where the

* R. Taylor.—New Zealand, p. 48.
† Gill.—Myths and Songs of the South Pacific, 148.
‡ Livingstone.—Travels in Africa.
§ Wilkes.—Exploring Expedition, 254.
| "Records of the Past," III, p. 129.
** Rosellini — I Monumenti del Egitto.
†† See Isaiah XXVII, 6; Job XL and XLI.
‡‡ Landrin, p. 112.
§§ Landrin.—Les Monstres Marins, p. 112.

devil is called Hydros, or water-serpent. This is Typhon of old. *El Kazwini says that monstrous serpents came out of the China sea, to devour elephants.

But it is to Norse accounts that we must turn for more circumstantial accounts of the sea-serpent. †In Eddaic mythology, Jörmundgandr, the great Midgard serpent, brother of Hel, the northern Pluto, lies at the bottom of the seas, forever trying to bite his own tail, and is so large that he encircles the world. When he heaves up the coils of his immense body, storms arise. At the destruction of the world, he will burst over the land, and infect the very air. Thor, the northern Hercules, is said to have caught this serpent, and to have struck its head off with his hammer.

PONTOPPIDAN'S SEA-SERPENT.

Mediæval Norse traditions represent the seas as full of serpents, formerly living on land, and only taking to the sea after a visitation of the Black Death. Olaus Magnus thus describes the sea-serpent: ‡"All seamen say there is a sea-serpent two hundred feet long, and twenty feet thick, who comes out at night, to devour cattle. It has long black hair hanging down from its head, and flaming eyes, with sharp scales on its body." He says there is a "worm," on the coast of Norway, over forty feet long, yet hardly so thick as the arm of a child. It is harmless, except that its skin is poisonous to the touch.

*Marvels of Creation.
†Thorpe.—Northern Mythology.
‡History of the Goths, 1658.

*Pontoppidan describes the sea-serpent as being six hundred feet long; its body so large that its folds appeared like a string of hogsheads on the water. The earlier editions of his work give illustrations of this monster, seen rising mast-high from the water. They were called Soë-armen. In 1350, two are said to have appeared in the Foksö, and two years afterwards, one was stranded on the coast.

Modern Norse accounts repeat these descriptions. A sea-serpent was fabled to appear in the Lister, to announce some great calamity, such as the death of a king. † Similarly, an ill-omened messenger of like shape, whose body was as thick as a calf, and whose tail was two ells long, appeared at Svansviksö; and one was said to arise from the sea at Bollarvatr, in Sweden. There is a folk-tale that a sea-serpent lies coiled about the great sunken bell at Hammer, in Norway.

At Miös, serpents occasionally were seen, only to vanish immediately. One, brilliant in appearance, lay coiled on a rock, where it was killed. Tradition reports that its body lay there for many years.‡ Nicholas Lamins, a minister at Loudon, saw on the 6th of June, 1650, a great sea-serpent come out of the sea, during an inundation. It had lived in the rivers Miös and Branz, and crawled into the fields from the banks of the latter. It advanced like the long masts of a ship, overthrowing trees and huts in its progress. Its whistles and cries made all shudder who heard them, and the fish disappeared or died. Many fishermen of Odale were so terrified that they renounced their calling, and did not dare even to walk the beaches. Its head was like a great cask, its body great in proportion.

The Archbishop of Bergen says he learned from sailors, who traversed northern seas, that the sea-serpent would cast himself in the tracks of vessels, rising suddenly and seizing one of the frightened crew or passengers as a prey. Pichot gives us further details: "The movement of the sea-serpent is very swift, the Norwegian poets comparing it to the flight of a rapid arrow. When fishermen see it at the surface, they row fast, toward the sun, the monster not being able to see them when his head is turned toward that luminary. It is said that he sometimes throws himself into a circle about a ship, and then they find themselves sur-

* Mangin.—Mysteries of the Ocean, p. 297.
† Thorpe.—Northern Mythology, Vol. II. p. 28.
‡ Horpeifus.—" Mundus Mirabilis."

rounded on all sides. Experience of the sailors has taught them not row toward the open places left by the folds of his body, for then he will move on and so overturn the bark. It is safer to steer for his head, for it is probable that the animal will plunge in and disappear, above all when one can spread on the deck the essence of musk. So the boats do when they cannot avoid it. But when they discover it at a distance, they proceed to the shore or the mouth of some creek inaccessible to the formidable enemy."

*Thorpe says it can hardly be denied that great snakes are sometimes seen on the northern coasts, and gives many instances. Commander Laurence de Ferry gives his sworn testimony that he saw a serpent in August, 1749, near Molder. It had a head like a horse, rising some two feet from the water, and was gray in color with deep brown mouth, black eyes, and long white mane about its neck. Its coils were about a foot apart, and it was moving very rapidly.

Rev. P. W. Demboll, in 1845, obtained the testimony of several persons who had seen the serpent. Lars Jorenson saw one at Smölen from six to seven feet long, and two feet in diameter, with its head as large as a ten-gallon cask. Three men of Molde saw a serpent some forty to fifty feet long in the same year.

†A sea-serpent, Turenfax, living in an island in the ocean, and devouring a maiden each year, appears in a folk-tale.

‡Arnanson tells an Icelandic legend of a great serpent that grew from a heath-worm by the power of gold, until it filled the sea. Its appearance predicted great calamities.

§ Ruysch, a Dutch naturalist, figures and describes a sea-serpent, said by him to have been found and preserved. He represents it as being twenty-six to thirty feet long, and says it changes its skin.

| Landrin says a mariner, F. Legnat, wrecked and abandoued on a desert rock in 1708, killed a sea-serpent.

**Bellforest gives minute accounts of the sea-serpent He says it clings to barks and small ships, striking men off the deck with its tail, and devouring them. Should the

---

* Landrin.—Les Monstres Marins, p. 118.
† Snipp, Snapp, Snorson.
‡ Icelandic Folk-lore.
§ Histoire Naturelle (1718); in Landrin, 112.
| Landrin.—Les Monstres Marins, 113.
** Cosmographie.

ship prove too great for its powers, it was accustomed to draw it toward the shore, and, when the crew tried to escape, it seized them. It is described as having a wolf-like head and scaly body.

A serpent was seen from the French ship Le Havre, near the Azores, and one is figured in *Le Monde Illustré*, of October 8, 1881, as having been recently seen at sea.

Serpents of the sea figure in Sicilian stories, where they bring great gifts, and possess wonderful power.

* In a Basque story, a sea-serpent tells the master-mariner to get a ship at any price, then embarks in it, saving it from a storm, and eventually proving to be a king's son.

A monster serpent is believed to live in the Rhine.

† In a Russian story, "The Water-snake," serpents in the land become men and women beneath the waves, and one gets a wife, by getting possession of her shift while she bathes.

‡ Scott, speaking of Shetland and Orkney fishermen, says: "The sea-snake was also known, which, arising out of the depths of the ocean, stretches to the skies his enormous neck, covered with a mane like that of a war-horse, and with his broad, glittering eyes, raised mast-head high, looks out, as it seems, for plunder or for victims." "The author knew a mariner, of some reputation in his class, vouch for having seen the celebrated sea-serpent. It appeared, so far as could be guessed, to be about a hundred feet along, with the wild mane and fiery eyes which old writers ascribe to the monster; but it is not unlikely the spectator might, in the doubting light, be deceived by a good Norway log on the water."

§ Hibbert describes them as seen by Shetlanders, and says that the skeleton of one that came ashore was sent to the Edinburgh Museum. This was found to be the remains of a shark.

Rev. —— McLean, pastor of a Hebrides parish, describes, in a letter to the Wernerian Society, a sea-serpent seen in 1808, while he was in a boat some two miles from the land. The serpent followed him, but he finally escaped to a rock. It had a large head and a slender neck, with no fins, and tapered towards its tail. It moved by undulations up and down. "Its length might be seventy to eighty feet."

* Webster.—Basque Legends.
† Ralston.—Russian Folk-lore, p. 116.
‡ Notes to "Pirate."
§ Shetland Islands.

Marryat makes Huckabuk say, in the "Pasha," " Nor
has the animal been seen before or since, except by the
Americans, who have much better eyes than the people of
Europe boast of." But this statement is not borne out by
the accounts given of its appearance.[*] The surgeon of an
English ship, Davidson, testified that he saw one in India in
1829. A Dr. Barclay saw the body of one some months
later, it being about fifty feet long, and eighteen feet in circumference, with a mane on its neck, and fins on its shoulders.

In 1867, the officers of the steam sloop "Halifax," saw
one eighty feet long; and in 1848, a serpent was seen near
the African coast by the officers of the "Dædalus," where
captain McQuhae made and published sketches of it.[†] Accounts of this monster forwarded to the Admiralty, stated
that it passed close under the vessel's counter, so as to be
plainly seen by all, swimming rapidly. It was in sight
some twenty minutes; was some sixteen inches in diameter,
with no fins, but having a sort of mane on its neck. Its head
and shoulders were some four feet in the air, its dark brown
body on the surface.

A sea-snake was seen by a Captain Steele, in 1852, and
an account of another is given in the London Times of February 5, 1857.

The officers of the ship Castilian saw one near St. Helena
in 1857. Captain Harrington says, [‡] "While myself and
officers were standing on the lee side of the poop, looking
towards the island, we were startled by the sight of a huge
marine animal, which reared its head out of the water within twenty yards of the ship, when it suddenly disappeared
for about half a minute, and then made its appearance in
the same manner again, showing us distinctly its neck and
head, about ten or twelve feet out of the water. The diameter of the head was about seven or eight feet in the largest
part, with a tuft of loose skin circling it about two feet from
the top. The water was discolored for several hundred feet
from its head, so much so that my impression was that the
ship was in broken water: . . . but the second appearance
completely dispelled these fears, and assured us it was a
monster of extraordinary length, which appeared to be
moving slowly towards the land. . . . From what we saw

* Jones.—Broad, Broad Ocean, p. 256.
† London Illustrated News, October 28, 1848.
‡ Jones.—Broad, Broad Ocean, p. 257.

from the deck, we conclude that it must have been over two hundred feet long; . . . it was of a dark color about the head, and was covered with several white spots."

*The captain, officers and crew of the bark Pauline of London, also made deposition before a magistrate in 1875, that they saw, in July, an immense serpent twined about a large sperm whale, that whirled the latter over as if it had been a toy, and finally carried it down to the sea-depths. Again, later, by a few days, they saw a similar monster, skimming along the sea, head and neck out of the water several feet.

Another serpent was seen on the 10th of August, 1881, by the Dowley, an English ship.

Sea-serpents have always been a treasured fancy of American sailors, many of whom, like Whittier's skipper

" Had seen the sea-snake's awful form."

He appeared as early as 1639. Josselyn says: †"They told me of a *sea-serpent* or *snake*, that lay coiled upon a rock at Cape Ann; a boat passing by with English on board, and two Indians, they would have shot the serpent, but the Indians warned them, saying that if he were not killed out-right, they would all be in danger of their lives."

The New England coast became a famous habitat of the strange monster.‡ One was seen in 1809 by Rev. W. Cummings, in Penobscot bay. This one was some fifteen rods off, and was sixty feet long. §Six years previously, three officers carried out into Halifax bay in a boat, saw one from eighty to one hundred feet long, with a black body, streaked with white. In 1781, a Captain Little encountered one in Broad Bay, some forty-five to fifty feet in length, and fifteen inches in diameter. In 1817, it again appeared in Massachusetts bay. A Mr. Nash testifies that it was some seventy to one hundred feet long, in eight portions or bunches, each the size of a barrel, and rough and dark in appearance, with its tongue, that protruded some two feet, shaped like a harpoon. It was swimming some twelve to fourteen miles per hour, playing around in circles. Some ten depositions of its appearance were made. Several persons also saw one the same year, in Long Island sound.

In 1819, many witnesses of its appearance near Marble-

* Sobele de Vere.—Wonders of the Deep.
† Josselyn's Voyages, in Mass. Historical Coll., Vol. XXIII, p. 228.
‡ Babson.—History of Gloucester.
§ C. Nordhoff.—Harper's Monthly, Vol. XIV.

15

head, and at Nahant, gave their testimony. *Mr. N. D. Chase, of Lynn, writes: "At this time he was about a quarter of a mile away; but the water was so smooth that I could plainly see his head, and the motion of his body. Later in the day I saw him again, off 'Red Rock.' He then passed along about one hundred feet from where I stood, with his head about two feet out of the water, and his speed was about the ordinary one of a common steamer. What I saw of his length was from fifty to sixty feet. It was very difficult to count the bunches or humps upon his back, as, by the undulating motion, they did not all appear at once. The color of his skin was dark." Five reliable persons were with him at the time. One of these, Mr. Cabot, writes: "My attention was suddenly arrested by an object emerging from the water, at the distance of about one hundred or one hundred and fifty yards, which gave to my mind, at the first glance, the idea of a horse's head. It was elevated about two feet from the water, and he depressed it gradually to within six or eight inches, as he moved along. His bunches appeared to me not altogether uniform in size. I felt persuaded by this examination that he could not be less than eighty feet long."

†James Prince, Esq., says: "His head appeared about three feet above the water. I counted thirteen bunches on his back. . . . I had seven distinct views of him from the Long Beach (so called), and at some of them the animal was not more than a hundred yards distant." Other creditable witnesses stated the same. John Marston, a seaman, deposed upon oath that he saw, "within two or three hundred yards of the shore, a singular-looking fish in the form of a serpent." He was an old fisherman, and declared his belief that it was the veritable sea-serpent. ‡Drake tells us that whaling-vessels were fitted out, boats cruised after the serpent, and the revenue cutter's double-shotted nets were spread to catch the "fish," and one venturesome hunter fired a load of duck-shot into its eye. The Boston Linnæan Society sent ten members to see it, who reported: "The monster was from eighty to ninety feet long, his head usually carried about two feet above water; of a dull brown color; the body with thirty or more protuberances, compared by some to four-gallon kegs, by others to a string of buoys," etc.

* Letter to C. H. Holder, in Lippincott's Magazine.
†C. H. Holder.—Lippincott's Magazine.
‡S. A. Drake.—Legends of New England.

Brainard wrote an ode to the sea-serpent, in which he says,—

> " But go not to Nahant, lest men should swear
> You are a great deal bigger than you are."

In 1830, a sea-serpent was seen by three men near the mouth of the Kennebec river, in Maine. Another was reported on our coasts in 1860, and the mate of the sloop "Concord"* informed the Linnæan Society that he saw one in 1863, rising seven feet out of the water, its body being in sections, like a chain of casks. A recent account of the appearance of the serpent is given in this newspaper extract,—

"While the boats of the bark Hope On, commanded by Captain Seymour, were on the watch for whales off the Pearl Islands, between forty and fifty miles from Panama, the water broke, a short distance away, and Captain Seymour made ready for a whale. But a head like that of a horse rose from the water, and then dived. The creature was seen by all the boat's crew. Captain Seymour describes the animal as about twenty feet long, with a handsome, horse-like head, with two unicorn-shaped horns protruding from it. The creature had four legs, or double-jointed fins, a bronzed hide, profusely speckled with large black spots, and a tail which appeared to be divided into two parts. It was seen on two different days, and, if whales had not been about at the time, an effort would have been made to catch it. Captain Seymour and his officers agree that the creature is peculiar to the locality, and that it could easily be killed with lances and guns. It is important to notice that officers of the Pacific Mail Company state that they have seen the animal on several occasions, but not so closely as did officers and men of the Hope On."

This story is credited by an authority as able as R. A. Proctor, the English astronomer.

An officer long employed on the coast survey told me of the appearance of a serpent off Cape Cod. At first, it stood straight up out of the water, like a hogshead; then, on its re-appearance, some three hundred feet away, about thirty feet of its body was seen out of the water, rising angularly from it, and moving with great speed.

The sea-serpent has appeared in Asiatic waters. Chinese

* Maugin.—Mysteries of the Ocean, 300.

stories are told of them. *Denys tells a tradition of one so large that a ship was a whole day in sailing round it.

A dragon-snake is thought to live in Kwangtung lake. Another, one hundred and twenty years old, appeared off Chapoo. It was one hundred feet long and twenty wide, showing ten feet of its length above the water. Giles tells a tale of a sea-serpent, that towered like a hill out of the water. A serpent is said to live in the Chien Tang. Chen was the governor of the province, who, unable entirely to stop the leak in the dyke, threw himself into the lake. Chinese reports claim the capture of a serpent three hundred feet long, during the present century.

Stories of sea-serpents and water-snakes occur in modern Hindoo folk-lore.†

They also occur in the traditions of our American Indians. Hundreds of water-snakes opposed Hiawatha's progress. ‡Creeks, Algonquins, and Iroquois believed that a monstrous serpent lived in the great lakes, and broke the ice, if irritated. Iroquois legends also tell of a horned serpent, who lived in the lake, and was slain by a thunderbolt. Ojibways sacrificed to a water-serpent, and Onondagas had a legend of a great horned water-snake. Huron magicians pretended that a great serpent, *Angoub*, dwelt in seas, lakes, and rivers. §The channel of the Fox river was traditionally formed by a great serpent who passed from the Mississippi to the lakes.

∥Piutes said a great demon-snake abode in Pyramid lake, and caused the wind-storms that sweep its surface. The Pueblos believed in a great water-snake, whose body was as large as a man's.

In the sculptured front of Uxmal palace, is figured an animal, half fish, half serpent, covered with feathers.

Araucanian Indians believe in a large water-serpent. **A great fierce serpent, Yaca-mana, is believed to lurk in the Amazon. Indians approach no nearer than a hundred yards in their canoes, and blow horns to frighten the monster. Smith says the Brazilian Indians, believe in another serpent monster, the " Mother of Waters " (Mai d' Agoa), and say she drinks the water from evaporated ponds. ††Verne

* Folk-lore of China.
† Lal Behari Day.— Folk-lore of Bengal.
‡ Brinton.— Myths of the New World.
§ Schoolcraft.— Algic Legends.
∥ Bancroft.— Native Races, Vol. III, 135.
** Herbert Smith.— Brazil.
†† *Giant Raft*, Chapter XI.

says it is called Minhocao, and the Amazon rises when it plunges in.

Notwithstanding the mythical element evidently present in the formation of these legends of sea-monsters and serpents —notwithstanding the evident readiness in the middle ages to find animals in the mysterious ocean similar to those on land, and the consequent incentive to the imagination to people unknown waters with monsters—in spite of the exaggerations of seamen and landsmen, there is apparently some foundation for the belief in the existence of such beings. I have alluded to the sun-myths, that evidently have had a share in originating the idea of devouring monsters. Mythologists generally agree that the many maiden-devouring monsters, man-swallowing fish, and rain-causing dragons, are but the vaporous clouds arising from the sea, and that the hero, be he Perseus, Apollo, Hercules, Sigurd, Rinaldo or St. George, is the sun himself, who vanquishes the cloud-monster. This element was doubtless assisted by the representations of monsters accompanying Poseidon and the other lords of the deep, which became common in later Greek art. Originally nature-myths, definite form was thus given them by the artist, who but transfers them to the stone.

There is an obvious tendency in the human mind to exaggerate wonders. This has been especially true with regard to those wonders found in the great ocean, where a limitless horizon sets no bounds to thought, and where the smallest object, often by atmospheric causes, will easily be magnified. Thus it must have been with the Island-fish, and the other giant fish, accounts of which have been given. It is improbable that sailors ever landed on such a fish, mistaking it for an island. Doubtless larger whales existed in the ocean, before the days of whaling fleets. It is well known that shells and sea-weed grow on the skin of the whale, and this would aid in the deception.

As to the Kraken stories, and those of giant squids, and cuttle-fish, who shall say that they are not without some foundation? The great Linnæus, in the first editions of his work, avows his belief in the Kraken. *Pennant and Shaw think the cuttle-fish is meant, when the Kraken is described. † In 1824, Peron saw, near Van Dieman's Land, a calamary whose body was as large as a cask, and the naturalists‡ of

* Kent.—Gigantic Cuttle-fish, p. 13.
† Mangin.—Mysteries of the Ocean, p. 290.
‡ Landrin.—Les Monstres Marins, p. 38.

the " Urania," found the remains of one, weighing one hundred pounds, and deposited them in the Paris Museum.

* Steenstrup describes one, found in Jutland, whose body filled a cart, and there are accounts of the finding of other specimens of these monstrous Cephalapoda.

Kent describes such an animal, who attacked fishermen in a boat, and whose tentacle, severed by them, measured some nineteen feet. Its body could have been no less than twenty feet in diameter, and its arms thirty feet long. Another was captured entire, in St. Johns, Newfoundland, and described in a journal of the date. Its body was eight feet long, five feet in diameter, and its long tentacles twenty-four feet in length. Reliable evidence of the finding of others, measuring forty, forty-seven and eighty feet in stretch of limb, are given by the same author. One, whose body was fifteen feet long, was found on the Grand Banks, by Captain Campbell, of the schooner B. D. Haskins. Another was found alive, whose body was ten feet in length, and its arms forty feet in extent. Other interesting accounts of these veritable giants are given in the work alluded to, and Mr. Kent concludes: "It further appears obvious that the numerous tales and traditions that have been current from the earliest times, concerning the existence of colossal species of this race, though in some instances unscrupulously exaggerated, had, in all probability, in the main, a groundwork of fact, and can be no longer passed over as the mere fabrications of a disordered mind."

There is certainly a basis of truth in the stories of curious fish, although the imagination has played strange tricks with men. Such strange animals as the hammer-headed shark, the walrus, the polypus, and many well known varieties of fish, were doubtless seen in all ages, and lent a color of probability to the stories of the existence of the sea-monk, and other animals similar to forms terrestrial.

Again, as a probable element in the origin and growth of these beliefs, comes the recent testimony of geology and paleontology, to the existence of monstrous and enormous marine animals in former ages, especially in the Mesozoic time. The elæomosaurus, had a body thirty feet in length, tapering to a long tail, propelled by paddles or flippers, and a neck twenty feet in length, surmounted by a large, flat head, with terrible teeth and fierce eyes. The ichthyosaurus, or

* Mangin.—Mysteries of the Ocean, p. 287.

fish-lizard; the plesiosaurus, and the teleosaurus, similar monsters, even surpassed this in size; and the mosasaurus was at least sixty feet in length, with a narrow, serpent-like body, and a long and lance-shaped head. Who shall say that these monsters may not have existed in antiquity, or at least traditions of them, and may not their degenerate descendants even now exist at the bottom of the great depths of the ocean?

All these things are to be borne in mind in the case of the much-derided sea-serpent. In antiquity, Oceanus was at first a river, easily imagined a serpent, and this is, as Keary shows,* the same as Jörmundgandr, of Norse myths.

But later accounts of the appearance of this reptile would seem to have an undoubted real basis. They are so circumstantial, they resemble one another in their particulars, most of them come from seamen, more accustomed to the element in which these animals are found, and are in many cases supported by reliable testimony. Naturalists are now disposed to think that a foundation in truth exists, accordingly, for these tales. Remains of serpentine monsters have been found in the rock. † The titanophis was at least thirty feet in length, and another, the clidastes, was even eighty feet long, serpentine in body, and carnivorous in habits. Existing water-snakes of great size have been described. ‡ Tape fishes (gymnetrus and regalecus) from thirty to sixty feet long, have been found, resembling a serpent. The basking shark attains a length of from thirty to fifty feet, and this, says Sir Charles Lyell, must have been thought a serpent.

Some of these giant serpents have been seen by seamen. The master of the bark Georgina saw, on May 21, 1877, in the Indian ocean, a large serpent, forty or fifty feet long, and ten or eleven inches in diameter, of a gray and yellow color. Dawson, the Canadian naturalist, gives an account of a sea monster seen by many in the Gulf of St. Lawrence. It was black, with a rough skin, and was from eighty to a hundred feet long; and another seen in Nova Scotian waters, was sixty feet long, and three feet in diameter. Both these are described as having along the back a series of humps or protuberances.

A recent authority says, "I have no idea that we shall

---

* Outlines of Primitive Belief, p. 71-74.
† Holder, in Lippincott.
‡ Wilson.—Sea-serpents of Science.

ever find a huge unknown lung-breathing saurian as a foundation for the stories. The existence of types of extinct sauria of various geological periods is possible but improbable. Within a few years our imperfect apparatus has secured from great depths a host of strange creatures, but none of the largest or strongest. In fact, we have had scarcely more than mere suggestions of what may exist; and, in view of them, should not be surprised at anything that may come up. If there is a sea-serpent yet unknown to scientists, it is likely to prove a deep-sea fish or Selachian." *

Finally, many accounts of the sea-serpent have perhaps been due to the presence of enormous sea-plants. Such a one was seen by the ship Peking, near Moulmain, in 1848.† This had been previously seen by another vessel, and reported as being an enormous sea-serpent. The Peking sent her boats, and found it to be a sea-plant, some one hundred feet long. These enormous plants, as thick as a man's body, floating on the waves, undulating, serpent-like, with their motion, may easily be taken for serpents.

* Gorman, in Fish Commission Report, 1884.
† Mangin.—Mysteries of the Ocean, p. 308.

CHAPTER VI.

LEGENDS OF THE FINNY TRIBES.

" His hook he baited with a dragon's tail,
And sat upon a rock, and bobbed for whale."

William King.

"For seas, as well as skies, have sun, moon, stars,
As well as air, swallows, rooks and stares,
As well as earth, vines, roses, nettles, melons,
Mushrooms, pinks, gilly-flowers, and many millions
Of other plants more rare, more strange than these
As very fish living in the seas."

Du Bartas, Divine Weeks and Works.

MANY legends and curious tales have been current among mariners and fishermen concerning the finny inhabitants of the deep, from the huge whale to the smallest perch. These legends, as far as they relate to enormous and curious whales and fish, have been reported in the last chapter. There existed in antiquity some very strange ideas concerning whales, apart from the general exaggeration in respect to size. *Nearchus encountered a school of these animals, many of them very large, in the Persian Gulf, and they so terrified and alarmed his crews, that he formed his ships in line, and charged upon them, blowing horns to frighten them away.

†Aldrovandus figures some strange looking objects for whales. In one cut, such a monster is biting off the entire stern of a ship. It is spouting water out of the entire top of its head, in a cataract sufficient to submerge the vessel.

* Goodrich.—Man upon the Sea, p. 77.
† Landrin.—Les Monstres Marins, p. 152 and 153.

Another animal is pig-snouted and saucer-eyed, having a remarkable fringe or mane about its neck, and, projecting from the top of its head, two tubes or funnels, from which it spouts water.   Another has a curious sort of external spine, with bag-like appendages along it.   It is attacked by two smaller animals with pig's heads, and spine-like projections from the middle of its back.

*An old "Bestiare d' Amour " says the whale has a shell on its back, whose folds are like a valley, and that it attracts fish by its smell.

†Munster says whales near Iceland destroyed ships. ‡Arnanson reports many curious Icelandic notions concerning whales.   There are said to be two classes of these animals.   Good whales spout high, and are favorable to men, defending them from the attacks of bad whales, which latter

WHALE AND ORCAS.

are known by their short, quick "spouts" or "blows." Should the defender, in such cases, suffer harm, vengeance is sure to overtake the ungrateful person harming him. Gisli was thus attacked by a bad whale, and delivered by a good one.   The ox-whale was said to be like an ox.   The sword-whale had a fin on its back, like a sword.   The lingback has ling, or heather, growing on its back.   The redmaned whale has a particularly bad name, and its thirst for human blood is said only to be quenched by that of seven brothers, but it also proves to be its destruction.   The Rauthkembingr, or Red-comb, is also very malicious and blood-thirsty, and the Buhwahlr can easily bite a ship in two.

*Landrin.—Les Monstres Marins, p. 50.
†" Cosmography."
‡ Icelandic Legends.

*In the Norse Heims Kringla, a warlock assumes the shape of a whale, in order to carry news from Iceland to Norway. †So in an Icelandic folk-tale, a man is changed into a whale by a water-woman whom he had married and deserted. He causes death to many persons, and wrecks many boats. Finally, after swallowing the daughter of a priest, he is decoyed by him into shallow water, where he dies, and it is said that his immense skeleton is still seen on the sands. Ahts say the whale, Quahteaht, is the incarnation of a certain great deity.

We have spoken of the whale that carried Astolpho. So in a Norse tale a youth is carried on the back of a whale. ‡A Miniako hero, Glooscap, was carried to the sunset land on the back of a whale.

WHALE ATTACKING SHIP.

§ "Then the water grew so shoal that the whale heard the song of the clams as they lay under the sand, singing to her that she should throw him off and drown him. For these clams were his deadly enemies. But Bootup, the whale, did not understand their language, so she asked her rider— for he knew Clam—what they were chanting to her. And he replied in a song."

Presently the whale ran high and dry on the beach, and begged him to get her off. "Then, with a push of his bow against her head, he sent her off into deep water. And the whale rejoiced greatly. But ere she went she said, 'O my grandson, hast thou not such a thing as an old pipe and some tobacco?'" He replied,—

* Conway.—Demonology and Devil-lore. Vol. I, p. 166.
† Arnanson.—Icelandic Legends. See also Powell and Magnusson, p. 409.
‡ Conway.—Demonology and Devil-lore, Vol. I, p. 46.
§ Leland.—Algonquin Legends, 1884, p. 34.

" ' Ah yes.
You want tobacco,
I behold you.'

"So he gave her a short pipe and some tobacco, and thereunto a light. And the whale being of good cheer, sailed away, smoking as she went, while Glooscap, standing silent on the shore, and ever leaning on his maple bow, beheld the long low cloud which followed her until she vanished in the far away."

In an Italian folk tale, a whale teaches a man how to succeed in certain tasks. * There is a New Zealand tale of a whale that obligingly allowed a man to cut steaks from its body. A magician finally killed it, by stopping its blowholes.

According to the Norse " Book of Kings," certain whales drove the fish into the nets, so long as the fishermen did not quarrel. † Cardinal Maffei says a whale seriously menaced a ship, while on a voyage to the East Indies, until it was exorcised by a priest, when it went away.

‡ In a Greenland tale, a girl is carried off by a whale, who is a man in disguise. Another whale is lured into shallow water by a magic lay. Esquimaux said that a certain whale, having two black spots on either side, was reserved for the spirit of the moon, and must not be killed.

A Waikato (New Zealand) story represents a whale as stranding on the coast, that contained, or was the body of a deified man. Any one eating of it became spiritualized.

§ In the Georgian islands, whales were sacred, and were not killed. Tongans and Kamtchatdales sacrificed to them.

Whales also furnish prognostications. ‖Aubrey says a whale came up the Thames during Cromwell's protectorate, and greatly alarmed that iron man, who thought it forboded trouble.

Fishermen on our own coast say that it is a sign of storms, if whales lie about, blowing and puffing.

** Swift says, "Seamen have a custom, when they meet a whale, to fling him out an empty tub, by way of amusement, to divert him from laying violent hands (sic) on the ship." This custom is also mentioned in Brandt's "Ship of Fools,"

* Grey.—Polynesian Mythology.
† Jones.—Credulities.
‡ Rink.—Tales and Traditions of the Esquimaux.
§ Tylor.—Primitive Culture, Vol. II, p. 270.
‖ Miscellanies.
** Tale of a Tub, Preface, 1704.

and there is a picture in Munster's "Cosmography," of men on board ship throwing a tub overboard to a whale near by.

* Scotch whalers had a legend of an invulnerable whale, two centuries old, whose back was covered with algæ and shells. † Melville says similar traditions existed concerning sperm whales, and a famous white whale, the hero of his story, "Moby Dick."

Both the authors last quoted record a superstition long existing among whalers, that these animals had some excessively rapid means of locomotion; that they were able mysteriously to transport themselves long distances, and that whales were found in the South Seas with harpoons in them, which had been struck in Greenland.

Hovas of Madagascar say, when an earthquake occurs, "The whale is turning over." "The whales are playing with their children."

WHALES FOLLOWING SHIP.—ALDROVANDUS.

Tales of men swallowed by whales, sharks, and fish, are numerous. In Welsh mythology, the whale is Kyd (Cetus). ‡ Taliesin says, "Who brought Jonas out of the belly of Kyd?" Davies, the Arkite mythologist, says it typifies the Ark.

§ Pradyumna, son of Vishnu, was swallowed by a fish, and restored to life. According to a modern Hindoo story, a maiden jumped into a fish's mouth, and remained there twelve years, causing the monster so much trouble and distress, that a crow, a jackal, and a serpent are sent down his throat, to liberate her.

* Mangin.—Mysteries of the Ocean, p. 209
† Moby Dick.
‡ Celtic Mythology.
§ Gubernatis.—Zoological Mythology. Cox.—Aryan Mythology, Vol. I, p. 28.

*In an Italian folk-tale, a little girl is received in the belly of an enchanted whale, where she finds a garden, palace and people. †In a Roman story, it is a queen who is thus swallowed, and who speaks, is heard, and liberated. In a Russian tale, a whale swallows a whole fleet, and a forest grows out of its back. It aids the hero of the tale to find a casket, and can then get rid of the fleet. In a Mongol tale, *Ai-Khan*, a sorcerer, assumes the shape of a cup, and falls into the sea, where he is swallowed by a fish, but is eventually rescued from its stomach.

Traditions of North American Indians tell of similar occurrences. ‡Boin, an Indian hero, like Glooscap, was carried to paradise in the belly of a whale, paying tobacco as a fee for his passage. Hence, say Nova Scotia Indians, when you see the whale spout, it is the smoke of Boin's tobacco.

Indians of Shoalwater Bay had a tradition that a certain man was swallowed by a whale, and cut out by his brother. §So, in Ojibway legend, a great hero, the Little Monedo, was swallowed by a great fish, and liberated by his sister.

‖Manabozho, the Algonquin hero (Longfellow's Hiawatha), was swallowed by a whale, but wedged his canoe across the monster's throat, and killed him. Gulls then pecked a hole in its body, and liberated him.

Plutarch says a Greek hero lived three days in a shark's stomach. Lycophron asserts that Hercules was imprisoned in a whale's belly, and Eneis de Gaza says Hercules' cup was a whale.

In the first chapter of Jonah, we are told that a storm arose, and that lots were cast to see whose fault it was, and the lot fell on Jonah. He offered himself as a sacrifice, and was cast into the sea, where a great fish swallowed him. "And Jonah was in the belly of the fish three days and nights." He was finally delivered, by praying to the Lord. **In Mussulman legend, the ship was mysteriously stopped at sea, and lots were cast for a sacrifice, which fell on Jonah. He was accordingly thrown overboard. A huge fish swallowed him, and he remained inside it forty days, being finally delivered by prayer.

*Pentamerone.—Bk. VIII.
† Gubernatis.—Zoological Mythology, Vol. II, p. 337.
‡ Farrar.—Primitive Customs.
§ Tylor.—Primitive Culture. Vol. I, p. 398.
‖ Schoolcraft.—Algic Researches, Vol. I, p. 46.
** Weil.—Legends of the Koran.

* These comparative examples conclusively show the man-swallowing whale to be a myth, and we are here, as mythologists agree, confronted by the same idea as was shown in the case of the sea-monsters—a conflict between light and darkness, or day and night. As the sun was swallowed up at night in the ocean, a monster was easily imagined as doing it, and the whale being the greatest monster, he was credited with these feats. All these heroes are solar heroes, and represent the sun.

† The Narwhal is called in Iceland Nähvalhr, or Death-whale, and it is fabled only to appear above water to foretell destruction by wreck. In Greenland tales, it is the embodiment of the soul of a certain woman, condemned at death to do penance thus.

This animal was by some fabled to be the unicorn, generally deemed a land-animal. ‡ Its horn was supposed to be an antidote to poison, long before the animal was known to exist. Its very presence was thought to detect the most subtle essences. Cups were made of it, and enormous prices were paid for the horn itself,§ six thousand ducats being mentioned. Ambrose Paré, a celebrated French physician, says that pieces of it were placed in the king's drinking cup, so late as 1606.

Dekker tells us of—

| "The Unicorn whose horn is worth a city."

alluding to the great price paid for them.

Many strange notions have been entertained concerning spermaceti, amber, and ambergris. Spermaceti, as its name indicates, was long supposed to be the sperm of the whale. ** Sir Thomas Browne says it was, in his time, thought to be a bituminous substance, floating on the surface of the water.

El Idressee says ambergris flows from the bottom of the sea, and we are told by a Mahometan traveler of 851 A.D., that the Hindoos then believed it was generated by the whale. Sindbad found a spring of crude ambergris, which, he says, fish swallow and then disgorge, after it has been congealed. In the seventeenth century it was used in the

* Tylor.—Primitive Culture, Vol. I, p. 340.
† Arnanson.—Icelandic Legends.
‡ Landrin.—Les Monstres Marins, p. 122.
§ Jones.—Credulities, p. 160.
| Gull's Hornbook.
** Vulgar Errors.

compositiou of love-powder. *A chemist, Nicholas Lémery, in 1675, says it is a sort of bitumen, found on sea-beaches.

† O'Reilly mentions a legend current among whalers, that amber (ambergris?) is a petrifaction of some interior part of a whale. There were stories of whales that nearly turned to amber, such as he celebrates in " The Amber Whale."

Josselyn in his " Second Voyage " says, "Amber-greese, I take to be a mushroom. Monardus writeth that amber-greese riseth out of a certain clammy and bituminous earth under the seas, and by the seaside, the billows casting up part of it aland, and fish devour the rest. Some say it is the seed of a whale. Others that it springs from fountains as pitch doth, which fish swallow down; the air congealeth it."

It is now well known that ambergris is the indurated fæces of the whale, deposited by disease. When the whale is struck, it vomits some of it up. Amber is the petrified resin of a tree, found on sea-beaches, but is often confounded with ambergris.

The shark has been connected with many superstitious ideas. Its French name *requin*, indicates its deadly nature, the requiem being often sung over its victims.

‡ Sailors have long thought it an ill-omened animal. § It was believed able to scent a victim, and would follow a ship for miles, in which a dead body lay. ‖ To see one follow a ship was an ill-omen.

** Cheever says, "A sailor always regards the presence of a shark about a ship a most fatal omen to the sick on board. The highest exultation I ever witnessed on board a man-of-war, was occasioned by harpooning a shark that was hanging about while a favorite was sick."

†† Plutarch says, the shark is kind to its offspring, taking it into its stomach in case of danger.

Pearl divers in Ceylon employ shark charmers, to protect them while at work   ‡‡ Marco Polo first told us of them. He calls them Brahmans or Abræmani. Their charms only operated in daylight, and they received as wages a twenti-

---

* Landrin.—Les Monstres Marins, 221.
† Songs of the Southern Seas.
‡ Cooper.—Homeward Bound.
§ Carnes.—Voyage to West Africa.
‖ Grant.—Mysteries, p. 309.
** Sea and Sailor, 1827.
†† Landrin, p. 89.
‡‡ Yule.—Marco Polo, Vol. II. p. 261.

eth of the gains of the fishermen.   Colonel Yule says the modern snake charmers have taken their places.   They are called Kudal, or Timmal (sea-binders) or Haibandi (shark-binders).   The chief operator is pensioned by the government, and receives ten oysters daily from each boat.   At Aripo, these charmers all belong to one family.   * Two go out, one in a boat, the other on the beach.   The latter has a basin filled with water, and in it several silver fish.   He shuts himself up with them, and declares that the fish will fight, should any harm come to the divers.   The man in the boat performs certain incantations in the bows, while progressing seaward.

† Tahitians deified the blue shark, dedicating to it temples and a priest.   These were called *akua maoo* (shark gods), and were supposed to recognize their priests.   ‡African negroes worship it, calling it Joujou, and sacrifice rabbits to it.   At certain times, they bind a child, ten years old, decorated with flowers, etc., to a post on the beach at low tide, and leave it to be devoured by sharks, drowning its cries with the noise of drums.

§ Sharks' teeth were formerly set in gold as a charm, and when powdered and mixed with the brain, became a medicine.

‖ There have been many legends of its voracity.   Labat, a French naturalist, asserts that it prefers white men, and Englishmen above all.   A shark cut open at Marseilles is said to have contained a man, clad in armor, in its stomach, and another, a horse.

The Dolphin and the Porpoise have long been associated with many curious legends.   The dolphin was fabled to be fond of men, of music and of company, and had prescience of coming storms.   Ælian tells of children riding on their backs and playing with them.   **An ancient Roman tradition averred that a dolphin in the Lucrine lake had a great fondness for a child, feeding from its hand, and carrying it on its back.   Pausanias says he saw one at Paros, which, wounded by a fisherman, and aided by a child, afterwards came at its call, and served it as a vehicle.   Many tales of its carrying men ashore from wrecks were told.   Telemachus

* Jones.— Broad, Broad Ocean, p. 148.
† Ellis.—Polynesian Researches, Vol. I, p. 178.
‡ Landrin.—Les Monstres Marins, p 192.
§ Landrin.—Les Monstres Marins, p. 89.
‖ Landrin.—Les Monstres Marins, p. 78.
** Pliny.—Natural History, Vol. IV, p. 8.

was saved by one, and Plutarch † recounts a similar tale of a
certain Hesiod.   He also tells a story of two lovers, one of
whom leaped overboard to escape being sacrificed, followed
by the other, when both were carried ashore, and saved by
a dolphin.   Arion, condemed as a sacrifice by the mariners,
taking his harp and charming the fish, leaped overboard,
and was carried safely ashore by a dolphin.   So Spencer,—

> † "That was Arion, crown'd,
> Who, playing on his harp, after him drew
> The ears and hearts of all that goodly crew;
> That ere yet the Dolphin which him bore
> Through the Ægean seas, from pirates' view,
> Stood still by him, astonished at his lore,
> And all the raging seas forgot to roar."

THE MONKEY AND THE DOLPHIN.

And Ovid,—

> ‡ "But past belief, a dolphin's arched back,
> Preserv'd Arion from his destin'd wrack.
> Secure he sits, and with harmonious strains,
> Requites his bearer for his friendly pains."

In La Fontaine's Fables, a tale is told of a dolphin who
picked up a monkey from a wreck, and carried him nearly
to the shore, but suddenly dropped him, on discovering that
he could not speak.

* Morals.—Goodwin's Trans.
† Marriage of the Thames and Medway.
‡ Metamorphoses. See also Ford.—Lovers' Melancholy, Act I, scene I.

Other stories were told of the intelligence of man-loving animals.* Seneca tells a tale from Babillus, of a conflict between crocodiles and dolphins at the Heraclite mouth of the Nile, in which the latter vanquished their formidable adversaries by diving under them, and plunging the fin on their backs into the soft bellies of their opponents.

† Pliny says they aided fishermen on the French coast near Nimes to catch tunny, by driving them into their nets, and by intercepting and devouring them, when they attempted to escape. For these services, they were rewarded with bread soaked in wine.

Ptolemy Soter, when driven out of his course by contrary winds, is said to have been directed to the right course by a dolphin. Both dolphins and porpoises were attendant on Poseidon, Amphitrite, and the other sea-gods. Two dolphins are said to have carried off Amphitrite, and brought her to Poseidon.

‡ One of the titles of Apollo was Delphinios, given him after he had assumed the form of a dolphin, in order to guide a ship's crew to his temple at Delphos.

Bacchus, when carried off by Tyrrhenian pirates, transformed the crew into Dolphins.§

> " All my crew, transformed, around the ship,
> Or dive below, or on the surface keep,
> And sport the wave, or wanton in the deep.
>
> * * * * * * * * *
>
> A shoal of useless dolphins round her play."

Pliny and Ælian assert that the dolphin sleeps on his back, sinking until he touches the bottom, then rising to the surface, thus being continually in motion.

Later antiquity represented the dolphin as a sign of good fortune. They were to lead souls to happiness, to carry men on their backs to the Fortunate Isles. Thus in the middle ages, and in early Christian art,‖ it became the symbol of Christ, who was to lead souls through the waters of baptism. So it is found on early Christian tombs, with the word "philanthropos," in keeping with its ancient character, as well as with the new ideas. It often accompanies the Saints in early representations, as an emblem of

* Landrin.—Les Monstres Marins, p. 208.
† Landrin.—p. 212. Pliny.—Book XIV, p. 9.
‡ Cox.—Aryan Mythology Book II, Chapter 2.
§ Ovid.—Metamorphoses.
‖ Lindsay.—Christian Art.

fortunate existence.   It was still reported, however, to carry men on its back.

*St. Arlan and St. Théodique, martyrs, were said to have been carried ashore by them.   The body of St. Lucien, of Samosata, was likewise thus transported, and the body of the dolphin who carried his remains was long exposed in a temple.   A Persian author asserts its carrying propensity, and a Breton folk-tale says a dolphin carried men ashore from a wrecked boat.

The dolphin was a symbol of other qualities.   Sir Thomas Browne says it is the hieroglyph of celerity, and Sylvanus Morgan, that of society.   It was also an emblem of fortune, and became the symbol of certain cities.   To dream of a dolphin, however, was to lose your lover, according to dream-lore.

†Stow says: "A dolphin came forth of the sea.   These dolphins are fishes of the sea, that follow the voices of men, and rejoice in playing of instruments, and are wont to gather themselves at musick."   "The seas contain nothing so swift nor nimble, for oftentimes, with their skips, they mount over the sailes of the ship."

‡Olmstead records a modern sailor superstition, which is shown by the name common among them for the porpoise, of sea-hog (German *Meerschwein*): "The mouths of all varieties of the porpoise have some resemblance to that of a swine, from which circumstance sailors have assigned a rather fanciful origin to this class of Cetacea.   According to an opinion prevalent among them, when the evil spirits were cast out of the unfortunate man near the lake of Genesaret, and entered into the herd of swine, the whole herd ran violently down a steep place into the sea, and were changed into porpoises."

The blood of a porpoise, mixed with a little of the heart, pulverized, and placed under the armpit, was, in the middle-ages, believed to bestow great judgment upon the wearer.

§Cotton Mather assures us that it is the providence of God that sends these animals to be caught by people at sea, in distress for want of food.

The dolphin is often figured along with the Chinese god of the sea.   Esquimaux say dolphins were once men.

* Landrin.—Op. cit. p. 211.
† Chronicles.
‡ Notes of a Whaling Voyage (1841).
§ *Magnalia* Christi Americana.

Ruskin says that the dolphin in Greek art is the sea itself, and is also typical of the rising and setting sun, its arching back being taken as a sign of these.

The dolphin in mythology and folk-lore typifies the moon, the weather-maker, and, as Gubernatis shows, is a symbol of the soul journey and of the new birth, as also above-stated.* "The dolphin, that watches over Amphitrite by order of Poseidon, in the Hellenic myth, is the same as the dolphin, the spy of the sea, or the moon, the spy of the nocturnal and misty sky. Inasmuch as the sky of night or winter was compared to the kingdom of the dead, both the dolphin and the moon, according to the Hellenic belief, carried the souls of the dead."

As the dolphin and the shark are often seen together about the ship, the latter gloomy, watchful, and malicious, and the former playful and mild in appearance, there would naturally grow up, alongside of the tradition of the ill-omen of the one, that of the man-loving qualities of the other. This, with the notion of their usefulness as weather-indicators, has perhaps given rise to these many myths.

With these animals was connected the seal, in many legends. Its peculiarly human look, its soft and mild eyes, and its child-like cry, were early noticed, and doubtless led it to be imagined a mermaid, who could, by rejecting the seal garment, assume the human shape, and dance on the strand. Many of the stories of the docility and friendliness of the dolphin may have arisen from confounding it with the seal, which is well known as susceptible of being well tamed. So of the music-loving qualities of the two animals. Captain Scoresby and other Arctic travelers remark on the acute hearing of the seal, and its fondness for music, one writer having drawn them out by a few notes of his flute. † In Iceland, the seal is a Sjövite, or animal that will come when called. They are also called Pharaoh's men, and are fabled to come ashore and dance on the strand, on St. John's night. On the west coast of Ireland,‡ fishermen fear to kill them, as they possess "the souls of them that were drowned at the flood." § Greenlanders also think that the souls of people inhabit seals' bodies after death. The Umiarak, a spectral boat, is filled with seal-rowers, when too

* Zoological Mythology, Book II.
† Maurer.—Islandische Sagen.
‡ Froude.—Short Studies.
§ Rink.—Tales and Traditions of the Esquimaux.

many have been killed in a season. *Esquimaux believe that seals will be frightened away, if the heads of those taken are thrown into the water, so they burn them, or pile them up on shore.

† Weddel says a man left temporarily on a rock in South Shetland heard a mournful cry, and, on looking up, saw a seal. He declared it was a sea-ghost, and begged to be taken on board ship, deeming the appearance of the seal an ill-omen. Melville also says that sailors considered the cries of seals an omen of disaster.

A host of legends have been current concerning fish, and so remarkable have been many of these, that it has grown into a saying to characterize an unusually improbable tale, as a fish story. These legends are of various kinds, some mythical, others fanciful notions-of fishermen and sailors, and others embracing false ideas of the shape, habits and characteristics of these animals.

Fish have been the incarnation of various deities and heroes. ‡ According to Hindoo lore, Agasti was born a fish. Vishnu, Buddha, Indra, and Adrika were at one time fish, and the sons of the latter were Matsyas (male fish), and her daughters Matsya (female fish). Vishnu was at first a small fish in a pond, and become gradually larger and larger, being transferred from tank to lake, and from lake to ocean, where he saved man from destruction, by towing the ark. Eros and Aphrodite, escaping from Typhon, became fish.

In Norse legend, Loki became a salmon, and Andvari a pike.

Oriental Mahisars, evil demons, had fish-heads, and fish, in the Arabian Nights, become efreets, or evil genii.

Gavran, a Welsh sorcerer, transformed himself into a fish, to gain certain ends. Tuan McCorreal was three hundred years a fish. Isembart, a hero of the legends concerning William of Orange, was a fish, and was transformed into a man by a fairy. Fairies themselves became fish, in Hindoo, Greek, and French folk-tales.

Japanese have a tradition that fish are the embodiment of the souls of naval officers.

Thorstein, an Icelandic magician, was condemned to become the greatest fish in the sea, and as such he wrecked nineteen ships.

* Farrar.—Primitive Customs, 28.
† Voyage to South Shetland (1825).
‡ Gubernatis.—Zoological Mythology, Vol. II, p. 330.

* Fish in Clear lake are transformed from grasshoppers by a Coyote fiend. Xalote, in Mexican legend, became a fish, and a certain tribe claimed the fish of a river as their relations, and would not kill them. † Tlailottakans represented that all drowned at the deluge became fish. A West Indian legend says that the prime minister of a certain revolted prince was turned into a flying-fish, and the former inhabitants in the shapes of dolphins chased him.

THE SHARK CHARMER OF CEYLON.

African negroes think that magicians assume the shapes of fish, and come to their nets to work evil.

‡ Fijians suppose that certain deities reside in fish.

Besides the Fish-gods and demons spoken of in a previous chapter, many fish were sacred, and some demonical. In ancient Egypt, they were Typhonic, and priests could not eat them, while in Catholic belief they are allowed to be eaten when flesh is forbidden. Jews of the middle ages cast a fish in the sea, to carry away their sins.

§ T h e Oxyrhynchians worshiped the *Oxyrhynchus*, and the Latopolitans the *Lato*. ¶

Ten fish guarded the tree which produced the *Soma*, or heavenly nectar, according to the Vedaic beliefs.

* Bancroft.—Native Races, Vol. III, p. 57.   ‡ Williams.— Fiji, Vol. I, p. 217.
† Bancroft.—III, p. 67.   ¶ Tylor.—Prim. Cult., Vol. I, p. 288.

* Indians at Qu'Appelle river caught a strange fish, in 1858. They at once threw it back into the river, and sacrificed dogs to it, declaring it a manitou, or deity.

Tahitians, Fijians, ancient Peruvians, and natives of other South Sea Isles, all worshiped or reverenced fish. Guinea negroes selected the bonito and sword-fish as deities.

The turbot and halibut are still regarded with veneration by Shetland fishermen. † Blind says they are both holy fish. The turbot takes its name from the Northern deity Thor (Thor's butt). Folk-lore stories represent them as all-powerful. A fish-prince is brought out of the sea, in one of these tales, by the power of the charm,—

> " Little man, little man, Timpe Te,
> Little butt, little butt, in the sea."

It is called in German Heiligen Fisch (holy fish). A correspondent in Shetland told Blind that fishermen there, when they get a "bite" from a turbot, keep perfect silence, not allowing anyone to speak. Should anyone pronounce the name of this fish, he was thought the cause of a day's ill-luck, and was punished for it. The halibut (holy butt) was the object of similar superstitions.

‡ So the salmon is held in great veneration by Scotch fishermen. Its name must never be spoken, and it is called instead, "So and so's fish," "the spey codlin" or "the beast." To speak of it at sea, or to catch either it or trout in the nets, was a bad omen.

§ Fish typified the faithful in early Christian art, and were also symbols of Christ. Anciently they were placed on tombs as symbols, and also on baptismal fonts. Greeks put round dishes with fish on them in tombs to feed the dead. The word " Ichthus " (fish), was placed on charms, because its letters formed the initials of the words " Jesus Christ our Savior."

Fish have also been consulted as oracles. Those in a fountain in Syria gave responses by leaping up, or floating upon the water. They are frequently said to predict storms. ‖ Cornish fishermen place their fish in barrels, and they occasionally make a squeaking sound, when their air-bladders

* Brinton.—Myths of the New World.
† Scottish and Shetlandic Water-gods. Cont. Rev., 1882.
‡ Gregor.—Folk-lore of Scotland.
§ Lindsay.—Christain Art.
‖ Bottrell.—Traditions of West Cornwa'l.

burst. This predicts good luck. * Jinnu, a Japanese queen, fished for an auspicious omen on the first day of the fourth month, and caught a fish. Ladies fish on that day.

In Tobit, a fish is boiled to raise a vapor charm, which drives away evil spirits. A mediæval legend represents a magician as using the blood of a fish in his conjurations and incantations. Fish entered into the composition of the witch broth.

Strange transformations of fish are spoken of. In the story of the Fishermen in the Arabian Nights, Mussulmen are transformed into white fish, Persians into red fish, Christians into black fish, and Jews into yellow fish.

† The saints often worked transformations with fish. St. Augustine, in passing through a village, was reviled by some men, and so caused fish tails to grow on them. St. Ulrich turned flesh into fish. ‡ An odd story is told of St. Patrick. He was quietly helping himself to a tender chop on a fast-day, when an angel unexpectedly came up. The saint, not wishing to be caught sinning, quickly popped the chop into a tank, signed the cross over it, and it became fish. In many parts of Ireland, meat is dipped into water, christened "St. Patrick's fish," and eaten on fast-days.

The same saint, when reviled by fishermen, cursed their stream, and thereby forever banished fish from it.

§ Glooscap changed a witch into a fish Kegunnibe, an evil fish, with a fin on its back.

Many legends and tales record the intelligence of fish, and their gift-bringing and beneficial deeds.

‖ There is an old Persian story that fish brought clay to build an island for Adam to live on.

A Moslem instance of their sagacity represents them as coming out in crowds, on observing that no one fished on Sundays. St. Anthony, to convince certain skeptics, preached a sermon to a shoal of them, as any one may see by a picture in the Borghese palace at Rome. ** A Talmudic legend says Solomon tried to feed all the fish in one day. One hundred thousand came the same number of miles, and all were satisfied except the whale.

Fish once gathered to choose a king, and did so by ac-

* Mitford.—Tales of Old Japan.
† Jones.—Credulities, p. 57.
‡ Jones.—Credulities, p. 61.
§ Leland.—Algonquin Folk-lore.
‖ Baring Gould.—Legends of the Prophets and Patriarchs.
** Weil.—Legends of the Koran.

clamation. *A certain fish, the grunter, can talk, according to German legends. Its theme is a lament for its fish-shape, and for past happiness in another form. They were traditionally inhabitants of Helgoland, transformed to fish for yielding to the devil.

† Shoals of fish are said to have aided a Japanese fleet in their progress to Corea, by pushing their ships ahead.

Indians of British Columbia were wont to meet the salmon in their way up the river, and make a speech to them to conciliate them.

Marco Polo tells us a curious fish story, and its counterpart is told by Willbrand of Oldenburg, of a river in Cilicia, and by another author, of a lake in Georgia. ‡ Polo says: "There is in this country a certain convent of nuns called St. Leonards; near the church in question is a small lake, at the foot of a mountain, and in this lake are found no fish, great or small, throughout the year, till Lent comes. On the first of Lent, they find in it the finest fish in the world, and great store thereof, and these are certain to be found till Easter eve. After that they are found no more till Lent come again."

§ Another old traveler tells us: "In the land of Siria there is a river having a great store of fish like unto salmontrouts, but no Jew can catch them, though either Christian or Turk shall catch them in abundance with great ease."

∥ An old Arabian writer says fish came out of the Red Sea, to tempt the Jews to violate the passover. David punished them for it, by making them into apes.

** Hoare tells us: "The fish of a certain pool near Seez, in Normandy, fought so furiously that the noise attracted many people there, and many fish were killed, thus by a wonderful and unheard of prognostic, foretelling the death of one by that of many." Who that one is, we are not told.

All fish were anciently reported to be fond of music. Plutarch says: †† "Certain fish are caught by means of dancing, for during the dance they lift their heads above water, being much pleased and delighted with the sight, and thrashing their tails this way and that, in imitation of the dance."

* Schmidt.—Seeman's Sagen und Schiffer Märchen.
♦ Mitford.—Tales of Old Japan.
‡ Yule.—Marco Polo, Bk. VI p. 60, Vol I.
§ E. Webbe.—Travels (1590).
∥ Ai Zamokti, in Brewer's " Readers' Hand-Book."
** " Giraldus Cambrensis," in Jones' Credulities, p. 53,
†† Morals.—Goodwin's Trans.

Ælian and Aristotle reported that fish, particularly skates, were attracted and caught by carrying in a boat a musical instrument and net. *Jones says this is said to be practiced yet by boatmen on the Danube, who use bells. Carp have been known to answer the call of a bell.

Arion and Orpheus charmed fish by their lyres. Horant, in the Gudrun lay, charmed them when he sang, and later heroes have been accorded the same powers. Wainamoinen, the Finnish hero, charmed birds, beasts and fishes with his harp, made from the bones of a pike. Maurice, the Irish piper, piped fish from the water, and the lady of Pengerswick, according to Cornish legend, still attracts the fish by the sounds of her harp.

In a German tale, Tiberias, Emperor of Rome, finds a fisherman, vainly trying to charm the fish with his fiddle, and he teaches his unskilled hands how to do it.

A fisherman in Cornwall whipped a hake, and put it back into the water. According to the legends, they never came any more.

†Fish in a mill-pond, according to Russian stories, employed a magician to remove an obnoxious mill.

Fish often, in folk-lore tales, bring benefits in gratitude for being put back in the water when caught, or for other considerations. In a German story, it is a ring that a fish restores to a youth. ‡In a Norse tale, it is the egg at the bottom of a well that incloses a giant's heart. In a Russian tale they assist a man to find his friends, and in another, they guide ashore a cask in which a woman has been thrown into the sea, and liberate her. In a Wallachian tale, they carry a man to the bottom of the sea, to shield him from pursuers. §In German and Italian tales, fish bring many benefits to fishermen who restore them to the water.

‖In another German tale, a man is almost upset by an enormous fish, who reproaches him for fishing in the pond, and only agrees to liberate him, by the promise of his daughter. The maiden is carried down to wonderful palaces below the sea, whence she is finally delivered by her brother, after many perils.

Remarkable stories are also told of the regenerative powers of fish. In the Pseudo Callisthenes, a fish returns

* Broad, Broad Ocean.
+ Ralston.—Russian Folk-lore.
‡ Dasent.—Popular Tales from the Norse.
‖ "Straparolo" and " Der Kossat und Süne fru."
‖ Wuttke.—Deutsche Aberglauben.

to life when nearly ready to cook. *Abd-ul-Cassim, an
eastern traveler, says of a certain river near the Black Sea:
"Every year, there arrives in this part of the river a great
quantity of fish. The people cut off the flesh on one side of
them, eat it, and let the fish go. The year following, the
same creatures return, and offer the other side, which they
had preserved untouched. It is then discovered that new
flesh has replaced the old."

†A more wonderful story is told by Dr. Walsh: "At the
distance of a quarter of a mile from the walls is.Balatka, or
the church of fishes. The church is so called from a legend
that has rendered it very celebrated among the Greeks.
There stood on this place a small Monastery of Greek
Calayers, when Mohammed laid siege to Constantinople,
who, it seems, were not molested by his army. On the day of
decisive attack, a monk was frying some fish, when news
was suddenly brought to the convent that the Turks had
entered the town through the breach in the walls. 'I would
as soon believe,' said he, 'that these fried fish would spring
from the pan, and become again alive.' To reprove the in-
credulous monk, the fish *did* spring from the pan into a
vessel of water which stood near, and swam about as if they
had never been taken out of it."

An eastern story asserts that the Angel Gabriel restored
a sole to life, to assure the Virgin Mary of the truth of the
miraculous conception.

‡Purchas says: "In the Moluccas there is a river stored
with fishes and yet so hote that it flareth off the skinne of
any creature that entereth it."

St. Corentin had a fish caught each day which miraculously renewed itself. §St. Neot had been told to take from
a well one fish each day, for his support. During his illness,
his servant cooked two. On his discovering it, the saint
caused the extra fish to be thrown back into the water,
when it came to life again.

Probably on account of its regenerative powers, the fish
was anciently a remedy for diseases. The carp was a well-
known remedy. Van Helmont says the Dutch used to
apply a split herring to the bite of a rabid dog,‖ and a live
trout was, not very many years ago, used to lay on the

* Jones.—Credulities. p. 51.
† Travels of Macarius, in Jones' Credulities, p. 50.
‡ "Pilgrims."
§ Jones.—Credulities, p. 50.
‖ Henderson.—Folk-lore of the Northern Counties of England, p. 154.

THE EMPEROR TIBERIAS CHARMS THE FISH.

stomach of a child troubled with worms, in Cleveland, Yorkshire.

Fish in many stories have an undoubted phallical character. These tales, numerous in folk-lore, represent them as causing women to conceive, when eaten, often at their own request. *The phallus is called in Neapolitan dialect *pesce* (fish). Eels share the same character with fish. †Gubernatis says the French "poisson d'avril (April-fool fish) has a phallical meaning. This same idea would seem to be indicated by the accounts of their regenerative power.

Miraculous draughts of fish are reported in many places. St. Bonita and St. Anne were each favored with one. A clergyman in the north of England became unpopular in his parish, but regained his position by going out in the fishing-boats, when just one hundred and fifty-three fish, the miraculous draught, were caught.‡

Other miraculous supplies of fish are also recorded. §St. Thomas-a-Becket, when passing a certain stream, hearing that fish would be scarce, said, "the Lord will provide," when a bream jumped out into his lap. |St. Peter is said to have visited Westminster at its foundation, crossing the Thames in a fisherman's boat. This man, complaining of the scarcity of fish, the apostle told him he should have plenty, if he would not fish on Sunday, and would pay a tithe to the church. A salmon was long presented annually to the church.

A shooting-star is said to have rained fish in 519 A.D., and there are several later accounts of showers of fish.

There are other miraculous occurrences recorded, as connected with fish.

Pisces, the fish transferred to the constellations, reappears in the Esquimaux tradition that stars were once fish. **Greenlanders, however, said they were made from chips thrown into the water by a male sorcerer, and bits of cloth by a female. In the Finnish Kalevala, they are changed into foam by a magician. ††An Icelandic legend states that Christ created the stone grig by spitting into the sea, and St. Peter, in the same manner, the hake. Satan imitated them, but produced the devil-fish.

* Gubernatis.—Zoological Mythology, II, 347.
† Gubernatis.—Zoological Mythology, II, 250.
‡ Henderson.—Folk-lore of the North of England.
§ Jones.—Credulities, p. 50.
| Jones.—Credulities.
** Hans Egede.
†† Maurer.—Isländische Sagen.

*Mahometan writers say fish come ashore with their throats cut, since Mohammed blessed a knife and threw it into the sea.

An Orkney conjurer fished up cooked fish from the sea, and St. Moet caught them on dry land.

†A small fish, the Chrysofrus or Aurata, was said formerly to allow women and children to take it out of the water, and handle it. It was sacred to Venus, and Gubernatis says this is why we eat fish on 'Friday, Venus' day.

‡Leonard Vair, an old writer, says that in 1583, there was a pond near a cloister in Burgundy, in which there were fish, corresponding in number to the monks. When a monk fell sick, a fish was observed to do the same, and, when the monk died, the fish was sure to be found dead on the shore.

Closely connected with the stories of fish swallowing men, recounted in the present chapter, are the numerous tales in which fish swallow rings, pearls, or other valuables, and restore them, or are caught, and these gems restored. These tales are very ancient. §A Talmudic legend says Asmodeus, the evil spirit, stole from Solomon the signet-ring that conferred upon him so much power and wisdom. The evil genius threw it into the sea, but Solomon recovered it in the belly of a fish that was caught soon after.

‖A Hindoo nymph, Sakuntali, lost her ring while bathing, but found it again in the belly of a fish. **In "Aboo-Seer," a ring is found in a fish's throat, and in another tale, a diamond worth one hundred thousand dollars. ††Another Talmudic tale is of a wealthy Jew, who bought a fish, containing a wonderful diamond. This had been the property of a neighbor, who had sewed it into the rim of his turban, to keep it, as it had been predicted that all his property would become Joseph's. He had dropped the turban into the sea, and the fish swallowed the gem.

⁂Polycrates, being too fortunate, was advised to cast away some valuable thing, and threw his ring into the sea. It was found, some days afterward, inside a fish that came to his table.

* Jones.—Credulities. p. 54.
† Gubernatis.—Zoological-Mythology.
‡ Jones.—Credulities.
§ Al Zamokti.—Brewer's Readers' Hand Book.
‖ Gubernatis.—Zool.-Mythology.
** Lane.—Arabian Nights.
†† Jones.—Credulities. 107.
` Brewer.—Readers' Hand Book. p. 353.

*A bas-relief in the church of St. Maria della Anima, at Rome, commemorates the following occurrence: St. Benno, bishop of Meissen, closed the doors of the cathedral in 1075, against Henry IV., who had been excommunicated, and threw the key into the Elbe. On his return from Rome, he is said to have recovered the key, by directing a fisherman to cast his net, and then cutting open a fish that was caught.

St. Francis Xavier, according to Portuguese authorities, once dropped his crucifix while preaching, during a voyage to India, into the sea, but a lobster bronght it to the surface in his claws, at the saint's earnest request.

† So St. Cadoc is fabled to have lost his manual-book at sea, but it was restored by a salmon.

§ The key of the church door at Norham, on the Tweed, was thrown into the river by a boy, who wished to escape threatened punishment. St. Cuthbert appeared in a vision to the priest, to inquire why vespers had not been said, and, on learning the loss of the key, told the priest to buy the first haul of fish caught in the river the next morning. In the stomach of a large salmon was found the key.

‖ A salmon with a ring in its mouth figures in the arms of the city of Glasgow. A certain woman gave her lover a ring belonging to her husband. The latter stole it, threw it in the river, and required her to find it. She, in her extremity, applied to St. Kentigern. Spottiswoode adds, "Not long after, as the saint walked by the river, he desired a man who was fishing, to bring him the first fish he caught, and from its mouth was taken the lady's ring, which he immediately sent to her."

A mediæval English story is told of a knight, who threw a ring into the sea to avoid a bride, telling her she must find it. A cod-fish caught it, and brought it to the shore. This fish and ring appear in the arms of Rebecca Berry, in St. Dunstan's church, in London (Stepney). John of Horslett is said to have shot with an arrow a fish, that had in its stomach his lady's ring.

In many Bohemian and German stories, rings lost at sea are restored by fish. Du Cange reports a tradition that a certain gem is found in a fish's brain.

* Jones.—Credulities, 106.
† Sikes.—British Goblins and Welsh Folk-lore.
§ Reginald of Durham. Jones.—Credulities, p. 106.
‖ Jones.—Credulities, p. 107.

A newspaper account was given in 1870, of the finding of a ring in a fish's stomach, by a fisherman of St. Johns, Newfoundland, that had been lost in the wreck of the "Anglo-Saxon," in 1861.

Modern mythologists agree that these tales, like the Jonah stories, originated in mythical ideas. * "Out of the cloudy, nocturnal, or wintry ocean, comes forth the sun, the pearl lost in the sea, which the gold or silver fish brings out," says Gubernatis.

There are many legends in folk-lore to account for the peculiar shapes of fish. When the fish assembled to choose a king, the skate delayed, to make himself pretty, and his mouth is now one-sided, from not being chosen king. Several legends are given concerning the flounder's wry mouth:

> " Haddock, cod, turbot and ling,
> Of all the fish, the sea-herring's the king.
> Up started the flouk and said, ' Here am I,'
> And ever since that his mouth stands awry."

A Scotch rhyme gives another legend of its crooked mouth,—

> "Said the trout to the fiuke,
> ' When did your moo crook?
> ' My moo was never even
> Since I came by John's haven.'"

† The sole owes its shape, according to a Russian story, to the fact that the Queen of the Baltic ate one half of it, and threw the other back. Or, says another legend, it was restored to life, after half of it had been eaten, by the angel Gabriel.

‡ A Ranatonga myth asserts that the knob on the head of a certain fish is where Ina, a goddess, stamped on it when it was carrying her. Another fish has a blue mouth, and the sole but one eye, from the same cause, and a fourth fish was made black for upsetting her.

The pilot-fish has been the subject of many legends. It was anciently called *Naucratis* (ship guide), and was thought to guide vessels safely into port, and hence was sacred. Ovid says, " Halieuticon, the pilot-fish, the companion of the vessels, who always follows in the white foam of the tracks that they make along the ocean." It was also fabled to at-

* Zoological Mythology. Vol. II.
† Ralston.—Russian Folk-lore. p. 330.
‡ Gill.—Myths and Songs of the South Pacific, pp. 91-92.

tend on the movements of the shark, and to guard it from
danger, by giving it warning. Oppian says, substituting
the whale for the shark, probably through ignorance of the
difference between them,—

" Bold in the front, the little pilot glides,
    Averts each danger, every motion guides;
    With grateful joy the willing whales attend,
    Observe the leader and revere the friend."

Seamen still think they guide sharks to their food,
but it is only true that they attend them, in order to seize
upon any food that may be rejected.

A far more widely spread legend was current concerning
the echeneis, a fish of the Remora or Sucker family. It
was thought to adhere to the sides or bottoms of ships, im-
peding their progress, and even stopping them.

* Plutarch tells us this tale: "Chaeremomanus, the Trall-
ian, when we were at a very noble fish-dinner, pointing to

ECHENEIS OR SHIP STOPPER.

a little, long, sharp-headed fish, said the echeneis (ship-
stopper) was like that, for he had often seen it as he sailed
in the Sicilian sea, and wondered at its strange force, for it
stopped the ship when under full sail, until one of the seamen perceived it sticking to the outside of the ship, and
took it off."

Athenæus alludes to the same belief. Oppian says,
describing its effects,—

* Morals, Goodwin's Trans., Vol. III.

> " But though the canvas bellies with the blast,
> And boisterous winds bend down the cracking mast,
> The bark stands firmly rooted on the sea
> And all unmov'd, as tower, or towering tree."

* Pliny says, " Why should our fleets and armadas at sea make such turrets on the walls and forecastles, when one little fish is able to arrest and stay, per force, our goodly and tall ships?"

Lucan says this fish stops ships in the middle of the ocean, and Ovid, " There, too, is the little sucking fish, wondrous to behold, a vast obstruction to ships."

† This is alleged as a reason for the delay of Mark Antony's ship in getting into action at ‡ Actium, and this fish is said to have also stopped Caligula's galley at sea.

Poets in times more modern, have alluded to this belief. Du Bartas says,—

> § " The remora, fixing its weak snout
> 'Gainst the moist bottom of the stormy ship,
> Stops it suddenly in midst of the fleet."

> " Tell us, O remora, in what place thou hidest
> The anchor that at one stroke stops the progress
> Of a vessel tossed by all the elements?"

‖ Mayne, an old dramatist thus sings,—

> " No remoras that stop your fleets
> Like sergeants' gallants, in the streets."

And Spenser,—

> ** " All suddenly there clove unto the keel
> A little fish that men call remora,
> Which stopp'd her course, and held her by the heel."

And again,—

> " Strange thing, me seemeth, that so small a thing
> Should able be so great an one to wring."

†† Many superstitions are connected with a little fish, the John Dory. Its name is derived from the French " Jaune Dorée " (yellow gilt). The " dorée " came, say some, from

* Nat. Hist., Vol. XI, p. 41.
† Jones.—Credulities, p. 15.
‡ Mangrin.—Mysteries of the Ocean.
§ Landrin.—Les Monstres Marins p. 61.
‖ "The City Watch," 1699.
** Visions of the World's Vanity, 1591.
†† Jones.—Credulities, p. 52.

adoreé, worshiped, and it is still hung up in places of worship, by modern Greeks. Others say the name is from *Janitore*, doorkeeper, as St. Peter was the keeper of the gates of heaven. It was called Peter's fish, from a legend that in its mouth was found the penny with which the temple tax was paid, and that the spots on either side of its mouth were caused by the apostle's thumb. * In "Metellus his Dialogues" we find these lines,—

> " O superstition's dainty, Peter's fish,
> How cam'st thou here to make so goodly dish?"

Its name in Latin, Deus Faber (God worker), indicates its superior gifts.

The haddock disputes with the John Dory the honor of being the fish indicated in these legends, and its spots are due to the same cause, according to some legends. Others say they were caused by St. Christopher. † A Yorkshire story gives another origin to these spots: " The evil spirit, in one of his pranks, determined to build Filey bridge for the destruction of ships and of sailors, and the annoyance of fishermen. In the progress of this work, he accidentally let his hammer fall into the river, and in his haste to pick it up, grasped a haddock instead, leaving the black marks on it."

Haddock's bones should not be burned, in Scotland. A haddock once said,—

> ‡ " Roast me an' boil me,
>   But dinna burn my behns,
>   Or than I'll be a stranger
>   Aboot yi'r hearth-stanes."

The flounder comes in for its share of legends. In Iceland, it was called " Holy Fish." § In Finland, its white side is said to have been caused by the Virgin Mary's laying her hand on it.

∥ The salmon is held in great veneration by Scotch fishermen. Its tail is pointed, since Loki became a salmon, and was caught by that appendage while slipping through a net set for him by the gods. A Finnish legend says its spots are balls of fire, which fell from heaven and were rashly swallowed. It is also the fish of Wisdom.

* Jones.—Credulities.
† Hone.—Table Book, Vol. II, p. 637.
‡ Brand.—Pop. Antiq. III, p. 362.
§ Finnish Folk-lore, in Notes and Queries, December 15, 1863.
∥ Blind.--Contemporary Review, August, 1863.

* Fionn, a Celtic hero, was cooking one, when he dropped a spark from it on his finger, and burned it. He hastily clapped the finger into his mouth, and found that he had acquired the gift of knowledge.

There are other similar stories in folk-legend. The pike is also an important fish in legends. Monstrous and powerful pikes appear in † Finnish, Russian, and Lithuanian stories. In the legends of the latter people, one rules in a lake, and causes storms and wrecks boats.

The herring is, in many countries, the first fish eaten on Easter day. At Oxford, England, it formerly graced the center of the table, surmounted by a corn salad. ‡ Simrock says that you must eat herring or mullet on New Year's day in Markland, or herring-salad in Wittemberg, to have gold all year round. In Limburg, on New Year's day, a herring was formerly hung at the church door, and men tried to jump up and bite it, with their hands tied down.

§ Indians on the Northern lakes said white-fish were the embodiments of a maiden, drowned in the lake.

The bream was called choke-children, in Cornish. ‖ St. Levan caught two on one hook, three times in succession, after throwing them back into the water, and finally took them home to his sister, but they choked her children. This tradition is perpetuated by a carving in the Saints' Church. ** In Hungary, it is said to attack men voraciously.

The perch is a favorite fish, in Russian legend. The hero, in one tale, is afraid of nothing, until a perch jumps into his boat, when he drowns himself. The †† *Jorsh*, or little perch, triumphs over many fish, in these legends. He gets the pike drunk, evades punishment, etc.

Plutarch says, "In Gaul is a fish, the clupea, which is white when the moon increases, black when it wanes."

‡‡ Ælian says the alopex swallows the hook, and then vomits it up, with its own intestines, and Oppian says the trugon kills men with a dart. §§ The gold-fish were formerly supposed to live on gold.

* Jones.—Credulities.
† Gubernatis.—Zoological Mythology, Vol. II.
‡ Deutsche Mythologie, p. 56.
§ Schoolcraft.—Algic Researches, p. 190.
‖ Jones.—Credulities, p. 49.
** Gubernatis.—Zoological Mythology, Vol. II, p. 344.
†† Gubernatis.—Zoological Mythology, Vol. II, p. 346.
‡‡ Gubernatis.—Zoological Mythology, Vol. II, p. 344.
§§ Conway.—Demonology, Vol. I, p. 223.

Kircher says flying-fish were fabled to come out of the sea in summer, and become birds.

Eels are the subject of many legends.   New Zealanders say they were once dwellers upon earth.   It is a phallical animal.   Fishermen of Folkestone formerly said, when they found conger-eels frozen on the snow, that they came out to look at the moon.   Others say they are blinded by the snow.

In the imaginary land of Cocaigne,* the beams of the house are made of sturgeons, and the house is wholly built of fish,—

> " With dabs, with salmon, and with shad
>   The houses round are fenc'd,
>   Whose beams of sturgeons firm are made."

According to another romantic legend, Carnival and Carême had a battle, and all the fish and sea-animals assisted the latter.   He was thus attended and accoutred,—

> "All, from the matchless whale's unwieldy form
>   To the brook fry that in the shallows swarm,
>   Fir'd at the summons, join, a vengeful host,
>   And quit th' unpeopled waters for the coast,
>   Armed cap-a-pie, on signal vengeance bent,
>   On a short mullet rides imperial Lent.
>   His shield a cheese, a trenchant sole his blade,
>   His prick-spear of well-temper'd fish-bone made,
>   A ray's sharp hide, his armor'd corse adorns,
>   With tubercules all rough and hornèd thorns."

* Ellis.—Early English Poets, p. 88.

CHAPTER VII.

STORIES OF OTHER ANIMALS.

" The barnacles with them, which wheresoe'er they breed,
  On trees or rotten ships,—yet to my fens for feed
  Continually do come, and chief abode do make,
  And very hardly forc'd my plenty to forsake "

Drayton.—Polyolbion.

HE other animals of the sea were not forgotten in legend, and there were many superstitions connected with the animals of the land, not hitherto recited.

The Argonaut, or Pompylia, was fabled to rise to the surface, raise its tentacles for masts, spread membrances on them for sails, and use oars to propel itself along. * Pliny says it was favorable to men at sea, " Oh fish, justly dear to Navigators! Thy presence assures winds soft and friendly! thou bringest the calm and thou art the sign of it! "

† Schmidt also says the sight of a Portuguese Man-of-War announces a calm. Sailors generally believe that it floats on the surface of the sea.

Scotch peasants believed formerly that sea-crabs danced at the witches' sabbats. Some Russians will not eat them, as they say they were made by the devil.

The turtle is the subject of various myths. Vishnu was a tortoise. Many peoples believed that a tortoise supported the earth. ‡ Chelone was transformed into a turtle (Chelona), for laughing at Jupiter and Juno.

* Natural History, Bk. XI, c. 47.
† Seeman's Sagen und Schiffer Märchen.
‡ Ovid.—Metamorphoses.

Maui, the Polynesian hero, was carried to the sea by a jelly-fish.

* Moore says,—

> " Like the first air of morning creeping
> Into thin wreathing Red-sea shells,
> Where love himself of old lay sleeping."

† Wilsford explains, " This idea was not unknown to the Greeks, who represented the youngest Nerites, one of the Cupids, as living in shells, on the shore of the Red sea."

A Fiji god was a shell-fish, called *Uva*. Greenlanders have tales of enormous shell-fish. ‡ Carreri, a traveler in the Phillippines, in 1696, says rings and chaplets made of certain shells are an antidote to poison, becoming shattered in its very presence.

§ In an old work, it is said that certain shells (*voluta musica*) found at Curaçoa, are filled with musical notes, so that they may be used in singing. Moore refers to this superstition in his ode to a sea-shell, which falls from a siren's bosom.

‖ Scollop shells are said in another old work to be engendered solely by the dews of the air. This was anciently affirmed of the oyster. Pliny says the pearl oyster feeds on dew, which the sun ripens into pearls. Another old author says, " These mussels, early in the morning, when the sky is clear and temperate, open their mouths a little above the water, and most greedily swallow the dews of heaven, and after the measure and quantity of the dew which they swallow they conceive and breed the pearl."

** Pliny's words are, " The pearl is produced by the dews of heaven falling into the open shells at the breeding time; the quality of the pearl varies according to the amount of dew imbibed, being lustrous if that were pure, and dull, if it were foul. Cloudy weather spoils its color, lightning stopped the growth, and thunder made the shell-fish unproductive, and to eject the hollow husks called bubbles." He also says they have a king who aids them to escape the divers, but if he is caught, they are easily entrapped.

†† It is still believed in parts of the East that these pearls

* Lalla Rookh.
+ Nature's Secrets.
‡ Landrin.—Les Monstres Marins, p. 40.
§ Histoire Naturelle des Antilles. Notes to Moore.
‖ Gmelin.—Display of Heraldry. Brewer's Reader's Hand Book.
** Natural History, Bk. XI, c. 54.
†† Jones.—Broad, Broad Ocean, p. 151.

are drops of rain swallowed by the oyster.   An Oriental poet, quoted by Jones, * says, " Every year, on the sixteenth of the month Nisan, the pearl oysters rise to the sea and open their shells, in order to receive the rain which falls at that time, and the drops thus caught become pearls."

Shakespeare was well acquainted with the superstition. In Richard III. (Act IV, scene 4), he says,—

> "The liquid drops of tears that you have shed
> Shall come again, transform'd to orient pearl."

Moore alludes to it also:†

> "And precious the tear as that rain from the sky
> Which turns into pearls as it falls in the sea."

‡Da Gama's sailors reported that oysters at the Cape of Good Hope grew on trees.   This was un old superstition. §A sailor who visited the island of Yezo in 1645, reported that great quantities of oysters were found on the coast which were, for the most part, one and a-half ells in length.

In the reports of the voyage of Nearchus, it was said that they were found, a foot in length.

‖Pliny says of another mollusk, " The sea-pen (pinna) flourishes in muddy bottoms, and is never found without its companion, called by some pinnatheres, and by others pin-nophylax.   It is a little sea-leek, a sort of crab, and to nourish themselves is the object of their union.   The shell-fish, blind, opens, showing its body to the little fish which play around it.   Emboldened by impunity, they fill the shell. At this moment the crab, which is on the watch, warns the sea-pen by a little bite; it closes, crushing everything found between its valves, and divides its prey with its companion."

Olaus Wormsius says (1865) that the Medusæ are the seed or spawn of the Kraken, in the existence of which beast he devoutly believes.

An old adage says, " Whoever eats oysters on St. James' Day (August 5th), will never want."

But far more wonderful legends were related concerning the barnacle.   **Sinbad is the first to chronicle this belief. "And I saw a bird that cometh forth from a sea-shell, and

* History and Mystery of Precious Stones, p. 116.
† Lâllâ Rookh.
‡ Goodrich.—Man upon the Sea, p. 255.
§ Landrin.—Les Monstres Marins, p. 12.
‖ Natural History, Bk. IX, c. 67.
** Lane's Arabian Nights.

layeth its eggs, and hatcheth them upon the surface of the water, and never cometh forth from the sea, upon the face of the earth." Although Lane thinks the Nautilus is meant, we shall see that this resembles the stories afterward told of the barnacle.

* Boëce, a Scotch author, makes an early allusion to it. "Some men believe that thir (these) claiks (fowls) grow on trees by the nebbis (bills)." †Holinshead, writing some forty years later says he saw the feathers "hang out of the shell at least two inches."

‡The old chronicler, Giraldus, asks, "Who can marvel that this should be so? When our first parents were made of mud, how can we be surprised that a bird should be born of a tree?" The first complete account we have of this marvel is from Gerard: §"There is a small island in Lancashire, called the Pile of Foulden, wherein are found to be broken pieces of old and bruised ships, some whereof have been cast thither by shipwrackes, and also of the trunks and bodies, with the branches, of old rotten trees, cast there likewise; whereon is found a certain spume or froth, that in time breadeth into certain shells, in shape like those of a muskle, but sharper pointed, and of a whitish colour; one end whereof is fastened to the inside of the shell, even as the fish of oysters and muskles are; the other end is made fast unto the belly of a rude masse or lumpe, which in time cometh unto the shape and form of a bird. When it is perfectly formed, the shell gapeth open, and the first thing that appeareth is the aforesaid lace or string; next comes the legs of a bird hanging out, and as it groweth greater, it openeth the shell by degrees, till at length it is all come forth, and hangeth only by the bill; in a short time after, it cometh to full maturity, and falleth into the sea, when it gathereth feathers, and groweth to a fowle bigger than a mallard, and less than a goose, having black legs and bill, or beak, and feathers black and white, spotted in such a manner as is our magpies, called in some places a pilannet; which the people of Lancashire call by no other name than a tree-goose, which place and all those parts adjoining, do so much abound therewith, that one of the best may be bought for three-pence."

* Cosmographie of Albioun (1541).
† Chronicles of Englande, Scotlande and Irelande (1586).
‡ Giraldus.—In Jones' Credulities, p. 77.
§ Herbal (1597).—Jones' Credulities, p. 18.

*Scaliger says: "There was brought to Francis I., a shell, not very large, in which was a little bird entirely formed. He hung to the shell by the end of his bill and his feet." The Abbé Valmont, Francis' confessor, thought these birds deposited their eggs on the surface of the water, where they were hatched, and then they clung to the wood.

†Du Bartas, who records so many nautical superstitions of the age, thus writes:

> "So, sly Bootes, underneath him sees
> In y cycles, those goslings hatcht of trees,
> Whose fruitful leaves, falling into the water,
> Are turned (they say) to living fowles soon after.
> So rotten sides of broken ships do change
> To barnacles. Oh! transformation strange,
> 'Twas first a greene tree, then a gallant hull,
> Lately a mushroom, now a flying gull."

Cardan and Munster tell of these goose-trees and shell-birds, and a certain Count Mayer wrote a whole volume concerning them, which he named "Volucris Arborea," and in which he goes so far as to tell the food of the shell. Albertus Magnus, Æneas Sylvius, and Roger Bacon had long before this contested these superstitions, but Aldrovandus gave graphic representations of the goose-tree.

Another old author says, when the leaves of the tree fall in the water, they become fish, but when on land, a bird.

Barentz, the Dutch navigator, again refuted the notion in 1594-6. But people were still credulous. Marston, in the Malcontent (1604), says:

> "Like your Scotch barnacle, now a block,
> Instantly a worm, and presently a great goose."

And Hall,—

> ‡ "That Scottis barnacle, if I might choose,
> That of a worm doth wax a wingèd goose."

§Baptista Porta tells us: "Late writers report that not only in Scotland, but also in the River of Thames, near London, there is a kind of a shell-fish, in a two-leaved shell, that hath a foot full of plaits and wrinkles. They commouly stick to the keel of some old ship. Some say they come of worms; some, of the boughs of trees, which fall

* Landrin, p. 134.
† Divine Weeks and Works.
‡ Virgedemarium, Lib. IV, Sat. 2.
§ Natural Magic.

into the sea; if any of them be cast upon shore, they die, but they which are swallowed still into the sea live, and get out of their shell, and grow to be a duck or such like bird."

Shakspeare alludes to this belief, in "The Tempest" (iv-1), where Caliban says,—

> "We shall lose our time,
> And all be turn'd to barnacles."

Another old writer, quoted in the London *Athenæum*, tells us: "Fowles, lyke to wylde ghees, whiche growen wonderly upon trees, as it were nature wrought agayne kynde. Men of religion ete bernacles on fastynge dayes, bycause they ben not engendered of flesche, wherein, as we thinketh, they are."

An anonymous writer, quoted in a work cited by Landrin, says: *"Near Pomonic, in Scotland, on the seashore, gather and breed certain birds called crabans or cravans, which birds are not hatched, nor have feathers, nor moult, but arise, grow, and are engendered by the rotting and decay of old timber, masts, and oars from ships, which rot in the sea, and breed them thus. When this old wrack of ships falls in the sea, it is rotted and corrupted by the salts of the sea, and from this decay breeds birds, hanging by the beaks to the wood; and when they are all covered with plumage, and are large and fat, then they fall .into the sea; and then God, in his grace, restores them to their natural life."

To prove the truth of these assertions, an old author published a book, in which he compares this miracle to the immaculate conception. † Scribonius, Torquemada, and Parthenopex allude to the superstition.

‡ Butler sarcastically speaks of those

> "Who, from the most refined of saints,
> As naturally grow miscreants
> As barnacles turned Soland geese
> In the islands of the Orcades."

Southey defines the word "Barnacle:—A bird breeding on old ships' bottoms."

§ Sir Robert Moray, in a scientific paper, in 1678, writes:

* Les Monstres Marins, p. 130.
† Landrin.—Les Monstres Marins, 131.
‡ Hudibras (1663).
§ Transactions of the Royal Society.

"In every shell that I opened, I found a perfect sea-fowl; the little bill, like that of a goose, the eyes marked, the head, neck, breast, wings, and feet formed; the feathers everywhere perfectly shaped and blackish-colored, and the feet like those of a water-fowl."

*Another old writer says: "There is the bird engendered by the sea, out of timber by long lying in the sea. Some call these birds clakes, and soland geese, and puffins; others, barnacles; we call them *girrinn*."

Turner, an English naturalist, thus wrote: "When, at a certain time, an old ship, a plank, or a pine mast rots in the sea, something like fungus at first breaks out therefrom, which at length puts on the manifest form of birds." He also gives the testimony of a Scotch physician, Octavianus: "This clergyman then professed himself ready to take his oath upon the gospels, that what Gyraldus had related of the generation of these birds was most true, for he himself had seen with his eyes, and also handled, these half-formed birds."

So late as 1801, there was exhibited in London the "Wonderful Goose-tree, or Barnacle-tree, a tree bearing geese, taken out of the water."

Notwithstanding this mass of testimony, it is well known that the resemblance of the barnacle to a bird is very slight indeed, and, if closely observed, would fail to give rise to such beliefs. Whence then did they originate? Imperfect observation doubtless strengthened the notion, but could hardly have given it birth. Dr. Brewer is perhaps right in attributing the whole superstition to a linguistic error. The bird meant, in the greater part of these accounts, is the soland goose, although the writer in Duret says it is the Black Diver. This bird is in Latin *bernacula*, while *pernacula* means a small limpet. From these to the French bernacle, Portuguese bernaca, and finally to the Scotch *bren-clake*, the name of this goose, is not an unlikely transition.

Superstitions concerning birds, both of the sea and of the land, have been numerous. Many of these have been recounted. Divination by the flight of birds was a favorite method in antiquity. Sailors and nautical men, particularly, watched sea and land birds for indications of prosperous voyages and favoring winds. †As Aristophanes says:

* R. Flaherty.—Description of West Connaught (1684).
†Aves, I, 557.

> " From birds in sailing, men instruction take,
> Now lie in port, now sail, and profit make."

As they were imagined to fly through the air to heaven, they easily became messengers or diviners of the will of the gods. Du Cange says the custom was continued to the middle ages, and a Tuscan author says the peasants still augur the coming weather by the song of the birds. Their sensitiveness to atmospherical changes makes them good barometers. We have seen them prominent as storm makers and calm bringers, but there are other superstitions connected with them.

* The kingfisher boded good or evil, as its cry was to the right or left, said negroes of West Africa.

† In Oxfordshire, England, fishermen say that a kingfisher, suspended to the mast by its beak, will swing its breast in the direction of a coming wind. So Shakspeare, in " King Lear,"—

> " Disown, affirm, and turn their halcyon beaks
> With every gale and vary of their masters."

‡ Dyer says it is still seen suspended in cabins on the sea shore, and Collin de Plancy says this is still a belief in France. §Stover writes in 1599,—

> " Or as a halcyon with her turning breast
> Demonstrates wind from wind, and east from west."

And Marlow, in the " Jew of Malta" (1633),—

> " But how now stands the wind?
> Into what corner peers my halcyon's bill?"

‖ Sir Thomas Browne, in " Vulgar Errors," remarks, "That a kingfisher hanged by the bill sheweth what quarter the wind is by an occult and secret property, converting the breast to that part of the horizon from whence the wind doth blow. This is a received opinion, and very strange, introducing natural weather-cocks and extending magnetical positions as far as animal natures—a conceit supported chiefly by present practice, yet not made out by reason nor experience."

Kircher says the sea-swallow and the orbis hung up by

* Burton.—Wit and Wisdom from West Africa.
† Jones.—Credulities, p. 8.
‡ English Folk-lore.
§ Life and Death of Sir Thomas Wolsey, Cardinal.
‖ Book III, Chapter 10.

the back will point the bill to the wind. He says the custom arose from hanging these birds up, expecting that they would renew their feathers, as if alive.

* The kingfisher was formerly kept in chests to keep off moths.

† Moore's lines,—

> "And weary as that bird of Thrace
> Whose pinions know no resting place,"

refer to the kingfisher. ‡ A traveler at Constantinople says immense numbers of aquatic birds appeared on the shores of the Black sea, and were deemed a bad omen, being the souls of certain persons in purgatory, "Ames Damnées."

§ Cheever alludes to this: "If the spirits of those whom Moslem jealousy have murdered and sunk in the Bosphorus, still float the stream in the form of complaining birds, which never rest," etc.

The Fish-hawk and the Gurnet were esteemed bringers of good luck to English fishermen. Wilson says:

> "God bless the Fish-hawk and the Fisher."

|So with the tern, among northern fishermen,

> "Let nimble tern, and screaming gull
> Fly round and round, our net is full."

And the Osprey, on our own coast,—

> "The Osprey sails above the sound,
>   The Geese are gone, the gulls are flying,
> The herring-shoals swarm thick around,
>   The nets are launched, the boats are plying."

This bird was also able to fascinate the fish, and Shakspeare is supposed to allude to this in Coriolanus, Act IV, scene 7. ** While Drayton says,—

> "The Osprey, oft here seen, though seldom here it breeds,
> Which over them the fish no sooner do espy,
> But betwixt him and them by an antipathy,
> Turning their bellies up, as though their death they saw,
> They at his pleasure lie, to stuff his gluttonous maw."

* Sir Thomas Browne.—Vulgar Errors.
† Lalla Rookh.
‡ De Mormay.—Constantinople Ancient and Modern, Vol. I, p. 137.
§ Cheever.—Sea and Shore (1827).
| Jones.—Credulities, p. 9.
** Polyolbion, XXV.

There was an old superstition that gulls were never seen bleeding:

> "The stricken sea-mew dives that none may see her bleed."

During the middle ages, shooting stars were supposed to be the half digested food of winter gulls.

On the Croisic coast of Brittany, women go to the sea-shore, dressed in their finest apparel, and, strewing the waves with flowers, say to the gulls:

"Göelans, Göelans, bring us back our children and our husbands, from the sea."

*Pennant says: "The great auk is a bird observed by seamen never to wander beyond soundings; and, according to its appearance, they direct their measures, being then assured that land is not very remote."

The tropic-bird was reverenced by Fijians. Ellis says that, on one occasion, one of these birds perched on the mast of a boat, when all the natives fell down and worshiped it.

The ancients believed that the petrel hatched its eggs under its wings, and never rested. The albatross is believed by sailors to sleep on the wing. The eider-duck is sacred to St. Cuthbert, and is not eaten in many parts of England. †A sea-bird called the lavy was thought to indicate the weather by its motions, and was watched by Hebrides islanders for that reason.

‡Chinese junks frequently carry at their sterns a broad and high board, having on it a representation of a bird, which they call *Foong*, a sort of phœnix. It stands on a rock in a stormy sea, and is regarded as an emblem of speed and safety, materially aiding the ship in her progress.

In Scotch legend, the water-spirit comes as a bird, the § Boobrie. The daughters of Lir, a Celtic Neptune, were traditionally turned into sea-birds.

> "And we live in the water forever,
> By tempests driven from shore to shore."

So also Alcyon and Ceyx, and the Meleagrides were turned into sea-birds. Amber was said to be a concretion of the tears of the latter.

*Zoology.
†Smyth.—Sailors' Word Book.
‡Jones.—Credulities, 47.
§Campbell.—Stories of W. Highlands.

BRÉTON WOMEN STREWING THE SEA WITH FLOWERS.

"Around thee shall glisten the loveliest amber
That ever the sorrowing sea-birds have wept."

*The Ahts of Nootka Sound say the loon gets its plaint-
ive cry from its being the soul of a young man, whose
tongue was cut out by a mischievous fiend, so that he could
only utter such a cry.

We must not forget the Rukh or Roc, which, in Sindbad's
third voyage, crushes ships with stones. El Wardee relates
similar stories.

Land-birds have also been the subjects of many superstitious ideas. †Swallows were, in antiquity, thought unlucky at sea, although they are lucky on shore. Cleopatra
abandoned a voyage, on seeing a swallow at the masthead
of her vessel. Mancinus, a Roman consul, presaged defeat
from one of these alighting on the antenna of his galley;
and a similar omen led soothsayers to predict the speedy
death of Mark Antony.

‡Shakspeare alludes to the superstition:

" Swallows have built
In Cleopatra's sails their nests; the augurers
Say, they know not—they cannot tell; look grimly,
And dare not speak their knowledge."

It was at one time thought that these birds, in their
migrations, passed under the waters in the shape of an
animated ball. §Olaus Magnus says they fall down into
lakes and pools during winter, and are sometimes fished
out by fishermen, in the form of lumps or clods of a soft,
sloughing substance.

‖The Roman general, Fabian, regarded it as a favorable
omen that a *Buteo*, or kite, perched on the mast of his
galley.

**Pliny says crows were used as guides by navigators, as
they were carried out to sea by the inhabitants of Tapro-
bane, and then let loose, to indicate the direction of the
land by their flight. Norsemen used them for this purpose. Flock, in his voyage from Shetland to Iceland, is
said to have let them fly when at sea.

The crow and the raven are proverbially birds of ill-

* Bancroft.—Native Races, III, p. 97.
† See Chapter XIII.
‡ Antony and Cleopatra, IV, 12.
§ History of the Goths.
** Jones.—Credulities.
†† Natural History, VI, 24.

omen. Cicero regarded it as such that a raven perched on the ship that bore him across the sea.

*An old Scotch ballad illustrates this belief. The crow speaks:

> "As I sat on the deep sea-sand,
> I saw a fair ship right at hand;
> I waved my wings, I beat my beak,
> The ship sank—and I heard a shriek."

†In China, when crows perch on the mast, crumbs of bread are thrown to them, to gain favorable winds. This is illustrated by a tale in Giles' collection, where a man is changed into a crow, and is sustained by being fed, to insure good winds.

‡Another old ballad shows the raven's bad character:

> " 'Ah! well-a-day,' the sailor said,
> 'Some danger doth impend;
> Three ravens sit in yonder glade,
> And evil will happen, I'm sore afraid,
> Ere we reach our journey's end.'
>
> 'And what have the ravens with us to do?
> Does their sight betoken us evil?'
> 'To see one raven's lucky, 'tis true,
> But it's certain misfortune to light upon two,
> And meeting with three is the devil.' "

§ Archdeacon Gray says sailors on the Yangtze, in China, feared disastrous consequences in case the ravens were troubled, passengers having threatened to shoot them.

The magpie shared this evil reputation with these two birds. Sir Walter Scott relates a story of traveling in a stagecoach with a seaman, who, seeing a magpie, said, "I wish we may have good luck on our journey; there is a magpie." Upon inquiring, he further said: "All the world agree that one magpie bodes ill-luck, two are not bad, but three are the very devil itself. I never saw three magpies but twice, and once I nearly lost my vessel, and afterwards I fell off my horse and was hurt." Bourne says that three magpies augur a successful voyage.

The wren was long a sacred bird in England. |A Yorkshire couplet runs thus:

> " He that hurts a robin or a wren,
> Will never prosper, sea nor land."

* The Twa Corbies.
† Tales by Sung Ping Ling.—Giles' Translation.
‡ C. G. Lewis.—"Bill Jones," in Jones' Credulities, p. 10.
§ Jones.—Credulities, 47.
| Folk-lore Record.

* On the Isle of Man, it was formerly a custom to hunt the wren on a certain day. Feathers acquired at this time were treasured up as charms against shipwreck. McTaggart, a local author, says: "Manx fishermen dare not go to sea without one of these birds, taken dead with them, for fear of disaster and storm. Their tradition is of a sea-spirit, that haunted the herring-track, attended always by storms, and at last assumed the figure of a wren, and flew away, so that they think that when they have a dead wren with them, all is snug."

† We are told in an old work: "When there are great storms upon the coasts of Lybia Deserta, the sea casts up great tunnies on the shore, and these breed worms for fourteen days, and grow to be as big as flies, then as locusts, which, being augmented in bigness, *become birds called quails.*"

A small land-bird came aboard the Vanguard, Nelson's flag-ship, at the battle of the Nile, and was deemed a promise of victory, and a happy omen. ‡ Miss Knight says she saw it hopping about, petted and well-cared for.

A notable instance of the belief in bird-omens is seen in the following story by Captain Johnson, of the Norwegian bark Ellen, who, in 1857, picked up forty-nine of the wrecked crew of the steamer Central America. § "Just before six o'clock in the afternoon of September 12, I was standing on the quarter-deck. Suddenly a bird flew around me, first grazing my right shoulder. It soon flew at my face, when I caught hold of it, and made it a prisoner. The bird was unlike any bird I ever saw, nor do I know its name. As it strove to bite everybody, I had its head afterward cut off, and the body thrown overboard. When the bird flew to the ship, the bark was going a little north of northeast. *I regarded the appearance of the bird as an omen,* and an indication to me that I must change my course. I accordingly headed to the eastward direct. I should not have deviated from my course, had not the bird visited the ship, and, had it not been for this change of course, I should not have fallen in with the forty-nine passengers, whom I fortunately saved from certain death."

The dove was long a bird of good omen at sea. Among Roman sailors, it was the custom to let one fly after the

* Dyer.—English Folk-lore.
† Magick of Kirwan, King of Persia, and of Harpocratian (1685).
‡ Autobiography, in Jones' Credulities, 14.
§ Jones.—Credulities, 12-13.

CAPTAIN JOHNSON ATTACKED BY A BIRD.

sacrifice, when the ship was leaving port, as its "homing *
was deemed a certain omen of a speedy voyage. Cortez's
sailors in 1590, augured well of its appearance. The account says: "Their victuals waxed skant, and their fresh
water wanted, so that they prepared themselves to die.
Some cursyed their fortune, others asked mercie at God's
hand, looking for death, and to be eaten of the Carives.
And in this time of tribulation came a dove flying to the
shippe, being on Good Friday at sunsett; and sat him on
the shippe top—whereat they were all comforted and took
it for a miracle, and good token, and some wept with joy;
some said that God had sent the dove to comfort them;
others said that land was neare, and all gave beartie thanks
to God, directing their course the way the dove flew."

* In the legends of Queen Radegonde, she comes in the
shape of a dove, to rescue sailors from wreck In an Italian
folk-lore story, a dove perches on the crosstrees of a ship,
and is received as a favorable omen. A dove, we remember,
guided the Argonauts through the Symplegades, and another
bore good tidings of land to Noah. Vellerus Paterculus
says a dove guided Greek colonists to Cumae. Thus it anciently came to be a mariner's bird. That fanciful mythologist, Bryant, thinks the dove typifies the ark (as do a hundred other things to him), and its name Jonah, is the same
as Jonah, and also as the *Yoni*, the mother of all. It has
always been a bird of mystery—the incarnation of the Holy
Ghost, and the sign of immortality to the christian.

Four-footed animals and insects are also connected with
superstitious beliefs among sailors.† Many things have already been said about the cat, the wickedest animal in folk-
lore. It was not only a storm-bringer, but could bring good
or evil luck.

‡ Rockwell tell us: "Two men fell from the mast head
(of a naval vessel) and were killed. The crew, finding that
one of their number had killed a cat, regarded him as the
bringer of misfortune, and he had to be flogged and finally
set on shore to appease them." We have given some reasons for the cat's unpopularity at sea. §Karl Blind says much
of it, in connection with Shetland Folk-lore. We know from
Egyptian sculptures that the cat anciently represented the
sun and the moon, its glowing eye figuring them. So

* Gubernatis.—Zoological Mythology, Vol. II, p. 303.
† See Chapters II, III and XIII.
‡ Sketches of Foreign Travels, 1842.
§ Contemporary Review, September 1882.

* " When lo! a bright cerulean form appears,
  The fair Eidothea, to dispel my fears;
  Proteus her sire divine."

And so to Ulysses, when shipwrecked, Leucothea came, bringing a life-saving veil, that enabled him to reach the shore,—

† " Swift as a sea-mew springing from the flood,
  All radiant on the raft, the goddess stood."

Menelaus, in Euripides' " Orestes," is made to say,—

" for from the waves
The sailors' prophet, Glaucus, who unfolds," etc.

And Apollonius, in the " Argonauts," says he was the comforting apparition seen by sailors in distress.

In the "Æneid," Somnus appears in the guise of Phordas, and gains possession of the helm, by casting Palinurus overboard.

Apparitions of the Virgin and saints on shipboard are recorded in numerous Middle Age legends. ‡ In the eleventh century, an angel appeared to Æthelsige in a storm, and enjoined him to keep the Feast of the Conception. On his promising to do so, the storm ceased.

A crusading fleet set sail from Dartmouth, in 1190, to carry the troops of Richard I. from Marseilles to the Holy Land. One of them had a visit from St. Thomas of Canterbury, St. Edmund, and St. Nicholas, during a storm.

A twelfth century legend of Marseilles § chronicles the appearance of Notre Dame de la Garde upon the summit of a rock in the harbor, to aid a fisherman whose boat was in peril, and the same luminous apparition is said to have been seen by others. At one time, she saved a storm-beaten ship, by taking the helm in her own hands.

‖ In 1226, the Virgin is said to have appeared to Lord Salisbury at sea, in a storm, shielding a light. On his vowing a taper to her shrine, the gale abated.

Saint Cuthbert appeared to the crew who were carrying his body away. ** " And also the same shippe that they were in, by the grete storme and strong raging of the sea, as is aforesaid, was turned on one syde, and the booke of the

* Pope.—Homer's Odyssey, Bk. IV.
† Pope.—Odyssey, Bk. V.
‡ Jones.—Credulities of All Ages. Ch. 1.
§ Collin de Plancy.—Legendes Pieuses du Moyen Age.
‖ Jones. —Credulities. Ch. 1.
** Chronicles of the Monastery of Durham.

Holic Evangeliste fell out of the shyppe into the bottom of the sea. The which booke, being all adorned with guild and presious stones of the outsyde, and they being all troubled with great sorrow for the losse of the said booke, one Hunredin, being admonished and commanded by the vision of Sancte Cuthbert to seeke the booke that was lost in the sea, iij (3) miles and more from the land, and as they were so admonishede, they found the booke much more beautiful than before."

We have already related the legend concerning the appearance of Jakushai Niurai, a Japanese saint, to a devoted priest on board a storm-beaten junk, and further instances of apparitions of saints are given in the chapter devoted to them.

* Archbishop Bruno, of Wurtzburg, saw a spectral visitant, while at sea with Henry III., which announced itself as his evil genius, and he died shortly afterward.

† The crew of a French crigantine at Zante, averred they saw the figure of a horned and monstrous seaman plunge into the water with one of the crew, who had defied the Virgin by playing dice.

In Norse legend, Thor appeared to King Olaf Tryggvason in the guise of a red-bearded man, boarded his ship, laughed and joked with the crew, and finally jumped overboard.

We find among early navigators, an almost universal belief in a spectre at the Cape of Good Hope.

The spectre appears thus in the immortal song of the Lusian bard,—

> ‡ " Robust and vigorous in the air appear'd,
> Enormous and of stature very tall,
> The visage grim, and with squalid beard,
> The eyes were hollow, and the gestures all
> Threatening and bad, the color pale and sear'd."

He threatens ships with destruction.

> "The next proud fleet that think my drear domain
> With daring hand t'invade, and hoist the streaming vane,
> That gallant navy, by my whirlwinds toss'd,
> And varying seas, shall perish on my coast."

Thus this cape, the place of the punishment of the spectre captain, is also that of Adamastor, the cape spectre,

* Grant.—Mysteries of all Nations. 298.
† See Chap. II.
‡ Camoens.—Lusiad. Canto V.

and to this day, the mariner, beating about its windy headlands, sees, spread over its flat tops, the "Devil's Tablecloth," cloudy premonitor of coming tempest and possible wreck.

Around it and the opposite cape have for years clustered the legends of sailors, and many still refer to wonderful experiences in "coming round the capes."

There were other spectres that terrified the mariner. *Scot says: "Innumerable are the reports of accidents unto such as frequent the seas, as fishermen and sailors, who discourse of noises, flashes, shadows, echoes, and other things, nightly seen or heard upon the waters."

Ghosts are encountered at sea. †We read in an old work: "I look upon sailors to care as little of what becomes of themselves as any people under the sun; yet no people are so much terrified at the thought of an apparition. Their sea-songs are full of them; they firmly believe in their existence, and honest Jack Tar shall be more frightened at the glimmering of the moon upon the tackling of a ship, than he would be if a Frenchman were to place a blunderbuss at his head."

The same work tells us a tale of a ship's crew that had not only *seen*, but *smelled* a ghost. A few judicious lashes dispelled the belief, but the smell proceeded from a dead rat, found in the place indicated as a haunt of the ghost.

‡An anecdote is related, in Moore's life of Byron, of a Captain Kidd. He told Byron that the ghost of his brother (then in India) visited him at sea, and lay down in his bunk, leaving the blankets damp with sea-water. He afterward found that his brother was drowned at that exact hour and night.

§We find a nautical ghost as early as the time of Columbus: "The prince would have gone there in person, if it had not been that one of the crew of the galley of the marquis had said, more than a month before, that there appeared to him three times, in a nocturnal vision, a woman dressed in white, who said to him that he should say to the prince that he should take good care of his life, that he should not place his person in danger by sea, above all on St. Michael's day; or, otherwise that he should receive some harm."

* Scot.—Dict. of Witchcraft, 1665, in Jones' Credulities, 7.
† New Catalogue of Vulgar Errors (1751), in Jones' Credulities, 86.
‡ Jones.—Credulities, 87.
§ Memoires de Guillaume de Villeneuve (1496).

*Cotton Mather tells us of a spectre that visited a colonial ship, carrying off, in a ghostly canoe, seven of the crew at a time. He also says: "Many persons, who have died at sea, have been seen, within a day of their death, by friends at home."

Mary Howitt relates a story of a remarkable vision, as seen by Captain Rogers, R. N., who, in 1664, was in command of the "Society," bound from England to Virginia. He was heading in for the capes, and was, as he reckoned, after heaving the lead, three hundred miles from them. A vision appeared to him in the night, telling him to turn out and look about. He did so, found all alert, and retired again. The vision appeared again, and told him to heave the lead. He arose, caused the lead to be cast, and found but *seven* fathoms. Greatly frightened, he tacked ship, and the daylight showed him to be under the capes, instead of two hundred miles at sea.

In Sandys' Ovid (1632), a story is told of an old Bristol quartermaster, who saw the spectres of four Bristol witches playing dice in the cock-pit of his ship, at Gibraltar. They, perceiving him, disappeared, leaving him lame, and the ship was said to have been mysteriously stopped at sea by their power.

†Sir Walter Scott has a story of the captain of an English ship, who was assured by his crew of the nightly visit of the ghost of a murdered sailor. The crew refused to sail, but a close watch resulted in catching a somnambulist. Scott relates another incident of a captain who killed a man in a fit of anger, and, on his threatening to haunt him, cooked his body in the slave kettle. The crew believed that the murdered man took his trick at the wheel and on the yards. The captain, troubled by his conscience and the man's ghost, finally jumped overboard, when, as he sank, he threw up his arms, and exclaimed, "Bill is with me now!"

‡Scott also tells us of a Mrs. Leakey, who was said to have appeared after her death, standing on deck near the mast of her son's ship, raising storms by her incantations, and eventually wrecking the ship.

Glover, in a poem, "Admiral Hosier's Ghost," embodies an old belief concerning the wonderful appearance of the

* Magnalia Christi Americana.
† Scott.—Letters on Demonology and Witchcraft, p. 19.
‡ Notes to Rokeby, 16.

brave old admiral and all his fleet, after the taking of Porto
Bello, in 1740. He had been refused permission to assault
the place, and, when his successor took it,—

> "A sad troop of ghosts appeared,
> All in dreamy hammocks shrouded."

Many West India Keys were formerly supposed to be
the haunts of ghosts of murdered men, and Coffin Key was
especially feared by sailors after sunset. Sir Walter Scott
says the Buccanneers sometimes killed a Spaniard or a slave,
and buried him with their spirits, believing that his ghost
would haunt the spot, and keep away treasure hunters.

> * "Trust not, would his experience say,
> Captain or comrade with your prey,
> But seek some charnel, when at full,
> The moon gilds skeleton and skull,
> There dig, and tomb your precious heap,
> And bid the dead your treasure keep.
> * * * * kill some slave
> Or prisoner on the treasure grave,
> And bid his discontented ghost,
> Stalk nightly on his lonely post."

Caves in the shores of the Caspian were haunted by apparitions, in the belief of mariners of fifty years ago, and
Moore says,—

> † "And such the strange, mysterious din,
> At times throughout those caverns roll'd,
> And such the fearful wonders told,
> Of restless sprites imprison'd there
> That bold were Moslem who would dare,
> At twilight hour, to steer his skiff,
> Beneath the Gheber's lonely cliff."

‡ An old traveler tells us: "There is in this neighborhood
an extraordinary hill, the Kobé Guebr, or the Guebre's
mountain. It is superstitiously held to be the residence of
deaves, or spirits, and many marvelous stories are recounted
of the injury and witchcraft suffered by those who essayed
in former days to ascend or explore it."

§ In Brand's "Antiquities" there is a ludicrous tale of a
sea-ghost. The ship's cook, a lame man, died while at sea,
and was thrown overboard. Some days afterward his ghost

* Rokeby, II, p. 18. See also Canto II, v. 12 and Note 19.
† Lalla Rookh.
‡ Pottinger.—" Beluchistan."
§ Vol. III, p. 86.

was seen, walking on the water, ahead of the ship. On oomi̇g up with it, it proved to be part of a ship's mast, with the top attached, that simulated the lame man's walk by bobbing up and down on the waves.

This nautical ghost is often a malevolent spirit, as in Shelley's " Revolt of Islam,"—

> " The captain stood
> Aloof, and whispering to the pilot, said,
> 'Alas! alas! I fear we are pursued
> By wicked ghosts. A phantom of the dead,
> The night before we sail'd, came to my bed
> In dreams like that.' "

* Marryat relates a sailor story of a murdered man's ghost appearing every night, and calling all hands to witness a piratical scene of murder, formerly committed on board the ship in which he appeared.

† There is an account of the appearance, to an officer of a man-of-war, of his sister's ghost. He became unaccountably insensible, when the spectre touched him with her cold hand. She died the same hour, and on the next cruise he said he saw her again, this time disappearing over the ship's side during a storm. He lost his life shortly after, in the same manner. ‡A similar tale is told of a brother's ghost visiting an officer, at the hour of his death.

§ Symondson tells of the visit of the ghost of a former captain of the ship, at one time, to certain members of the crew, to prescribe a change of course, at another in wet and calm weather, quietly seated in his usual place on the poop-deck.

‖ Cheever says: " The sailor is a profound believer in ghosts. One of these nocturnal visitants was supposed to visit our ship. It was with the utmost difficulty that the crew could be made to turn in at night. You might have seen the most athletic, stout-hearted sailor on board, when called to take his night-watch aloft, glancing at the yards and tackling of the ship for the phantom. It was a long time, in the opinion of the crew, before the phantom left the ship."

Cheever tells of another ghost, returning to warn the

* Pacha of Many Tales.
† Blackwood's Magazine, 1860.
‡ Grant.—Mysteries of all Nations, 604.
§ " Two Years Abaft the Mast."
‖ "Sea and Sailor."

BUCCANEERS OF THE SPANISH MAIN.

men to repent of their sins, and the captain to desist from severe punishments.

* The crew of the ship Pontiac, not many years since, averred that they saw the ghost of a man that had been stabbed by a Greek. On one man's laughing at the notion, he was mysteriously stabbed. The men thereupon deserted the ship, on arriving in port, but the Greek was afterward convicted of both murders.

† Melville tells us of a man who was accidentally burned in his bunk, after having died there. The berth was sealed up, but the superstitious crew would not remain in the forecastle at night, nor sing nor joke while there.

An account of a haunted ship is given in the Nautical Magazine.‡ On the last voyage of the Lord Clive, a number of Lascars had mutinied, and were summarily hanged at the yard arm. Her story became known, and it was difficult to get a crew. Shortly after she sailed, during a night watch, the mate insisted that he heard groans in an empty cabin, and rushed terrified on deck. The crew afterward left the cuddy, likewise reporting a ghost, that of a Malay. Various accidents occurred, and the spectre was often seen in the rigging. Finally, the master saw the ghost on the yard arm, laid in wait for it, and captured a Lascar, who was playing these ghostly tricks, in revenge for the punishment of his comrades.

The spectre of a lady, drowned on the coast, is believed by fishermen to appear on the beach at Lyme, England. § A similar spectre is said to haunt the beach at St. Ives, Cornwall, during storms. It is called "the Lady and the Lantern." She and her child had been saved from wreck, but the child was swept away and drowned, and she is supposed to be hunting for its body. She is dressed in silks, and coins are always found where she has been seen.

‖ Popular tradition asserts that the ghost of a young man lost at sea appeared to his mother in Cornwall, and that of an officer of the navy appeared to his wife. At Morra, in Cornwall, the Lady Sybilla sits on the rocks, looking seaward for wrecks. The apparition of a smuggling crew, dripping wet, was also seen, portending the wreck that followed. A pilot at St. Ives received a ghostly

* Grant.—Mysteries, 584–5.
† White Jacket.
‡ 1871.
§ Bottrell.—Traditions and Fireside Stories of Cornwall.
‖ Hunt.—Romances and Drolls of the West of England.

warning, in the vision of a man, his mouth filled with seaweed, and his shoes with sand.

*In a Cornish legend, the spectre of a privateer captain goes off in a thunder-cloud in a mysterious ship. In the same story, the ghost of a shipwrecked sailor appears. In another tale a similar spectre appears, and carries off his waiting bride. The ghosts of shipwrecked mariners are seen, and their cries heard, from the waves, in a certain bay, on the Cornish coast.

Scotch fishermen and sailors have many stories of these ghosts. The ghost of a murdered lady appears to her lover at sea, in a tale by Gregor,† coming in the shape of a bright light, assuming the human form as it draws nearer. She finally calls him, and he springs into her arms, and disappears, in a flash of fire. In another legend, an officer sees, in a vision, two boatmen bringing in the body of a third. Soon afterward, this actually occurred, the boat in which they were having been capsized. The spectre of a woman, who died on the scaffold, is said to have appeared to her sailor lover, who had promised to be faithful to her, living or dead. It came in a gale, accompanied by a storm-cloud, accompanied by a gigantic figure. The vessel was meanwhile sorely stormbeaten, but was delivered, when these apparitions obtained possession of the sailor. On Solway Firth, the ghost of a murdered lady appears in a blaze of fire.

On a small island, near Windemere, Scotland, called Ledge's Holm, there is a quarry called "The Crier of Claife." An old legend says a ferryman was hailed on a dark night from the island, and went over. He came back, after a long absence, having seen some horrible sights, which he ever after refused to relate, and soon after he became a monk. Afterward the same cry was heard, and the monk went over, and succeeded in laying the ghost in the quarry, where it still is.

There are many stories of Irish banshees, some of which are aquatic ghosts. The Banshee of O'Carrol appears on Lough Dearg, gliding over the surface.

‡In various Danish legends, the ghost of a Strand Varsler, or coast-guard, appears, walking his beat as when alive. It was formerly considered dangerous to pass along

*"The White Witch."—Bottrell.
†Folk-lore of Scotland.
‡Thorpe.—N. Mythology, II, 166.

unconsecrated beaches, believed to be haunted by the spectres of unburied corpses of drowned people, also called
Strand-Varsler. Stories are told of encounters with them
by a peasant, near Sambek, and by a woman, near Niveröd.

THE SAILOR LAD'S GHOST.

*A mediæval East Prussian story is told of Father
Anselm, a Lusenberg monk, who, obtaining strand rights
on the coast, forbade the gathering of amber without the
payment of a heavy tax. It had always been free, but a
decree was obtained that any one caught secretly gathering
it, should be hanged to the nearest tree. In popular

*Bechstein.—Deutsches Märchenbuch.

legend, his spirit cannot rest in its grave, but is often seen, wandering on the beach, and crying, "Oh, my God! free amber!"

*In North German folk-lore, "Gongers" are ghosts of persons drowned at sea, who visit remote kindred, and announce their own death, always appearing at evening twilight, in the clothes in which they were drowned, and again in the night, leaving a track of water on the floor, and wet covers on the bed. In Schleswig, it is said they do not enter the house, but linger about to announce their sad errand, and always tell it to a relative in the third degree.

A young lad was forced to go to sea with his father against his will. He said to his mother, before he went, "As you sit on the shore by the lake, think of me." His ghost appeared to her there soon afterward.

†An island, Hörnum, near Silt, is traditionally peopled by the apparitions of murdered men, robbers, murderers, and ship wrecked sailors.

‡In Schmidt's stories, the ghost of a wronged maiden appears in a ship at sea, on board of which the crew are perishing with thirst. It comes in a cloud, traversing the vessel from boom to mizzen, when it finally overwhelms ship and crew.

§In one of Arnanson's tales, ghosts of dead men appear, to aid in moving a boat, in which is traveling a former benefactor of these spirits.

There are many such ghosts found in the legends of our own land. The West Indian superstitions have been recounted.

|On the New England coast, they were also found, and Whittier says the Old Triton,—

" Had heard the ghost on Haley's Isle complain,
Speak him off-shore, and beg a passage back to Spain."

**These ghosts are those of the crew of the Spanish ship Sagunto, lost here early in the last century, sixteen of whose graves are still to be seen there.

A more celebrated ghost is that of the "Shrieking

*Thorpe.—N. Mythology, III. p. 10.
†See also H. C. Andersen, Fairy Tales, " Anne Lisbeth."
‡Schmidt.—Seeman's Sagen und Schiffer Märchen.
§Icelandic Legends.
|Garrison of Cape Ann.
**Drake.—Legends and Folk-lore of New England.

Woman," long thought to haunt the shores of Oakum Bay, near Marblehead. This was a Spanish woman, murdered here by pirates in the seventeenth century. Whittier thus sings of her,—

> *" 'Tis said that often when the moon
>   Is struggling with the gloomy even,
>   And over moon and star is drawn
>   The curtain of a clouded heaven,
>   Strange sounds swell up the narrow glen,
>   As if that robber crew was there,
>   The hellish laugh, the shouts of men—
>   And woman's dying prayer."

† Drake says this spectre is still believed to haunt the spot, by many intelligent people, and a learned jurist stated that he had often seen it.

‡ Roads says there are stories told in Marblehead of the appearance on the water of loved ones, who had died at home.

§ Lights are often seen coming and going near old wrecks on Sable Island, and, with the leaping flames, ghosts of wicked people appear. One is especially renowned, that of the "Lady of Copeland," wrecked and murdered by pirates, from the Amelie transport. She has one finger missing on her hand.

∥ A Block Island tradition declares that the ghosts of certain refugees, drowned in the surf during the revolution, are often seen, these "harbor boys" struggling to reach the shore, and sometimes making their cries heard.

** Among Maine fishermen, there are legends of spectres. "There was particularly the story of the Hascall. She broke loose from her moorings during a gale on George's banks, and ran into and sank the Andrew Johnson and all on board. For years afterward, the spectres of the drowned men were reported to come on board the Hascall at midnight, and go through the dumb show of fishing over the side, so that no one in Gloucester could be got to sail her, and she would not have brought six pence in the market."

†† There is a legend of a ghost of a former wreck, pirate,

---

* Legends of New England.
+ Drake.—Legends of New England. p. 212.
‡ History of Marblehead.
§ Secrets of Sable Island. Harper's Magazine.
∥ Livermore.—History of Block Island.
** Fish and Men in the Maine Islands. W. H. Bishop, Harper's Magazine, September, 1880.
†† Drake.—Legends of New England.

THE SHRIEKING WOMAN OF MARBLEHEAD.

295

etc., at Ipswich. When storms come, the howling of the wind is Harry Main. The legend is embodied in a verse by A. Morgan:

> "He blasphemed God, so they put him down,
> With his iron shovel, at Ipswich Bar,
> They chained him there for a thousand years,
> As the sea rolls up, to shovel it back.
> So when the sea cries, the good wives say,
> ' Harry Main growls at his work to-day?'"

He is occasionally seen, hard at work on the bar.

* Fishermen on the Isles of Shoals, said that ghosts guarded treasures buried by Kidd on Appledore Island, and their luminous forms were often seen. On another island, the ghost of the mistress of one of the freebooters faithfully guards the treasure.

In Dana's Buccaneer, a spectral horse appears on the water, and the pirate is forced to mount him, see the spectre ship burn, and finally to ride him away.

╪ Rockwell says there was a superstition among sailors in our navy, in 1842, that when a man had been hanged at the yard arm, a voice would be heard that night, returning the hail, from each yard-arm, one being the ghost of the person hanged.

A certain island on the Japanese coast is traditionally haunted by the ghosts of Japanese slain in a naval battle. ╪Griffis says, " Even to-day the Chosen peasant fancies he sees the ghostly armies baling out the sea with bottomless dippers, condemned thus to cleanse the ocean of the slain of centuries ago." Mariners feared to anchor near, and thought the phosphorescent sea the forerunner of these ghosts.

§ An old Chinese legend reports that the ghost of the captain of a man-of-war junk, who had been murdered, reappeared, and directed how the ship was to be steered to avoid a nest of pirates. The ghost of a Canton man-of-war repeatedly visited his ship, promenading the deck, and drilling his men.

We should not wonder at the belief in ghosts and spectres at sea, when we hear of the belief formerly existing, that when ghosts were laid, they were banished to the Red Sea. In one of Addison's plays, we read, " There must be a power of spirits in that sea." When such exiled ghosts did reap-

* Drake.—Legends of New England, p. 346.
╪ Sketches of Foreign Travel.
╪ The Mikado's Kingdom.
§ Dennys.—Folk-lore of China.

pear, they were thought more audacious, appearing by day instead of by night.

But these are not all the spectral shapes that come to the credulous mariner. As the mysterious abodes of the spirits of the deep and of the air, he had a ready fear of the shapes of mist, cloud, and fog. The Fata Morgana of Messina Straits is little less than the "Bahr el Sheitan" (*Devil's Sea*), the deceptive and often disastrous mirage of the Arabian desert.

So the Argonauts were encompassed by fog when relieved by Apollo. The spectre ship is often attended by a fog, cloudy spectres hovered about many a headland, many unusual occurrences, as narrated in these pages, are attended by a fog or mist, and are often easily accounted for by the unusual resonance given to sounds in fogs, and to the trang feelings often experienced when locked in from the outside world by a fog-bank.

The Chinese call the mirage the "Sea Market," and evidently regard it as more substantial than fog, for we hear of visits to palaces in the sea-mist.

* Japanese legend asserts that the mirage is the breath of a clam, which lies in the bottom of the sea. The mirage is called *Shin-Kiro,*—"The vision of the palace of the god of the bottom of the sea."

† A mist over the river Cymal, in Wales, is traditionally the spirit of a traitress, who perished in the lake near by. She had conspired with pirates to rob her lord of his domain, and was defeated by an enchanter.

. In Icelandic belief, the fog is a king's daughter bewitched.

A certain lake in Sweden is said, when the sun is warm, to send up a mist like a human form. It is called spectre-water (Spökvatten).

The occasional reflections of mountains, cities, or ships in mirage or fog-bank, the land-look of such banks themselves, coupled with the superstition of the mediæval mariner, doubtless gave rize to the many stories of mysterious lands at various places and times, and these were aided by the belief in the existence of an earthly heaven or hell, generally reached by crossing the water.

The names yet existing in sailor-tongue of such mysterious places as Cape Fly-away, No-man's land, Lubber land,

* Greey.—The Wonderful City of Tokio.
† Sykes.—British Goblins and Welsh Folk-lore.

Dutchman's land, and Butter-land (German Smörland), are but faint reminiscences of many tales of wonderful lands in unexplored seas.

These fables are as old as Homer's time. For Æolus, dispenser of the winds, lives in a floating isle.

Delos, the sacred island, traditionally floated in the Ægean, and was anchored by Poseidon.

(Merry suggests that Æolia, like the Symplegades, was a floating iceberg of the glacial period.)

* Ovid tells us of a maiden, Penmele, who was turned into an island bearing that name, by Neptune, and there were similar Grecian traditions concerning other islands.

Navigators in early times thus brought home tales of many fanciful lands, and especially chose islands as the seat of many of these stories, the influence of which extended to the times of Columbus.

These tales were assisted in their growth by the fanciful descriptions of authors of the middle ages, and of the revival of letters. Scarcely one of them undertook to describe a sea-voyage, without creating numerous wonderful islands.

These islands are encountered in the Arabian Nights. On that seen by Sindbad, where King Mihrage lived, sounds of revelry were heard at night. †So El Kazwini reports that sailors say sounds of drum and tambourine were often heard from Bartail, a certain East Indian island, and say El Dezjàl, the Antichrist, lives there. Hole, in his comments, thinks these sounds made by waves in hollow rocks. He also says the island on which lived the old man of the sea, who so greviously oppressed Sindbad, was full of such beings, having no bones in their legs, and always ready to jump on the shoulders of an approaching mariner, and drag him down.

The Island of Apes is also described by El Kazwini, and both he and El Wardee tell of another island, where there were cannibal men with dog's heads.

King Bedr, when wrecked, finds an enchanted city, Lob, on an island.

‡ Moses sent Al Sameri, the maker of the golden calf, to an island in the Red sea, and there his descendants reign, plague-stricken. If a ship comes to the island, they run to the beach, and cry, "Touch me not."

* Metamorphoses.
† Marvels of Creation.
‡ Well.—Legends of the Koran.

Ariosto places the gardens of Armida in a wonderful island in the Atlantic, and Fata Alcina carries Astolfo to another enchanted island. *Angelina was exposed to be devoured by the Orc, on another island, to the west of Ireland, where that monster had already destroyed the inhabitants, descendants of Proteus.

No extended allusion to the various imaginary islands of Swift and Rabelais are necessary. †The fleet of the bottle visit in turn Nowhere island, Triangle island, Lipservice island, Desolation island, Monks' island, Sly land, Favorable Wind island, and others, and cross a frozen sea, where the noise of a conflict that had occurred twelve months previous was just beginning to be heard.

In the "Speculum Regale," we are told of an island that sometimes approached the Danish coast, on which grew herbs that could cure all ills. But no more than one person could land on it at a time, when it would disappear for seven years, and, on bringing back its burden, it sank, and another island arose in its place, similar to it. Giraldus tells us of an island that appeared and then vanished, but finally became fixed, on some one landing on it. ‡A French author, Pichot, says there were legends among northern sailors of floating islands, covered with grass, trees, etc., which sank in the sea at intervals. They regard them as the abode of malicious spirits, who cause them to rise and float about, so as to embarrass navigators. This statement is confirmed by Torfoeus. Gummers' Ore, just in sight of Stockholm, was one of these islands, and it is figured in the charts of Baroeus, a geographer. Baron Grippenheim relates that he long sought it in vain, but finally saw it by chance, as he raised his head when fishing, it appearing as three points of land. The fishermen informed him what it was, and said that its appearance prognosticated storms and plenty of fish, and added that it was but a reef, inhabited by sea-trolls, or, perhaps, shapes assumed by the trolls.

A floating island appears on Lake Derwentwater, in England. §"Some call it the devil's barge, and assert that it only appears in years of calamity; from this premise deducing the fact that England is about to be visited by the cholera. This prophecy is strengthened by the fact

* Hoole.—Ariosto. XI—240.
† "Pantagruel."
‡ Landrin.—Les Monstres Marins, 88.
§ London World, January 1866.

that it appeared in the last great cholera year. It matters not that it has also appeared since. Others—among them the oldest inhabitants—state that it presages three months' continual frost."

*Marco Polo tells us of islands inhabited by men alone, and of others inhabited by women alone. Colonel Yule says many ancient traditions of such islands were told. Mendoza heard of such in Japan, where there is still a legendary woman's island; and Columbus heard the same legend, of Martinique.

† Near Formosa lies Mauriga Sima, said, in Japanese lore, to have been sunk for the crimes of its inhabitants, and yet peopled by their souls. Kaempfer says the vessels and urns which the fishermen have brought from it are sold at an enormous price in China and Japan. ‡ So Moore sings:

> "And urns of porcelain from that isle,
> Sunk underneath the Indian flood,
> Whence, oft the lucky diver brings
> Vases to grace the halls of kings."

The Chinese have similar traditions of islands, near Formosa, called Sân-Chen-Sân (Isles of the Genii). §An expedition is said to have sailed to them, in 219 B. C., but wa mysteriously driven back by adverse winds, on sighting them.

Cocaigne, or Cookery island, was the subject of many legends and ballads. It is a gourmand's paradise, where abound stores of wine, game, and fish.

> ‖ "Far in sea, by West Spain,
> Is a land yhote Cockayne."

One authority calls it Lubber-land.

Schmidt, in his sailor legends, tells of a wonderful island, inhabited by fairies.

The Galapagos islands were formerly said to be enchanted, probably, as Melville suggests, because of the currents and eddies found near there.

An old ballad "The Enchanted Isle," reads thus:

* Yules' Marco Polo, Vol. II.
† Kaempfer.—Japan.
‡ Lalla Rookh.
§ Conway.—Demonology and Devil-lore, I, 166.
‖ Ellis.—Early English Poetry.

"From that daie forth, the isle has beene
By wandering sailors never seene;
Some say, 'tis buryed deepe
Beneath the sea, which breakes and roares
Above its savage rocky shores,
Nor e'er is known to sleepe."

Strange tales were long told of the Bermudas. *As Dekker says:

"Bermudas, called the Iland of Divels, by reason of the quantity of swine heard from thence to the sea."

We also read in the "Crudities" (1611).

"Of the Bermudas, the example such,
Where not a ship until this time darst touch,
Kept, as suppos'd by hel's infernal dogs;
Our fleet found there most honest courteous hogs."

†An account of these islands by Jourdan, in 1610, tells us: "For the Islands of the Bermudas, otherwise called the Isle of Divels, every man knoweth that hath heard or read of them, were *never inhabited* by any Christians, but were esteemed and reputed a most prodigious and inchanted place, affording nothing but gusts, storms and foul weather; which made every mariner and navigator to avoid them as Scylla and Charybdis, or as they would shun the devil himself." The Colony of Virginia supplemented this account thus: "These islands of the Bermudas have ever been accounted an inchanted place, *and a desert inhabitation for devils;* but all the fairies of the rock were but flocks of birds, and all the devils that haunted the woods were but herds of swine." In the addition to Stowes' Annuals, by Howes, we further read: "Sir George Somers espied land, which they judged it should be the dreadful coast of the Bermudas, which island men of all nations said and supposed to be enchanted and inhabited with wittches and devils, which grew by reason of accustomed monstrous thunder-storms and tempests near to these islands." Marryat says there was a sailor tradition that the crust of these islands was so thin, that there was constant danger of breaking through.

‡"Who did not think till within these foure years, but that these islands had been rather a habitation for Divells, than fit for man to dwell in."

* Strange Horse-Race (1600).
† A Discovery of the Bermudas, otherwise called the "Isle of Divels."
‡ A Plain Description of the Bermudas (1613).

302

LEGENDS AND SUPERSTITIONS

* "And whereas it is reported that this land of the Bermudas, with the islands about, are inchanted, and kept with evil and wiched spirits—it is a most idle and false report."

† Josselyn says: "*June*, the first day in the afternoon, very thick foggie weather, we sailed by an inchanted island, saw a great deal of filth and rubbish floating by the ship."

None of the tales told of ghostly shapes or shadowy lands in the ocean world have found so many credulous believers as those of the ghostly lights, that burn about the tops of the ship's spars in the heavy atmosphere preceding a storm, or in the agitated air near its close. Under various names, and connected with numerous legends, this appearance has been the joy or terror of mariners for centuries. It bears the same relation to the Will-o'-the-Wisp on shore that the Phantom-Ship bears to the Wandering Jew.

‡ Horace says of them:—

> " Soon as their happy stars appear,
> Hush'd is the storm, the waves subside,
> The clouds disperse, the skies are clear,
> And without a murmur, sleeps th' obedient tide."

Its earliest appearance is in the first celebrated voyage of the Argonauts. Here, during a storm, it appeared, in answer to the prayers of Orpheus, about the heads of Castor and Pollux, as a reassuring sign. Later, its appearance became common. § Xenophanes says they are small clouds, burning by their peculiar motion. Metrodorus thinks that they are luminous emanations from the eyes of spirits. Plutarch, quoting these, also thinks them spirits.

║ Pliny says, "I have seen, during the night-watches of the soldiers, a luminous appearance, like a star, attached to the javelins on the ramparts. They also settle on the yard-arms and other parts of ships while sailing, producing a kind of vocal sound, like that of birds flitting about. When they occur singly, they are mischievous, so as even to sink the vessel, and if they strike on the lower part of the hull, setting them on fire. When there are two of them, they are considered auspicious, and are thought to predict a prosperous voyage, and it is said they drive away the dreadful and terrific meteor named Helena. On this account their efficacy

* News from the Bermudas (1617).
† Voyage to New England (1865).
‡ Carmina, 1-12-25.
§ Plutarch Morals. Goodwin, Chapter xviii.
║ Natural History, Lib. II. Chapter xxxvii.

is ascribed to Castor and Pollux, and they are invoked as gods."

Euripides speaks of the appearance of these lights, in "Helena," and Ovid also alludes to them.

*Maximus, of Tyre, says, "I have seen on a ship, the Dioscuri, brilliant stars who reconduct into the right path the ship driven by tempests." Euripides and the Scholiast on Statius bear testimony similar to that given by Pliny. Lucian tells of a ship warned off a shoal by one of the twins. Hesychius and many of the poets speak of their appearance to mariners. Porphyrion, in a note to Horace, says, "It is on the contrary asserted now among sailors, that the stars of Castor and Pollux are generally a menace to the ship."

†Solin alludes to a vile incantation against the light, not of a nature to be here described, and it is further confirmed by a passage in ‡Pliny, indicating a method for avoiding all atmospheric dangers.

§Castor and Pollux were reputed sons of Zeus, or, some say, of Tyndareus, by Leda, and assisted in the Argonautic voyage. ‖At their death they were made stars in the constellation Gemini, and are invoked by mariners, as in Hor., Od. III, Bk. I.

" Sic Fratres Helenæ, lucida sidera!"

For Castor and Pollux were brothers of Helen, whose dire influence in the Greek fortunes gave her name to the single unpropitious flame.

**Dr. Anthon thinks the origin of these names is realistic. Leda means *darkness*, Tyndareus, *light-giving*. So their offspring are Helene, or Selene, the *moon* (always evil in its influence), or *brightness*, Castor, the *adorner*, and Pollux (Polleuces) *lightful*. Thus they are appropriate names, whether for these lights at sea, or for the stars that guide the mariner. As the Cabiri, or Dioscuri, the twins became early maritime deities. Another authority thinks Helena is elene, *light*, or elenas, *shipwreck*.

In the middle ages, mariners especially noted this apparition with superstitious joys or fears.

††El Masudi tells us: "Those who are to be saved fre-

* " Melusine." August 5, 1884.
† Polyhistor, Ch. I, p. 17 and 18—Mommsen's Ed.
‡ Hist. Nat. XXVIII, 23, q. by H. Gaidos, Melusine, September 1, 1884.
§ Smith.—Classical Dictionary.
‖ Diodorus Siculus.
** Classical Dictionary.
†† Golden Meadows, 954 A. D., Chapter xvi.

quently observe something like a luminous bird at the top of the mast. This appearance on the top of the mast is of such brightness that the eye cannot behold it, nor can they make out what it is. The moment it appears, the sea becomes quiet, the gale lulls, and the waves subside. Then the brightness vanishes, and no one can perceive how it comes, or how it disappears. It is the sign of safety, and the assurance that they have escaped."

*When the Earl of Salisbury, in 1226, was visited by the Virgin, as alluded to above, the light appeared, guarded by her, at the summit of the mast, at the moment of greatest danger.

Gregorius (1352) records the appearance of these lights, and the usual prognostications from them.

† M. Jal gives the following quotation from an old work: ‡"A vow being made, in invoking Holy Pope Urban, suddenly appeared to them the light of Saint *Elemi;* and, seeing this sign, they were exceedingly content."

M. Jal also gives an extract from a Spanish MS. in the Paris Naval library, called, "Relacion del Viajem del Flote." "The next day we had a great tempest, and some sailors assured us that they saw Santo Telmo in the tops with a light."

§ The same phenomena are recorded by a later writer, who calls the vision St. Helm.

Italian mariners of the fifteenth and sixteenth centuries regarded the light as a luminous emanation from the body of Christ.

‖ In the account of the second voyage of Columbus, we find this passage: "On Saturday, at night, the body of St. Elmo was seen, with seven lighted candles in the round top, and there followed mighty rain and frightful thunder. I mean the lights were seen which the seamen affirm to be the body of St. Elmo, and they sang litanies and prayers to him, looking upon it as most certain that in these storms, when he appears, there can be no danger. Whatever this is, I leave to others, for, if we may believe Pliny, when such lights appeared in those times to Roman sailors in a storm, they said they were Castor and Pollux."

* Jones.—Credulities, p. 64.
† Glossaire Nautique, Art. St. Elmo.
‡ History of the Miracles of Urban V. (1362-70).
§ Voyage du Seigneur du Caumont (1418).
‖ Historia del Almirante.

*Ariosto says,—

> " When sudden breaking on their raptur'd sight
> Appear'd the splendor of St. Elmo's light,
> Low settling on the prow, with ray serene
> It shone, for masts and sails no more were seen;
> The crew, elated, saw the dancing gleam,
> Each on his knees ador'd the fav'ring beam,
> And begg'd, with trembling voice and watery eyes,
> A truce from threatening waves and raging skies;
> The storm (till then relentless) ceased to roar."

†Erasmus says: "A certain ball of fire began to stand by the mast, which is the worst sign in the world to sailors, if it be single, but a very good one, if it be double. The ancients believed it to be Castor and Pollux. By and by the fiery ball glides down the ropes, and it rolls over and over, close to the pilot. It stopped a little there, then rolled itself all around the sides of the ship, afterward slipping through the hatches, it vanished away."

‡We have alluded above to the appearance of Ariel, in "The Tempest," on board the king's ship. He comes as the dread spectre light.

He says,—

> " I boarded the king's ship; now on the beak,
> Now in the waist, the deck, in every cabin,
> I flamed amazement; sometimes I'd divide
> And burn in many places: on the topmast,
> The yards, and bowsprit, would I flame distinctly,
> Then meet, and join," etc.

>   " Not a soul
> But felt a fever of the mad, and played
> Some trick of desperation. All, but mariners,
> Plunged in the foaming brine, and quit the vessel,
> Then all afire with me."

§ Douce says Shakspeare probably consulted Stephen Batman's "Golden Books of the Leaden Goddes," where it is thus written,—

"Castor and Pollux were figured like two lamps, or cresset lights, one on the toppe of a maste, the other on the stemme or foreshippe," and he further says that if the light ascends from the prow, it is a good sign; if it descends from the masthead, a bad one.

* Orlando Purioso (1516). Hoole's Trans.
† "Colloquy of the Shipwreck " (1522).
‡ Act I, scene 2.
§ Illustrations of Shakspeare (1830), p. 3.
20

* Psellus names the first class of demons, fiery devils. They displayed their power, he says, in blazing stars, in fire-drakes, in mock-suns and moons, and in the *Corpo Santo*.

In Pigafetta's history of the voyage of Magellan, we find this account:

"In stormy weather we frequently saw what is called the Corpo Santo, or St. Elme" (another account has it St. Anselmo). "On one very dark night it appeared to us like a brilliant flambeau, on the summit of the mainmast, and thus remained for a space of two hours, which was a matter of great consolation to us during the tempest. At the instant of its disappearing, it diffused such a resplendent blaze of light as almost blinded us, but the wind ceased immediately." In another place he says, " In this place we endured a great storm, and thought we should have been lost, but the three holy bodies, that is to say, St. Anselmo, St. Ursula, and St. Clare appeared to us, and immediately the storm ceased."

A foot-note in Pinkertoh's " Voyages " says the English sailors call the light Davy Jones, but he does not state his authority, nor does † Goodrich, who calls it the same.

‡ Camoens, in the " Lusiad," records the appearance of the light. It is in 1572, and Da Gama speaks,—

> " That living fire, by seamen held divine,
> Of Heaven's own care in storms the holy sign,
> Which midst the horrors of the tempest plays,
> And on the blast's dark wings would gayly blaze;
> These eyes distinct have seen that living fire
> Glide through the storm, and 'round my sails aspire."

§ Linschoten also tells us, " The same night we saw upon the main yard, and in many other places, a certain sign, which the Portuguese call *Corpo Santo*, or the holy body of the brother Peter Gonsalves, but the Spanish call it *San Elmo*, and the Greeks (as ancient writers rehearse, and Ovid among the rest), Helle and Phryxus. Whensoever that signe showeth you the mast, or main yard, or in any other place, it is commonly thought that it is a sign of better weather. When they first perceive it, the Master or Chief Boatswain whistleth, and commandeth every man to salute it with ' Salve Corpo Santo,' and a *miseracordia*, with

* Collin de Plancy.—Dictionnaire Infernale.
† Man Upon the Sea.
‡ Mickle's Translation, Bk. V, ver. 159.
§ Relation of a voyage from Goa to Enkhuisen (1588).

MAGELLAN'S SHIP AND THE ST. ELMO LIGHTS.

807

a very great cry and exclamation. This constellation, as
astronomers do write, is engendered of great moisture and
vapors, and showeth like a candle that burneth dimly and
skippeth from one place to another, never lying still. We
saw five of them together, all like the light of a candle,
which made me wonder, and I should hardly have believed
it, but that I saw it, and looked very earnestly at it. . . .
These five lights the Portuguese call 'Coroa de Nostra Senhora,' that is, 'our lady's crown,' and have great hope therein when they see it."

Sir Humphrey Gilbert tells us, "We had also upon our
main-yard an apparition of a little fier by night, which seamen call Castor and Pollux."

In Lord Bacon's "Apothegms," Gonsalvo says to Diego
de Mendoza, "It is Saint Ermyn, who never appears but
after a storm."

* Hakluyt in his Voyages (1598) saw the light. He says,
"I do remember that in the great and boisterous storm of
this foul weather, in the night there came upon the toppe
of our maine-yard and maine-mast a certaine little light,
much like unto the light of a little candle, which the Spaniards call the Suerpo Santo. This light continued aboord
our ship about three hours, flying from maste to maste, and
from top to top; and sometimes it would be in two or three
places at once."

† An old writer says,—

"As when a wave-bruised bark, long tost by the winds in a tempest,
Strains on a forraine coast, in danger still to be swallow'd,
After a world of feares, with a winter of horrible objects,
The Shipman's solace, fair Leda's twinnes, at an instant,
Signes of a calm are seen, and seen, are shrilly saluted."

‡ De Loier also says, "They shall see the fires which say-
lors call St. Hermes, fly uppon their shippe, and alight upon
the toppe of maste."

In that diverting work, Burton's "Anatomy of Melancholy (1624), we read, "Fiery spirits and devils are seen, as
commonly noted, by blazing stars, fire-drakes, or *ignes-fatui*,
which lead men often *in flumen aut præcipitu;* likewise they
counterfeit sun and moon, stars oftentimes, and sit on ship's
masts. *In navigiorum summitantibus visuntur,*§ and are called

* Vol. III, p. 450.
† Greene in Conceit (1598).
‡ Treatise of Spectres (1605).
§ " They are seen at the top of ships."

Dioscuri, as Eusebius informs us, in which they never appear, saith Cardan, but they signify some mischief, or ill to come unto men, though some will have them to portend good, and victory to that side they come towards in sea-fights. St. Elme's fire they commonly call them, and they do likewise appear after a sea-storm. * Radzovillius, the Polonian duke, calls this apparition Santo Germani Sidus (Holy German Star), and saith, moreover, that he saw the same often in a storm as he in his sailing, 1582, came from Alexander to Rhodes. Our stories are full of such apparitions in all times."

In a letter from a priest in Peru to his superior, written in 1639,† we find a curious account of this light. I translate, " But we passed through it (the storm) happily, since at its beginning, which was about 11 or 12 P.M., the Santelmo (*sic*) appeared to us at the main-topmast head, in the shape of three distinct lights, mild and beneficent to the sight, the form in which the Saint appears on like occasions to afflicted mariners. We all bade it thrice good speed, none in the ship omitting it, and then we knew that it understood our actions, and were not left in ignorance of the protection and special assistance that it afforded us, as it gave us an indication of this, the Saint passing from the main-topmast head to the fore-topmast head, and in the same form, and then we again bade it good speed three times, and the Saint, as if to show us that it afforded us a like protection and assurance, appeared the third time at the mizzen-topmast head, and there shone in the threefold form of three burning lights, which made a marked impression on all, and all at once wished good speed three times again, and saw it no more, but gave ourselves the greatest assurance and confidence in making a good voyage."

‡ Bartolomeo Crescentio records the light, and says it was called Saint Telme, or Saint Helm, because of its reflection in the helmets, or *helms*, of the soldiers.

Fournier, in his " Hydrographie " (1643), relates many curious stories of the light. He says it was named after a saint, familiarly known as Saint Telme, but who was San Pedro Gonzales de Tuy, in Gallicia, who had been a mariner, then was canonized, and became a patron saint of sailors.§ Gallician sailors called the light San Pedro Gonzales.

* Herosolymita Perigrinatio (1601), p. 230.
† Duro.—Disquisitiones Nauticas (1876).
‡ Nautica Mediterrannea (1607).
§ Acta Sanctorum, April 11, and June 1.

Varenius, a Dutch writer, in 1650, says of these lights, "They usually wander with an uncertain motion from place to place, sometimes appearing to cleave close to the sails and masts; but they frequently leap up and down with intermission, affording an obscure flame like that of a candle burning faintly. They are produced by some sulphurous and bituminous matter, which, being beat down by the motion of the air, above, and gathering together is kindled by the agitation of the air, as butter is gathered together by the agitation of the cream; and from this appearance we infer that storms come from sulphurous spirits that rarefy the air and fuel into motion."

*A work written in 1652 calls it "St. Ermyn, that never appears but after a storm."

Hazlitt, quoting an unpublished manuscript of the seventeenth century, says it was called Castor and Pollux, and Fermie's fire.

†Dampier encountered them: "After four o'clock, the thunder and the rain abated, and then we saw a Corpus Sant at our main-topmast head, on the very top of the truck of the spindle. This sight rejoiced our men exceedingly, for the height of the storm is commonly over when the Corpus Sant is seen aloft, but when they are seen lying on the deck, it is generally accounted a bad sign." "A Corpus Sant is a certain small glittering light; when it appears as this did, on the very top of a mainmast or at a yard-arm, it is like a star, but when it appears on the deck, it resembles a great glow-worm. The Spaniards have another name for it, and I have been told that when they see them, they presently go to prayers, and bless themselves for the happy light. I have heard some ignorant seamen discoursing how they have seen them creep, or as they say, travel about in the scuppers, telling many dismal stories that hap'ned at such times, but I never did see one stir out of the place where it first was fix'd, except upon Deck, where every sea washeth it about. Neither did I ever see any but we had rain as well as wind, and therefore I believe it to be some jelly."

‡Josselyn records these meteors: "About eight of the clock at night, a flame settled upon the main mast; it was about the bigness of a great candle, and is called by seamen

* Herbert's Remains.—Brand, III, p. 402,
† Voyages (1697),
‡ Voyages.

St. Elmo's fire; it comes before a storm, and is commonly thought to be a spirit; if two appear, they prognosticate safety."

Heyrick, in "The Submarine Voyage" (1691), says,—

> "For lo! a sudden storm did rend the air,
> The sullen heavens curling from its brow,
> Did dire presaging omens show,
> Ill-boding Helena alone was there."

In another place, Heyrick calls it Corposant, and so we find it named in John Coad's "Memorandum" (1690), and in Fryer's "Travels," of about the same period. *Fryer says, "In a storm of rain and hail, with a high and bleak wind, appeared the sailors' deities, Castor and Pollux, or the same it may be, gave light to those fables, they boding fair weather to seamen, though never seen but in storms, looking like a candle in a dark lantern, of which there were divers here and there, above the sails and shrouds, being the *ignis fatui* of the watery elements; by the Portuguese christened Querpos Santos, the bodies of saints, which by them are esteemed ominous."

Coad tells us: "God was pleased to give us a sign of the storm approaching, by a *corposant* on the top of the main mast."

†The writer of "Forbin's Memoirs" also relates that some thirty were seen in the Mediterranean. The French mariners thought that so long as they remained aloft, they were beneficent spirits, but if they descended, a gale would appear, and the wind would blow in proportion to their descent.

The St. Elmo appeared in answer to the prayers of some sailors in 1700, who called on Notre Dame de Deliverance, whose shrine is near Caen.

A belief existed in the Isle of Man, about the same period, that lights over water presaged drowning, and rested over drowned bodies also. Similar beliefs are recorded of the river Dee, according to Aubrey.

Dr. Caldecott says that when a Christian is drowned in that river, lights hover over the water to point out the location of the body, and hence it is called the Holy Dee.

A curious account of the meteor is contained in a work

---

* Jones.—Credulities, p. 76.
† Jones.—Credulities, p. 76.

quoted by Brand.[*] It calls them "fiery impressions that appear usually at sea, called by mariners Castor and Pollux; when thin, clammy vapors, arising from the salt water and ugly slime, hover over the sea, they, by the motions in the winds and hot blasts, are often fired; these impressions will oftentimes cleave to the masts and ropes of ships, by reason of their clamminess and glutinous substance, and the mariner by experience find that when but one flame appears, it is the forerunner of a storm, but when two are seen near together, they betoken faire weather and good lucke in a voyage. The natural cause why these may foretell fair or foul weather is, that one flame alone may forewarn a tempest, forasmuch as the matter, being joyn'd and not dissolv'd, so it is like that the matter of the tempest, which never wasteth, as wind and clouds, is still together, and not dissipate, so it is likely a storm is engendering; but two flames appearing together denote that the exhalation is divided, which is very thick, and so the thick matter of the tempest is dissolv'd or scattered abroad, by the same cause, but the flame is divided, therefore no violent storm can ensue, but rather a calm is promised."

Cotgrave, in his dictionary, defines Feu d' Helene, Feu d' Hermes, St. Helen or St. Hermes' fire as a meteor that often appears at sea.

"Furole, a little blaze of fire appearing by night on the tops of soldier's lances, or at sea on the sayle-yards, where it whistles and leapes in a moment from one place to another. Some mariners call it St. Hermes' fire, if it come double, 'tis held as a signe of goode lucke, if single, otherwise. If five of them are seen together, they are called by the Portuguese Cora de Nostra Senhora, and are looked upon as a sure sign that the storm is almost over."   ·

Aubin, in his Dictionary (1702), says: "The sailors draw presages from its appearance; for, if this light appear on the mast, yard, or rigging, they conclude that, the air being agitated by no wind which can dissipate these lights, there would ensue a profound calm; but, if the fires fly about, it is, according to them, a sign of bad weather." He calls them Feu St. Elme, Vree Vuuren (free fires), or Castor en Pollux.

[†] Becchi, writing of naval affairs in 1705, calls the lights

---

[*] Vol. III, p. 401.—Wonderful History of all the Storms, Hurricanes, Earthquakes, etc. (1700).
[†] De re Navali.

St. Elmo, and thinks they may be caused by phosphorescent marine insects scooped up into the air.

He says: "Wishing to invoke this light, and not knowing any name for it, they called it saint." He also says: "The Gallicians call this same light San Pietro Gonzales de Tui (Tui is a city of Gallicia, near Baiona), who was at first a sailor, and then, dying as a monk, so they called him a saint."

A writer in the "British Apollo" (1710), says: "When this light appears, it is a sign that the tempest is accompanied by a sulphurous spirit, rarefying and moving the clouds."

Thos. Chalky, in a journal of a voyage from Barbadoes to Philadelphia, says: "In this storm, December, 1731, we saw divers lights, which the sailors call corpusants. One of them was exceeding bright, about half an hour, on our main-topmast head, plain to the view of all the ship's company, divers of whom said they never saw the like, and I think I never heard of or saw the like before."

*Dr. Shaw tells us: "In the like disposition of the weather (thick and hazy), I have observed those luminous bodies, which at sea skim about the masts and yards of ships, and are called corpusance by the mariners—a corruption of Cuerpo Santo, as this meteor is called by the Spaniards."

A work, "A Wonderful Test of all Stones" (1760), has it: "They are seen rising in thin vapors from the surface of the waters, and then changing to the vessel's spars. One presages a storm, and two, fair weather." The author gives a whimsical explanation of their origin.

In a work, "Hostes Furioso," written about the same time, these lights are alluded to, and Ariosto's lines, above-quoted, are repeated.

Falconer, in the "Shipwreck" (1760), thus sings,—

> "High on the mast, with pale and lurid rays,
> Amid the gloom, portentous meteors blaze."

†An Italian brochure, published about 1768, gives an account of them, and relates the usual omens as to their number.

Nineteenth century science has not thoroughly dispelled the mariner's belief in the supernatural character of these

* Travels in the Levant (1738).
† Brand, III, 398.

weird lights. For, as is said in Scott's "Rokeby," numerous stories are still

"Told of Eric's cap and St. Elmo's light."

*German sailors say it is the spirit of a defunct comrade. When it mounts up, it is a good omen, and the contrary is shown by its descent. It is fatal to any one, when it shines on his head.

†In a modern French romance, the lights called by a sailor St. Elme, plays at the yard-arms, and, it is declared, would accompany the mariner to the yards, and aid him in his labors. It was said to be the soul of a shipwrecked sailor, which comes to warn of thunder-strokes and lightning. It was a profanation to touch it, but it disappeared when the sign of the cross was made.

‡Other sailors say it is a soul in purgatory. If the lights are double, it is a good sign, and they are called St. Elme and St. Nicholas. If they are single, it is a bad sign. A third light is called St. Anne.

§In Brittany, it is called the wandering candle (goulaouewn red), and is a menace. It is sometimes a lost soul, for whom prayers are asked. Others say it is an evil spirit.

"St. Elmo's fire upon the deep,
Death calls loudly there."

|It is called *Telonia*, in modern Greece—a word meaning, primarily, a demon taxgatherer, from an old Christian superstition that demons hindered souls, in their heavenward journey, to gather toll. Hence, this light is a bad omen. It breaks masts, destroys ships and crew; and, hence, prayer and incense are used against it. Incantations from the Clavicle of Solomon are said, a loud noise is made, and guns fired. If a pig is on board, its tail is pulled, as its diabolical cries will expel the demon.

**"The Telonia is a species of electricity, appearing during storms at the mastheads which the Greek sailors personify as birds of evil omen, which settle on the masts with a view to destroy the ship and sailors."

* Werner.—Erinnerung und Bilder, in Melusine, February, 1885.
† E. Corbière.—Le Negrier.
‡ De la Landelle.—Dernier Quarte de Nuit.
§ L. F. Sauvé, in Melusine, September, 1884.
| N. G. Politis, in Melusine, August, 1884.
** J. T. Bent.—McMillan's Magazine, March, 1885.

*A traveler in a Spanish ship, in 1808, says: "When retiring to rest, a sudden cry of 'St. Elmo,' and 'St. Anne,' was heard from those aloft, and fore and aft the deck. I found the topsail yards deserted, the sails loose, and beating in the inconstant wind; the awe-struck mariners, bare-headed, on their knees, with hands uplifted, in voice and attitude of prayer to St. Elmo and St. Anne."

† Cheever says: "A corpusant is a mass of phosphorescent jelly, that clings to the rigging and mounts the mast."

‡ Dana tells us: "Upon the maintop-gallant mast was a ball of light, which the sailors name a corpusant (Corpus sancti). They were all watching it, for sailors have a notion that if the corpusant rises in the rigging, it is a sign of fair weather, but if it come lower down, there will surely be a storm. It is held a fatal sign to have the pale light thrown in one's face. It passed to the foretop-gallant, and then to the flying jib-boom end."

§ Douce says these lights lead men to suicide. He says they were called Saint Helen, Saint Elm, St. Herme, St. Clare, St. Peter, and St. Nicholas.

‖ Melville says these lights were called corpusants. The mate feared them, and the men all avoided oaths while they were burning.

** Macaulay's lines embody ancient beliefs:

> "Safe comes the ship to haven
>   Through billows and through gales,
> If once the great twin brethren
>   Sit shining on the sails."

†† We are told by Thoms: "That the *ignis fatuus* is the spirit of some woman, who is destined to run *en furolle*, to expiate her intrigues with a minister of the church, and it is designated from that circumstance, La Fourlore, or La Fourolle."

Davis, in the "American Nimrod," says that the whalers call the light Ampizant, and have a tradition that it is the spirit of some sailor that has died on board. So the Will-o'-the-Wisp is said to be the spirit of evil-doers, of unbaptized children, etc.

* Jones.—Credulities, p. 76.
† Sea and Shore (1857).
‡ Two Years Before the Mast, Ch. 39.
§ Illustrations of Shakspeare, p. 3.
‖ Moby Dick.
** Battle of Lake Regillus.
†† Three Notelets to Shakspeare.

* Longfellow's lines, quoted here, are repeated in Swainson's " Weather-Lore," as a weather prophecy:

> "Last night I saw St. Elmo's stars,
>   With their glimmering lanterns all at play,
> On the top of the masts, and the tips of the spars,
>   And I knew we should have foul weather to-day."

† An old channel fisherman said to Buckland, " It never does any body any harm, and it always comes when squally weather is about."

In the account given of the destruction of the Gloucester, in early colonial times, a corposant is related to have appeared, standing over the house of each widowed wife. In the " Salem Spectre-Ship," too,—

> "The night grew thick, but a phantom light,
>   Around her path was shed."

Connected in legend with these spectral lights, we also find other luminous appearances. All apparitions at sea, material or ethereal, are usually represented as being attended by lights, even if fog or cloud is at the same time seen. Some of these have been alluded to. ‡Gregor tells a tale of a sailor, who murdered his lady-love. One stormy night, a bright light was seen, which finally took the human shape, and bore off the murderer.

A light hovers about a stone on the coast of Cornwall, called Madge Figg's Chair. § It was said to be the ghost of a wrecked lady whom Madge stripped of her jewels.

A light is said also to appear in Sennen Cove, which is thought to be an ill-omened apparition, the Hooper (from the whooping sound emitted). A fisherman once passed in his boat, when it had sounded, but never got back again.

Flames are reported as issuing from the Eider river, and from several lakes, in Germany, generally portending drowning.

Lights were seen in a spectral ship that appeared off a port in Cornwall. They were called Jack Harry's lights, from a pilot who discovered them. ‖ Hunt tells the tale, in this pilot's words: "Some five years ago, on a Sunday night, the wind being strong, our crew heard of a large

* Golden Legend.
† Curiosities of Natural History.
‡ Folk-lore of Scotland.
§ Bottrell.—Traditions and Fireside Stories of W. Cornwall.
‖ Romances and Drolls of the West of England.

vessel in the offing, after we came out of chapel. We manned our little boat, the *Ark*, and away we went, under close-reefed foresails and little mizzen, the sea going over us at a sweet rate. We had gone off four or five miles, and we thought we were up alongside, when lo! she slipped to windward a league." She slipped away again, the delusive light appearing further out each time.

* The spectre of a lady hunting for her child on the beach at Cornwall, referred to above, is accompanied with lights.

The appearance of these lights over water portends drowning, in the west of England.

"Corpse candles" are said to have rested near the graves of a drowned boat's crew at Penrose, such as Moore describes.

> † "Where lights, like charnel meteors, burned the distant wave,
> Bluely as o'er some seaman's grave,
> And fiery darts, at intervals,
> Flew up, all sparkling, from the main."

Drake says (1817) that the superstitions with regard to those corpse-lights were belived in France, Italy, Germany and England, in his time.

‡ Captain Leather, Chief Magistrate of Belfast, being wrecked in 1790, on the Isle of man, was told that thirteen of his crew were lost, as thirteen corpse candles were seen moving towards the churchyard. Thirteen men had been drowned.

§ Sikes, in his recent work, "British Goblins," relates a tale of passengers in a coach, seeing lights over a ford, and, a few days after, just as many men were drowned there, confirming the current belief that these "corpse-candles" portend drowning.

There is a Welsh tale of a spectre, the *Cyhyreath*, that appears on the beach, in a light, with groanings and cries, and always foretelling wreck. Corpses always come ashore after it is heard, in Glamorganshire.

An Irish story of an enchanted lake records the appearance of these lights over drowned bodies.

Many of the tales of spectre ships, given in another chapter, also include the appearance of these lights, especially

* Bottrell—Traditions and Fireside Stories of W. Cornwall.
† Lalla Rookh.
‡ Sacheverell.—Isle of Man.
§ P. 229.

in those of Solway Firth, and in other Scottish tales, as well as of those on our own coast.

* French sailors have a curious legend to account for the phosphorescence of the sea.   Satan, they say, constructed a three-masted ship, out of wood cut in his domain.   This ship smelled of sulphur, and sowed a pest for a hundred leagues around.   Satan assembled therein many souls of those who died in a sinful state, which gave him great joy, for when a fresh lot fell into his coppers, he laughed extravagantly.   This laugh irritated St. Elmo, who, finally enraged by these things, and by the piracies of the vessel's master, pierced the hull by a sudden stroke.   The devil, buzily engaged in counting a fresh accession to his spoils, was barely able to save himself by swimming.   The saint made a toothpick of the mast, and a handkerchief of the main-sail.

So when the night is dark and the air warm, the ship burns again, the smell of sulphur is noticed, and the flames mount to the sky.

Pomeranian sailors say it is the devil voyaging in a burning cask of tar, and presages great disasters.   In Scotch waters, it is also a bad omen, when appearing at night, and is called " sea-fire," " water-fire," " water-burn," etc.

In Scotland, the apparition of a spectral " lady of the golden casket," was attended by a phantom light.

Mariners said that St. Ninian's Kirk, standing in a desolate bay, was occasionally filled with lights, and they feared to enter there, as they portended wreck and disaster.

The Palatine light on Block Island, on our own coast, connected by Whittier with the legend of the spectre ship Palatine, is declared by Livermore † to have no connection with it, but is asserted by many to have been seen, a luminous emanation from the surface of the water.   A letter written by a resident, in 1811, describes it as now small, now high and extended like a ship, pyramidal, or in three streamers like a ship, flickering and reappearing, but not lasting longer than three minutes.   It is seen before easterly and southerly storms, and at all seasons.

‡ Flames are said also to issue from old wrecks on Sable Island, the surface of the ocean being covered with them, some being twenty feet in altitude.

* Dubarry.—Roman d'un Baleinier, in Mel., August, 1884.
† History of Block Island.
‡ Secrets of Sable Island.—C. Halleck, in Harper's Mag., Vol. V, p. 34.

Spectral lights are seen in two places in the Gulf of St. Lawrence. In one place, they were seen by an emigrant ship, burning for two hours from midnight, and looking.like a burning vessel. They were a sign of impending wreck. A French pilot described them as early as 1811.

* Lights, said to indicate a northwest gale, are seen in Chaleur Bay, even coming on ice. They are described in the *Colonial Times* (Miramichi), of November 2, 1801, "It appears as if the hull of a vessel was on fire." A ship is said to have been wrecked in a northwesterly gale, and afterwards some of the crew, who had murdered others, were again wrecked and destroyed. Another legend says the latter were pirates.

But to return to the St. Elmo light. We find a belief in the supernatural character of the lights among the Chinese. † Doolittle says they believe that their sea-goddess, the "Mother of Heaven," appears in these lights. If they rise, the indications are evil; if they descend, the portent is good. They thus reverse the European rule, as in many other things.

As we have seen, the lights have been called after a variety of names.

Helena, St. Helène, Helenen feuer and Heleneneld; Castor and Pollux, Leda's twins; St Elmo, St. Elemi, St. Anselmo, St. Ermyn, Santelmo, St. Telme, St. Helm, St. Ermo, and St. Elmo feur; Hermes, St. Hermes, St. Nicholas, St. Peter, St. Claire, and St. Elias feur; Corposant, Cormazant, Comazant, Ampizant, Corpusant, Corpusanse, Cuerpo Santo; Fermies' Fire, ‡ Capra Saltante, Sainte Herbe, La Feu des Gabiers, Corbie's Aunt, Helenen Feuer, Friedefeuer, Elmo vuer, Zee Licht, Fire Drake, Dipsas fuole, Looke fuole, Furoles, Flammeroles, and Flambars; San Pedro de Gonzales; Coroa de Nossa Senhora; Vree vuuren, Wetterlicht, Veirlys, and Helle and Phryxus, comprise these varied titles.

We have given some reasons for calling it St. Elmo. Its French titles would seem to point to the ancient name, but the St. Helena of the middle-ages was the empress of Constantine the Great, who, undertaking a voyage to Palestine in search of the true cross, was venerated by mariners. § Mrs. Jameson says St. Elme is St. Erasmus, who is shown

* Le Moine.—Chronicles of the St. Lawrence.
† "Chinese."
‡ See Mélusine, August, 1884.
§ Legends of the Madonna and the Saints.

in early art with a lighted taper on his head. * Ruscalli says St. Ermo was buried at Gaeta, and his tomb was venerated by mariners two centuries ago. Becchi says he was a Sicilian bishop. At sea, in a storm, he was taken very ill. He promised the distressed mariners, in dying, that he would appear if they were destined to be saved. After his death, a light appeared at the mast-head, and was named for him.

Another authority says St. Elmo is St. Erasmus, a Christian martyr (A.D. 303), who is usually invoked by Mediterranean mariners.

Saint Claire, or Santa Clara, was a virgin of Assisi, the patron saint of sailors, as was, above all, St. Nicholas. We may strongly suspect that *clair*, clear, is the origin of *that* name.

Corpo Santo, and its variations, means the Holy Ghost, supposed to appear, as in the instances we have given, and in the French phantom-ship story.

Buckland thinks Corposant comes from the French *coin blazant*, "blazing wedge." The Fire-drake was originally a sort of fire-works. In German tradition, Für Dräk is the evil one, "often seen passing through the air as a fiery stripe."

The other names have been explained, or indicate their own origin. St. Elias is a favorite Eastern saint, and Hermes, or Mercury, a classical messenger.

All the attempts, ancient and modern, to explain these lights as supernatural, seem now ridiculous, in the light of modern science. As over marshes and pools on land, so at sea, these electrical manifestations only occur in the rarefied air-gases, before or during a storm. These are naturally adherent to the iron of the spars, but, if touched, will harmlessly stream from human fingers, or at the most, give a slight shock to the experimenter.

* Notes to Hoole's Ariosto.

CHAPTER IX.

THE DEATH-VOYAGE TO THE EARTHLY PARADISE OR HELL.

"Upon a sea more vast and dark
The spirits of the dead embark,
All voyaging to unknown coasts."
Longfellow—The Golden Legend.

"There Charon stands, who rules the dreary coast,
*.   *   *   *   *   *   *
He spreads his canvas; with his pole he steers;
The freight of flitting ghosts in his thin bottom bears."
Dryden's Æneid, B. vi.

THE mysterious islands described in the last chapter, do not comprise all that was thought and written concerning such lands in the waste of waters encompassing the globe. Many such are reserved for the present chapter, as they are inextricably interwoven with the legends of mysterious voyages, ghostly barks, and spectral forms that suffice to fill a volume.

Legends of a voyage at the end of life's journey, where a river is to be crossed, or an ocean, are found in remote antiquity.

* The dead bodies of the Egyptians, after embalming, were conveyed by water through the canals, across the lakes toward the setting sun, where lay the sepulchres, in many cases. And to the westward lay the Earthly Paradise. The Greek Charon, ferrying souls over the Styx, is familiar to most readers. Sometimes the water was Avernus, Cocytus, Acheron, or the Acherusian lakes of the lower world.

* Keary.—Outlines of Primitive Belief, p. 272.

* In the Vedas, the river is Vaiterañi, "*hard to cross*," and the dead were not long since committed to the care of the sacred Ganges in a boat, with a funeral fire kindled in it. But the Greeks transferred these rivers to the under world, and so they named the

> 'Abhorred Styx, the flood of deadly hate,
> Sad Acheron, of sorrow black and deep
> Cocytus named of lamentation loud."

These names themselves, Acheron and Acherusia, are supposed to be derived from the same root as *aqua*, water.

These were under-world rivers. But the stream of death was more commonly on earth. It was earliest a river of death, and only became a sea later in men's history.

Among the early Aryans, this river was often an aerial stream, in the great air-sea above us.

The soul, which, with the spirit, the breath or ghost, was identified, as we have seen, with the wind, was thus, at death, borne along through the watery element to some unknown land, either Hades or Hel (the concealed, or hidden), or to Paradise (the *high land*). In time, the aerial stream, as well as the under-world river, became rivers of earth, and the abodes of souls were localized also in various remote parts of the earth's surface.

These river-myths grew into a great tribe of similar legends, even extending into a sea of death, the path (Pontus) to the abode of souls. The sea of death appears in all the Aryan folk-lore, in forms and legends too numerous to mention here.

As Miss Harrison aptly puts it: "We remember that for centuries the sea voyage has been the symbol of the troublesome waves of this world, and the transit to the next."

On Greek tombs, the words "Euploia" (favorable voyage) show the popular ideas on the subject. For this, modern Greeks substitute a pair of oars, laid on the grave.

The first great sea epics are now supposed to be accounts of the soul voyage.† The Odyssey, since it has been carefully studied, has been declared a succession of tales of such voyages, and the famous Argonautic expedition is as certainly a myth of the sun voyage or of the soul's migration. Both were made in the western sea, although later legends represent Jason as sailing to the eastward in the Euxine.

* Keary.—Outlines of Primitive Belief, 261.
† Keary.—Outlines of Primitive Belief.

Both were doubtless to the westward, the home of the setting sun, whose night journey was early typical of the soul voyage. So, in Egyptian sculptures, Osiris, the sun god, journeys in the under-world in his golden bark, attended by the hours. An invocation to the sun-god in a papyrus reads,—

* "Oh thou ruler of the waters, that cometh up out of the river,
   Sit thou on the deck of the solar bark."

Thus these imaginary voyages are to the westward, and have ever continued in that direction.

The mysterious Argo, which bore the Greek heroes in their search for the golden fleece, which, like the golden apples of the Hesperian gardens, lay across the waters, will be alluded to again. Ulysses' ship, in which he journeys from Circe's Island to Hades, was a true death ship. Circe says,—

† "Soon shalt thou reach old Ocean's utmost bounds,
  *   *   *   *   *   *   *
There fix thy vessel in the lonely bay,
And enter there the kingdoms void of day."

‡ The Phæacian ships in the " Odyssey " are also ships of the dead. "No pilots have they, no oars, no rudders, and they know the thoughts of men." They carry souls to Alcinous's gardens of Paradise. In one, Odysses is laid asleep, and returned to Greece.

The Ichthyophagi and the Lotophagi, according to Ptolemy, buried their dead in the sea. Hector was buried in an ark-shaped boat, or *Larnax*.

Popular belief shrouded Pontus with darkness. This is indicated by its modern title of Black Sea, which it gets in most European tongues. This Pontus was the *path* or way to the new home of the Aryan, as well as to the under world.

These legends, as men became more and more acquainted with navigation, were transferred to the west, as the earthly paradise was so transferred. So the sea became in later times the River of Death.§ That it was early so regarded we may believe, for from a Sanscrit root are the two words, *meer*, sea, and *mors*, death, derived, and Ulysses sails across

* Records of the Past.
† Pope's Odyssey, Book X.
‡ Keary.—Outlines of Primitive Belief, p. 322.
§ Keary.—Outlines of Primitive Belief, p. 344.

the Western Sea to Hades, and to other Hells and Paradises. From being a river around the world, Oceanus became a sea, and thus a sea of death was to be traversed.

Similar myths of the sea of death exist in all Aryan mythology. Ancient Norsemen called it Gjöll (the sounding). * Thorpe says Gjöll is the horizon, and has reference to the sun sinking with a sound. Here the sea is again mixed up with the myths of death.

† The Norseman named the home of the dead, *Nava*, which word seems to hint at the ship and nautical origins. In the legends of Baldur, the great hero, he is set afloat in his ship " Hringhorn " and in a pyre, set adrift at sea.

This ship Hringhorn was the greatest of all ships. The Edda say: ‡ "After their sorrow was a little appeased, they carried the body of Baldur down toward the sea, where stood the vessel of that god, which passed for the largest in the world. But when the gods wanted to launch it into the water, in order to make a funeral pile for Baldur, they could never make it stir, wherefore they caused to come from the country of the giants a sorceress." This sorceress was Hyrrokin (smoking fire). "Then the sorceress, bending over the prow of the vessel, set it afloat with one single effort, which was so violent that the fire sparkled from the keel as it was dragging to the water."

§ We have here another myth of the sun and of death. Baldur is the Sun-god, Hringhorn the Sun's disk, and this burial the sunset, typifying the journey of the dead.

‖ Sigmundr carries his son Sinfiötli, and puts him in a boat brought by a stranger, leaving him to his fate.

** Jarl Magus was conveyed, with his widow, to the Holy Land in a ship. †† Flosi was abandoned, in a leaky ship, to the mercy of the waves.

Scyld was also so buried. Beowulf says: "They bore him to the sea-shore, as he himself requested. There, on the beach, stood the ring-prowed ship, the vehicle of the noble, ready to set out. They laid down the dear prince, the distributor of things, in the bosom of the ship, the mighty one beside the mast. They set up a golden-ensign high overhead. They gave him to the deep."

* Northern Mythology.
† Keary.—Myths of the Sea and River of Death, Cont. Rev., 1882.
‡ Grimnismal.—Saemundr Edda, 39.
§ Keary.—Outlines of Primitive Belief, p. 401.
‖ Saemundr Edda, 170.
** Jarl Magus Saga, 45.
†† Dasent.—Burnt Njal.

*Sceaff (Skiff), another hero, was found, when a child, floating in a ship, with a treasure in the vessel. Traditionally, he was a descendant of Odin, and a progenitor of the Danish Royal Skyldings. At his death, he also was placed, as William of Malmesburg says, "According to a custom of parts of Scandinavia," in a boat, with a sheaf of corn at his head, and set adrift on the sea. The Saxon Chronicle says he was a son of Noah, born in the ark.

We read in the Heimskringla: "King Hake had been so grievously wounded, that he saw his days would not be long; so he ordered a war-ship which he had, to be loaded with his dead men, and their weapons, and to be taken out to sea, the tiller to be shipped, and the sails hoisted. Then he set fire to some tar-wood, and ordered a pile to be made of it in the ship. Hake was almost, if not quite dead, when he was laid upon this pile of his. The wind was blowing off the land, the ship flew, burning a clear flame, out between the islets, and into the ocean."

Asmundr, Geimundr, and others, were buried in ships, and such burial became so common that an early law prescribed the number of slaves to embark in the boat with a chieftain's body, varying in number from one to ten. †Odin has a golden ship in which he conveys souls to Valhalla. The river to be crossed was there Gurungu-gap, and Valhalla, the hall of heroes, was in Godheim, or Paradise.

‡This vessel is traditionally buried in Runemad, in Sweden.

The Vikings' boat, found in 1881, in a mound near Sandefjord, Norway, has in it a sepulchral chamber, in which a man's bones were found. It was pointed with its prow to the sea.

These death-ships abounded in the middle ages. They · move of their own will, without oars, sails, or rudder sometimes, are of all sizes and shapes, and some, like "Skidbladnir," fold up, or diminish into small space. King Arthur is borne to Avalon in such a death ship.

§Layamon says: "There approached from the sea a little short boat, floating with the waves, and two women therein wondrously formed, and they took Arthur anon, and bare him quickly, and laid him softly down, and forth

* Keary.—Outlines of Primitive Belief. p. 459.
† Grimm.—Teut. Mythology.
‡ Afzelius.—Svenska Folks Visor, I., 4.
§ Brut.

they gan depart."   The tale is told in full, in the old chronicle of the Arthurian deeds.

*Sir Galahad goes in one, in search of the Holy Grail, and legends represent this soul-carrying bark as telling the life-story or the wrongs of the souls embarking in it, and in the story of the "Fair Maid of Astolat," Hermanic became the ship of Faith, warning the mistrustful not to embark. It carries Sir Parsifal to the spiritual place.

† The Demoiselle D'Escalot "begged to have her body put into a ship richly equipped, that would be suffered to drift at the mercy of the winds."

So Tennyson represents Elaine as set adrift in a barge, with a mute slave at the helm.

The old German tribes generally believed in a ferryman of souls.   ‡ The Rhine became the German Styx in one of these stories, a fishermen being called upon one calm night to ferry monks across, his boat each time mysteriously wafted back by a gale.   Mysterious persons, in other tales, call fishermen at night, and leave quantities of gold to pay for their passage.

Such stories are told of ferrymen or fishermen at Spires, and at Saalfeld, in the Weser.   It is Perchta, goddess of death, who calls the boat, in the last story.

§ The bodies of St. Maternus, in the Rhine, and of St. Emmeranus, in the Danube, were mysteriously borne up these rivers in rudderless boats.

A Cologne legend says a certain learned Jew, Rabbi Amram, left the following request behind him: "When I am dead, place me in a coffin, and put it in a boat on the Rhine, and let it go where it will."   This was done, and the boat is said to have floated *up* the Rhine to Mayence. When it arrived, if a Christian tried to touch it, the boat would drift back, and Jews only were able to remove the body.

There is a bay of the departed in Brittany, near Cape Raz (Baie des Trépasses), where boats were summoned, according to the fishermen, to convey souls, especially of drowned men, to Isle au Sein, or the Isle of the Dead. ‖ This boat is, in local tradition, crowded with invisible passengers, whose wails and cries are heard.   Later, this

* Cox.—Aryan Mythology, Bk. I, Chap. 6.
† Romance of Lady of the Lake, 1801. Grimm, I, 831.
‡ Wolf.—Deutsches Sagen.
§ Keary.—Outlines of Primitive Belief, 459.
‖ Villemarqué.—Barzas Breiz, vol. I.

tradition was applied to Great Britain, then to Ireland, and so on to the westward; and the inhabitants and fishermen are represented as serving as ferrymen.

* At Guildo, on the Breton coast, small skiffs are said to come out at night, from under the cliffs, and row away with the souls of mariners, who have been drowned. All fear to pass the spot at night.

The Rhone was also a death-stream, and was sacred as late as the twelfth century, the dead often being committed to its care.

Philip of Rennes, was traditionally carried from St. Vilaine to Rennes in an oarless boat.

† Middle-age legends represent that the soul of Dagobert was wafted to the terrestrial paradise in a ship. As Walter of Aquitaine, was sailing to Ireland, he met a ghostly ship, with a black crew and captain, which latter, when asked where he was going, replied: "I flee from the archbishop, and I go to Hades."

According to a legend of 1585, the devil engaged all the children in Holland to go on a crusade, and got them on board ship, but they never came back.

‡ Old Finnish legend represents Wäinamöinen, the great hero, as being rowed to the lower world by Tuoni, goddess of death, in a black boat, built by Manata, daughter of the king of death.

There is a Spanish legend of a certain Count Arnaldos, who saw at sea a galley slowly drawing near the land, and in it an old sailor, who sang a wondrous sweet song. When asked to stop and sing the song, he replies:

§ " I can tell the Song to no one
Save to him who Sails with me."

Longfellow has a poem on this subject.

‖ A tradition exists that Pope Pius II. (Piccolomini) found at the bottom of the river Numicius a galley coated with bitumen, iron, and lead, and in it a coffer and amphora, believed to contain the ashes of the Roman emperor Tiberius.

** An Irish legend relates that a boat, moved by a hun-

* Sébillot.—Contes des Paysans et Pécheurs.
† Ludlow.—Popular Epics.
‡ Le Duc.—Kalevala.
§ Poems.—" Sea and Shore."
‖ Renard.—Les Merveilles del'Art Naval, 177.
** McPherson.—Int. to History of Great Britain.

dred self-impelled oars, and white sails, but with no crew, appeared out of a dark cloud in a storm, to a certain Druid, at Skerr. A voice said, "Behold the boat of the heroes!" He entered in it, and journeyed seven days to the westward, arriving at Flath Innis, or Noble island, a terrestrial paradise.

*Boat burial has been common among many nations. Keary gives an account of an early instance of this, among the Russ people in 942–76. The bodies of the poorest and richest alike were buried in boats. After burial in a ditch for ten days, a boat is prepared. "I went to the banks of the stream on which was the vessel of the dead. I saw that they had drawn the ship to land, and men were engaged in fixing it upon four stakes, and had placed around it wooden stakes. On to the vessel they bore a wooden platform, a mattress and cushions, covered with a Roman material of golden cloth." When the time came, the body, richly attired, was placed thereon, and with that of a strangled female slave, a dog, two horses, and three fowls, was buried along with the weapons of the deceased.

† Ralston says all Slavonic people believe in the voyage and river of death, and coins are still placed in graves.

‡ Scheffer says Lapps and Ostiaks buried their dead in boats, or boat-shaped coffins.

§ The Garrows of Bengal still burn their dead in a boat, four days after death. Borneo Kanowits set adrift a canoe containing some worthless property of the deceased, to typify the whole of his possessions. The sea Dyaks also place their dead in a canoe, with some property, and set it adrift. |The boats used in the funeral procession of Thrien Thri, a king of Cochin China, in 1849, were burned on his pyre. The dead are still carried to the grave in boats or barges, in Siam, just as in the Parish of Plougoel, in Brittany, they are rowed by a longer way than the land route, through a passage called "passage of hell."

Canoe burial is reported of many Indian tribes. The Musquitos burned their dead in a canoe, or cut the boat up, and placed it in the grave. The Aleuts used boat-shaped coffins. **The Shokomishes, Clallams, Chinooks, Flat-

* Outlines of Primitive Belief, 405.
+ Songs of the Russian People, pp. 107-6.
‡ Lapponia.
§ Tyler.—Anthropology.
| Tyler.—Primitive Culture, p. 489.
** Bancroft.—Native Races, Vol. I, p. 208.

SEA DYAK'S BOAT SACRIFICE.

heads, Nootkans, and some Columbia river tribes buried their dead in canoes elevated on poles.

Swan says some old boats lying on a point of land in Shoalwater Bay, were deemed the property of departed spirits, and were never molested. Wilkes found 3,000 canoes in one cemetery.

* The Cherokees and Chinooks sometimes buried their dead in the sea, as did the Ilzas of Guatemala, and the Aleuts.

Esquimaux often placed a kayak in or near the grave, or at least a model of one, to assist the deceased in his journey.

The Greeks early invented a traditional fare for the dead ferryman (the *naulas*), and an obolus was put into the mouth of the corpse to pay the passage. This custom existed in the Middle Ages in France and Germany, and bodies were found in a church-yard in France in 1630, with coins in the graves. The Chinese put a coin in the coffin, to pay the passage or fare of the corpse. † The custom is not yet extinct in Burgundy, and in Altmark, Havelland, and other parts of Germany it also survives, although the coin is now a charm to keep away a vampire (Nachzehrer).

In Markland, when several deaths occur in a family, it is because the penny was omitted in the case of the first one.

Wallachians still put the *obolus* in the mouth of the corpse, and Baring Gould says a man was buried not long ago in Yorkshire, with a penny, a candle and a bottle of wine in his grave.

We find in " Hamlet," the grave-digger says,—

> "And hath *shipped* me intill the land,
> As if I had never been such,"

possibly alluding to this belief of a death-ferryman. Nor are the savage tribes without such legends. In " Hiawatha " we find he

> "Came unto the Lake of Silver,
> In the Stone Canoe was carried
> To the Islands of the Blessed,
> To the lands of ghosts and shadows."

‡ The Athabascas and Chippeways had also a stone canoe in which souls crossed the waters. Many Indian tribes cross the water, on their way to heaven.

A Dacotah tale is of a youth who journeyed south in

* Bancroft.—Native Races. Vancouver's Voyages, Vol. II, p. 545.
† Grimm.—Teutonic Mythology.
‡ Jones.—Traditions of the American Indians, p. 256.

search of the abode of souls, the entrance of which is guarded by Chibiabos. A canoe of shining white stone conveys souls across the lake.

* The Fijians embarked from the northwest cape of their island, being rowed by a Charon to Mbula, a land of spirits. As the soul approaches, a paroquet gives warning of it.

† Mangaians journeyed to the west in a mystic canoe, called in a song, Puvai's canoe. Williams and Mariner were told by Fijians that they could see the *souls* of canoes floating down a spirit stream.

New Zealand tribes have their death-bark, and a woman was said to have made the final journey, and returned to earth.

In the Soloman Islands, a canoe comes to the West Cape, and carries all the dead to Gotogo, their heaven.

‡ Chilian souls went westward in a death-bark, and Australian legends embody similar fictions. § The Chinese, sixty days after death, place on the water an egg-shell, and an image of a duck with a man astride of it; the duck and boat are to assist the soul—represented by the small figure —in its voyage.

Thus we see, there has existed from antiquity, a belief in the death voyage, and as a consequence, we shall find numerous myths of a terrestrial abode of souls.

Mythologists claim that the ideas of primitive nations as to these abodes of the soul or breath (psyche) became localized gradually to this earth from their former aerial or heavenly positions. There is generally a water to be crossed, be it Styx, Acheron, or the Atlantic, and then the soul arrives at an island or continent, generally to the westward. The ancient Egyptian rowed across the Nile, or over the lake to the westward, and to the westward lay the evening mirage, and the desert became the sea of death to the inland tribes. In fact, philologists tell us that sea and desert were once identical, and possibly both corresponded to death, in the mind of the Aryan.‖ For the same word gave rise to *mare*, sea, *meru*, desert, and *mors*, death (*murder* also). Rivers were at first the death-streams, and even the Caspian, the first sea known to the Aryans, was a river around the world. The Ægean, or Pontus, next became the *path* of souls, and across

---

* Gill.—Myths and Songs of the South Pacific, 94.
† Gill.—Myths and Songs of the South Pacific.
‡ Tylor.—Primitive Culture II, p. 61.
§ Doolittle.—Chinese.
‖ Keary.—Myths of the Sea and River of Death.

the circumambient Ocean lay the Cimmerian land, which abode of shades Ulysses visits in the "Odyssey."

These fabled islands early became the traditional homes of souls, lost or saved, and thus we have, in all ages, stories of Isles of the Blessed across the waters of death. The terrestrial abodes of condemned souls, Hades, or Hel (both words meaning *unseen* or *concealed*), were early reputed to be islands, and the belief was closely connected with the Charon-boat and the sea of death. At first these islands were reported as being in the Ægean Sea, and only as the other parts of the Mediterranean became known, were these fabled islands removed farther and farther from the seats of Grecian civilization, even into the Atlantic.

These many fictions of mysterious islands would be strengthened and localized by the tales of wandering Phœnician and Greek mariners. So, many of Homer's myths of foreign lands seem to be compounded of real and imaginary experiences.

The prevalence of Sun-worship doubtless aided in forming these myths. We have seen how this is apparent in the early myths of the sea of death. Homer says the sun rises and sets in the ocean, and travels along the surface in his shining bowl. *The Jewish Midrash compares the course of the sun with that of a ship with three hundred and sixty-five ropes in it, coming from Great Britian, or one from Alexandria with three hundred and fifty-six ropes in it (Lunar year). Egyptians represented him as performing his night journey in the ocean, and hence it was to them accursed.

The Homeric books give us the first tales of such mysterious islands. The first purgatories are Ogygia (Ocean place) and Æae (land of wailing).

The islands of Calypso and of Circe were mysterious abodes. † Keary has shown them to be homes of the dead. Calypso (from kalyptein, *to conceal*) is none other than the Norse Hel, the concealer, and is death dwelling in her cave by the sea-side. Circe is the hawk, or death in bird-shape.

From her island, or Purgatory, Ulysses sails direct to Hades, just beyond the Cimmerians. Scheria, Lotos-land, and Hesperia, were Homeric paradises, the first and last fabled islands remote from Ulysses' Ithacan home. Scheria, the land of the Phæacians, means *shore*, and lies "at the end

*Goldhizer.—Myths Among the Hebrews, 101.
† Outlines.—Primitive Belief.

of the watery plain." The trees of Alcinous' garden are perpetually green, and we have seen that the Phæacians were carriers of souls.

This Paradise, at first in the east, was transferred to the west, among the Blameless Ethiopians or Hyperboreans, following the course of the Sun again. " By a train of fancy easy to follow, it is often held that the home of the dead has to do with that far west where the sun dies at night."

So Hesperia, at first in Africa, was finally transferred to Spain, and then to the Atlantic islands.

An early locality for these mysterious abodes was in the North. *There lay Olympus, home of the gods. There were the Hyperboreans, the Cimmerians, and Æolia, the abode of the god of the winds. Aristotle and Indicopleustes say the sun goes northward in his under-world journey, and Pytheas confirms this, by saying that he was shown the place where the sun dwelt at night; that is, he saw the midnight sun. Diodorus says there was a feast among the Hyperboreans in the Island of the Gods, every nineteenth year. Amber, says Pliny, comes from this garden of the gods, dropping from the trees, and drifting to northern shores. Avalon, to which Arthur was taken, was to the northward.

†Two recent authors discuss the subject of the Northern Paradise, from a scientific standpoint. •

So fixed in the minds of men became these traditions of earthly paradises, just out of sight of African headlands, that ages afterwards these islands were still sought, to the westward of the Azores and Madeiras, although the fabled Atlantis had been overwhelmed in the waves.

In the middle ages, these legends became abundant, doubtless aided by saintly authority and church sanction. Justin Martyr says Paradise is in the Western Atlantic. Claudian says an island exists near Gaul, ruled over by Ulixes, where the spirits of the departed abide. •

In Norse mythology, Jötuuheim, or giants' home, a cold region beyond the ocean stream, was, like Cimmeria, a sort of purgatory.

Many fables were related of these Atlantic, and of the Panichæan, islands. The golden apples of Hesperic gardens are, perhaps, oranges brought by Phœnician mariners from far-off Africa or Spain. Proclus says, on the authority of

* Keary.—Myths of the Sea and River of Death.
† Warren.—Paradise Found—1886. Scribner.—Where Did Life Begin?

Marcellus, that there were seven Atlantic islands,—one dedicated to Pluto, one to Ammon, and one to Poseidon. Euhemerus tells us of Panichæan islands, inhabited by god-like men.

These Atlantic islands, elsewhere numbered as ten, were appropriately governed by Neptune's sons, and it was further said that weeds and debris long impeded ships, and their sinking traditionally accounted for the Sargasso Sea of weeds.

*Plato tells us this, "For in those days the Atlantic was navigable, and there was an island situated in front of the strait which you call the Columns of Hercules. . . . But afterwards there occurred violent earthquakes and floods, and in a single day and night of rain, all your warlike men in a body sank into the earth, and the island of Atlantis in like manner disappeared and sank beneath the sea. And that is the reason why the sea in those parts is impassable and impenetrable, because there is such a quantity of shoals and mud in the way, caused by the sinking of the island." Plato further says the Egyptians (from whom these accounts were derived) told Solon that this occurred 9,000 B.C.

Hesiod calls the Western Islands the Isles of Souls. †Proclus says, "There life is easiest unto men; no snow or wintry storms, or rain at any time is there."

Diodorus says Panchaia was southward from Arabia Felix, and was also sunk in the sea.

Thor was rowed across the death stream by Harbarth,‡ whose boat would not bear the weight of a living person. Gortu the Wise also sailed to the West with three ships. They landed on an island of flocks and herds, from which they took more than they needed, and in consequence were pursued by a band of fearful monsters, who only left them when three men were sacrificed to them. In another island, Biarmia, they found the paradise and purgatory.

Leonardo de Argensola says there is a desert, rocky island, Poëlsetta, near Italy. Cries, roarings, groanings and other sounds were heard in it, and it was fabled to be peopled by devils.

Marco Polo represents Cipangu as a sort of terrestrial paradise, a city of golden streets, and of white-robed inhabitants.

* Timæus, II, 617.
† Boeck.—Fragments.
‡ Keary.—Outlines of Primitive Belief.

*Onogorojima, the island of the congealed drop, was a fabled Japanese Paradise.

†Allusion has been made to a traditionary isle of the dead near Cape Raz, in the Bay of Deposit. This "Isle au Sein" was said to be peopled by souls of the departed, and fishermen were said to be called to ferry souls over.

Another spot on the coast of France is traditionally inhabited by the souls of drowned persons, and fishermen fear to approach the opposite beach, at night, where phantoms are believed to wander.

‡A Breton legend is told of a fabled island of souls, and a death ferryman at Carnoët ferry, in a Breton stream. A young couple came along to cross the ferry, but the lover lingered behind, and the maiden was induced to enter the boat, while waiting for him. She was spirited away in the boat, forgetting to make the sign of the cross.

§ In Norse mythology, Heligoland, as indicated by its name, was a sacred island, the abode of the gods, and was reverenced by early mariners.

There was a sacred fountain on it, where early Christians were baptized.

‖Hörnum, near the Danish coast, is said to be inhabited only by the ghosts of murderers, strandwalkers, sea-women, fiends, etc. **A group of islands near Norway are also represented as being inhabited by elves, and fit only for grazing.

††Russians believe in an island paradise, Boyan, to the eastward.

The Cimbri called the Northern Ocean Mari Mortuus (sea of the dead), and German-lore gave us a Dumslaf (frozen sea) of wondrous properties.

Helvoetsfuis, at the mouth of the Maas, was another fabled islet of souls, and many legends concerning it were current.

‡‡These fancies of antiquity descended to later times. Procopius, an early Gothic historian, says Brittia, in the Northern Ocean, was in his day the fabled abode of souls.

* Warren.—Paradise Found, p. 140.
† Cam ry.—Voy. dans la Finnisterre, II, p. 240.
‡ Th. and K. McQuoid.—Pictures and Legends of Normandy and Brittany, p. 19.
§ Grimm.—Deutsche Mythologie, Vol. I, p. 150.
‖ Thorpe.—Northern Mythology, Vol. II. p. 8.
** Landrin.—Les Monstres Marins.
†† Ralston.—Songs of the Russian People, p. 375.
‡‡ History Goths, Bk. IV, Ch. 40. Keary, p. 487.

The home of the dead was beyond, noxious to living beings, but peopled by souls ferried across by fishermen from the opposite coast. These, called in turn at night, find barks laden with souls, and are wafted over by mysterious winds.

*Tzetes, another chronicler, says: "On the coast of the ocean opposite Brittania (England), dwell fishermen who are subjects of the Franks, but they pay them no tribute, on account, as they say, of their ferrying over the souls of the departed. They go to sleep in their houses in the evening, but after a little time they hear a knocking at the door, and a voice calling them to their work. They get up and go to the shore, not knowing what the need is; they see boats there, but not their own, with no one in them; they get in, row away, and perceive that they are heavy as if laden with passengers, but they see no one."

† England long remained the abode of spirits. German witches were thought to rendezvous there; and Ireland succeeded to England as the Blessed Isle.

‡ In German stories, the nightmare says her mother is in England, and German mothers still say, referring to the dead, "How my children are crying in England." In Armorican belief, the dog of the parish priest of Braspar carries souls to Great Britain.

§ Welsh legends tell of the "Green meadows in the sea," islands in the Irish Sea, the abode of souls of Druids, and they also call them White Man's Land. Gallic traditions speak of them as the Noble Land.

Pembrokeshire sailors, in the eighteenth century, told of an Island of Green Meadows in the Irish Sea, and they say some visited them in the present century, but when they re-embarked, these islands suddenly disappeared. ‖ Fairies are said to inhabit them; and Welsh traditions represent them as visiting Milford Haven, coming through a tunnel under the sea.

Other Welsh legends are of voyages in search of Blessed Isles, by Merlin and by Madoc, the latter reputed to have found our own shores, in his search.

Merlin (Merdyn Ennis) sailed with twelve companions, and Gavran sailed westward to find the Gwerddonan Llian (Green Islands of the Sea). These islands were fabled the

* In Fraser's Mag., Vol. II, p. 228.
† Wright.—St. Patrick's Purgatory, pp. 66 and 128.
‡ Kuhn.—Westphälische Sagen, p. 154.
§ Sikes.—British Goblins and Welsh Folk-lore, p. 8.
‖ Sikes.—British Goblins and Welsh Folk-lore, p. 9.

abodes of the Tylwith Teg, *fair family*, the souls of certain Druids, who abode in this lower heaven. They were said to revisit Wales, and to carry men to their island. These, when they returned, thought an absence of ten years but a day. These islands could be seen from a turf in St. David's churchyard, but they disappeared when sought. One man conceived the happy thought of sailing in search of them on a sod from the churchyard, and found them.

*Madoc's voyage has been immortalized by Southey:

> "Themselves, immortal, drink the gales of bliss,
> Which o'er Flath Innis breathe eternal spring."

Irish souls crossed Lough Derg, and, in Loch Cre, was one island where all lived forever, and another where none could live. After Arran was blessed, no corpse could decay.

The Norse, in the tenth century, called Ireland Hvit-manna Land (white man's land).

The traditional Green Isle, or the Isle of the Dead, lay beyond the Isle of Youth, and between Scotland and Ireland lay Caire Lewan, another mysterious island.

† There were numerous Druidical stories of such islands. Sir-na-m-Beo, Isle of the Living, and Hy-na-m-Balla, Island of Life, were of these, and were traditionally inhabited by the Firbolgs. By many, they were said to be inhabited by the ghosts of drowned men.

‡ The Landnama bók tells us: "Ari was storm-cast on the White Man's Land, which some call Great Ireland. This lies in the western sea, near Vinland, the good; it is called six days' sail west from Ireland."

§ Maildun, a Celtic hero, also undertook a voyage in search of these Blessed Isles. He sailed in a "Coracle," large enough to accommodate sixty-four people. He found islands of demons and monsters, a Circe, and finally the terrestrial paradise. So, in McGee's poem, we read of Eman Oge, who also sailed in search of these islands. St. Patrick is said to have set a neophyte adrift in a boat, with the boat-chain wrapped about him; and he, too, found this earthly paradise.

‖ But a more widespread tradition was of the voyage of St. Brandan, an early saint. He sailed, with twelve fellow-

*Southey.—Madoc, XI.
†Kennedy.—Fictions of the Irish Celts.
‡In B. Gou'd.—Curious Myths, 550.
§Sikes.—British Goblins, p. 9.
‖Voyage Mervellleux de St. Brandan, Ed. Michel.

monks, in search of the Isles of the Blessed.   He was fabled
to have found the holy island, inhabited by twenty-four
monks.   Besides, he found an island of birds (fallen angels),
an island of sheep, and an island inhabited by fiends, who
attacked him.   This is like the Island of Birds and Island
of Sheep, in the "Arabian Nights."   One version of the
story calls the islands *Hy-Breasil.*

*"Seven dayes they sayled awaye in that clere water.
And thenne there came a southe winde, and drof the shyppe
northward, wheras they sawe an ylonde full dirke and full
of stench and smoke; and then they herde grete blowinge
and blasting of belowes, but they might see noothynge,
but herde grete thunderynge" . . . "and soone ther
came a greate nombere of fendes, and assayled them with
hokes and brennying yron mattys, whiche rannen on the
water, following theyr shyppe faste in such wyse that it
seemed all the see to be in a fyre."   He also saw other
wonderful islands, and met Judas floating on a rock in the
sea.   He sailed east, then north, then west, then east to
Ireland.   Before him, a monk (Meruuke) had found the
earthly paradise, sailing three days to the eastward, until
a dark cloud came up; when it cleared, he found an island.
"In that ylonde was joye and mirthe enough."   So St.
Brandan finally found the Blessed Island, thenceforth to
bear his name, or that of Hy Brazil (Royal island).

> †"On the ocean that hollows the rocks where ye dwell,
> A shadowy land has appeared, as they tell;
> Men thought it a region of sunshine and rest,
> And they called it O'Brazil, the isle of the blest."

These islands were long believed to lie west of Ireland,
or of Spain.   In an old chart of 1751, one is put down three
hundred miles to the westward of Ferrol, in latitude
twenty-nine degrees.   After the discovery of the Canaries
and Madeiras, these islands were supposed to lie still farther
to the westward, and the loom of land was thought to have
been seen, but they would fade as fast as they were neared.

‡A Lisbon pilot of the fifteenth century, storm-beaten,
was said to have found them, and a noble Spanish lord
fitted out an expedition to find them.   Separated from his
fleet in a storm, he is said to have been driven to them, and,

* Wynklin de Worde.—Golden Legend.
† Gerald Griffin.—Hy Brazil.
‡ W. Irving.—Chronicles of Woolfert's Roost.

after a Rip Van Winkle sleep of years, returned to Spain, reporting that they were ruled by descendants of Rodrigo, the last king of the Goths.   * The Portuguese called the isle St. Sebastian, and alleged that some Wednesday of holy week, a fog would come up, and in it the fleet of that monarch, bringing him back to his kingdom.

†Canary islanders thought they saw it, and, on the globe of Martin Beheim, it was figured two hundred leagues to the westward of Canary.

Many other accounts of the island were given by early writers.   Irving's story, "The Adelantado of Seven Cities," is founded on these old traditions.

It was even mentioned in the treaties between Portugal and Spain.   The Spanish retained traditions of it in the sixteenth century, calling it the island that "*quando se busca no se halla.*"   An expedition sailed in search of it as late as 1721.

‡Irving says it was also called aprositus (inaccessible)

There are many early accounts of it.   William of Worcester twice mentions Brasyle.   He says his brother sailed to it, in 1401, from Bristol, steering due west for nine (?) months; but scarcely had he discovered the island, when they were driven back by storms.

§One of the maps contained in the work of an Italian geographer of 1605 has Hy Brazil figured in it.

║A manuscript in Trinity College library, Dublin, dated 1636, states that "many old mappes lay down O'Brazile in longitude 03.00; latitude 50.20."   Werdenhagen, an old Dutch author, gives a chart, in which an island is figured near this spot.

Hardiman quotes a letter from a Mr. Hamilton to a cousin in London, in which he says he was told by a Captain Nisbet that one of his ships had sailed to this island, in 1614.

**Jeremy Taylor alludes to O'Brazile, or the Inchanted Isle, in 1667.

††Dr. Guest says a work was published in London, in 1674, entitled, "The Western Wonder; or, O'Brazile," giv-

* Brewer.—Reader's Hand Book.
† Irving.—Voyages of Columbus, Vol. II. note 25.
‡ Irving.—Chronicles of Wolfert's Roost.
§ G. Bronero Broneri.—Relazione Universali.
║ Jas. Hardiman.—Irish Minstrelsy, V. 358.
** Discussion Against Popery, 1671.
†† Notes and Queries, October 26, 1868.

ing an accurate description, in the style of DeFoe, of a visit to the island.

* A Mr. Fraser published a paper in 1879, giving an enlarged map in which the island is distinctly laid down. It is from a work by the Royal Geographer, Tusser, in 1674. Fraser thinks the island occupied the spot where Porcupine shoal now is, as shells have been found there, requiring regular atmospheric exposure to have attained their development.

† Hy Breasil appears in a map of Andreas Bianco, and in others down to the time of Coronelli. Humboldt says it is on an English map, and it is found in an old map of Purdy's.

The legends concerning Bermuda have been related. ‡ An Italian chart of Jacomo di Gaetaldi, in 1550, calls Newfoundland "Isola dei Demonii (Isle of Demons), and figures demons near it. Thevet says the Indians were tormented by demons residing there. Champlain tells of a diabolic island near Miscou, on the St. Lawrence, where lived an ogress, taller than the tallest ships.

§ Baring Gould says Lambertus Floridus, in a MS. of the twelfth century, locates Paradise in the Indian Ocean, and a map in Cambridge library figures it at the mouth of the Danube, while the Hereford map of the thirteenth century also places it near India, but separated it from the continent by a wall of brass.

Even savages have such mysterous isles. Near Raratonga Island, in the Hervey group, in an islet reputed the home of souls, is "No-land-at-all," and souls embarked from the West Cape.

| A Tongan home of souls was Bolotoo, an island to the northwest. Here mortals lived forever, and plants and animals were also reproduced. A canoe of warriors once reached it, but were instantly bidden to depart. They died from the effects of the air of this paradise. Naicobocoo was another island paradise, to reach which souls embarked from a certain cape. ** Pulola was the Samoan heaven, under the sea.

In Mangaia, the abode of souls was an island to the

* Notes and Queries, December, 1888.
† Yule's Polo II, 318.
‡ Le Moine.—Chronicles of the St. Lawrence.
§ Myths of the Middle Ages.
| Tyler.—Primitive Culture II, p. 62.
** Gill.—Myths and Songs of the South Pacific, p. 168

northwest. When bodies were thrown from cliffs into the sea, souls found their way to these islands.

Fijians thought souls went westward. Their Islands of the Blessed lay to the northwest, and were named Boluta. The crew of a tempest-driven boat are said to have landed on it, but never returned.

They also spoke of a paradise below the sea. When a thunder-clap was heard on the distant horizon, they said it was a soul descending to this paradise.

Australians, and other Polynesian tribes believed in Islands of Souls, generally to the westward, toward the setting sun.

Nor are our own uncultured races without such traditions. The Athabascans believe that their Isles of the Blessed lie in Lake Huron; and in " Hiawatha " we find the poet saying that Chibiabos went

> " To the islands of the blessed,
> To the land of ghosts and shadows."

* Algonquins' souls paddled in a white stone canoe across a lake, where storms destroyed wicked souls, to a Blessed Island. Hurons and Sioux believed a river must be crossed, and Dacotahs, a crystal lake, while Choctaws, and Massachusetts Indians went west to Kiehtan.

† The Indians of Lake Superior have a tradition of an island with golden sands, about whose shores waves ceaselessly beat. Mortals landing on it, never return.

This island is in Lake Manitobah, where a Manitou, or speaking God, is heard at night.

Chilians and Peruvians believed that the abodes of souls lay to the westward. Sacred islands existed in Mexico and Guatemala. ‡ To the westward lay Coaibai, the Haytien paradise. Brazilian souls went west, and there in the ocean lay the paradise of the Aronco Indians, whose Charon was Tempalazy, the sailor.

The Khonds say the Judge of the dead is in a rock beyond the sea. To this " leaping rock " all must jump, across the black and muddy stream.

§ The Okanagans had traditions of a White Man's Island (Samahtumiwhoolah), from whence their ancestors came,

* Tyler.—Primitive Culture, II, p. 62.
† Schoolcraft.—Indian Tribes,
‡ Tyler.—Primitive Culture, II. p. 62.
§ Bancroft.—Natives Races, III, p. 158.

having been banished on a floating piece of the island, by its ruler, Scomalt, a woman. A southern *California tribe also believed in island paradises near Monterey.

The discoveries of modern navigators have banished all thoughts of real islands mysteriously located, and inhabited by the souls of men. Since the remotest corners of the temperate ocean have been explored, and no terrestrial heaven, or earthly purgatory has been found, no shadowy lands remain on our charts to vex the night-wearied mariner, save such spectral rocks as are from time to time located in mid-ocean, by some careless skipper. Well may we then ask,—

> † " Where are they, those green fairy islands, reposing
>   In sunlight and beauty, on Ocean's calm breast?
> What spirit, the things that are hidden disclosing,
>   Shall point the bright way to their dwellings at rest?"

‡ And we may answer these queries by this verse:

> " Here, 'mid the bleak waves of our strife and care,
>   Float the green Fortunate Isles,
> Where all the hero-spirits dwell and share
>   Our martyrdom and toils."

* Bancroft.—Native Races, III, p. 525.
† Mrs. Hemans' Poems.
‡ J. R. Lowell's Poems.

CHAPTER X.

THE PHANTOM SHIP.

"'Tis the Phantom ship, that, in darkness and wrath,
Ploughs evermore the waste ocean path,
And the heart of the mariner trembles in dread,
When it crosses his vision like a ghost of the dead."
Ayres.—Legends of Montauk.

" 'A ship's unhappy ghost,' she said,
'The awful ship, the Mystery.' "
Celia Thaxter.

THE legend of the Flying Dutchman is the most picturesque and romantic of the many tales current among sailors half-a-century ago. It is also, perhaps, the best-known nautical legend. Novelists have used it as their theme; poets have embellished the tale with their verse; dramatists have familiarized the public with it, and it has been the subject of modern opera. The tale is told with variations in nearly every maritime country, and folklore tales of wonderful spectral and phantom ships are abundant.

The usually accepted version of the story is thus given by M. Jal: *"An unbelieving Dutch captain had vainly tried to round Cape Horn against a head-gale. He swore he would do it, and, when the gale increased, laughed at the fears of his crew, smoked his pipe and drank his beer. He threw overboard some of them who tried to make him put into port. The Holy Ghost descended on the vessel, but he fired his pistol at it, and pierced his own hand and paralyzed his arm. He cursed God, and was then condemned by the apparition to navi-

*Scénes de la Vie Maritime, Vol. II, p. 60.

gate always without putting into port, only having gall to drink and red-hot iron to eat, and eternally to watch. He was to be the evil genius of the sea, to torment and punish sailors, the sight of his storm-tossed bark to carry presage of ill fortune to the luckless beholder. He sends white squalls, all disasters, and tempests. Should he visit a ship, wine sours, and all food becomes beans—the sailor's *bête noir*. Should he bring or send letters, none must touch them, or they are lost. He changes his mien at will, and is seldom seen twice under the same circumstances. His crew are all old sinners of the sea, sailor thieves, cowards, murderers, and such. They eternally toil and suffer, and have little to eat or drink. His ship is the true purgatory of the faithless and idle mariner."

*This is the Phantom Ship, of which Scott sings:

"Or of that Phantom Ship, whose form
Shoots like a meteor through the storm;
When the dark scud comes driving hard,
And lowered is every topsail yard,
And canvas, wove in earthly looms,
No more to brave the storm presumes!
Then, 'mid the war of sea and sky,
Top and topgallant hoisted high,
Full spread and crowded every sail,
The Demon Frigate braves the gale;
And well the doom'd spectators know
The harbinger of wreck and woe."

As the hero is a Dutchman, we should properly refer to Holland for the true version of the tale.

†Several authorities give this as follows: "Falkenberg was a nobleman, who murdered his brother and his bride in a fit of passion, and was condemned therefor forever to wander toward the north. On arriving at the seashore, he found awaiting him a boat, with a man in it, who said, '*Expectamus te.*' He entered the boat, attended by his good and his evil spirit, and went on board a spectral bark in the harbor. There he still lingers, while these spirits play dice for his soul. For six hundred years the ship has wandered the seas, and mariners still see her in the German ocean, sailing northward, without helm or helmsman. She is painted gray, has colored sails, a pale flag, and no crew. Flames issue from the masthead at night."

* Rokeby, Canto II, v. 2.
† Bechstein.—Deutches Sagenbuch. Wolf.—Niederländische Sagen, No. 188.
Thorpe.—Northern Mythology, III, 206.

THE PHANTOM SHIP.

345

Some of the features of this tale seem to be borrowed from a Norse tradition, that Stöte, a Viking, stole a ring from the gods, and when they sought him they found him a skeleton, in a robe of fire, seated on the mainmast of a black spectral ship, seen in a cavern by the sea. This legend is embodied in Bishop Tegnér's Fridthjof's Saga.

*Marryat, *facile princeps* in matters maritime, has woven out of the legend the plot of his phantom ship. The captain of the ship, Vanderdecken, relates to his wife in Holland the cause of his wandering. He had tried for nine weeks to weather the stormy cape, but after battling against adverse winds and currents, and after throwing overboard the pilot, who opposed him, he finally swore on a relic of the true cross that in spite of wind and weather—storms, seas, lightning, etc.—he would beat until the day of judgment, to pass the cape. His oath brought upon him the punishment. The hero of the tale, his son, finds a letter describing all this, after his mother's death, and, in addition, saying that a return of the cross-relic on board by a mortal would insure the termination of the punishment. To the execution of this task, the son, Philip, devotes his life. The phantom ship appears in the story many times in the son's search after her, and embodies the main points of the legend. One says that to meet the phantom ship is worse than to see the devil, such ill luck follows thereby. Others, that letters must not be taken, or the vessel receiving them will be lost. Her first appearance is in a cloud at sunset, surrounded by a pale-blue light. It was fine weather, but she was under storm-sail, pitching and tumbling about as in a sea. The whistles of the mates were heard, and orders from her decks, but she soon disappeared in the gloom and mist. Again she was seen in a good breeze, only the loom of her hull appearing in a fog, but a gun was fired, and voices heard. Again she came in a gale, sailing tranquilly with all sail set, and still again she sails over the bar and shore, decoying the pursuers on shoals, and again in a typhoon, when she ran right through the pursuing son's vessel.

In her last appearance she rises gradually out of the water, a true demon-ship, and heaves to, awaiting a message. A boat appears, boards the pursuing ship with letters, which are thrown overboard. As a result of the machinations of Philip's evil spirit, he is set adrift by the superstitious sailors

* Phantom Ship, *Passim.*

of his ship, and finally gains the deck of the phantom ship, restores his father the relic, and terminates the wanderings of the blaspheming captain.

* In a poem by Leyden, the ship is thus described. It is thought to be a slave-ship attacked by the plague, and refused a refuge in the various ports,—

> "Repelled from port to port, they sue in vain
> And track with slow, unsteady sail the main,
> Where ne'er the bright and buoyant wave is seen
> To streak with wandering foam the sea-weeds green.
>
> * * * * * * *
>
> The Spectre-Ship, in livid glimpsing light,
> Glares baleful on the shuddering watch at night,
> Unblest of God and man!"

† Brewer says the Phantom ship is called Carmilhan, and the goblin Klaboterman sits on the bowsprit smoking his pipe. ‡Longfellow sings of

> A ship of the dead that sails the sea,
> And is called the Carmilhan,
> A ghostly ship, with a ghostly crew.
> In tempests she appears,
> And before the gale or against the gale
> She sails, without a rag of sail,
> Without a helmsman steers.
>
> And ill betide the luckless ship
> That meets the Carmilhan!
> Over her decks the seas will leap,
> She must go down into the deep,
> And perish, mouse and man."

§And so sings O'Reilly,—

> " But Heaven help the ship near which the demon sailor steers!
> The doom of those is sealed, to whom the Phantom Ship appears,
> They'll never reach their destin'd port, they'll see their homes no more,
> They who see the Flying Dutchman never, *never* reach the shore."

‖ Brachvogel has written a tale, "Die Fliegende Holländer," of the time of the Spanish Armada. In Dietrichson's career is reproduced the tale of Vanderdecken.

** There is another English tale, "The Flying Dutchman," in which mutineers seize a man-of-war and rig her to simu-

---

* Scenes of Infancy.
† Reader's Hand-book.
‡ Poems.—Tales of a Wayside Inn.
§ Boyles O'Reilly.— Songs of Southern Seas.
‖ Die Fliegende Holländer.
** Monroe's Seaside Library, No. 508.

late the spectre-ship, by so arranging her sails that they are but net works of rope and canvas, while they seem firm and substantial. This is done to terrify a pursuing vessel, but the real spectre-ship is encountered by her, terrifying the mutineers, and furnishing an omen of their final capture and condemnation.

* Thomas Gibbons, in an interesting volume recently published, gives a poem from some nautical pen recapitulating the main events of the usual tale.

† Cooper says she is said to be a double-decker, and is always to windward, sometimes in a fog during clear weather, often under all sail in a gale, and even sailing among the clouds.

‡ H. Fitzball dramatized the story, and it was performed many times in New York. The usual story, with slight variations, is embodied in the drama. The story has also furnished a theme for opera. In Wagner's "Fliegende Holländer," a Norwegian brig meets the spectre-ship at sea, on his own coast. He is induced, by promises of great treasure, to pledge his daughter to the captain of the "Flying Dutchman," here nameless. The captain says, relating his tale, that he must wander seven years without ceasing, but may now, a respite being at hand, claim an earthly bride.

The ships proceed to port, where we find the intended bride and her maidens. In a ballad, Senta recalls the Dutchman's fate.

§ "There sails a ship o'er stormy main,
    With blackened mast and blood-red sail;
On deck, and ever suffering pain,
    The captain watches without fail.
Around a cape he once would sail,
He strove, and swore 'gainst wind and hail,
' Forever will I strive to pass.' "

But he is to be saved if he finds a true maiden. The lover appears, and endeavors to dissuade the maiden, in an impassioned duet. Finally the maiden hesitates, when the captain of the spectre-ship, thinking her faithless, goes to sea again, revealing himself thus:

* Boxing the Compass.
† "Red Rover," Chapter xiv.
‡ "The Flying Dutchman" a Drama.
§ R. Wagner.—Die Fliegende Holländer.

> " ' Thou know'st me not; thou think'st not what I am;
> Go ask the seas of every zone;
> Go ask the sailor who those seas doth roam;
> He knows this ship, the subject of his tales,
> The Flying Dutchman am I nam'd.' "

Such are the main features of the story of the Flying Dutchman, with its many variants. But there are a host of other legends concerning spectral ships, which serve to illustrate the ideas of the seafaring man concerning such illusions.

* Danish sailors have a legend of a spectral ship, often seen in the Baltic, and believe it is a sign of disaster to meet with it.

A Schleswick-Holstein tale is told of a maiden who was carried off by her lover in a spectral ship, as she was sitting on the shore bewailing his absence. Fishermen aver they see m Katzeburg lake spectral boats and nets, which suddenly disappear when approached.

† The old Frisians thought the world a great ship ("Mannigfual"), the mountains its masts. The captain went about on horseback giving his orders. Sailors going aloft when boys came down gray headed men, and in blocks about the rigging were dining-halls, where they meanwhile sustained life. This ship was afterward lessened, but still remained gigantic. She stuck in the Straits of Dover, but her ingenious captain smeared the port side (she was bound north) with soap, and she scraped through, but left the "white cliffs of Albion" as a reminder. Getting into the Baltic, that sea proved too narrow, and the huge ship was lightened. ‡ The island of Bornholm was formed by metal ballast then thrown overboard, and Christiansö from ashes and rubbish. This ship was known in England but a century ago as the "Merry Dun of Dover."§

North Frisian mariners still tell of her wonders. She scraped off a regiment of soldiers with her head-booms, at Dover, while, at the same time, her spanker-boom projected over Calais' forts, as she tacked in the Channel.

∥ She is not unknown to the French mariner, as we are told of the grand "Chasse Foudre," or "lightning-chaser," so large that she is seven years in tacking. When she

* Thorpe.—Northern Mythology,Vol. II, p. 275.
† Thorpe.—Northern Mythology, III, 28.
‡ Muellenhoff.—Sagen aus Schleswig, 216.
§ Brewer.—Reader's Hand-book. Folk-lore Journal, 1884, p. 23.
∥ Jal.—Scènes de la Vie Maritime, 1832, II, p. 89, etc.

rolls, whales and other large animals are found high and dry in the channels. The nails of her hull are a pivot for the moon. Her signal-halyards are larger than our greatest hempen cables. It took more than thirty years to dig the iron for her hull, and many enormous forges, blown by Arctic tempests, to fabricate her plates and frames. Her cables are the circumference of St. Peter's dome, and would extend around the globe. Her lower masts are so high that a boy becomes a white-headed man before he reaches the futtock-shrouds. Her mizzen-royal is larger than the whole of Europe; twenty-five thousand men can manœuvre on her main-cap, and the rainbow serves as a streamer. There is a tavern in each block, the pipe of the smallest boy is as large as a frigate; the quid of a tar would supply the crew of a frigate eighteen months in tobacco. Her cabin is a true paradise. In one corner is a large patch of ground planted with trees and greensward, and elephants, tigers, and other huge beasts, abound in it. She is the opposite of the spectral ship proper, as her crew are the good and deserving men, and their tasks are light and fare superb. She has ports, but no guns, for want of material. *Gargantua made a ship like this, which it took a whole forest to build.

The Normans believed that if their offerings for souls in purgatory were not acceptable, a spectral bark would sail in to the wharf, with crews of the souls of those who had perished years before at sea. Friends on shore recognized lost ones, but at midnight the bell would strike, and lights and ship disappear as suddenly as they came.

†Chapus says it is believed that this boat comes on All Saints' day. "The watchman of the wharf sees a boat come within hail at midnight, and hastens to cast it a line; but, at this same moment, the boat disappears, and frightful cries are heard, that make the hearer shudder, for they are recognized as the voices of sailors shipwrecked that year." Hood describes this event in "The Phantom Boat of All Souls' Night."

There are various German traditions of phantom ships. ‡Falkenberg still cruises in the northern ocean, and plays at dice with the devil for his soul. Murder on the high seas is said to have been the cause of his punishment.

*Sébillot.—Gargantua dans Les Traditions Populaires, 18.
†"Dieppe et ses Environs" (18'2).
‡Thorpe.—Northern Mythology.

*A spectral lugger is seen in a pool, on Lizard promontory, with all sails set.

An English revenue cutter reported, in 1845, that she had seen at sea a spectral boat, rowed by a bearded man, a noted wizard of the west of England.

Near Penrose a spectral boat, laden with smugglers, was believed to appear at times on the moor, in an equally-spectral sea and a driving fog.

The spectre of a ship, that had sailed from a Devonshire port, was one day seen coming in in a cloud, disappearing little by little. The real ship soon after came in.

†In the "Ancient Mariner," the spectre-ship is seen by the narrator, after killing the albatross, coming

" Without a breeze, without a tide,
She steadies with upright keel."

" Those her sails that glance in the sun,
Like restless gossameres?"

On board is Death, playing at dice with a woman—Life-in-Death—for the possession of the mariner's crew. She wins, whistles thrice, and

" Off shoots the spectre-bark."

The mariner's own bark is a spectre-ship, moving without wind; for

" The loud wind never reached the ship,
Yet now the ship moved on,"

and the ghosts of the dead crew work the ropes and steer her, she sinking on arriving in the home port, and only the Ancient Mariner escapes.

‡Cunningham gives us, in his charming story, the legend of the haunted ships of the Solway. Two Danish pirates, who had permission, for a time, to work deeds of crime on the deep, were at last condemned to perish here by wreck, and were seen coming in, one clear night, one crowded with people, the other having on its deck a spectral shape, flitting about. Thus they approached the shore, and four young men put off in a boat, that had been sent from one ship, to join her, seeking to participate in the revels. When they reached her, both vessels sank where they were.

* Bottrell.—Traditions and Fireside Stories of West Cornwall.
† Coleridge's Poems.
‡ Traditional Tales of the English and Scottish Peasantry, p. 388.

Other wrecks lay here also, but only these two remain unbroken. If boats approach too near, fishermen say they will be drawn down to join the reveling crews. One night, a man was seen to approach the shore, dig out of the sand a brass slipper, and whirl it on the water, when it became a boat, in which he went to the wrecks, and, striking them with his oar, they rose to the surface, all equipped and sails set. Lights were seen, and both vessels stood out of the harbor, sailing over Castletown shoals, like true phantom barks. On the anniversary of their wreck, they are believed to come in again, and the whole scene is re-enacted. Work is said to be done on them on dark, stormy nights.

They are generally seen before a gale. Whoever touches these wrecks will be drawn down below to them. Any one approaching them as they rise and sail out, is lost.

*Another spectral vessel appears in the Solway, always coming near a ship that is doomed to wreck, and guided by a fiend. It is the ghostly bark of a bridal party, who were maliciously wrecked,—"the spectral shallop which always sails by the side of the ship which the sea is bound to swallow."

†There is a Highland legend of a great ship (the Rotterdam) that went down with all on board, and that appears from time to time, with her ghostly crew, a sure omen of disaster.

A Scotch tale, related in many books of folk-lore, is of "Meggie of the Shore," a kind of witch, who saw and showed to others a spectral boat with lights in the harbor, and that night a boat was lost there.

There are also tales of spectral ships on this side of the water.

‡In an Ojibway tale, a maiden is about to be sacrificed to the spirit of the falls, by drifting her over them in a canoe. But at the last moment, a spectral canoe, with a fairy being in it, takes her place and serves as a sacrifice.

Whittier, " The Cruise of the Jessie," describes a spectral canoe,—

> "While perchance a phantom crew,
> In a ghastly birch canoe,
> Paddled dumb and swiftly after."

There is a legend of a spectre-ship near Orr's Island, in

* Cunningham, p. 288.
† Gregor.—Folk-lore of Scotland.
‡ Lanman.—" Haw-hoo-noo."

Maine, embodied in verse by Whittier, in "The Deadship of Harpswell," where

"The ghost of what was once a ship
Is sailing up the bay."

The conclusion to the narrator of this tale by the Bookman—

"Your flying Yankee beats the Dutch"—

is good. Whittier gives us another American legend in the "Palatine,"—the spectre of a ship wrecked on Montauk Point, which is said to appear on the anniversary of its destruction, when

THE BURNING PALATINE.

"Behold! again with shimmer and shine,
Over the rocks and the seething brine,
The flaming wreck of the Palatine."

It is a warning to sailors, too,—

"And the wise sound-skippers, though skies be fine,
Reef their sails when they see the sign
Of the blazing wreck of the Palatine."

*The Palatine was a Dutch trader wrecked on Block Island, about 1752. Wreckers are said to have burned her as she drifted to sea, with one woman on board, who had refused to leave her. †Livermore gives the testimony of several persons who had heard the story from their ancestors, and stoutly maintains that the wreck was not plundered. Whittier gives as his authority a Mr. Hazard. It was long supposed that Dana's "Buccanneer" also described this deed, but the author says it is a work of the imagination. Another authority says the Palatine was not wrecked then, but afterward, in 1784. Drake, in his recent work,‡ repeats the story of her wreck, and says she was burned by the wreckers.

§ In his poems, Whittier also alludes to

"The spectre-ship of Salem, with the dead men in her shrouds,
  Sailing sheer above the water, in the loom of morning clouds."

‖ In an early and now scarce work, he tells the story of another spectral bark of Salem. In the seventeenth century a ship about to sail for England had as passengers a strange man and a girl of great beauty. So mysterious were their actions, that they were supposed to be demons, and many feared to sail in the ship. The vessel sailed on Friday, and never reached her destination, but reappeared as narrated, after a storm that lasted three days:—

'Near and more near the ship came on,
  With all her broad sails spread,
The night grew thick, but a phantom light
  Around her path was shed,
And the gazers shuddered as on she came,
  For against the wind she sped."

On her deck were seen the spectral forms of the young man and woman. This spectral bark disappears at the prayer of the minister.

Whittier gives us another story of a phantom ship, in a recent poem.** The young captain of the schooner visits the Labrador coast, where, in a secluded bay, live two beautiful sisters with their Catholic mother. Both fall in love with the handsome skipper, who loves the younger alone. She is confined in her room by her mother, just as she is to meet

* Drake.—Legends of New England.
† History of Block Island.
‡ Legends of New England (1883).
§ Garrison of Cape Ann.
‖ Legends of New England. See also Blackwood. Vol. XXI, p. 463.
** "The Wreck of the Schooner Breeze."

her lover and fly with him. Her elder sister, profiting by her absence, goes in her stead, and is carried to sea in the vessel. The disappointed lover, on learning the deception, returns at once, but finds his sweetheart dead. The schooner never returned home, says the poem,—

" But even yet, at Seven Isle Bay,
Is told the ghastly tale
Of a weird unspoken sail.
She flits before no earthly blast,
With the red sign fluttering from her mast,
The ghost of the Schooner Breeze."

*Cotton Mather gives us a legend of a Colonial spectre-ship—the New Haven ship. A new ship was sent out from New Haven in January, 1647, but was never heard from again. In June, about an hour before sunset, and after a thunder-storm, a ship like her was seen sailing up the river against the wind, disappearing gradually, and finally fading out of sight, as she drew near. This vision was declared a premonition of the loss of the vessel—even from the pulpit. Longfellow has illustrated this tradition:

†" On she came, with a cloud of canvas,
Right against the wind that blew,
Until the eye could distinguish.
The faces of the crew."

" Then fell her straining topmasts
Hanging tangled in the shrouds,
And her sails were lowered and lifted,
And blown away like clouds."

" And the masts, with all their rigging,
Fell slowly, one by one,
And the hulk dilated and vanished,
As a sea-mist in the sun."

‡Bret Harte relates a legend of a phantom ship, in one of his poems. Children go on board a hulk to play, but it breaks loose, and drifts out to sea, and is lost.

" But they tell the tale,
That when fogs were thick on the harbor reef,
The mackerel fishers shorten sail,
For the signal, they know, will bring relief,
For the voices of children, still at play,
In a phantom hulk that drifts away
Through channels whose waters never fail."

* Magnalia Christi Americana.
† Poems.—The Ship of the Dead.
‡ Poems.—A Greyport Legend (1797).

*Celia Thaxter has also published a poem, "The Mystery." She is a slaver, whose cargo of two hundred, penned below hatches, perish there, and their corpses are thrown overboard. The wicked captain tries to regain his port, but a calm comes up, and the ghosts of the murdered slaves come, and bind the captain to the mast. The crew hastily desert the ship.

"And they were rescued; but the ship—
The awful ship—the Mystery,
Her captain in the dead men's grip,
Never to any port came she.

"But up and down the roaring seas,
Forever and for aye she sails,
In calm and storm, against the breeze,
Unshaken by the wildest gales."

Roads, in his History of Marblehead, relates tales current of spectre-ships, premonitory warnings of some vessel's loss.

†In Dana's "Buccaneer," a spectre-ship appears. Lee, the pirate, carries a lady to sea, who jumps overboard, and her horse is thrown alive after her. On the anniversary of this deed, the phantom-ship and horse appear.

"A ship! and all on fire! hull, yards, and mast,
Her sails are sheets of flame; she's nearing fast!"

The third time the vision comes, it sinks, and the horse takes its place.

‡Irving tells of a spectral boat, seen in the Hudson. "The prevaient opinion connected it with the awful fate of Ramhout van Dam, of graceless memory." "He had danced and drank until midnight (Saturday), when he entered his boat to return home. He was warned that he was on the verge of Sunday morning, but he pulled off, nevertheless, swearing he would not land until he reached Spiting Devil, if it took him a month of Sundays. He was never seen afterward, but may be heard, plying his oars, being the Flying Dutchman of the Tappan sea, doomed to ply between Kakiot and Spiting Devil until the day of judgment."

§Like the Palatine, is the "Packet Light," in the Gulf of St. Lawrence. The packet was wrecked, with loss of life,

*Our Continent, 1881.
†Poems of R. H. Dana.
‡Chronicles of Wolfert's Roost, Chap. 2.
§Capt. Hall.—Adrift in the Ice Fields.

near Prince Edward's Island. When a storm is threatened from that quarter, a ball of fire emerges from the sea, rises, sways about and expands, becoming a burning vessel, then sinks and disappears.

"The lumbermen of the St. John tell with bated breath of an antique French caravel, which sails up the Cadelia falls, where no steamer or sail-vessel dare follow. And the farmers and fishermen of Chester Bay still see the weird, unearthly beam which marks the spot where the privateer Leach, chased by an overwhelming English force, was hurled heavenward by the desperate act of one of her own officers."

* A Phantom ship is seen at times at Cap d'Espoir, in Gaspé Bay, Gulf of St. Lawrence. Lights are seen on it, and it is crowded with soldiers. On the bowsprit stands an officer, pointing shoreward with one hand, with a female on the other arm. Suddenly the lights go out, a scream is heard, and the ship sinks. It is said to be the ghost of the flagship of a fleet sent to reduce the French forts by Queen Anne—which fleet was wrecked here, and all in it lost.

† Moore wrote a poem describing a spectre-ship seen at times in the vicinity of Deadman's Island, where wrecks were once common:—

> "To Deadman's Isle, on the eye of the blast,
> To Deadman's Isle, she speeds her fast,
> By skeleton shapes, her sails are furled,
> And the hand that steers is not of this world."

‡ A Chinese form of the story is told by Dennys. A party of tiger-hunters found a horned serpent in a tiger's cage near Foochow. They shipped it to Canton, but during the voyage, lightning struck the cage and split it, the serpent escaping. As he rapidly consumed the cargo of rice, the master offered a thousand dollars to any one who would kill the monster; but two sailors attempting the task were killed by the serpent's noxious breath, and, finally, the junk was abandoned. It is still believed to cruise about the coast, and knowing natives will not board a derelict junk. ·

§ Ibu Batuta tells of a "Ship full of Lanterns," which appears near the Maldive Islands. It was formerly a demon, to whom a virgin was sacrificed, but who has no power at

* Le Moine.—Chronicles of the St. Lawrence, p. 36.
† T. Moore.—Phantom Ship of Deadman's Isle.
‡ Folk-lore of China.
§ Voyages, 125, q. Mélusine, December, 1884.

present.   He says he saw the ship, and that people drove
it away by chanting the Koran and beating gongs.

We may even find earlier traditions of spectral ships.

* We first find a fully-developed legend of phantom-barks
in the Sagas.   A certain Geiröd sets adrift a boat, after he
lands, with the words, "Go hence, in the power of the evil
spirits"; and thus the spectral ship has since cruised.

† During the plague in Europe, in Justinian's time, people
said that spectral brazen barks, with black and headless men
as crews, were seen off infected ports, and this is the first
appearance of the phantom-ship.

‡ There is an old Venetian legend, of 1339, of the ring
with which the Adriatic was first wedded, that alludes to a
spectral ship.   During a storm, a fisherman was required to
row three men, first to certain churches, then out to the entrance of the port.   There a huge Saracen galley was seen
steering in, in the storm, with frightful demons on board.
These three caused the spectral craft to sink, thus saving
the city.   On leaving the boat, a ring was given to the boatman, and by it these men were ascertained to be St. Mark,
St. George and St. Nicholas.   In the Venetian Academy is
a painting, by Giorgione, of this spectral ship, with a demon
crew, who, in terror of the Saints, jump overboard, or cling
affrighted to the rigging, while masts flame with fire and
cast a lurid glare on the water.

Such are the many legends current among sailors and
seafaring folk, of phantom ships, spectral boats, and finally
of the Flying Dutchman.   Spectres, apparitions and ghosts,
as we have seen, are as abundant at sea as on land, and it
requires no greater effort of the imagination to see a ghostly
ship than to see a ghostly shipman.   Many would and have
argued, in fact, that the spectral bark exists only in the imagination of the sailor, created as a natural accompaniment
to those weird lights, often seen before a storm.   It is true
in one sense that these ghostly barks are none other than
the nautical manifestations of the same restless spirit that
wanders on shore as the wild huntsman, the headless horseman, or the ghostly night-walker.   A curse is, in these cases,
supposed to be pronounced on the restless spirit, and so
here, one of the first alleged causes of the curse upon the
ceaseless wandering spectral ship is murder and piracy at

sea, and the whole story is the type of that of the Wandering Jew on land.

* "The curse of a deathless life has been passed on the Wild Huntsman, because he desired to chase the red deer forevermore; on the Captain of the Phantom Ship, because he vowed he would double the cape, whether God willed it or not; on the Man in the Moon, because he gathered sticks during the Sabbath"; etc.

So of the Wandering Jew, whose prototype at sea is Falkenberg. †As Conway shows, there is a great class of such wanderers in legend. Undying ones have been reported in all lands. Arthur, Charlemagne, Tell, Boabdil, Sebastian, Olger the Dane, and others, will readily be recalled by students of folk-lore. The myths of these wanderers work the one into the other, forming a network of legends. Cain is a wanderer in many eastern lands, and Cain is the Man in the Moon in other legends. Cain's wind is the hot Khamseen in Bedouin tongue, and the Wandering Jew passes in the Wild Hunt, in Picardy. Odin is a famous leader of the Wild Hunt, and Odin became Nick.‡ "Nikke was a Wild Huntsman of the Sea, and has left many legends, of which the Flying Dutchman is one." Another wanderer is Judas, and he, too, is a wanderer on the sea. St. Brandan saw him on a rock in the sea, during his voyage. §Al Sâmeri, maker of the Golden Calf, was banished to an island in the sea; in another is Arthur. If the spectral ship comes in storms so in whirlwinds is Elias, an eastern wanderer, and in storms the Wild Huntsman. Attendant on the Phantom Ship is often seen the phantom light, and the Will-o'-the-Wisp is called the Wandering Jew. The appearance of the Phantom Ship in a calm is a bad omen. ‖So the sound of the Wild Huntsman's hounds are thought to be evil portents, and the "Seven Whistlers," also called "Wandering Jews," prognosticate storms by their whistling cries. These analogies are sufficient to show to what class the legend under consideration must be referred, and what an element in its formation these widespread ideas concerning a deathless punishment have been.

The ship was well chosen as the theme of these ghostly manifestations. Around it cluster many maritime legends,

* Baring-Gould.—Myths of the Middle Ages, p. 39.
† Legend of the Wandering Jew, Chapter VII.
‡ Conway.—Demonology and Devil-lore, II, 112.
§ Sales.—Koran.
‖ See Chapter III.

and it is often the subject of mythological and legendary traditions. As we saw in the last chapter, it was the chosen carrier of souls—the bark that wafted the immortal part across the water of death.

Many of these, and other mysterious barks of story and of legend, move of their own will, without sails or oars, often, as the Phantom Ship, against wind and tide, frequently obeying some charm, or some well-known voice. There is nothing strange in this, since the sailor has ever accredited intelligence and life to his ship. "She walks the waters—a thing of life" to him, and is not "a painted ship upon a painted ocean." He refuses a neuter name, and his vessel is "she"; or, when a fierce fighting vessel, a "man-of-war." These ideas are illustrated by numerous folk-lore legends, showing that the sailor is not alone in his ideas concerning the ship. Self-moving ships frequently occur in middle-age legends; and such, generally, are the death-barks spoken of above.

*So, priestly legends represent St. Mary and St. Mark as coming to Marseilles in a drifting, self-impelled ship; and, in Spanish sacred legend, †the body of St. James the Greater is said to have been conveyed in such a mystical ship; and a vessel is represented, with an angel at the helm, in a cathedral in Spain dedicated to him; and the legends of the foundation of Westminster Abbey relate that when St. Peter entered a fisherman's boat, to cross the Thames,‡—

> "As when a weed
> Drifts with the tide, so softly o'er the lane,
> Oarless, the boat advanced."

Rinaldo, in middle-age legend, is given a ship by a conjurer, that moves of itself to the island-paradise.

§We are told of three mysterious boats that entered the harbors of Rue, Dorn and Lucca (?), having borne from the Holy Land three sacred crosses.

Twardowski, a physician of Cracow, was believed to sail in the Vistula in a boat without oars or sails; ‖and ships in Russian tales move of their own accord.

**A fakir gives a prince a paper boat, in one of Miss Stokes' Hindoo tales, which also moves of its own volition;

*Collin de Plancy.—Légendes Pieruses du Moyen Age.
†Brewer.—Reader's Hand-book, fr. España Sagrada.
‡Jones.—Credulities.
§Marquis de Paulny.—Legends of Picardy.
‖Afanasieff, in Ralston, Russian Folk-lore, 123.
**Stokes.—Hindoo Fairy Tales.

and river-nymphs gave a certain Chinaman a wonderful boat, *"No sails or oars are used, but the boat sped along of itself."

Boats and ships that obeyed the voice of their master, or which went only at the sound of certain words, are also numerous. Such a boat, which requires a charm-word to make it move, occurs in "Quaddarmi and His Sister," a Sicilian tale.

† A Hindoo tale is told of a boat made of hajolwood, which goes with three snaps of the finger, and the words

> " Boat of Hajol
> Oars of Mompaban
> Take me to ——."

‡ In a Russian story, a boat moves only at the words

> "Canoe, canoe, float a little farther."

or

> "Canoe, canoe, float to the water side,"

and an elf-queen at Leije, in Holland, had a fairy ship, which moved when she said,

> " Wind with four."

§ The boat of " Big Bird Dan," in the Norse story, sailed at the words " Boat, boat, go on," or " Boat, boat, go back home."

Such a boat was the magic canoe of the Indian hero, moving only at the words " *N'chimaun Poll*," according to Ojibway‖ legend, or " *Manjaun Chemaun*," in Saginaw story. This hero was Manabozho,** or Hiawatha:—††

> " Paddles none had Hiawatha,
> Paddles none he had or needed,
> For his thoughts as paddles served him
> And his wishes served to guide him."

A famous boat in Greenland ‡‡ fable rises into the air, or moves on the water, controlled by a magic lay sung by its possessor, but if this is forgotten while the boat is in the air, it tumbles to the ground and is no longer useful.

* Giles.—Tales by Sung Ping Ling.
† Lal Behair Day —Folk-lore of Bengal, p. 68.
‡ Ralston.—Russian Folk-lore. p. 163.
§ Dasent.—Tales from the Norse.
‖ Schoolcraft.—Algic Researches, Vol. II, p. 94.
** Schoolcraft.—Indian Tales, Vol. I, p. 324.
†† Longfellow.—Hiawatha, Vol. VII.
‡‡ Rink.—Tales and Traditions of the Esquimaux,

According to Arthurian legend, Pridwen, his ship and his shield, obeyed his voice.

Many of these barks possessed the power, according to legend, of sailing over sea and land.

*In two Breton tales, Peau D'Anette and Jean del Oara, such mysterious barks occur, and in an Italian story, St. Joseph aids a young man to make such a boat.

Further intelligence is also accorded to these boats and ships of legend and story. Many speak, others refuse to move when certain things are forgotten, and various acts of intelligence are otherwise recorded of them.

Ellide, a famous Icelandic ship, was of these. She was shaped like a golden-headed dragon, with silver tail and blue-and-gold belly. Her planks magically grew together, and were probably of ash, sacred to Ran, the amphitrite of the North. She had black sails, bordered with red, and flew fast over the seas. She was sent as a present by Ægir, a marine deity who had been picked up at sea. So

> " Ellide, his dragon-ship. pulled impatient at her cable,
> And spread her wings, all eager for the sea."

Fridthjof sailed in her to the northward, when he was attacked by two demon spirits, described elsewhere. He appeals to Ellide,—

> † " Hearken to my calling,
> If thou'rt Heaven's daughter,
> Let thy keel of copper
> Sting this magic whale!"

She hears and heeds,—

> " Heed Ellide giveth
> To her lord's behest,
> With a bound she cleaveth
> Deep the monster's breast."

Lemmiakainen,‡ a Finnish hero, created a boat out of an old distaff and spindle, which would, at his command, fly over the sea. It laments and weeps because it is constructed for no useful purpose, and is therefore employed in useful deeds by Waïnamoïnen.

§ In the Italian stories, " Pot of Rue " and " Ceneterola,"

* Sébillot.—Littérature Orale do Haute Bretagne.
† Taylor.—Tegnér's Fridthjof Saga.
‡ Le Duc.—Kalevala.
§ Busk, R. H.—Folk-lore of Rome.

ships refuse to move: in the former, because a rose is forgotten; a bird, in the latter tale.

*The same is alleged of boats in Hindoo tales.

As to speaking ships, an ancient example is furnished in the Argo, which was built by Argus, son of Phryxus, an ancient navigator on the golden-fleeced ram. In its prow was inserted a piece of the speaking oak of Dodona, long an oracle in northern Greece, by Athena, a daughter of the sea, and reputed inventor of navigation. Of her we are told,—

> †"Sudden the vessel as she sail'd along,
> Spoke! wondrous portent, as with human tongue,
> Her steady keel of Dodonian oak,
> By Pallas vocal made, prophetic spoke."

According to the Floamana saga, the ships Stajakanhofthi and Hunagantur, possessed human speech. ‡Greenland tales are told of speaking ships in a lake in the under world.

§Arnanson reports an Icelandic tradition of the "Skipamal," or speaking ships. Vessels are said to creak even in still water, and when on the ways, in ship houses. This is called the speech of the ships, and but few are given to understand it. But such a favored one heard the following conversation one evening, between two ships lying in the harbor. The first one said, "We have long been together, but to-morrow we must part." The second one said: "That will never be. Thirty years have we been together, and grown old together, but when one is worn out, the other must lay by." The first: "That will not really be, for although it is good weather this evening, to-morrow morning will it be bad, and no one will go to sea but thy captain, while I and all other ships must remain. But you will sail out and never come back, and our companionship is at an end." "Never, for I will not stir from this place." "But you must, and this is the last night of our companionship." "When you go not, I will not go, the Devil himself must take a hand in it else." The tale goes that the captain of the second ship tried to go, but his ship would not sail, and his crew rebelled. He shipped another, but they could do no better. He called on Christ's name with

* Miss Stokes.—Hindoo Fairy Tales, and L. Behair Day, Folk-lore of Bengal.
† Ap. Rhodius.—Argonautics. Fawkes' Trans.
‡ Rink.—Traditions of Greenland Esquimaux.
§ Icelandic Legends.

no success, then on the Devil's, when his vessel flew before the raging storm, was lost, and thus the prediction of the wiser ship realized.[*]

A writer in the "Spectator," of 1852, says: "Ships no longer sea-worthy, when about to break up, between the strains of wind and wave, have been known to give forth moaning sounds like wailing; the sailor cannot conjecture how the noise is made, or the exact spot whence it proceeds, but he knows too well its import, and his heart fails him." [+] Cooper makes Fid say, "A ship which is about to sink makes her lamentations just like any other human being."

[‡] Sailors always personify ships and boats, and this was carried so far by a certain Cochin Chinese magnate as to put his boats in the stocks when they did not sail well.

Southey says, "Our own sailors sometimes ascribe consciousness and sympathy to the ship." He tells of a Captain Adkins, who thought his ship would sail faster after a French ship than after any other, and who would talk to her, urging her to greater speed, by promising her a new coat of paint.

A venerable commodore in our own navy, still living (in 1881), was won't to talk to the mizzenmast of his ship, asking it what sail to carry, when to reduce it, etc.

This is a common idea among old sailors, who often believe, as the old captain said, "She can do anything but talk," and sometimes, as we have seen, she can even do that.

These mysterious ships of legendary tales are wonderful in many other respects. They are not made of ordinary materials. Such was the famous Norse ship Skidbladnir, [§] large enough to contain all the gods and their war-equipment, but folding up like a cloth. It belonged to Frey, and always had a fair wind. Gangler says to Har: "You have told me of a vessel called Skidbladnir, that was the best of all ships.[‖] "Without doubt, it is the best and most artfully constructed of any. They were dwarfs who built Skidbladnir, and made it a present to Frey. It is so large that all the gods, completely armed, may sit in it at their ease. As soon as ever its sails are unfurled, a favorable gale arises, and carries it of itself to whatever place it is destined. And when the gods have no mind to sail, they can take it to

[*] See also Powell and Magnussen, Icelandic Folk-lore, 1866.
[+] Red Rover, Chapter XXIV.
[‡] Bastien.—Oestlich Asien, 157.
[§] Thorpe.—Northern Mythology, Vol. I, pp. 38, 199.
[‖] Snorre   Edda, p. 48. Mallet's Trans.

pieces so small, that, being folded upon one another, the whole will go into a pocket."

* Folk-lore tales preserve a reminiscence of this ship. A dwarf gives such a one to Hans, which grows and diminishes at the words "grow ship," and "lessen ship." † An old witch gives Lillekort a similar vessel, which will fly over land and sea, and which expands upon setting foot on her decks. In "Shortshanks," a similar vessel appears, able to carry five hundred men, and which dives and rises to the surface at will.

‡ Curiously enough, we find the Algonquin hero Glooscap possessed of such an expanding vessel, which he constructs out of Granite Island. § But larger than "Skidbladnir" was "Näglfar," belonging to Muspelheim, made of dead men's nails, and carrying souls at the end of the world, Rymer her pilot; and when one dies with uncut nails, the Sagas say he aids in the repairs of this huge ship.

‖ At the end of the world, says the prose Edda, "The ship Naglefara is set afloat. This vessel is constructed of the nails of dead men, for which reason great care should be taken not to die with unpared nails; for he who dies so, supplies material toward the building of that vessel, which gods and men will wish were finished as late as possible."

The Voluspa Saga also tells us at the last day,

> "The ship of Nails is loosened,
> It floats from the East."

** This strange vessel is also preserved in modern beliefs. Arnanson tells us that there is still a belief in Iceland, that, in removing the nails, you should cut them in two or more pieces, or Satan will use them to make a Ship-of-the-Line.

Near Jokul, a strange crew left the harbor in a strange vessel, pursued by an Icelandic ship. Just as the latter was nearing the strange craft, she sank with all on board. Her pursuers reported that she was made of men's nails, fastened together.

* Powell and Magnussen.—Icelandic Legends, 1866.
† Dasent.—Tales from the Norse.
‡ Leland.—Algonquin Folk-lore, 1884.
§ Thorpe.—Northern Mythology, Vol. I, pp. 79 and 80.
‖ Snorre Edda, 89.
** Arnanson.—Icelandic Legends.

24

Glass is also reported as a ship-building material. Merdyn Ennis sailed westward in a ship of glass (Ty Gwidwlo). * Southey says:

> "In his crystal ark,
> Whither sailed Merlin with his band of bards,
> Old Merlin, master of the mystic lore."

Arthur was conveyed to Avalon, says one legend, in a glass ship, and the Welsh Noah, Hu, was fabled to have journeyed in a similar vessel.

We also read of stone vessels. † Greenland tales are told of elves journeying in a stone canoe, and a giant comes in a stone canoe, in an Icelandic tale. A block of stone, on Upalo island, in the Hervey group, is still pointed out as a great ancestral canoe.

A sacred stone galley or boat is found in China, and I have a photograph of this, which is supposed to have been connected with some religious worship formerly.‡

§ The trunk of a tree often sufficed. A somewhat celebrated boat thus constructed was "Guingelot," which Chaucer says was that of Wade, made for him by his sire, Wayland the smith. Chaucer says old women "Connen so moche craft in Wade's bote," here probably in an obscene sense. It was made from the trunk of a tree, with a glass window in front.

More wonderful metal ships and boats are frequently described. ‖ Wainamoinen, the Finnish hero, makes one of brass, with an iron bottom, and in it makes his apotheosis:

> ** "In his shining ship of copper,
> In his galley made of metal,
> Sought the higher earthly region,
> And the lower realms of heaven."

In a Samoyed tale, a magic boat is made of copper, and goes at command of her captain.

In a Greek folk-tale, a king has a gold ship, with a crew of forty maidens. In a Welsh tale, it is a golden boat, with golden oars; in a Russian tale, a golden boat, with silver oars.

More unsuitable materials than these were sometimes used. A ship of ivory and ebony, encased in plates of gold,

* "Madoc."
† Rink.—Tales and Traditions of the Esquimaux.
‡ See also Scott.—Marmion, II, 14.
§ Thorpe.—Voluspa Saga, in Northern Mythology. Vol. I, p. 88.
‖ Castren.—Finnish Mythology.
** "Kalevala."—Schiefner's Translation.

and with oars of sandal and aloes wood, appears in the Arabian tale, "The King and His Son." In a Danish tale, "Mons Fro," a youth has a mahogany ship.

* A great chief in a savage land builds a canoe of bark, hollowed out by birds, sewed with the aid of the claws of others, through holes punched by the long beaks of others, and launched by birds also. In this he voyages, and, after many adventures, discovers, and settles the Hervey islands.

A Guaraco legend of Guiana, relates that the first navigator formed a ship of wax, and sailed in it. † Queatzal-

CHINESE STONE BOAT.

coatl, a Mexican demigod, had a magic boat made of serpent-skins. ‡ In Algic legend, there is a boat of a sorcerer, whose ribs are formed of living rattlesnakes.

Kircher says Cosmiel gave to Theodactus, a boat of asbestos, in which he sailed to heaven.

So Moore sings,—

> "Oh! for the boat the angel gave
>   To him, who, in his heavenward flight,
> Sail'd o'er the sun's ethereal wave,
>   To planet isles of odorous light."

* Gill.—Myths and Songs of the South Pacific, 144.
† Bancroft.—Native Races, 111-349.
‡ Schoolcraft.—Algic Researches, Vol. II, p. 73.

Paper boats figure in Miss Stokes' Hindoo tales, fore-shadowing modern inventions.

In a French anonymous fairy-story, the fairies make a giant ship of light buoyant woods. It is covered over with peacock-feathers, so that the plumes serve as sails, and such feathers line its walls and render it invisible.

*Grimm, quoting an old writer, tells of a boat made of feathers and straw, which was launched in the air from a height.

Boats and ships are likewise, in folk-legend, created mysteriously out of strange materials.

Leaves are thus transformed, to convey the soldiers of Prester John to Charlemagne, by the warrior Arnolfo:

> †"Soon as the waves the scatter'd leaves receiv'd
> They swell'd in bulk, and (miracle to view!)
> Each long, and large, and curv'd, and heavy grew;
> The fibres small to cables chang'd appear'd;
> The larger veins in solid masts were rear'd:
> One end the prow, and one the steerage show'd,
> Till each a perfect ship the billows rode."

Rods or chips served the same purpose. A magician in one of Campbell's Highland tales creates a ship out of a rod thrown into the sea; and two hazel wands become a boat, in one of Kennedy's Irish stories. ‡Sir Francis Drake is said to have thrown blocks into the water, and thus created a fleet to oppose the Armada. §In a Shetland tale, a Finn escapes with a captured bride, from his pursuers, by cutting off chips and throwing them in the water, thus creating a fleet, and puzzling them.

‖Dryden says of Oberon,—

> "What was his club, he made his boat,
> And on his oaken club doth float
> As safe as in a wherry."

**On the Cornish coast, the Fraddam witch is still seen floating along the coast in a tub formerly used by her in her incantations, with a broom for her oar, and a crock attending her larger bark, as a tender. The hapless mariner who sees her will be drowned before many days.

*Teutonic Mythology.
†Hoole.—Ariosto, Bk. XXXIX, 210.
‡Mrs. Bray.—Legends of Devonshire.
§Blind, in Contemporary Review, August, 1882.
‖Nymphidia.
**Bottrell.—Traditions, etc., of West Cornwall.

Witches have been famous navigators, both of the air and the watery element. Sometimes they sailed in sieves, as in Macbeth.*

> " But in a sieve I'll thither sail."

Swift, and other old authors alluded to this belief.
† Montgomery says,

> ." To sail sure in a seiffe."

And Congreve:‡

> " They say a witch will sail in a sieve."

The sieve in folk-lore is a cloud, and witches ride it on the watery element, as well as in the air. The same cloud sieve was a sacred instrument formerly, and the test of the vestal virgin's purity, and hence it became a mystical bark, like other cloud-barks of story.

Egg-shells were also chosen by witches as instruments of navigation. § An old English writer here tells us,—

> " This witches
> Possess'd; even in their death, deluded, say
> They have been wolves and dogs, and sail'd in egg shells
> Over the sea."

And Another,—

> ‖" The devil should think of purchasing that egg-shell
> To victual out a witch for the Bermoothes."

** We are told in an old work: " It is a common notion that a witch can make a voyage to the East Indies in an egg-shell. or take a journey of two or three hundred miles across the country on a broomstick."

†† Reginald Scot also informs us: " They can go out at auger holes, and saile in an egge shell, a cockle or muscle shell, through and under the tempestuous waves."

‡‡ And T. Fielding: " Most persons break the shells of eggs after they have eaten the meat; it is done to prevent their being used as boats by witches."

This is still believed in some parts of Europe. §§ In Hol-

* Act I, Scene 3.
† The Witch.
‡ Love for Love.
§ Cotgrave.—English Treasury of Wit and Language, p. 298.
‖ Beaumont and Fletcher.—Women Pleased.
** The Connoisseur.—No. 100. In Brand's Popular Antiquities, Vol. III, p. 7.
†† Discovery of Witchcraft.
‡‡ Proverbs.
§§ Choice Notes, p. 7.

land, when eggs are eaten, the shells must be broken, for
this reason. *In Russia, the same is said, and in Portugal
also; while in Somerset, †England. "If you don't poke a
hole in an egg-shell, the fairies will put to sea to wreck
ships."

In an Italian tale, a cask in which a princess is inclosed
becomes first a ship, and then a palace.

‡In a Chinese tale, a boat is created out of a hairpin, by
a sea-fairy, and a Scotch witch was, for the same purpose, a
cast-off slipper. A fox, in one tale, becomes a boat, a
barque and a ship, and a Wallachian magician transformed
himself into a boat.§

These legends are surpassed by others of wonderful
magic, mystical and mysterious vessels, which illustrate in a
remarkable manner the tendency to ascribe to the ship
mysterious qualities.

❘Sir Tristram is challenged to play chess on board of a
ship by her captain. While thus engaged he is kidnapped,
and sail made; but contrary winds arise, sails split, and oars
break, until the knight is put on shore. In the legends of
the "Round Table," Sir Tristram is set afloat in a ship, with
a servant only as companion—Gouvernayl (Rudder)—certainly a trusty one. Mysterious vessels are connected with
the heroes of middle-age legend. Arthur, Tristan, Parsifal,
Gudrun, Horant, Orendel, and other lesser known heroes,
have these magic vessels.

Ursula and her eleven thousand virgins had a fleet of
eleven triremes, gorgeously equipped. In some representations of this mystical voyage, angels are depicted at the
helm.

**Ursula is Hörsel, the Moon-goddess, and we may believe,
with Fiske†† and others that we have here the moon and her
accompanying stars, journeying from England, the home of
souls, to Germany, and suffering martyrdom at the coming
of the lord of day.

In Spenser's "Faerie Queene," Phædra has a magic
gondola on an enchanted lake, in which she carries the
hero of the song. In the mediæval legend of St. Hippolite,
he is drawn by horses across the water in a magic boat.

* Ralston.—Songs of the Russian People.
† Choice Notes, p. 238.
‡ Giles.—Chinese Tales, by Ping Sung Ling.
§ Ralston.—Russian Folk-Tales, 169.
❘ Cox and Jones.—Legends and Romances of the Middle Ages.
** Grimm.—Teutonic Mythology.
†† Myths and Myth-Makers.

Folk-lore tales abound with these curious boats and ships, and even the Japanese, New Zealanders, and Fijians have their legends concerning them. *The former people say that on New Year's day, *Takarai-bune*, the treasure-ship, manned by the seven gods of luck, will enter every harbor, dispensing gifts and favors.

We see thus a universal tendency, in certain ages and among certain peoples, to make the ship the subject of marvelous tales and of curious transformations. Even in the times of Virgil and Ovid, this tendency appeared. †The ships of Æneas are turned to sea-nymphs:

> "Now, wondrous! as they beat the foaming flood,
> The timber softens into flesh and blood;
> The yards and oars now arms and legs design;
> A trunk, the hull; the slender keel, a spine;
> The prow, a female face; and by degrees,
> The galleys rise—green daughters of the seas."

The sailor is responsible for few of these ships. They are fireside inventions, tales of wandering minstrels, myths of the common people, or fancies of the poets.

Along with this mystical character, ascribed to the ship in legend and in song, was the equally mysterious awe with which the ocean was regarded. This has been abundantly shown in the preceding pages, and needs no further exemplification.

With such an element of mystery in the ship, and concerning the sea, they would well be chosen as the theater of such a supernatural occurrence as that imagined in the legend of the Flying Dutchman. As we have shown, the parallel legend of the Wandering Jew is reproduced in that of the Spectral Ship. The features of the legend prove this. Whether the curse is for blasphemy, for murder, piracy, or slave-dealing, it is all the same—there is a sin to be expiated. The propitiation may be a maiden for a wife, a return of a relic of the cross, or there may be none. So the Jew wanders, without relief. The ship is diabolic—that is, a sight of her brings storms and disaster. The Jew brought storms, as we have seen, in 1604; and, perhaps, in his name, as the Wild Huntsman, we have the key to the application of his story to the storm-bound Falkenberg. All ghostly appearances are bad omens, and we have especially seen that spectre-ships were such.

* Greey.—Wonderful City of Tokio.
† Dryden.—Æneid, Bk. IX.

There are those, with Cox, who would have these all cloud-ships, wafted hither and thither by the changing winds; and as the clouds presage storm, so the typical spectre-ship precedes disaster.

But the nature-myth theory will not explain enough here. Perhaps it has its influence, for we have seen the sun imagined as traveling in a ship, the clouds figured as barks moved by the winds, etc. Such nature-myths have doubtless played their part in the legends we have alluded to, and in others concerning strange and mysterious ships. In the last chapter, we traced the effects of the sun-myth in the formation of the death-ship legends. The Argo, that wandered in search of morning-beams, or, as later writers said, sought the evening-twilight land, is, like the golden cup of Helios, the sun itself.

So Mone thinks Skidbladnir, which belonged to Freyr, the summer-god, typifies the summer months; and Hring-horn, in which Balder, the sun-god, is buried, the nine long winter months of the northern lands. But perhaps Cox is more apt in his likening Skidbladnir to the cloud, since we find other cloud-ships of story and song. *Fiske remarks: "Clouds are in Aryan lore ships, are mountains, or rocks," as the Symplegades; and Kelly: "Sometimes they were towering castles, or mountains, or ships sailing on the heavenly waters." Many of the ships and boats of folklore, which move without sails or oars, are doubtless cloud-barks.

Natural phenomena have also had a prominent p rt in forming and perpetuating the wonderful story. †While the idea of a wandering curse seems to be an old one (Conway shows it to exist in early Aryan and Greek legend), and an equally ancient myth exists, of the Voyage and Sea of Death, connected closely with the course of the setting sun— while these gave the incentive to the formation of the legend, it does not seem to have been elaborated until the revival of navigation had familiarized the sailor with the outer ocean, where the phenomena of nature present themselves on a grander scale than in the narrow seas to which navigation had been confined.

A derelict and corpse-laden bark, a pest-stricken slaver, a wandering pirate, or all these, would furnish material for the origin of the story of the wandering punishment, and

*Myths and Myth-makers.
†Wandering Jew, Chapter III.

the wonderful images often seen in mirages at sea, the presence of mysterious natural lights there, the occasional remarkable resonance of the air, especially before storms, and other incidental causes, would aid thus in building up the complete legend. * "A ship seen upside-down in a mirage is called (in Denmark) the 'Ship of Death,' and is a bad omen.

† A particularly apt illustration of the effects of natural causes is given in a modern book of travels. One evening they beheld, close to Port Danger, on the South African coast, a well-known English man-of-war, a short distance away. They saw familiar faces on board, and a boat was lowered and manned, in sight of everybody. All recognized the "Barracouta," and they expected to find her at anchor, when they arrived, a short time after, in Simon's bay. It was a week, however, before she arrived, and then it was learned that she was at least three hundred miles from Port Danger, at the time referred to. The image seen was doubtless due to reflection or refraction in some cloud or fogbank. Arctic voyagers often speak of the very remarkable effects of refraction, and many of the *nautical* tales of phantom-ships are, beyond doubt, caused by the sight of images in cloud or fog-bank.

The locality of the legend is one that would be naturally chosen, and would give a coloring of truth to the main features of the story. Here at the "Stormy Cape," Diaz turned, fearing to advance farther, as his predecessors had at Capes Nun and Bojador. In the cloud that hung over Table mountain, still known to mariners as the "Devil's Table Cloth," hovered the spectre of the cape, the terror of mariners for many years. In the clouds that incessantly hover over the high peaks of land, would often be reflected strange sights, invisible else to the mariner.

There are also sufficient reasons why the hero of the tale should be a Dutchman. They were, at the time of the formation of the legend, foremost among the navigators of the world. They were cool and phlegmatic, in contrast with the excitable and volatile Portuguese and Spanish. Doubtless then, as now, they were superior seamen, in which case, in accordance with the spirit of the age, their superior skill would certainly be attributed to some league with the evil one. From the north also came the story of the spectral

* H. C. Andersen.—"O. T.," a novel.
† Owen.—Voyage to Africa, 1833.

re have seen, bore a great resemblance to the
'Falkenberg. This legend itself, we remember,
the North Sea—hence was probably older
rs. Perhaps here, also, the early conflict be-
nity and German Paganism may have had its
way* shows it did in perpetuating the legend
o the Dutch Van der Decken [on the deck (?)]
pirit, which, in the early form of
u, pa or his soul.
dvent forever banished the legend from
minds, and it terminated the punishment of
wanderer. One feature was destroyed when a ship
uld be able to move against wind and tide. But the
pectral captain had his revenge, for he seems to have taken
rith him the traditional sailor, almost as much a memory
f the past as the Phantom Ship.

*Wandering Jew, Ch. X.

CHAPTER XI.

SACRIFICES AND OFFERINGS.

"'Twas so, the ancient skipper spake,
  His face with terror pale;
 'There's here some murderous wretch on board,
  Hinders the ship to sail.
Up, men, we'll cast the lot about
  On whom it falls, we'll see,
And if their sails a villain here
  So overboard shall he!'"
—*Old English Ballad.*

" If any there be beneath the wave
  That hinder the ship to sail,
I'll give you silver and ruddy gold
  To send us a fav'ring gale."
—*"German Gladeswain"* (*Danish Song*).

WE shall not be surprised, after learning of the many deities, demons, ghosts, etc., believed in by the sailor, to find many usages resorted to to propitiate them. Among these, the most ancient, as well as the most natural to the primitive or superstitious mind, are sacrifices and offerings. These have been often alluded to in the preceding chapters, and are frequently referred to and described by ancient writers. Human sacrifices were doubtless the earliest of these, and seem to have been thought particularly efficacious by Semitic nations, who thought the sea typhonic, or diabolic. Animal sacrifices were, however, more common in antiquity, especially among the Greeks and Romans. But offerings were often substituted, either to the elements, to the gods imagined powerful at sea, or to the Virgin and Saints, in later times. It was frequently customary to offer these in the form of a libation or oblation, and we shall find in the next chapter a surviving relic of this usage, in the modern custom of breaking a bottle of wine over the bows of a ship in launching her.

Among the Phœnician mariners, human sacrifices were perhaps common, as in these lands the worshipers of Baal were accustomed to such horrid rites. Whatever we may think is meant by the story of Jonah, whether we believe it mythical or real, it certainly describes an occurrence not uncommon. *"Then the mariners were afraid, and cried every man unto his God. * * * And they said every one to his fellow, 'Come, and let us cast lots, that we may know for whose cause this evil is upon us.' So they cast lots, and the lot fell upon Jonah. So they took up Jonah, and cast him forth into the sea, and the sea ceased from her raging."

When Xerxes, in the course of his conquests, came to the sea, he availed himself, as other eastern conquerers had done before him, of the ships of the maritime nations of lesser Asia, and doubtless from them received also their customs in regard to sacrifices. †He sacrificed a human life to the Hellespont, and at Artemesium,‡ the handsomest Greek captive was slain over the bows of his admiral's ship. At Mycale, too, he was only induced to engage the Greeks by the fortunate omen of propitious sacrifices.

The Tauri, a Thracian tribe inhabiting the Crimea, had a temple dedicated to a goddess called by the Greeks Diana Taurica, and to her sacrificed shipwrecked persons. Here Iphigenia recognized and delivered Orestes, about to become a victim to the custom.

Idomeneus, king of Crete, is said to have vowed to sacrifice to Neptune the first living thing he should meet after a storm, and this happening to be his son, he fulfilled the vow religiously.

Such sacrifices were not unknown even among the more humane Greeks. Plutarch tells us of a virgin being sacrificed to Amphitrite. Iphigenia was near being sacrificed at Aulis by the Greek leaders whose fleet was there windbound on its way to Troy. When threatened with the Persian invasion, they made an extraordinary sacrifice to

* Jonah, Ch. I, v. 7.
† Herodotus.
‡ Parker.—Fleets of the World, p. 26.

Boreas, whose blasts thereafter destroyed the invading fleet at Artemesium. Medea nearly became a sacrifice, during the return voyage of the Argonauts.

We even find relics of this barbarous custom during the middle ages. * Mussulman chroniclers tell us that a virgin was then sacrificed to the river Nile, but was later replaced by a mummy's finger. Savary says an earthen figure was used in later days. † Moore refers to this custom:

> " Pallid as she, the young devoted bride
> Of the fierce Nile, when decked in all the pride
> Of nuptial pomp, she leaped into his tide. "

The old Norseman frequently offered human sacrifices to the gods. Saxo says: "Thorkill's ship was mysteriously stopped at sea, until a man was thrown overboard."

An old ballad from "Pedlar's Pack" illustrates the idea of a sacrifice to allay a storm,—

> " They had not sailed a league, but three,
> Till raging grew the roaring sea,
> There rose a tempest in the skies,
> Which filled our hearts with great surprise.
> The sea did wash, both fore and aft,
> Till scarce one sail on board was left;
> Our yards were split, and our rigging tore,
> The like was never seen before;
> The boatswain then he did declare
> The captain was a murderer,
> Which did enrage the whole ship's crew;
> Our captain overboard we threw. "

The gale, according to the story, then ceased.

‡ As recorded elsewhere, three men were sacrificed during Gorm's voyage to Biarmia, to free the ship from pursuing demons. There is an old Swedish tradition that St. Peter was once called upon to choose passengers for sacrifice from among fifteen Jews and fifteen Christians, and he so arranged them that Jews only were sacrificed. He chose every ninth man, and arranged them thus: 4 Christians, 5 Jews, 2 Christians, 1 Jew, 3 Christians, 1 Jew, 1 Christian, 2 Jews, 2 Christians, 3 Jews, 1 Christian, 2 Jews, 2 Christians, and 1 Jew.

Kinlock says that in ancient Scotland, "when a ship became unmanageable, lots were cast to discover who occa-

* Notes to Moore's Poems.
† Lalla Rookh.
‡ See Chap. II.

sioned the disaster, and the man on whom the lot fell was condemned."

Russian traditions tell of human sacrifices. The tale of Sadko was related in a former chapter. *A certain Cossack invader is said, in Muscovite annals, to have found it necessary to sacrifice a beloved Persian captive, at the crossing of the River Volga.

† German tribes anciently offered human sacrifices at the crossing of rivers.

Chinese have been known, says Jones, to fling men overboard in storms, to appease the offended deities. In 1465, several men are said to have been sacrificed, at the breaking of certain dykes, and in 1750, to prevent the tide from rising higher.

Many African tribes formerly sacrificed human lives to the sea. Such sacrifices were made to the Benin river, not many years since. ‡At Whydah, a man is chosen by the king, and sacrificed to *Hu*, god of the sea. He is carried down in a hammock, dressed in the dress, and having the stool and umbrella, of a minister of state, and is taken out into the sea, and thrown to the sharks. At Bony, it was also a custom to sacrifice a man to the shark deities.

Fanti negroes offer cattle and men to the fetich of the water.

§ Fijians and Samoans formerly sacrificed human lives to their shark deities. When a new canoe was built or launched in Tahiti, human blood was spilt. Ellis says Polynesian fishermen sometimes wrapped their dead in red cloth, and threw them into the sea, supposing that sharks would eat them, be animated by their spirit, and thus spare the fishermen, when out at sea.

‖ Human beings, gaily dressed, were sacrificed by ancient Mexicans to the spirit of a mountain torrent. Mendiez says boats were taken to a whirlpool in Lake Mexico, filled with children, and there sunk, a horrid propitiation to the gods supposed to dwell in subaqueous caverns.

Animal sacrifices were, however, the rule among early navigators, when human sacrifices were reserved for dire extremity of peril.

* Ralston.—Russian Folk-lore.
† Grimm.—Teutonic Mythology.
‡ Burton.—Dahomey. Vol. II, p. 141.
§ Ellis.—Polynesian Researches.
‖ Bancroft.—Native Races, Vol. III, p. 457.

The Greeks offered sacrifices when setting forth or returning from a voyage. After landing, it was to Jove Decensori; while at sea, to Poseidon, Athene, Amphitrite, Boreas, or some lesser sea or wind god.

Homer often describes

"These rites of Neptune, monarch of the deep."

Menelaus ascribed a calm to the fact that

ANCIENT BULL SACRIFICE.

* "No vows had we preferred, no victims slain!
For this the gods each fav'ring gale restrain."

And after arriving in Egypt, they

"There quit the ships, and on the destined shore,
With ritual hecatombs the gods adore."

And Minerva says to him,—

* Pope.—Odyssey, Ch. IV.

> *" Now immolate the tongues, and mix the wine
> Sacred to Neptune, and the powers divine."

But bulls, heifers or sheep were usually sacrificed to Neptune:

> "There hecatombs of bulls, to Neptune slain,
> High-flaming, please the monarch of the main."

Jason sacrificed two oxen, with a libation of honey, flour and oil, before sailing in the Argo.

† Herodotus says Kleomomes sacrificed a bull to the sea before embarking for Nauplia.

Ovid says, "Before the poop of the crowned vessel, crowned with flowers, they sacrifice a heifer without spot."

Virgil says of Æneis,‡—

> "Thus having said, the sacrifices, laid
> On smoking altars, to the gods he paid,
> A bull to Neptune, an oblation due
> Another bull to bright Apollo slew,
> A milk-white ewe, the western winds to please,
> And one coal-black to calm the stormy seas."

The Argonauts, too, sacrificed sheep:—

> § "The choicest sheep they bade their leader slay,
> And to the power benign, due honors pay,
> He to the galley's poop with speed convey'd
> The choicest sheep, and, as he offer'd, pray'd."

These sacrifices were offered by Greeks and Romans before and after a voyage, in time of danger, storm or calm, before going into action, and after a victory. Cymon offered victims to Apollo for his victory at the Eurymedon. Cicero says: |"Our generals, embarking on the sea, have been accustomed to offer a victim to the waves." The entrails of these victims were carefully inspected for omens of success or victory. The victim was eaten after the sacrifice. ** Hannibal sacrificed animals to Poseidon.

Phocæans sacrificed to Poseidon the seal, their patronymic animal. †† Livy says Scipio cast the entrails of an animal into the sea, before embarking.

Mariners and sea-faring people have been wont, in mediæ-

* Pope.—Odyssey, Ch. IV.
† History, Bk. VI.
‡ Dryden.—Æneid, Bk. III.
§ Appolonius Rhodius.—Argonautica. Fawkes' Trans.
| De Natura Deorum, Vol. III, p. 20.
** Tylor, from Herodotus, Vol. VI.
†† T. Livy.—History of Rome, p. 629.

val and modern times, occasionally to sacrifice some animal to the powers of the wave. Such sacrifices to the demons or spirits supposed to resided in the waters, have been alluded to in previous chapters. Many rivers, lakes and streams are still supposed to require an occasional victim, like the river in the couplet,—

> * " River of Dart! River of Dart!
> Every year thou claimest a heart!"

† Barbary corsairs sacrificed sheep and fowls to the spirits of the storm, and Arab navigators also dedicated an occasional cock to the evil spirit, accompanying it with an offering of wax candles and oil.· Ancient Norsemen devoted a black lamb to the water-spirits.

A singular instance of a popular belief in the efficacy of animal sacrifices is shown in the trial of Marian Ribchart, in the Orkneys, in 1629. "Ye cum to Stronsay, and asking almes of Andro Couper, skipper of ane bark, he said, 'Away! witch, carling, devil, nae farthing will ye fall!' quvairvpon ye went away verie offendit, and incontinentlie, he going to sea, the bark being vnder full sail, he ran made, and wold have luppen over boord; and his sone seeing him, got him in his armes, and held him, quvairvpon the seikness immediately left him, and his sone ran made; and Thomas Paiterson, seeing him tak his madnes, and the father to run veile, ane day being in the bark, took the dog, and bladdit him vpon the tuo schoulders, and thair efter flang the said dogg in the sea, quvairby these in the bark were saiffed."

‡ Russian tribes often sacrificed horses to the river spirits. A relic of human sacrifice is still visible in two ceremonies in Poland and Bavaria. In the former country, § a puppet of straw is flung into the water to propitiate the demons, with the words "the devil take you," and in Bavaria, a man wrapped in leaves is flung into a lake on Whit Sunday, and afterward allowed to swim out.

An old Prussian legend is told, to the effect that Albert the Elder, not being able, in 1520, to repel the fleet of Sigismund of Poland, consented that a certain courtier should sacrifice to the ancient gods. A steer was the victim, and it is recorded that the enemy's fleet was stopped by a shoal

* Dyer.—English Folk-lore.
+ See Ch. III.
‡ Grimm.—Teutonic Mythology, II, p. 542.
§ Conway.—Demonology and Devil-lore, Vol. I, p. 80.

25

mysteriously raised; but the fish, at the same time, were driven away, and it required the further sacrifice of a sow to bring them back again.

* Ostyaks hang a stone about a reindeer's neck, and cast it as a sacrifice into the river Obi.

At Assam, sacrifices were formerly made to the gods of the sea and wind.

Chinese still offer fowls at the shrine of the River Goddess, *Loong Moo*.† The captain stands before an altar in the bow, with three cups of wine on it. He takes a live fowl, cuts its throat, first pouring out wine from the cups, and then spills the blood upon the deck, and sprinkles with it bits of gilt paper.

Japanese legends of Jinnu record that that queen sacrificed to the sea-gods as early as 207 A.D.

Philippine Islanders formerly cast sacrifices to the alligators in the rivers. In many South-Sea Islands it was formerly a custom, when casting a new net, to offer animal sacrifices on the beach. Fijians threw overboard dogs, to remove ill-luck from their canoes. ‡ Tonga Islanders sacrifice to the whale when they meet one at sea § Polynesians sacrificed the first fish caught to the male gods, the second to the female ones. Peruvian tribes sacrificed to sacred fish.

Our own Indians frequently sacrificed animals to the spirits of the water. Hennepin saw sacrifices made at St. Anthony's falls, where a number of men had been drowned at one time. Sacrifices were also seen by early travelers on Lakes Winnipeg and Pend d'Oreille.

‖ Dogs were frequently thrown in, with their legs bound.
** Esquimaux offer foxes' tails, probably as a type of the living animal, to the water spirits. In passing certain capes, they always sacrifice to the spirits there resident. Kamtchatkans offered animals to the whale deities.

Instead of sacrifices, offerings of food, clothing, money, or gifts of equal value, were given, and even in antiquity were, as we have seen, joined to the sacrifices.

After the victory at Salamis,†† three Phœnician vessels, a statue holding the beak of a ship, and a brazen mast with three golden stars on it were given to the Delphic temple.

* Tylor.—Primitive Culture, Vol. I, p. 211.
† Jones.—Credulities, pp. 47-8.
‡ Manner.—Tonga Islands.
§ Grey.—Polynesian Mythology, p. 215.
‖ Charlevoix.—Nouvelle France, Vol. I, p. 304.
** Rink.—Tales and Tradition of the Esquimaux.
†† Parker.—Fleets of the World, p. 42.

Prizes were frequently dedicated to the gods. *Phormio, after his victory at Naupactus, offered a galley to Poseidon, and erected a trophy on Antirrhium promontory. The Consul Duilius, after a naval victory, erected a rostral column (so called from having affixed to it images of the *rostra*, or beaks of the captured ships); †Antigonus, after battle, linen, cloth, and entire fleeces; others cast in cheese, wax, bread, every one according to his ability.

‡An early traveler gives us an account of an offering made by sailors in the Black Sea. The ship had been long wind-bound near a rocky promontory, where a deity called Semès was supposed to reside, and the men said the vessel was charmed. The second mate declared that they would not get away without an offering. They were detained there four days; and after they got away, the mate said: "Ah, well! when I told you that you should propitiate Semès, you laughed at me; but, notwithstanding, if, during the night, I had not taken the resolution to climb secretly upon the rocks, you would never have passed them."

It was a custom in Germany, during the fifteenth and sixteenth centuries, to offer carp and pike to St. Ulrich, a fisherman's patron.

§Grimm shows, from old documents, that the Alemanni and Franks sacrificed horses at river-crossings.

‖Livonian fishermen, before putting to sea, propitiate the divinities by a libation of brandy, poured on the waters.

Norwegian sailors frequently made offerings to the water-spirits, as did Germans and Danes. A tradition exists that a man would offer a cake to the sea, but it was frozen over. He cut a hole in the ice, when a hand reached out and seized the cake.

**Fishermen of Folkstone formerly chose eight whitings out of each boat, and made a feast to a certain Saint Rumbald, at Christmas. In certain parts of Cornwall, they used to set aside a certain part of the catch, and leave it on the beach, as an offering to Bucca, a spirit greatly feared.

††Thévenot says he saw offerings to the sea, made in the East Indies, in 1689. A woman came to the seaside at Dabot, bringing a vessel of straw, with dishes of meat,

* Gravière.—La Marine des Anciens.
† Rénard.—L'Art Naval, p. 134.
‡ Sigismudi, L. Baroni.—Commentaria della Moscovia.
§ Deutsche Mythologie, Vol. I, p. 562.
‖ Farrar.—Primitive Customs, Vol. I, p. 185.
** Hasted.—History of Kent, Vol. III, p. 380.
†† Travels (1684), p. 249. Jones.—Credulities, 68.

fruits, etc., in a procession with music, banners, etc. The
vessel was cast into the sea, and the meats and fruits left
upon the shore.

* Navigators of Amboyna, passing by a certain coast of
Malacca, were in the habit of offering flowers and meats,
in a cocoa-shell by day, and, oil burning in a shell, by
night, to the demons of a mountain near the coast. †So
Moore tells us that lamps filled with cocoanut-oil were
formerly set afloat on the Ganges, as an offering for those
at sea. If they sank immediately, it was ominous; but a
good sign, if they floated until out of sight. The same
author speaks of sacrifices, which, Morier says, were made
by Moslem navigators:‡

> "While breezes from the Indian Sea
>   Blow round Selama's sainted cape
> And cool the shining flood beneath,
>   Whose waves are rich with many a grape
> And cocoanut and flowery wreath,
>   Which pious seamen, as they passed,
>   Had toward that holy headland cast
>   Oblations to the Genii there
>   For gentle skies and breezes fair."

§ Lampongs of Sumatra make an offering of cakes and
sweetmeats to the sea, on first beholding it, so that it
may not injure them. In many East India islands, it was
formerly the custom to set adrift proas laden with food,
etc., as an offering to the spirits of disease, to entice them
to sea.

The Siamese still float down the rivers small bamboo
rafts, with images, offerings, and a lighted taper on them.

A traveler in Cochin China tells us of a rock in the
rapids of a certain river, where the natives, in passing,
always made an offering. On one occasion, when he was
present, bananas and betelnuts were offered by the Indians,
and a biscuit for the traveler, while the pilot stood up and
made a speech. A raft afterward overturning there, the
natives claimed that the god of that spot, Berala Bonjok,
was offended at the white man's offering.

|Chinese sailors offer to the sailor-goddess bits of red
paper with votive prayers on them, tobacco and incense,

* Yule.—Marco Polo.
† Notes to Moore's Poems.
‡ Lalla Rookh.
§ Marsden.—Sumatra, 301.
| J. Verne.—Tribulations of a Chinaman.

and hang near the compass gilt-paper boats. Food is also offered, and afterward eaten. Chinese boatmen throw food to crows that may alight on the masts of their junks, as an offering to secure a good passage. *In a dead calm, gilt-paper boats are set afloat, to secure a breeze. The owners

"A HAND REACHED OUT AND SEIZED THE CAKE."

of junks also offer food at the shrine of the Queen of Heaven. Salt is thrown in the water, when any one is drowned. River sailors throw bread on the water, as an offering. This custom is said to have originated about 200 A.D., when a certain general was told by sooth-sayers

* Gray.—China.

to sacrifice forty-nine men, but substituted loaves of bread for them.

*A certain mandarin is said to have thrown overboard in a storm, in the Yangtze river, an inkstand, which he valued greatly as a gift. The storm ceased, and an island arose there, which is still known as Inkstand island.

†In one of Giles' tales, a fisherman obtains luck by a liberal libation to the deities. Archdeacon Gray says he saw, in a temple to the sailor-goddess, at Tientsin, bags of salt, with the donors' names on them.

Early travelers in Japan tell us of offerings to the sea-gods. ‡Japanese, saved from wreck, cut off their short queues, "a Japanese seaman's ordinary vow." A traveler says that in 1822, on the occasion of the detention of a junk by unfavorable winds, a barrel of "saki," or native wine, and many copper coins, were thrown overboard, to propitiate Kompira, a god of the elements, and to obtain favorable weather.

§Burkhardt, speaking of a voyage to Cairo, says: "An island near the coast contains the tomb of a saint, Sheik Hassan el Merabét, who is counted of great repute in the waters thereabout. Boats are sent from passing ships, with presents of dates, figs, etc., to propitiate the saint. When we sailed by, our reis made a large loaf of bread, which he baked in the ashes, and distributed a morsel of it to every person on board, who eat it in honor of the saint."

To propitiate evil spirits in the waters, he says: "They have the constant practice of throwing, at every meal, a handful of dressed victuals into the sea, and, before they sit down themselves to their repast, saying that the inhabitants of the sea must have their morsels, otherwise they will impede the vessel's course."

‖Madras coolies suspend a bag of coins, or other valuables, from the masthead, as an offering. They also cast refuse articles in the sea, as a propitiatory offering.

**Phillips, who visited Africa in 1693, says the king of the Caboceers, when they feared to embark because of the rough sea, made flattering speeches to it, telling it to be smooth, and offered oil, cloth, corn, rice and brandy.

*Jones.—Credulities.
†Chinese Tales.—Pin Sung Ling.
‡Kaempfer.—Japan.
§Travels in Arabia, Vol. II, p. 347.
‖Notes and Queries, December 13, 1884.
**Astley.—Voyages, Vol. VII, p. 411.

others hung here in gratitude by Crusaders, on their return from the fifth crusade.

* Grimm says a church in a village in Holstein has the image of a ship hung up in it, which, on the opening of spring, is gaily decorated with green plants, flags, ribbons, etc.

† The Lapps hang a small figure of a ship, stained with reindeer's blood, on trees at Christmas time.

Such offerings are seen in many seaside temples in Europe. In other countries, too, they are occasionally found. ‡ Commander Shore says there is at Tientsin a temple to the Queen of Heaven, and models of junks hang from the ceiling, votive offerings from grateful seamen.

§ Pictured ships, or scenes of wrecks, tempests, and so forth, were in antiquity common, and Juvenal says (Sat. XII.),—

> " As Isis temples show,
> By many a pictured scene of woe."

Bion says, "But this tablet, given by one after a shipwreck, pleased me." ‖

And Horace:

> ** " Me in my vowed
> Picture the sacred wall declares to have hung
> My dank and dripping weeds
> To the stern god of the sea."

An old scholiast to Horace tells us: "But we see some days certain ones who also paint their calamities in tablets, and hang them in the temples of marine gods."

†† Phædrus alludes to another custom:

> " Others their tablets
> Carry, begging alms ";

and other writers tell us that persons who had suffered from shipwreck, sometimes obtained aid by these means.

These scenes are common in the seaside temples and chapels of Europe, and a large collection may be seen in such marine temples as the church at Honfleur, Notre Dame des Flots, near Havre, Notre Dame des Gardes at Marseilles, at Rouen, Ciudadella at Minorca, or in other

* Teutonic Mythology, I, 289 (note).
† Grimm.—Teutonic Mythology, I, p. 285.
‡ Flight of the Lapwing, 1881.
§ Jones.—Credulities, p. 42.
‖ Hampton.—Medii Ævi Kalendarium.
** Ode V.—Milton's Translation.
†† Hampton.—Medii Ævi Kalendarium.

maritime places, accompanied sometimes by touching or
ludicrous inscriptions.

*Hampton says they were to be seen in England in the
early part of the present century.

†Cicero says Diagoras, being shown such votive tablets,
and being asked whether he did not now recognize the
power of the gods, said: "But where are the portraits of
those who have perished in spite of their vows?"

Vows to make these varied offerings became quite numerous, after Christianity had furnished so many saints
and shrines.

‡Grimm quotes an old saga to the effect that Norse
voyagers devoted three casks of ale to Freya for fair winds
to Sweden; to Thor, or Odin, for favoring breezes to Iceland.

§Erasmus relates instances of such vows: "There was
an Englishman there that promised a golden mountain to
Our Lady of Walsingham, so he did but get ashore alive.
Others promised a great many things to the shrine of the
saint which was in such a place; and the same was done by
the Virgin Mary, who reigns in many places. Some made
promises to become Carthusians. There was one who
promised to go on a pilgrimage to St. James of Compos-
tella barefooted and bareheaded, clothed in a coat of mail,
and begging his bread all the way."

"Did no one think of St. Christopher? I heard one, and
could not help smiling, who, with a shout, lest he should
not be heard, promised to St. Christopher, who dwells in
the great church at Paris, and is a mountain rather than a
statue, a wax image as great as himself. He had repeated
this more than once, bellowing as loud as he could, when
the man who happened to be next to him touched him
with his finger, and hinted: 'You could not pay that, even
if you set all to auction.' Then the other, in a voice low
enough that St. Christopher might not hear him, whispered,
'Be still, you fool! Do you fancy I am speaking in
earnest? If I once touch the shore, I shall not give him a
tallow-candle.'"

Equally ludicrous is the story told of a certain man,
who, greatly terrified in a storm, vowed he should eat no

*Medii Ævi Kalendarium.
†De Natura Deorum.
‡Teutonic Mythology.
§Colloquy of the Shipwreck (1523).

haberdine. Just as the danger was over, he qualified his promise with "Not without mustard, O Lord!"

*Such vows, made during peril at sea, were common among the seamen of Columbus' time. During a severe storm, he put beans in a cup, and lots were drawn to decide who was to make a pilgrimage to the shrine of Our Lady of Guadeloupe, with a taper weighing five pounds. The lot fell on Columbus himself, and he religiously performed it. At another time, the lot fell on him to make a pilgrimage to another shrine, and the third time it was one Pietro de Viela, who was chosen to go to Our Lady of Loretto. The crew then vowed to go to the first chapel, when they landed, which vow was performed at St. Mary's, in the Azores, as related in the next chapter.

We also read in the journal of his fourth voyage: "And being in great danger of perishing, they made a vow to send one of their number on a pilgrimage to the shrine of Nuestra Señora de Cintra at Guebra; and the lot fell on the admiral, showing that his offerings were more acceptable than those of others."

In the relation of Amerigo Vespucci's third voyage, we also read: "In this extremity, our sailors made many vows of pilgrimages for their safety, and performed many ceremonies, according to the custom of seafaring men."

†Admiral Howard wrote to Henry VIII.: "I have given him (Captain Arthur) liberty to go home, for when he was in extreme danger he called upon Our Lady of Walsingham for health and comfort, and made a vow that, an it pleased God and her to deliver him out of the peril, he would never eat flesh or fish until he had seen her."

Dieppe sailors, during the middle ages, were wont to vow pilgrimages to certain shrines in time of trouble or storm at sea.

‡Byron says, describing a storm at sea,

"Some went to prayers again, and made vows
Of candles to their saints."

The silver ship given by the queen of St. Louis was made in accordance with a vow. Joinville says: § "She said she wanted the king to beg he would make some vows to God and the saints, for the sailors around her were in the

---

*Gravière.—Les Marins du XV and XVI Siècles.
†Jones.—Credulities, 58.
‡Don Juan, Canto II.
§ Vie de St. Louis.

greatest danger of being drowned." 'Madam,' I replied, 'vow to make a pilgrimage to my lord St. Nicholas, at Varengeville, and I promise you that God will restore you in safety to France. At least, then, madam, promise him that if God shall restore you in safety to France, you will give him a silver ship of the value of five masses. And if you shall do this, I assure you that at the entreaty of St. Nicholas, God will grant you a successful voyage.' Upon this, she made a vow of a silver ship to St. Nicholas. She shortly afterward came to us to say that God, at the intercession of St. Nicholas, had delivered us from that peril."

* Scott says, "In very stormy weather, a fisherman (in Shetland) would vow an Oramus to St. Ronald, and acquitted himself of the obligation by flinging a sixpence over his left shoulder into the chapel window." He also tells us that St. Ninian's kirk was a noted shrine for the fulfillment of the vows of fishermen's wives, for the safety of their husbands at sea.

† Kingston gives us this sketch of mariners' ceremonies in Portugal, during the last century: "The vows most faithfully kept are those made by mariners on the stormy ocean, when their frail bark, tossed by the wave, is threatened each instant with destruction. As soon as they land, the captain and crew, frequently barefooted, form a procession, carrying their mainsail, tastefully decorated with flowers, to some familiar shrine. When mass had been performed, they reclaimed their sail, which of course belonged to the owner of the vessel."

Sacrifices and offerings have been made in all ages, and by savage as well as civilized people, to propitiate the gods and gain their favors. Sometimes the deity, in the case of the sea itself, is supposed to require and consume the gifts. When made to an animal, as the shark, it is supposed to be the incarnation of a deity. In any case, the sacrifice is a gift of homage to the supposed deity, and this is often something precious to the giver. Animals were substituted for men, after human sacrifices were abandoned, and offerings were in turn substituted for animal sacrifices. Many of the ceremonies described in the next chapter were undertaken to secure the same end—the favor of the deity.

* Notes to " Pirate."
† Lusianian Sketches.

CHAPTER XII.

MARITIME CEREMONIES AND FESTIVALS.

> "Neptune rules about the line
> Till sunbeams cease above to shine."
>
> *Newcome in the Navy.*

> "A seaman in a masquerade
> Such as appears to me from the deep,
> When o'er the line the merry vessels sweep,
> And the rough saturnalia of the tar,
> Flock o'er the deck in Neptune's borrowed car.
> And pleased, the god of ocean sees his name
> Revive once more, though but in mimic fame
> Of his true sons."
>
> *Byron—The Island.*

MANY superstitious observances have been common, from ancient to modern days, among mariners. We shall find these ceremonies addressed to the ship at various times in its history, to the paraphernalia of the seaman and fisherman, to the sea itself, and on certain occasions, to the saints, to Neptune or to lesser gods.

Ceremonies at the laying of the keel, or at the launch of the new vessel into her destined element, have always been performed. *Ancient authors state that the ship was launched with ceremonies, first decking it with flowers and crowns of leaves, and pouring out a libation. Similar practices prevailed during the middle ages. The vessel was decked with flowers, purified by a priest, anointed with egg and sulphur, consecrated and named for some saint, and then launched.

When a modern ship of any size or importance is launched, it is frequently made a gala occasion, the vessel

---

*Jal.—Glossaire Nautique. Bâptême.

being gaily decked with flags, and a band of music stationed on board. The principal shores are removed, and but one or two left, to retain the cradle in which the ship is launched, upon the ways. When ready, it is usual to break a bottle of wine over the vessel's bow, then the last shore is removed, and the vessel glides into her destined element, amid the cheers of the beholders, and the strains of music. It was always regarded as a bad omen should any accident happen, or if the ship refused to move, or the wine was not spilled, or especially if any lives were lost. This must have occurred frequently during the middle ages, for we read that slaves or criminals were usually appointed to remove the last shores. In our day, this is done by electricity, the gentle finger of some favored maiden manipulating the key. In 1878 a large excursion steamer was launched at Norfolk, Virginia, in presence of many invited guests. The wine was not broken over the bows, and many predicted disaster to the vessel, and regarded the omen as verified when the ship was lost while being towed to New York.

* "Perhaps it will be remembered that when a big yacht was launched last summer, without the customary waste of a bottle of wine on her bows, the omission was telegraphed all over the world, because it showed a very remarkable temerity on the part of the owner."

† Aubin says, "Most Roman Catholics give to their vessels the names of saints, under whose protection they have placed them; and in virtue of this choice that they have made of their protectors, it is to them that the prayers of the crews are addressed, in times of peril. They consecrate also, and baptize their ships, and attach a certain efficacy to this ceremony. Some among Lutherans baptize them also, but they attach no particular virtue to this baptism.

‡ Among the ancient Norsemen, victims were attached to the rollers on which the ship was launched. This ceremony is alluded to in the Eddas, under the name of "hlun-rod," roller-reddening.

Modern Greeks, in launching, decorate their ships with flowers, and the captain takes a jar of wine, puts it to his lips, and then pours it upon the deck.

In the North of Scotland, it was, a short time ago, a custom to launch a boat to a flowing tide. A feast of

* New York Daily, 1885.
† Diottonnaire de La Marine (1702).
‡ Corpus Poetarum Boreale, I, p. 419, in Mélusine, January 5, 1888.

and cheese is distributed, the boat is named, a bottle of whisky broken over its bows, and then it is launched. Sometimes this charm is said over it,—

> *" Frae rocks and saands
> An' barren lands,
> An' ill men's hands,
> Keep's free,
> Weel oot, weel in
> Wi a guede shot."

Fijians had certain ceremonies at the laying of the keel of a new canoe, as well as at launching it, generally involving a human sacrifice. †Mariner says, "Men were sometimes murdered, to wash a new canoe's deck with blood." We are also told that it was sometimes a custom to use men as living rollers, on which to launch a new canoe.

‡Ellis says, "The priest had certain ceremonies to perform, and numerous and costly offerings were made to the gods of the chief and of the craft or profession, when the keel was laid down, when the canoe was finished, and when it was launched."

Ships were consecrated or christened, even after launching. The term baptism, used by old authors, is applied to the christening either at launching, or afterward.

§After a boat is finished, in Pas-de-Calais, France, a priest blesses it under a tent made on board, out of the mainsail. Wine and cakes are then devoured by the crew, and one offers to passers-by on the quay, a drink of wine. A refusal to drink is considered a bad omen.

The choice of a name was always considered as of great importance. ‖Greek ships, always feminine, were often named for goddesses, while Romans made frequent choice of the appellations of the deities to serve as names for their galleys. **Appian describes such a ceremony, "On the shores of the sea, altars with their bases washed by the waves, are erected. The ships of the fleet are arranged in a semicircle, the crews keeping during the ceremony profound silence. The sacrificers enter the sea in boats, and row three times the round of the fleet, . . . adding prayers to the gods to take evil luck from the ships. Then

---

*Gregor.—Folk-lore of Scotland.
†Tonga.
‡Ellis.—Polynesian Researches, I, p. 176.
§Labille.—Les Bords de la Mer, in Mélusine, January, 1885.
‖Boeck.—Urkunden des Attischen Seewesens.
**Jal.—Glossaire Nautique, Art. Baptême.

returning to the shore, they immolate bulls or calves, whose blood reddens the sea and shore." * Livy recounts a similar ceremony, where a whole fleet was baptized.

As Aubin has already told us, a saint's name was pre-ferred in the middle-ages, and the fleets of the seventeenth and eighteenth centuries contained all the saints in the cal-endar. Hawkins' flag-ship was the Jesus, and the Holy Ghost was in Tourville's squadron, in 1692. The Santa Maria was one of Columbus' ships, and numerous other examples of this proclivity will occur to every reader.

We find in a work entitled "Construction of a Galley," by J. Hobier † (1622), the following description of a christening in the middle ages: "The galley being in this state on land, more or less finished in the upper works, it was launched in the water with more or less difficulty and labor, after hav-ing been first blessed by a mass, and given a name by a godfather or godmother, which they call baptism."

‡ In Scotland, a new boat is christened by a woman sprinkling barley or corn over it. One man seized a bride and marched her about his new boat, while still in the water.

§ When a modern Greek captain first goes on board of his new ship, he hangs laurel and garlic about it, and drinks a libation to it.

❘ Hindoo boatmen never build, launch, or man a new boat without a ceremony by a priest, entailing a heavy fee.

After a new Fijian canoe was launched, it became neces-sary to throw stones in the house in which it was built, to charm away the gods of the carpenters.

It was long a custom to bless ships before setting out on a voyage, especially on undertaking any expedition of great importance. ** The ships of the fleet of John de Outrema-rius were thus prepared for their voyage to the Holy Land. ††So the ships of the Armada were all publicly blessed, before their disastrous expedition against England.

‡‡ An item on the accounts of the English Rolls informs us that the Bishop of Bangor was paid five pounds for his expenses in going to Southampton, to bless the great ship Henry Grace de Dieu, in 1418.

* Ch. XXXVI.
† Jal.—Glossaire Nautique, Baptême.
‡ Gregor.—Folk-lore of Scotland.
§ Jones.—Credulities, p. 65.
❘ Forbes.—Oriental Memoirs.
** Jones —Credulities, p. 45.
†† Goodrich.—Man upon the Sea, p. 33.   ‡‡ Jones.—Credulities, p. 65.

* Before the Reformation, certain Yarmouth priests blessed the fishing boats, and preached an annual fishing sermon. Russian priests always bless the ships of the fleets leaving port for Siberia.

Scotch fishermen formerly sprinkled their boats with "forespoken," or holy water.

A traveler in a New Zealand canoe tells us, "The crew were in great strait because they had no priest to charm their canoe, to make it sail bravely when the wind blew."

Masses, prayers and other ceremonies, were often resorted to, both at the beginning of a voyage, and at its successful termination, and also in any time of unusual danger or peril. † Covilham, after making a lucky landfall at Calicut, in the sixteenth century, summoned all his ship's crew to prayers, and said over the "Salve Regina," and gave thanks.

‡ Da Gama and his entire crew passed the night in the Oratory, at Belem, near Lisbon, before setting out on their celebrated voyage, and § Columbus and his crew went in solemn procession to the convent of La Rabida, and he remained there all night, engaged in prayer, before his departure to discover new lands. When the fleet of Outremarius was overtaken by a storm, he requested the crew to pray for its safety, and we are told, the storm then ceased.

· ‖ The fleets of St. Louis of France, were provided with means for conducting masses, etc., when they went to the Holy Land. Each ship had an altar, and priests were carried in each one. When the flag-ship struck the ground at Cyprus, Joinville tells us, "Many on board were kneeling before the holy sacrament on the ship's altar." So before setting out on their voyage, he tells us, ** "when the priests and clerks embarked, the captain made them mount to the castle of the ship, and chant psalms in praise of God, that he might be pleased to grant us a prosperous voyage. They all, with a loud voice, say the beautiful hymn of 'Veni, Creator,' from the beginning to the end."

On another occasion, he tells us that a current, having kept the ship all night under a certain mountain on the Barbary coast, so as to be in danger of being driven ashore, they were told by one of the priests that, it being the third

* Folk-lore Record.
† Gravière.—Les Marins du XV et XVI Siècles.
‡ Goodrich.—Man upon the Sea, p. 171.
§ Goodrich.—Man upon the Sea, p. 140.
‖ Guérin.—Histoire Maritime de France, Vol. I, p. 48.
* Guérin.—Vol. I, p. 51.

Saturday in the month, they should march in procession
three times around the mast. " Now this day was a Saturday, and we instantly began a procession around the masts
of the ship."

Before embarking on an expedition against France,
Henry III, of England, visited the shrines of various saints,
to obtain their influence in his undertaking.

* Before a Spanish fleet sailed out of Vera Cruz harbor,
in 1639, according to a letter from a gentleman of Malaga,
a procession was inaugurated with a statue of the Virgin on
board a certain ship, while others, getting under way, fired
salutes in her honor.

† In the account from the travels of Oderic, quoted in a
previous chapter, prayers are mentioned as resorted to to
save the ship in the storm. " On this occasion, the idolaters
began to pray to their gods for a favorable wind, but which
they were unable to obtain. Then the Saracens as industri-
ously made their invocations and adorations, to as little
purpose. After this I and my companions were ordered to
pray to God, and the commander of the ship said to me in
the Armenian language, which the rest of the people on
board did not understand, that unless we could procure a
favorable wind from our God, he would throw both us and
our bones into the sea. Then I and my companions went
to our prayers, and we vowed to celebrate many masses in
honor of the holy Virgin, if she would vouchsafe us a wind."

‡ On one occasion, Drake's flag-ship grounded in the East
Indies. The whole crew went to prayers, and the sacrament
was administered to each one.

§ Erasmus, in his graphic picture, "The Shipwreck," says
mariners prayed to the Virgin and saints: "One sang his
'Hail, Queen!' another, 'I believe in God!' There were
some who had certain particular prayers, not without magical charms against dangers."

‖ West India buccanneers often had prayers said for their
safety, and the successful issue of their marauding expedi-
tions.

** Arab and Barbary corsairs, during the middle ages,
whipped their Christian captives, when other means of

* Letter of Juan de Lauros, in F. Duro's Disquisiciones Nauticas, Vol. II.
† See Chap. III.
‡ Goodrich.—Man upon the Sea, p. 220.
§ Colloquies (1516).
‖ Goodrich, p. 220.
** Dan.—History of Barbary.

quently had prayers at sea, preceded by a curious ceremony. A boy ran about the decks with a lighted candle in
his hand, inviting all to come upon deck, and crying, "The

WHIPPING CHRISTIAN CAPTIVES TO MAKE THEM PRAY FOR FAIR WINDS.

*Fishermen at Clovelly, in the north of Scotland, had a special service in church, at which the One Hundred and Seventh psalm, containing those sublime verses, "They that go down to the sea in ships," etc., was read. A special prayer was then said, too long for insertion here, but containing petitions for safety from storms and wreck at sea, and beseeching the Lord to send an abundance of fish to them.

When a Breton fisherman puts to sea, he says, "Keep me, my God; my boat is so small, thy ocean so wide."

†When a Breton boat is wind-bound, two of the crew are sent to a chapel of Ste. Marine at Combrit, to sweep the chapel, and throw the dust in the direction of the desired wind. This saint is also importuned by the families of absent fishermen, to return them safely home. A similar ceremony is practiced at a chapel in Penmarch, by sailors' wives, only the dust is swept in a corner of the church.

‡In the Isle de Sein, a little ship made of breadcrusts is suspended over the table, and, on Holy Thursday, it is lowered down and burnt, while all uncover, and the "Veni, Creator" is sung. Another bread-ship is then suspended over the table. This ceremony is called the "Ship-feast," and is designed to insure the safety of the family fishing-boat.

§In Sicily, on Ascension Eve, peasants go to the sea-shore, kneel, and repeat the following prayer as the waves roll in, stopping with the ninth:

" I salute thee, sea-fountain,
The Lord has sent me here;
You should give me good,
For I give thee my ills."

Each time the prayer is recited, a handful of sand is collected, which is afterward cast on the roofs of silk-worm raisers, while a certain formula is repeated.

‖Tyndall gives the following account of a ceremony performed by Sardinian fishermen: "Amidst the cheers of the men at having made a good capture of fish, a general silence prevailed; the leader, in his little boat, having checked the hilarity, and assumed a priestly as well as a

*Choice Notes.—Notes and Queries, p. 271.
†L. F. Sauvé, in Mélusine, December 5, 1884.
‡Mélusine, January, 1885.
§T. Gannizzaro, in Mélusine, December 5, 1884.
‖Jones.—Credulities, 36-7.

piscatorial character, taking off his cap—an example followed by all his company—commenced a species of chant or litany, in invocation of the saints, to which an 'Ora pro nobis" chorus was made by the sailors. After the Virgin Mary had been appealed to, and her protection against accidents particularly requested, as the ancients did to Neptune, a series of saints were called over, half of whose names I knew not, but who were evidently influential persons in the fishing department." Then follows a description of appeals to particular saints, which will be found elsewhere.* " Besides the saints of such undoubted authority and interest in tunny-fishing, the shrines of general saints, as well as local ones, were called over, and a blessing requested for the principal towns and places in the Mediterranean which purchased the fish." " The next day, the weather being unpropitious, a fresh invocation of the saints was made in church at vespers, and fishermen and others were assembled to implore a change of wind and a successful fish on the morrow."

† A similar ceremony to secure luck in fishing is described in the following words by an eye-witness, as having taken place among French fishermen at Etrétât, in Normandy, on St. Sauveur's day:

" When all was ready, the organ struck up, and through the open door the fishermen entered, carrying between them a floral pyramid surmounted by a model of a fishing-boat, over a huge loaf—a peculiar kind of light, sweetened bread, called *brioche*, which was to serve for the *pain beni*."

" Each fisherman carried a candle, not the long church-candle belonging to ecclesiastical ceremonies, but a primitive tallow dip, with a piece of paper wound round the end that it should not soil the hand.

" The leader, the village sailmaker, led in the *cantique*, which was almost as old as the church, praying for each part of the hull and rigging of the boats separately, and to be saved from the power of the Turks and pirates, while all joined in the repetition of the last line of each stanza not very strong or audibly, for strangely these fishermen, strong of lungs in the open air, were afraid of hearing their own voices in the church."

‡ Gibbons tells us, "A particular form of ceremony and

*See Chap. II.
† Letter in Boston Transcript, 1880.
‡ Boxing the Compass.

thanksgiving, and observed on the island of Capri, in honor of Madonna di Carmela, by the coral fishers previous to the departure of their fleet every spring. A somewhat modified form of the ceremony is observed by the Canton and Foo-chow sailors, who call at the island of Pootoo, in the Chusan Archipelago, on their passage up and down the China Sea, where they pray for fair winds and a prosperous voyage."

A *clavie*, or a blazing tar-barrel, was formerly carried deiseal (with the sun) about every ship in Binghead Harbor, Moray Firth, Scotland.

Nannie Scott, a Northumberland witch, prayed for fair winds for sailors' wives, during the last part of the eighteenth century.

* One of Paul Jones' biographers tells us that, on the occasion of his famous raid on the Scottish coast, the minister and people came down to the shore at Kirkaldy, and a prayer was offered, in which the Lord was begged to send a storm to repel the invader. One came soon after, and Jones was blown off the coast, and it was always believed that the prayer was directly answered.

† In a Russian folk-lore tale, a man calms the angry waves by prayer, and by promising to pay a debt.

‡ Joshua Coffin tells us that the privateers of Newburyport used to request the prayers of the congregation before setting out to sea, and always obtained them.

§ So the " Filibustiers " first fell on their knees at quarters (each group at their gun), to pray God that they might obtain both victory and plunder.

Society Islanders prayed to their god before launching their canoes. ‖ Fijians accompanied a libation to the sea-gods, with this prayer, " Let the gods be of a gracious mind, and send us a wind from the east." Samoans prayed to the sailing-gods before each meal.

Kamtchatdales prayed to the storm-god, sending a naked child around the village with a shell in his hand. ** Hurons prayed to a local god, " Oko, thou who livest in this spot, we offer thee tobacco; help us, and save us from shipwreck."

Many other ceremonies have been observed by sailors and sea-faring people, to obtain luck in winds, fish, etc.

* J. K. Laughton.
† Ralston.—Russian Folk-lore.
‡ Drake.—Legends of New England, p. 300.
§ Thornbury.—The Buccaneers.
‖ Williams.—Fiji.
** Tylor.—Primitive Culture, Vol. II. p. 206.

*Virgil testifies to a custom of Greek and Roman sailors, after escaping the dangers of a stormy voyage,—

> "So sailors, when escap'd from stormy seas,
>   First crown their poops, and then enjoy their ease."

And Ovid alludes to the same custom.

In the journal of Columbus' voyages, we find this description of the performance of a ceremony vowed, as seen in the last chapters, while in danger at sea, after arriving at St. Mary's, in the Azores: †"The Admiral and all the crew, bearing in remembrance the vow which they had made the Thursday before, to go barefooted and in their shirts to some church of our Lady at the first land, were of the opinion that they ought to discharge this vow. . . . They accordingly landed, and proceeded according to their vow, barefooted and in their shirts, toward the hermitage."

‡When Magellan's ship arrived at Seville, the crew performed penance, going barefooted and in their shirts, to Our Lady of Victory, with lighted tapers in their hands, in performance of a vow made while in danger.

§ William the Conqueror, before setting out for England, had the body of St. Vallery carried about to obtain favorable winds and a prosperous voyage to England.

‖At Fraserburg, in England, at the commencement of the fishing season, a procession of fantastically-dressed men, with bagpipes, part on horseback and part on foot, travel about the fishing village, preceded by a man with a tall crowned hat having a herring's tail stuck in it.

Another ceremony is thus described: **"The herring fishing being very backward, some of the fishermen of Buckie, on Wednesday last, dressed a cooper in a flannel shirt with burrs stuck all over it, and in this condition he was carried in procession through the town in a hand-barrow. This was done to bring better luck to the fishing."

††At Moray Firth, in Scotland, a new boat went to sea in advance of the others in the fleet. If it was found successful, it was deemed a good sign. The boats raced on their way home, and the first boat in was bound to provide a feast of bread and cheese.

*Georgic I.
† Gravière.—Les Marins du XV et XVI Siècles.
‡ Pigafetti, in Goodrich.—Man upon the Sea, p. 220.
§ Turner.—Anglo-Saxons.
‖ Folk-lore Record.
** Banff Journal.
†† Gregor.—Folk-lore of Scotland.

California Indians formerly propitiated the gods of the sea, by certain ceremonies at the commencement of the fishing season.

* Fijians built a new canoe as a final ceremony at the death of a king, and it was regularly put to sleep and waked by beat of drum.

Williams says all canoes approaching Mbui Island had to lower their sails and submit to many degrading ceremonies before they were permitted to land. It was said that a god once visited this island on a bamboo, guided by a superior deity in the shape of a rat, but he passed his guide on the way, and hence all canoes suffer degradation for his fault.

† In the Maldive Islands, it was formerly the custom to set a new boat on fire, and to perform certain other ceremonies with offerings before setting out on a voyage.

When Chinese vessels leave port, all other junks in the harbor burn crackers and incense and beat gongs, etc., to propitiate the gods. Offerings are made to them in temples, after arriving in port. During a squall, sacrifices and offerings are made, as detailed in the last chapter.

‡ Negroes on the West African coast, when the sea is stormy, form a procession, and walk toward it, sacrificing an ox or a goat, and spilling its blood on the sand, throwing a ring into the water at the same time, as a charm.

§ Du Chaillu says when the Mpongwee negroes go on a voyage, they fire guns, and wish a pleasant sail, with loud shouts, and they receive a vessel arriving safely, with similar ceremonies.

Greek and Roman sailors, when they hoisted their sails, were in the habit of consigning them to Castor and Pollux. ‖ Similarly, the mariner of the middle ages, in tacking ship, was wont, at the most critical part of the ceremony, to consign the vessel into the hands of God, lest the manœuvre fail. This was the origin of a command, corresponding to our " Helm's alee!" that is not yet entirely eliminated from marine vocabularies. ** The Provençal mariner said, " A Dieu Va," and the Spanish or Portuguese, " A Dios Va," directly committing the vessel into God's hands, while the Dutchman was content with saying, " Overstaag, in God's

* Williams.—Fiji Islands.
† Grant.—Mysteries of All Nations, p. 53.
‡ Tylor.—Anthropology.
§ Journey to Ashango Land.
‖ Jal.—Glossaire Nautique.
** Tecklenborg.—Marine Dictionary.

name." These commands are interesting examples of survivals of prayers for assistance in performing the evolution.
It was also a custom to say "Coupe, de par de Dieu" (Cut,
for God's sake), when a rope or sail was cut loose.

Not only was it thought necessary to consecrate the ship
or boat, but fishermen often thought it advisable to perform
some ceremony over their nets, or fishing gear. *Grant
says an English fisherman, not many years' since, had his
nets sprinkled, because they were bewitched. It was still in
1879 a custom to salt them, in the Tweed. Nets of Sardinian fishermen were formerly smoked with the smoke of
need-fires, kindled with sacred wood, by drilling, the motion
being "with the sun."

Hurons and Athabascan Indians married their nets to
young girls, to obtain luck in fishing.

These ceremonies have also been addressed to the sea
itself. Such was the famous annual wedding of the Adriatic. This was instituted in honor of a great naval victory
over the Saracens, †Pope Alexander III. giving a ring for
that purpose, in 1174. The Doge, in the magnificently decorated Bucentaur, or state barge, attended by a gay fleet
of gondolas and barges, proceeded to a certain spot in the
Lagoon, and there performed the ceremony. First, a large
cask of consecrated water was thrown into the sea, as a preventive against storms, etc. Then a priest, when the Doge
was ready with the ring, poured in a large ewer of holy
water, and the ring, of gold, containing precious stones of
onyx, lapis-lazuli and malachite, was thrown into the same
spot. Flowers were afterward strewn on the water, and
then all proceeded to St. Nicholas' church, where mass was
said. This festival took place on Ascension Day.

A ceremony was held in Venice, in 1569, to commemorate the deliverance of the naval arsenal from destruction.
Mass was said in a convenient church, after the sea had
been blessed, and races and festivities followed.

‡The Greeks cast a cross in the sea on the sixth of January, with certain ceremonies, to render it fit for navigation. §The waters are blessed at Constantinople on the
eighteenth of January, and on the same day the waters of
the Neva are blessed in Russia. A chapel is then built on

---

*Grant.—Mysteries of All Nations, p. 578.
†Jal.—Glossaire Nautique, Art. Bucentaur.
‡Jones.—Broad, Broad Ocean, p. 340.
§Jones.—Credulities, p. 66.

the ice, and the priest dips out water through a hole, making the sign of the cross three times, and then sprinkles the people with holy water. The people carry home bottles of the Neva water, for purifying purposes.

In Roumania, the New Year begins with a blessing of the waters, to exorcise the demons therein.

At Dieppe, not twenty years since, priests blessed the sea, sprinkling water upon it, signing the cross over it, and saying litanies for the repose of the souls of the drowned.

Kerry fishermen formerly had an annual mass performed in the bay.

*Every spring at Port Louis, France, a ceremony is observed by the fishermen, when a thousand boats form in a procession, and follow a gaily-decorated barge to the fishing-ground, where a priest, from the poop of the barge, blesses the sea.

Instances of ceremonies, sacrifices and oblations offered directly to the sea are given in the last chapter, and were numerous during the early days of navigation.

†Burnes says the sailors of Scinde sing songs to the saints, in passing certain dangerous spots in the rivers.

‡Many maritime ceremonies were performed on certain days, particularly on those set apart in the calendar as saints' days, and on the other holidays of the year. Many of these take place on St. Nicholas' day. Such a ceremony is described here as occurring at Bari, in Italy:—

"Tradition has it that the saint, when in life, came from Mira to Bari on this day; and, therefore, every year, on the eighth of May, his arrival is celebrated by embarking him on two rafts and transporting him to the very spot where he is said to have landed for the first time in 1085. A number of gaily-decked boats follow the saint by sea. Some are filled with kneeling pilgrims, singing hymns; others, on the contrary, are filled with pretty women, in pretty morning-dresses; whilst others are filled with young fellows, who follow the ladies."

§St. Peter's day was also frequently observed. An old account of the Lordship of Gisborough, in Yorkshire, tells us: "The fishermen on St. Peter's daye invited their friends and kinfolk to a festyvall kept after their fashion

* Pacini.—La Marine.
† Travels into Bokhara.
‡ Correspondent Boston Transcript, 1881.
§ Brand.—Antiquities, Vol. III, p. 353.

WEDDING THE ADRIATIC.

with a free hearte, and no show of niggardnesse. That day, their boats are dressed curiously for the showe, their masts are painted, and certain rytes observed amongst them with sprynklying their bowes with good liquor, sold with them at a groate a quarte, which custome or superstition, sucked from their ancestors, even continyeth doune vnto this present tyme."

*On the same saint's day, bonfires are lighted in Penzance, and other Cornish towns, to open the fishing season. This is also done on midsummer eve, and it is a survival of an extensive sun-worship, formerly prevalent.

Fishermen of Cleveland, Yorkshire, held a ceremony similar to that described above, dressing their boats with flags and streamers, and sprinkling liquor on them.

On New Year's day, in the Isle of Man, fishermen hunt the wren, to find the one that was traditionally a siren who deluded a young fisherman by her arts.

†On May day, in Dorsetshire, England, the children of each boat's crew deck the prows of their boats with flowers, and then march to the sea, and throw flowers in it.

‡Fishermen at Hartlepool, on the first Monday after Epiphany, parade the streets, dragging a fool-plough or *stot* (a small anchor), asking gifts and singing carols.

On Whit-Monday, the sailors at Arzoe, in Brittany, visit a shrine of St. Anne, in performance of a vow made by their ancestors, in a naval combat with the Dutch. They go in boats, ornamented with red sails, the leading one having flags and streamers flying, and carrying in its bows a priest with a crucifix.

§On Shrove-Tuesday, at Köpeneck, in Germany, fishermen go about from house to house, with ice-hooks, fish-hooks and other implements in hand, and sing a recitation, in which they beg food and money.

The Sunday before Shrove Tuesday, the proprietors of certain fisheries near Berlin were formerly in the habit of meeting and choosing their respective fishing-ponds by lot. The next day their men were wont to assemble, carrying about on a pole a gaily decked model of a ship, and singing a song similar to that at Köpeneck, visiting their patrons in turn.

---

* Bottrell.—Traditions and Fireside Stories of West Cornwall.
† Folk-lore Record.
‡ Jones.—Broad, Broad Ocean, p. 241.
§ Wolf.—Deutsche Märchen und Sagen.

* On Good Friday, Catholic mariners in many lands still cockbill their yards in mourning, and many scourge an effigy of Judas. Such a ceremony is described as follows, in 1810: "Good Friday was observed with the most profound adoration on board the Portuguese and Spanish men-of-war at Plymouth. A figure of the traitor Judas Iscariot was suspended from the bowsprit end of each ship, which hung till sunset, when it was cut down, ripped up, the representation of the heart cut into strips, and the whole thrown into the water, after which the crews of the different ships sang in good style the evening song to the Virgin Mary. On board the Iphigenia, Spanish flagship, the effigy of Judas Iscariot hung at the yard arm until Sunday evening, when it was cut down."

† An English paper describes such a ceremony as occurring so lately as 1881:

"The old Good Friday custom of flogging an effigy of Judas Iscariot was, after a lapse of two years, duly celebrated in the London docks on April 7, by the crews of three Portuguese and Maltese vessels. The effigy of the traitor, hewn out of a block of timber, was carried by chosen members of the crews round the quarter deck and hanged from the yard arm, and each man chanted his vituperation as he lashed the figure with knotted ropes. The scourging over, Judas was cut down, thrown upon the deck, spat upon, cursed, and kicked to the galley fire, where he was burned into a charred mass, and then hurled into the water, after which the sailors went in procession to church."

‡ On May 16, St. John Nepomuc is honored in Magyar lands, by throwing his image in the Danube, while people follow it in boats, playing musical instruments, etc.

§ In many Russian towns, the Rusalkas, or water-demons, are expelled by throwing straw figures into the lakes and rivers during Rusalka week.

Among miscellaneous observances are to be noted the following:

In the thirteenth and fourteenth centuries, it was the custom to place in churches boxes for collections, designed for seamen and their families. These boxes were labeled for each ship, and were opened at Christmas.

* Brand.—Antiquities, Vol. III, p. 153.
† Quoted in Boston Transcript, 1881.
‡ Magyar Folk-lore, Notes and Queries, December 27, 1868.
§ Ralston.—Songs of the Russian People.

Whalers were in the habit of suspending aloft a garland or wreath of flowers and leaves, and carrying it to sea with them. *Hone says: "A custom prevails among the seamen of these vessels, when traversing the polar seas, to fix, on the first day of May, a garland aloft, suspended midway on a rope leading from the main topgallant mast head to the first topmast head, ornamented with knots of ribbon, love tokens of the lads for their lassies, etc. This garland remains suspended till the ship reaches once more her port." It was regarded as an ill omen to detach this garland, or for it to receive any accident.

The ceremony best known among those practiced among sailors, and concerning which much has been written, is that observed in modern times, "on crossing the line," from north into south latitude, or vice versa, as the case may be.

This custom, still observed as a pastime among sailors, is another of those remarkable survivals of ancient practices begun as actual worship of some deity, and finally existing as mere customs, without any significance. Anciently the Greeks sacrificed, on nearing any prominent cape, on many of which temples to the deities were placed. During the middle ages, the present ceremony of receiving a visit from a fictitious Neptune, arose, when it was not, of course, performed at the equator, but on arriving within the tropics, crossing the Arctic Circle, and even in passing certain capes, etc.

†Aubin quotes some older writer concerning this ceremony: "It is a custom practiced from all antiquity, that those who are apprenticed to the sea, and who pass certain places, where they have never passed, undergo this penalty, under the favorable name of Baptism; that is, to be cast from the yard-arm into the sea. The ships also are subjected to this ceremony, so ridiculous (of Baptism). It may be said that is a recompense for the rejection by the Reformers, of that which, among the Roman Catholics, has remained an act of religion; these latter baptizing effectively their ships, the first time they are placed in the sea. When the occasion presented, and the ships arrived in these consecrated places, that is to say, where they had never been, the master was obliged to redeem them; otherwise the crew at once proceeded to cut off the ship's *nose*, or the whole outer part of the prow, or to disfigure or destroy some other part

*Table Book.
†Aubin.—Dictionnaire Nautique (1702). Art. Baptême,

of the ship. Those whom they will to cast from the yard-arms into the sea, could redeem themselves by giving money to the crew. As to the boys, instead of dipping them from the yard-arms, they put them under a basket surrounded by tubs full of water, and each one dipped it out with buckets and threw water on them."

In after times, the ruder features of this ceremony were dropped, while the essential ones, baptism and a penalty, were retained, and a more extended ceremony added.

The same author describes this ceremony as occurring in French ships about the middle of the seventeenth century: "As a preparation, there are ranged on the upper deck, on both sides, tubs full of sea-water, and sailors, formed in two rows, stand near, each with a bucket in his hand. The chief steward comes to the foot of the mainmast, his face full-bearded, and his body attired in gaskets, entirely surrounding him, and ropes' ends hanging from his arms. He is followed by five or six sailors, equipped in the same manner, and holds in his hand some marine book, to represent the Gospels of the Evangelists. The man who is to be baptized kneels before the steward, who, making him put his hand on the book, forces him to promise that whenever an occasion presented itself of baptizing others, he would impose upon them the same ceremonies which were inflicted on him. After this oath, the one to be baptized rises, and, marching between the rows of tubs, and the people who wait for him with buckets full, he reaches the bow, and thus receives what is called the baptism."

*A description of this ceremony, celebrated about the same time, and given by M. Jal, shows that the usages of the present time with regard to it were already observed: "The second mate, dressed as *Neptune*, wore a long cap on his head, and a fringed collar of parrel-trucks and small blocks. His long beard, and hair, made of tow, were matted with sea shells, and his face was *blackened*. In his hands he carried a chart-book (such a book was then called a *Neptune*), opened at the chart showing the position of the ship. Each one of the crew knelt before him, and swore by bread and salt that he had previously passed the line. If not, the mate dubbed them kneeling, with a blow of his wooden sword, and the crew then threw water over each victim until he paid a penalty of wine or money."

---

* Jal.—Glossaire Nautique, from Œxmelin, Histoire des Flibustiers.

The same authority tells us that in Dutch ships, during the seventeenth century, the roll was called by the clerk of the ship, when passing these places, and each man answered to his name, and indicated whether he had passed the place before or not. If he had not, he was fined, and compelled to pay fifteen sols, or else was attached to a rope, hoisted to the main yard-arm, and dipped three times into the sea. The officers were fined thirty sols, the passengers mulcted of all they would pay.

These are the earliest descriptions of this ceremony, but we learn that between the voyages of Columbus, in 1492, when no mention is made of it, and 1529, the French created a sort of an order of knighthood,* the "Chevaliers de la Mer" (Knights of the Sea), by giving novices an accolade on the shoulder when passing these places, and giving a feast after each ceremony.

During the middle-ages, the novice was often terrified at the horrible appearance of Neptune and his crew, and was usually bidden to watch for lights near the chosen spots.

† De Plancy says the Devil was caricatured in costume, in the Neptune ceremony, being brought on board in a cask.

It was especially the custom among Dutch mariners to observe these ceremonies at Capes Raz and Bailooges. Even admirals were compelled to pay these fines. The clerk bought wines for the crew with the money thus gained. So greatly was this privilege abused, that the ‡ Dutch East India Company prohibited these fines in 1669, and Charles IX. of Sweden, some years previous to this, abolished the right to claim fines, and allowed to each of the crew a bottle of wine on crossing the equator and the tropic circle.

This ceremony, as performed in modern times, has been often described. It is now observed merely as a pastime among sailors, only on crossing the equator, and officers and passengers are rarely troubled.

§ Hone describes it as performed on board whaling vessels, early in the present century, on the first day of May, or on crossing the Arctic circle. The novices were kept below decks, and a barber-shop was fitted up, with a sign,

* Journal of J. Parmentier, in Jal. Glossaire Nautique, Baptême.
† Dictionnaire Infernale.
‡ Jal.—Glossaire Nautique, Baptême.
§ Table Book, Vol. 1, 630.

" Neptune's Easy-shaving Shop, Kept by John Johnson."
Then a c , consisting of ten fiddlers, dressed in
mats and progss Neptune riding on a gun-carriage, with his
usual retinue of tritons, etc., was formed. On reaching the
quarter-deck, Neptune interrogated the captain, asking the
name of the ship, her destination, and similar questions,
and, on three quarts of rum being produced, drank the captain's health. The novices were then brought up, questioned
as to their names, ages, destinations, etc., and were then
put through the usual rough shaving process.

*Chaplain Rockwell tells us that among the usual feat-
ures of the procession during the early part of the present
century, was a trio composed of two bears led by a triton.
He says some explain this as a representation of Ursa Major
and Ursa Minor, disappearing under the horizon as the
equator is crossed, under the guardianship of Arctophylax
(Boötes).

†Marryat gives an excellent description of the modern
ceremony. Neptune appears, preceded by a young man,
dandily dressed in tights, riding on a car made of a gun car-
riage, drawn by six nearly naked blacks, spotted with yellow
paint. He has a long beard and ringlets of oakum, an iron
crown on his head, and carries a trident with a small dolphin between its prongs. His attendants consist of his
secretary, with quills of the sea-fowl; surgeon, with lancet,
pill-box, etc.; barber, with huge wooden razor, with its
blade made of an iron hoop, and his mate, with a small tub
for a shaving box. Amphitrite also appears, wearing a
woman's night-cap, with sea-weed ribbons on her head, and
bearing an albicore on her harpoon, carrying a boy in her
lap as a baby, with a marlinspike to cut his teeth on. She
is attended by three men dressed as nymphs, with curry-
combs, mirrors and pots of red paint. The sheep-pen,
lined with canvas, and filled with water, had been already
prepared. The victim was seated on a platform laid over
it, blindfolded, first shaved by the barber, and then plunged
backward into the water. Officers were expected to pay a
fine. Marryat says this ceremony was performed at the
tropics, if the ship *did not intend to cross the line.*

The ceremony is sometimes observed among the fishermen on Newfoundland banks. ‡ " Practical jokes are played

*Sketches of Foreign Travel (1847).
† Mildmay.
‡ Fish and Men in the Maine Islands. Harper's, May, 1884.

on greenhorns on their first visit to the banks, where Neptune, in a garment of rock-weed, sometimes comes on board to shave them with a broad hoop."

A traveler in Austria, in the early part of this century, tells us, that on board the regular passenger boat, on arriving at the whirlpool called Wirbel, the steersman goes about with water in a scoop, which he throws upon the passengers who have not passed before.

—— Many festivals have been observed at various times by sailors, fishermen, and maritime folk in all countries. Such festivals, connected with navigation, were not uncommon in antiquity. The Egyptians had several. Nile boatmen and mariners held an annual festival attended with great debauchery and license. On the 15th of December, offerings of grain, etc., were made to the river Nile.

In the annual festival of Isis, at the opening of navigation, or of spring, a small boat was set adrift, in which incense had been placed by the priests. A sacred boat was also carried about on men's shoulders, in this festival. In many of these festivals, such boats, dedicated to Ra, the Sun-god, were thus carried about.

*The numerous representations of these on the existing monuments show us golden barks, built of precious woods and inlaid with stones, with prow and stern adorned with sacred emblems, and the image of the god in a tabernacle in the center. These are found in the Oasis temples also, and they have images of priests and gods on them. Sacred boats were in use on the Nile, and are often spoken of as carrying the king on religious occasions. These were called Tum- or Ra-barks, and Baris.

† Plutarch describes the annual festival: " The Egyptians go down at night to the sea; at which time the priests and supporters carry the sacred vehicle. In this is a golden vessel in the shape of a ship or boat, into which they take and pour some of the river water. Upon this being performed, a shout of joy is raised; and Osiris is supposed to be found.

The Apis bull, when found, was also carried in procession on the Nile.

The worship of Isis, transplanted to Greece and Rome, was there continued. On the 5th of March, at the Festival of Navigation, her bark was carried in joyous procession.

* Rosellini.—I Monumenti. Lepsius.—Denkmaler, aus Ægypt.
† De Isidis et Osiris.

The Greeks had also their sacred barks, dedicated to Poseidon and to Athena, while the Romans carried about, in triumphal and sacred processions, the barks of Jupiter Redax, or of Neptune, god of the waters. *In the yearly procession of Athena, a bark proceeded from the Piræus to Athens, having her *peplos*, or sacred veil, as a sail.

Several festivals of a maritime nature were celebrated by the Greeks. Apuleius tells us that priests of Aphrodite yearly dedicated to her a new ship, laden with the first fruits of spring, as soon as the storms of winter were over. Lactantius also says that on a certain day, a ship was borne about in honor of Isis, to show that navigation was opened. Pausanius says Hercules was carried on a raft or float, in certain rites in his honor in Ionia. Aristides says a ship was carried in procession in the Dyonisiac festival in Smyrna. Clemens Alexandrinus says honors were paid to an unknown hero at Phalerus, seated in a ship.

†Two ships were sacred in another sense among the Athenians. These were the "Paralos" and the "Salaminian." The former carried tribute, messages, worshipers, etc., to the sacred temple at Delos, and the latter was used in festivals to promote the memory of the victory of Salamis. Antigonus consecrated a ship to Apollo after he defeated Ptolemy. The boat Esculapius carried to commemorate his arrival in that city in time of pest, was of stone, cut in the shape of a galley.

An annual festival was held at Delos, to which priests repaired, in these sacred ships.

The annual festival at Salamis is thus described: "Each year, a ship left Athens and came quietly to Salamis. Many people from the island came down in front of the ship, pell-mell, in great disorder, and an Athenian jumped ashore, with arms in his hands, and ran, crying aloud, toward those who came from on shore."

A yearly festival in honor of Isis was held at Rome, when the Isis ship, gaily decked with flowers, was launched on the Tiber before a multitude of people. who then repaired to the temples and sacrificed to the gods. Ausonius says: "I add the cult, sacred to foreign lands, the Hercules, or the ship of Isis, a naval ceremony."

The Roman naval triumphs, undertaken by conquerors after a naval victory, were festivals, in which were carried

*Murray.—Mythology, p. 54.
†Jal.-Glossaire Nautique.

in procession pictures of naval triumphs, trophies of battle, prows of conquered ships, etc.

* Tacitus tells us that the Suevi carried about in spring processions a model of a liburna, or galley, and offered it to Isis. Such a model was carried about in Germany in honor of Frey, and is found in the accounts of many German tribes.

Frey's name is connected with agriculture and navigation. Ziza, an old Teutonic goddess, was worshiped in a procession of boats.

† In Inda, or Corneliminster, in Germany, in 1133, a ship was made in a grove, set on wheels, and dragged by weavers to the Rhine at Maestricht, where it was embarked, fitted with masts and taken up the Rhine, with festive processions.

‡ The Council of Ulm prohibited such processions in 1530, and that of Tübingen, in 1584. These boats were, however, carried about in procession at Mannheim in 1865.

Similar processions were held in other places in the middle ages. Thor was carried about by the Northmen in a ship. § A ship with sails set is still carried in Christmas processions in Siberia, with a figure of a saint seated on it.

In 1825, they were carried about in processions in various cities in Belgium. ‖ At Brussels, there is a festival called Ommegarde, where a few years ago, a ship was drawn about by horses, to commemorate a miraculous appearance of the Virgin in a boat, from Antwerp.

Ships' models, carried by boys dressed as sailors, figure in a procession called the pardon of Guingamp, in Brittany.

In many places, the ship is superseded by the plough. As Keary suggests, this is natural, and plough is etymologically connected with the Greek *plous*, a sailing. So the ships of the Eddas "plough the waves."

Diego da Conto says the Siamese had an aquatic festival in 1542, at the "turn of the waters." The king came out in his barge accompanied by a large number of boats, and the waters were "turned" with great noise and shouting, boat races terminating the festival.

** Mohammedans of Bombay throw into the sea gilt-paper temples, in the festivals attendant on the Moharrum, or

* Cox.—Aryan Mythology, B. II, Chap. II.
† Grimm.—Teutonic Mythology, Vol. I, p. 258.
‡ Grimm.—Teut. Myth., Vol. I, p. 224.
§ Ralston.—Songs of the Russian People, p. 209.
‖ Simrock.—Deutsche Mythologie.
** Rousselot.—L'Inde et ses Rajahs.

FLOATING PAPER TEMPLES.

New Year. At the feast of Naryal Puranama, natives wade into the sea, throw cocoa-nuts into it, and invoke it, with prayers, to be favorable to voyagers.

At St. Malo, near Manilla, a festival was held, about the beginning of this century, on November 26, in honor of St. Nicholas, when large floating structures, brilliantly illuminated, and filled with people, were seen on the river, and pieces of paper with votive sentences on them, were thrown in at the same time.

The Chinese have several water festivals. On the fifth day of the fifth month,[*] long, light and narrow boats, made for the occasion, are pulled in races by forty or fifty men, and in the bows are three more, waving flags and beating drums, to frighten the dragon of the waters. The excitement is so great, that many boats are frequently overturned. It is said to have originated at the drowning of a certain courtier, Wat Yen, in 500 B.C. Another ceremony is described, in which his body is sought. Bamboo leaves, or silk bags filled with rice, are thrown into the water, gongs are beaten, and men in the bows of the boats stand throwing their arms about, and peering in the water for the appearance of the defunct.

[†] In the rivers of China, Taouist priests, from the fifth to the fifteenth of the month, go about in boats, throwing bits of paper, rice and other vegetables into the water, and chanting requiems for the repose of the drowned. Lights are set adrift at night, to show the way to the souls of such unfortunates.

[‡] On the 1st of August, boats from twenty to thirty feet long, made of bamboo, are born on the shoulders of men, in a night procession. These are preceded by men with torches, and others with gongs, etc., and followed by persons in grotesque costumes and masked faces. The boats are burned, and the ashes thrown into the sea, where they are supposed to carry certain diseases.

A similar procession, in which paper boats and a dragon some two hundred feet long are carried, is held on the 22d of December, to the sailor goddess. Boats of bamboo and paper are carried in a procession in honor of the fire elemental gods. They are dragon-shaped, and in them are images with offerings of rice, salt, etc.

[*] Doolittle.—Social Customs of Chinese, Vol. I.
[†] Grey.—China.
[‡] Doolittle.—Social Customs of the Chinese.

It is with the ceremonious observances as with the sacrifices,—they are addressed to the sea, or the sea-gods, to propitiate them, and gain their favor. Prayers, vows and votive offerings are simple substitutions for sacrifices, and are devoted to the same end—that of gaining good winds and speedy voyages.

CHAPTER XIII.

LUCK, OMENS, CHARMS, AND IMAGES.

"Some days, like surly stepdames, adverse prove;
Thwart our intentions, cross whate'er we love,
Others, more fortunate and lucky shine,
And, as a tender mother, bless what we design."

Hesiod. — Works and Days.

"I should be still
Plucking the grass to learn where sits the wind."

Merchant of Venice, Act I, Scene 1.

THE belief of the seaman in the numerous deities of sea and wind, and his reliance on sacrifices, prayers or other ceremonies to propitiate them, did not, at the same time, prevent him from having a firm belief in the operation of good or bad luck, and of omens warning him of danger or of success, while he also did not hesitate to use charms and amulets to bring about the desirable end. That

*"Fortune brings in some boats that are not steer'd,"

was part and parcel of his creed, and many seamen to this day are firm in these beliefs.†

A belief in the virtues of odd numbers was very prevalent, as shown in the usages of maritime nations with regard to salutes. All national, festal and personal salutes consist of an odd number of guns, a custom dating back to the beginning of modern history at least.

‡ Teonge wrote, in 1676, "This day, being the day of our

* Cymbeline, Act IV, Scene 3.
† See Cooper.—Red Rover, Chaps. XIV and XV.
‡ Voyages.

king's marterdom, wee show all the signs of morning as possible wee can, viz: our jacks and flags only half staffe high, and at 5 o'clock in the afternoon wee shot from 20 guns."

Minute guns are still the only even-numbered salutes. We often find in folk-lore that three, seven and nine, and their multiples, are considered lucky.

The traditional ill-luck of certain persons has been partially shown in previous chapters. Priests were most feared of all, and it is not only unlucky to have them at sea, or to speak of them there, in many maritime lands,* but in several, it is a bad omen to meet them on shore when about to set out on a voyage. He even brings bad luck to himself, for Arnanson † tells us Icelanders say you must leave the church-door open if the pastor goes out to row, or he may not return, nor should his books be aired during his absence.

‡ Women shared in this ill-favor both on board ship, as we have seen, and on shore. § Firth of Forth fishermen say if they meet a barefooted woman with very flat feet, it portends bad luck. A Cornish fisherman said a woman met him every morning, and wished him good luck, but he never had any, so long as she did so.

‖ Holinshead tells us, "Over against Rosse, on an isle named Lewis, sixtie miles in length, there is but one fresh river, and it is said that if a woman wade through the same, there shall be no more salmon seen there for a twelvemonth afterward; whereas, otherwise, that fish is known to abound there in greate plentie."

In the same island, a fisherman is sent out to the boats early in the morning, to see that women do not come down to them first, as there would then be no fish caught.

The statement of Holinshead as to the beliefs concerning the river is confirmed by Martin,** who says the fishermen of Barras send a man early on May-day to see that no female crosses the stream first, as salmon would not then be found in it for a year.

Women are unlucky in Cleveland, and other parts of England. †† In Sweden, if a woman steps over a fishing-rod, no fish will bite.

* See Froude.—Short Studies, p. 50.
† Powell and Magnusson.—Icelandic Legends.
‡ See Chapter III.
§ Jones.—Credulities, p. 116.
‖ Chronicles of England, Scotland and Ireland (1577).
** Account of the Western Isles (1716).
†† Jones.—Credulities, p. 134.

Children, according to some, are unlucky on board English ships, but others say they are considered fortunate.*

† In certain Scotch fishing villages, many family names are unlucky. Rosse, Cullie and White are mentioned as such in one village. These men were not allowed on the water, if possible, and wages were sometimes refused them, if the catch were small. They were even thought to bring ill luck by looking at the boats or nets, and it was an unfortunate omen to meet them first in the morning. It was the custom, in some villages, for an experienced man to rise early and prognosticate the weather. On one morning two of these unlucky ones happened to get up first, and soon met each other, but were so impressed with the ill-portent that each retired to his own home, and no one fished that day.

‡ John Smith records that he was deemed a "Jonah" while on a voyage to Rome. "They would never have fair weather while he (a heretic) was on board."

§ English sailors bestowed upon Commdore Byron (1750) the name "Foul-weather Jack," from his proverbial bad luck at sea; and a similar epithet was applied to Sir John Norris. The curse of the Flying Dutchman was upon these, and bad weather followed them everywhere.

This idea of personal luck probably led to the notion that a ship was safe, that carried some royal personage. So Cæsar, when his pilot feared shipwreck, said, "Why fearest thou? Cæsar thou carriest!"

∥ William Rufus was advised not to sail for France during a gale, but to wait for more favorable weather, for his campaign to Normandy. He answered: "I have never heard of a king that was shipwrecked. Weigh anchor, and you will see that the winds will be with us." He lost his nephew Harry at sea, nevertheless.

Henry II, embarking at Barfleur, and, seeing alarm at the state of the weather depicted on the faces of his courtiers, preferred rather to place his trust in God than to trust in kingly immunity.

The address of Cæsar to his pilot was graven on a medal of William III, who, when in a storm-tossed boat near Holland, said to his men, "How! should you think it hard to die with me?"

William I, of Germany, in placing his steamboat at the disposal of a young couple on Lake Constance, said to a lady who was afraid to embark, "Do not be alarmed! the steamer bears my name, and that ought to reassure you."

 * We have also seen many instances of the ill-luck in the presence of animals on board ship, and also at times, when encountered on shore. Hares, as weather-bringers, were especially ill-omened.

 † An old Cornish writer says: "To talk of hares, or such uncanny things, proves as ominous to a fisherman as the beginning of a voyage on Candlemas day, to a mariner."

 ‡ In Forfarshire, Eugland, fishermen would not go to sea if a hare crossed their path on their way to their boats. In Scotland, if the hare sat still, or ran toward the beach, it was not unlucky; but if she crossed the fishermen's path, he would catch no fish that day.

The cat, another wind-bringer, was also an unlucky visitor on board ship. § Speaking of Norman fishermen, a writer says: "The fishermen decline to take in their boats many things, such as priests and cats." ‖ When the cat plays, it is always a sign of a gale, especially if it has an apron or a gown to play with. ** In Sweden, says a recent writer, "Sailors will not go to sea in a ship having a cat or a spinning-wheel on board."

 †† Somerset fishermen would not go to sea if they met a pig, while on their way to the boats. ‡‡ One was once secretly introduced into a New Haven boat, but was immediately thrown overboard, when discovered by the fishermen.

 §§ English and Scotch fishermen thought it unlucky to mention any four-footed animal at sea. "Brounger" was a name they could not bear to hear. In one boat, a lad spoke the word "horse," and the fishermen at once threw their nets overboard, refusing to fish. ‖ Another incident is related, in which a boy says three forbidden words:— "There's a salmon-box on our weather bow. It would make a grand trough for our minister's pig." He narrowly escaped severe punishment from the enraged fishermen.

 * Chapter III.
 † Carew.—Survey of Cornwall.
 ‡ Jones.—Credulities, p. 118.
 § Bosquet.—La Normandie.
 ‖ Jones.—Credulities, p. 119.
 ** Swedish Folk-Lore, Notes and Queries, December 8, 1883.
 †† Choice Notes, p. 271.
 ‡‡ Grant.—Mysteries of all Nations, 592.
 §§ Gregor.—Folk-lore of Scotland.
 ‖ Notes and Queries, October 4, 1884.

*A dog anywhere near the nets or fishing-tackle brought ill-luck to the Icelandic fishermen, nor did they like one in the boats.

†Greenock fishermen say if a fly falls into a glass of water, it portends good luck.

‡In Iceland, a spider, when hanging down by its web, must not be disturbed; but you must say to it, putting your hand under it, "Up, up, fishing-carl! your wife lies ill in her child-bed"; or, "Row up from below, fishing-carl, if you betoken fair weather; row down, if you betoken foul."

§Fishermen at Santec, in Brittany, have a song, in which presages are drawn from actions of the cat. If it wipes the face with its paw, the omen is bad, and if it rubs the ear, the helmsman cannot steer. If it turns the back to the fire, the boat will upset, and if it burns its claws, the crew are lost. If it commences to purr, the omen is good.

‖Darwin says that when the surgeon of the Beagle killed ducks for sport, captive Fuegians said bad weather would certainly ensue.

**Hindoo boatmen keep venomous serpents in their boats. If these are dull and irritable, they will not sail; but if they are lively and good-natured, it is thought a sign of an extremely lucky voyage.

††In many Scotch villages it was deemed an unlucky venture to go to sea in any boat that had been overturned with loss of life. Such a boat would not be used again by the people of the village to which it belonged, although it might be purchased and used by another village.

Sailors have long implicitly believed in the luck or ill-fortune of certain ships, and a volume of curious anecdotes might easily be gathered, relating to the subject. So recently as 1879,‡‡ a sailor was fined in an English court for refusing to go to sea in a vessel, in which he had shipped, and he alleged that he dreamed that she was lost, and feared to sail in her, as a previous dream of like import had proven true. Naval officers in our own service will call to mind a like occurrence concerning a man-of-war, lost afterwards.

This unlucky character is thought to abide with the ship

*Powell and Magnusson.—Icelandic Legends.
†Choice Notes, p. 247.
‡Powell and Magnusson.—Icelandic Legends.
‖L. F. Sauvé, in Mélusine, January, 1886.
‖Voyage of the Beagle.
**De Feynes.—Voyage Jusque à la Chine (1630), p. 207; Mélusine, January,
††Gregor.—Folk-lore of Scotland.
‡‡ Credulities, p. 67.

from the first, and to pursue her name when bestowed on a successor. -

> " It was that fatal and perfidious bark,
> Built in the eclipse, and rigged with curses dark,"

says the Blind Poet.[*]

[†]A fisherman, in " Natasqua," says of a certain boat, "She's unlucky. She means mischief some day. There was a man killed at her launching, and the mark of the blood is on her bow." " If that's the case, there's no help for her," responds another.

We have already alluded to the belief that a ship will always be unlucky, if any one is killed in launching her.

Sometimes it is a whole letter of the alphabet that is affected by this unlucky character. It is often said, with reference to our own navy, that the letter S is an unlucky one, from the losses of the Suwanee, Sacramento, Saranac, San Jacinto, and many others. But a careful examination of the list shows that but one fifth of the ships whose names begin with that letter have been lost.

An old friend in Boston informs me that Dr. Bowditch, who was much consulted by underwriters, always declined to insure a ship whose name commenced with O, saying that such ships were an unlucky venture, that they were lost, their cargoes burned or damaged, and were in every way unfortunate risks.

It has been noted that the Royal George, and the Royal Charlotte, two English ships built at the same yard, and named after the reigning sovereigns, were both lost, with all on board.

Sailors on board of one of our first Monitors feared to go to sea in tow of the " Rhode Island," because she had lost the original monitor.

This belief in the good or evil luck of ships has had great influence in the choice of names. [‡]Spanish sailors will not choose a secular name, as it is considered unlucky. So ancient Greeks seem to have avoided a masculine name, as all their ships bore feminine ones, probably in deference to Athene, goddess of the sea.

So great is this prejudice against unlucky ships, that it is often difficult to get men officers, freight or passengers for

* Milton.—Lycidas.
† Scribner's Monthly, Vol. I.
‡ Sir Hugh J. Rose.—Spain.

her. * Rockwell says, "Ship owners will rarely purchase a vessel which, by meeting with repeated accidents at sea, had proven to be unlucky."

†A recent instance of this belief in the luck of ships is recorded in a daily paper. A man had fallen from the top-mast-head of a lake vessel, and after that another, until the men began to believe the ship an unlucky one. On arriving at Buffalo, "the men went ashore as soon as they were paid off. They said the ship had lost her luck. While we were discharging at the elevator, the story got around, and some of the grain-trimmers refused to work on her. Even the mate was affected by it. At last we got ready to sail for Cleveland, where we were to load coal. The captain managed to get a crew by going to a crimp, who ran them in, fresh from salt water. They came on board two thirds drunk, and the mate was steering them into the forecastle, when one of them stopped and said, pointing aloft, 'What have you got a figurehead on the masthead for?' The mate looked up and then turned pale. 'It's Bill,' he said, and with that the whole lot jumped on to the dock. I didn't see anything, but the mate told the captain to look for another officer. The captain was so much affected, that he put me on another schooner, and then shipped a new crew and sailed for Cleveland. He never got there. He was sunk by a steamer off Dunkirk."

Another instance is given in an account of the loss of a vessel whose name was three times changed, without losing her unlucky character.

‡"The steamer with the pretty name of Ianthe, was formerly the Rose, and before she was the Rose she was that most ill-fated ship which, if 'not built in the eclipse,' was certainly attended with 'curses dark,' the Daphne, whose launch on the Clyde, it will be recollected, caused the drowning of an appalling number of men. She sank in the Clyde as the Daphne; she was raised, and then sank in Portrush harbor as the Rose; she was raised again, and still, as the Rose, she ran ashore on Big Cumbrae. Then she was got off and lost sight of for a little, and now reappears as the Ianthe, comfortably lodged on the mud which she seems to love so well, and to which her instincts regularly direct her, after having threatened to go down in deep

water, and then changing her mind and plumping on a rock. She is evidently an unlucky ship. Common sense must yield to superstition, and partake of the sailor's view of such a vessel as this."

* In Pomerania, stolen wood is employed in building a ship, a small piece being inserted in the keel. Such wood makes the ship go faster at night. If the first blow struck in fashioning the keel draws fire, the ship will be lost on her first trip. A piece of silver, preferably an old coin, is placed under the heel of the mast of a new ship, as then she will make profitable voyages.

† In Iceland, it is deemed unlucky to use the wood of a certain tree, called *sorb*, in building ships. When used for such purposes, the ship will sink, unless willow or juniper wood is used with it, to counterbalance its ill influence, as they are inimical woods.

There are also many things connected with the belongings of ships that bring evil or good luck.

‡ It was long thought unlucky, on board of English ships, to turn a hatch cover upside down, or to lose a bucket or swab overboard.

§ Seamen think it a misfortune to lose or tear the colors, and it was unlucky in English ships to sew sails on the quarter deck.

To hand anything through a ladder is equally unlucky. ‖ Grant tells an anecdote of a ship-captain, who greatly offended a sailor, by passing him a mug of beer through a ladder.

Folk-lore traditions say any one passing under a ladder on shore will be hanged.

** When a basin is turned upside down, fishermen in the south of England will not go to sea.

‡‡ Aubin says the Dutch, in the fifteenth century, deemed it lucky if a ship, when laden, heeled to starboard, but unlucky, if to port, and Melville says whalers used to think it a lucky circumstance if they had a sperm whale's head at the starboard yard-arm, and a right whale's on the port side, as the ship would then never capsize.

* Tenne.—Volkssagen aus Pommern, p. 346, in Mélusine, January, 1885.
† Maurer.—Islandische Sagen.
‡ Jones.—Broad, Broad Ocean, p. 267. Brand.—Popular Antiquity, p. 240. Hazlitt.—Popular Antiquities of Great Britain.
§ Grant.—Mysteries, p. 345.
‖ Grant.—Mysteries, p. 503.
** Jones.—Credulities, p. 115.
†† Benard.—Merveilles de L'Art Naval.

*Among West India boatmen, overturning the calabash used to bail out the boat is unlucky, as the boat will certainly be upset.

There are many actions not to be performed at sea, or among sailors or fishermen.

† Sneezing has been regarded by people in all ages, and in all lands, as unfortunate. It was long a custom to salute one who sneezed, to remove the bad results thought to ensue therefrom.

Among Baltic fishers and mariners, it is still thought unlucky, on Christmas Day. Greeks and Romans thought a sneeze to the right hand lucky, to the left unlucky.‡ Themistocles is said to have conceived a good opinion of the result of a naval engagement in which he was about to participate, by a sneeze to the right, just as he was about to sacrifice to the gods. § Timotheus, on the contrary, would not sail because he heard a sneeze to the left of him. | Shetlanders still prognosticate the weather by sneezing.

Spitting to windward, prohibited for obvious reasons, in well regulated ships, was considered unlucky among Maldive Islanders. Chinese Junk sailors considered it unlucky, and a forerunner of fowl weather, to expectorate over the bows of the vessel, when starting on a voyage. Saliva has, however, generally been regarded as curative, and fishermen in **England often "spit on the hansel" for luck—a custom not yet extinct among schoolboys in our own land, while †† Peruvian fishermen put chewed coco on their hooks for a similar reason. ‡‡ In Germany, any one spitting on a pothook, and calling the devil by name, gets plenty of fish.

§§ Baltic seamen and fishermen held that you should not quarrel about the catch of fish, or envy another's luck, or your own would leave you. On the contrary, Esthonian fishermen thought it an extremely lucky thing to get up a quarrel with some member of the family, before setting out on their fishing trips. They often locked up store-rooms, overturned kettles, or committed some similar act, to irritate the housewife. Blows were extremely lucky, and, it was said, brought three fish for each one.

* Branch.—W. I. Superstitions, Cont. Rev. October, 1881.
† Tylor.—Primitive Culture, Vol. I, p. 97.
‡ Renard.—Les Merveilles de L'Art Naval, p. 236.
§ Jal.—Glossaire Nautique. Eternument.
| Nautical Magazine, 1870.
** Grose.—Antiquities of Great Britain.
†† Dorman.—Primitive Superstitions, p. 205.
‡‡ Folk-lore Record, 1879.
§§ Thorpe.—Northern Mythology, Vol. II, p. 275.

In Iceland, fishermen will not sing at the line, nor dredge with a net, as it is unlucky. Scotch fishermen think borrowed nets and fishing tackle bring luck.* This was also true in England, and in Sweden,† where also it was said

that pins found in church made the best fish-hooks. Indians prefer a hook that has caught fish, and never put two nets together, as they would be jealous.

* Fraser's Magazine.—Vol. LVII, p. 353.
† Afzelius.—Svenska Folkets Sagen.

*Pomeranians say you must not throw overboard a burning coal, or you will have a storm. So, when the wind is contrary, you must not sew or mend anything, or you sew up the wind. In a good breeze, you can do it, for then you keep it. You should not even speak of the wind when it is good, for it will then change, and even resents any fears as to its permanency. It is most risky to calculate when a good breeze will carry you in, as then it is sure to change.

Fishermen work all night before Easter, Pentecost, or Ascension Day, believing it especially lucky. They decline to tell the number of fish caught, or at least must understate the catch.

†Spanish sailors regard it as unlucky to place the left foot on shore first, or to enter a boat left foot first. They also say it is unlucky for a sailor's wife to put a broom behind the door, with the brush up, during her husband's absence at sea.

‡When Irish sailors passed a little island, Mac-Dara, they wet their sails three times in the water, to insure a good voyage.

§Marriages are unlucky among Scotch fishermen, bringing a tempest with each ceremony, and it is equally unfortunate to have eggs on board the boats.

∥Breton fishermen became angry, if wished a good voyage on setting out.

**Swedish fishermen also thought it unlucky for strangers to see how many fish they had, or to tell any one the number of the catch, or the locality of the fishing-ground.

††Scotch fishermen were equally unwilling to tell the number of fish caught, and considered it extremely unlucky to be asked where they were going. ‡‡It was also unlucky for any one to point at the boats with the finger, or to count them, or the fishermen while standing.

§§English fishermen say that if you count your fish, you will catch no more, and Scotchmen would refuse to sell the first fish of a catch to a person with broad thumbs. ∥∥White

*Tenne.—Volkssagen aus Pommern, pp. 347, 348, q. in Mélusine.
†Guichot.—Supersticiones Populares, p. 299, in Mélusine, January, 1885.
‡Folk-lore Journal, II. 259.
§Gregor.—In Mélusine, January, 1885.
∥L. F. Sauvé, in Mélusine, January 5, 1885.
**Thorpe.—Northern Mythology, Vol. III, p. 111.
††Jones.—Credulities, p. 117.
‡‡Jones.—Credulities, p. 119.
§§Jones.—Credulities, p. 116.
∥Gregor.—Folk-lore of Scotland.

stones must not be taken as ballast, nor those bored by certain animals, known as "hunger-steen," and it was thought unlucky for boats to touch the salmon cobble.

*Maurer says no ship will sail from Malmsey to Drangey in Iceland, in the spring, without carrying three stones, to be obtained by a stop at Thordarhöf. In the same Island, if a stone is cast over a ship, it will cause her to capsize as soon as she gets to sea.

†A heap of stones on a hill near Weston-super-Mare, in England, should receive an additional stone from each fisherman passing it on his way to the sea.

On New Year's day in Scotland, it was especially lucky to catch the first fish, or at least to draw blood first. A correspondent of "Notes and Queries" says: "Wife beating to the effusion of blood may be a novel method of securing luck in the herring fishery, but to 'draw blood' is practiced in some of the fishing villages on the north coast of Scotland, under the belief that success follows the act. This act must be performed on New Year's day, and the good fortune is his only who is the first to shed blood. If the morning of the New Year is such as to allow the boats of the village to put to sea, there is quite a struggle which boat will reach the fishing-ground first, so as to gain the coveted prize—the first-shed blood of the year. If the weather is unfavorable for fishing, those who are in possession of a gun, are out, gun in hand, along the shore, before daybreak, in search of some bird, no matter how small, that they may draw blood, and thus make sure of one year's good fortune."

The captain of a Newfoundland "banker" still casts a penny over the bow for luck, when starting on a fishing voyage.

When Greenock whalers left port, it was formerly a custom to throw old shoes after them, for luck. The same custom was also observed at Whitby, England. ‡Boatmen in Canton say you should not put your shoes on the deck bottom upward, or the boat will capsize.

§To see a flat footprint in the sand before embarking, boded ill luck to the English fisherman.

‖At the present day, the whale-fishers of Scotland, before leaving harbor, often burn effigies, to promote a lucky voyage.

* Islandische Sagen.
† Choice Notes, p. 175.
‡ Folk-lore Record, Vol. III.
§ Jones.—Credulities, p. 117.
‖ Grant.—Mysteries of all Nations.

* Rockwell says it was thought ill-luck to hear a death-march played by fife and drum on board of a men-of-war, in 1847, and some officers would not allow it, saying that death would certainly follow.

There is often but one way to turn a boat, among sailors and fishermen. † Orkney fishermen say it must go *with the sun*, i.e. from left to right, and ‡ Swedish boatmen will not turn the boat with the prow toward the shore. In Scotland, where witches went *widdershins*, or from right to left, around the cauldron, a boat must be turned *deiseal*, or with the sun.§ "On going to sea, they would reckon themselves in the most imminent danger, were they by accident to turn their boat in opposition to the sun's course."

Many of these beliefs with regard to luck were connected with articles of food.

∥ A loaf of bread should not be turned upside down, said fishermen in the north of England, for a ship would be lost for every loaf so placed.

Sunderland wives see that their husbands take some bread, baked on Good Friday, with them, to avoid ship-wrecks.

** At St. Michael, a piece of cake, eaten at a certain festival, is saved for each absent sailor, and is placed in a cup-board, carefully wrapped in a fine napkin. If a storm appear, it is regarded as unlucky to find the cake dried up.

So in the Isle of Man, in 1700, no seaman would sail without salt in his pocket, and fishermen in the Tweed salted their nets for luck, and threw some of it in the sea to blind fairies, as late as 1879. Bags of it were hung in temples, on Pescadore island, says Archdeacon Gray, as offerings by mariners. Salt was an ingredient of holy water, ever powerful over the waves. Mariners of 1600 swore by bread and salt, and threw some of the latter into the sea. English seamen think it unlucky to throw it about.

†† In Holland, it was thought unlucky to overturn a salt-cellar, as a ship would be wrecked each time it was done.

‡‡ Rice was long regarded with ill-favor. Sailors called

*Sketches of Foreign Travel (1847).
†∥Hazlitt.—Popular Antiquities of Great Britain.
‡ Jones.—Credulities.
§ Sir J. Sinclair.—Statistical Account of Scotland, in Brand, III, 442.
∥ Henderson.—Folk-lore of the Northern Counties of England.
** Bulletin of a Morbihan Society q. in Mélusine, Jun. 1880.
†† Choice Notes. p. 7.
‡‡ Hazlitt.—Popular Antiquities of Great Britain.

it "strike-me-blind," and there was a tradition that its continuous use caused blindness.

Icelanders regarded it as unlucky to eat the liver of a seal. Chinooks will not eat the heart of a fish at all. *Dutch fishermen eat no meat on Easter Sunday. †Cornishmen eat fish from the tail toward the head, so as to turn the fishes' heads toward the shore.

Fishermen in many parts of the world have tabooed words that must not be used at sea. We have already seen instances of this in speaking of animals, and also when treating of the ill-luck of priests. You should not wish a Swedish fisherman "good-luck," and Scotch fishermen do not like to have women wish them the same. Many family names, especially those of unlucky persons, must not be spoken at sea. This odd belief has led to the creation of many curious sea-words in Shetland and Scotland, where many circumlocutory words and phrases are used, to avoid the objectionable ones. ‡The sea was held in such dread in Shetland, that it must not be named. Blind says it was called "Holy toyt," and the *cat* (which he says was the sea) was called *Kasirt*, *Footie*, or *Saistal*.

§Swedish fishermen will not pronounce the name of a seal, but call it "brors lars"; and regard it as equally unfortunate to pronounce the name of an island toward which they may be sailing.

By far the greater part of sailor beliefs and usages in regard to luck is applied the luck or ill-luck of certain days. This idea of a choice of time, with regard to its influence on any undertaking, is not new, nor is it confined to the seaman alone. From antiquity the *Dies Nefasti*, or *Ægypticæ*, were known and regarded, and they still have their believers in many places.

> " By the Almanack, I think
> To choose good days and shun the contrairie,"

has been believed by many.

❙ Hazlitt quotes an old English manuscript:
" Yt be observed by some old writers, chiefly the canon astrologicum, who did alledge yt there were twenty-eight

---

*Thorpe.—Northern Mythology. Vol. III. p. 33.
† Hunt.—Romances and Drolls of the West of England, p. 148.
‡ Blind.—New Finds in Shetland and Welsh Folk-lore. Gentleman's Magazine, 1882.
§ Moman.—De Superstit. hodiernis (1752), in Mélusine, January. 1885.
❙ Popular Antiquities of Great Britain.

'days in the yeare, which were revealed by the Angel
Gabriel to good Joseph, which ever have been remarked
to be very fortunate dayes either to perrge, to let blood,
cure wounds, use marchandizes, sow seed, plant trees,
build houses, or take journees in long or short voyages, in
fighting or giving of bataille," etc.

*Another old work tells us: "There are fifty-three days
in the year, in which it is dangerous to undertake journeys," etc.

†Chief among these unlucky days were Cain's birthday
(first Monday in April), the anniversary of the destruction
of Sodom and Gomorrah (second Monday in August), and
December 31, when Judas hanged himself.

We are told in an early account of the Orkney Islands:
"In many days, they will neither go to sea in search of fish,
nor perform any sort of work at home."

‡Shakspeare says of a lucky day,—

> " But on this day let seamen fear no wreck."

Saadi, the Persian poet, relates the following illustrative
anecdote: "Some slaves were fishing, when one lost his net.
Being reproved, he said: 'Oh, brothers, what can I do!
Seeing that it was not my lucky day, and the fish had some
days remaining.' The moral given is, 'A fisherman without
luck cannot catch fish in the Tigris.'"

It was long thought unlucky to lay the keel or launch
the ship on certain evil days, or even to fell the wood.

§ Hesiod says of the 17th,—

> " In the same day, and when the timber's good,
> Fell for the bed-post and the ship, the wood."

Many days were unfortunate as sailing days, and sailors
in many countries have for ages paid particular regard to
this. As to Friday, we will speak more fully hereafter.
∥Forbes says Hindoo vessels will not sail on unlucky days.
**Bryant says the ancients thought it unlucky to sail at the
heliacal rising of the Pleiades or Doves. The dove was
regarded as a fortunate omen to navigators.

Saints' days and church holidays were generally unfort-

* Book of Presidents (precedents), 1666.
† Jones.—Credulities, p. 110.
‡ King John, Act III, scene 1.
§ Works and Days.
∥ Oriental Memoirs.
** Ancient Mythology.

unate. *Cornishmen say Candlemas is a bad day to put to sea. All-Hallow eve and All Saints' day were holidays among French fishermen. † Those who went to sea on the latter day were said to see double, and in the nets they would have nothing but a skeleton and a winding-sheet. ·The superstition that a spectral bark with the souls of those drowned at sea would come on that night, has been alluded to.‡ It was also said that a car was heard at midnight, drawn by eight white horses, and having eight white dogs ahead of it. Voices of sailors drowned during the year were heard, and any one seeing it, was doomed to die.

§ Baltic fishermen would not set their nets between All Saints' and St. Martin's days, or on St. Blaise's day.

Fishermen on Lewis Island do not go out to their work on St. Blaise's day. St. Peter's day (June 26) was observed as a holiday by many fishermen. ‖Finns used to say that any one making a disturbance on St. George's day would encounter storms and disasters. No fishing is done in Sweden, on Christmas, but the nets are set that night for luck. Abraham Brahe, in his Tankebok, says (December 24, 1618): ** "On this Christmas eve, God granted me a glorious haul of fish." At Ofveds' Kloster, it was the practice of the peasants, every Christmas eve, to go by torchlight and fish for their Christmas supper—first invoking the aid of the demon who lived at the bottom of the lake.

†† O'Reilly embodies in the following lines a superstition prevalent in Ireland:

> ' Upon St. Martin's eve, no net shall be let down;
> No fisherman of Wexford shall, upon that holy day,
> Set sail, or cast a line within the scope of Wexford Bay.''

A further legend says some men who violated this rule were visited by a demon, and never reached the shore again.

Many days of the month were marked as evil ones among sailors. In an old almanac,‡‡ we find that the 19th, 20th, 24th and 31st of July are marked "No good Anchorage."

§§ In an old manuscript, we read that the Saxons believed

* Jones.—Credulities, p. 110.
† Jones.—Credulities, p. 107.
‡ See Chapter IX.
§ Jones.—Credulities, p. 108.
‖ Jones.—Broad, Broad Ocean, p. 240.
** Jones.—Broad, Broad Ocean, p. 239.
†† Songs of the Southern Seas.
‡‡ A Newe Almanacke of Prognostication of the year of our Lord God, 1615.—Saxon Leechdoms, etc.
§§ Saxon Leechdoms and Wortcunning. .

the seventh day of the month good for fishing, the eleventh, for killing whales, walrus, etc., and the twelfth, good to go to sea.

Hazlitt says tempests were thought to come on the thirteenth of the month, and many sailors would not go to sea on that day.

Hesiod enumerates the days in which certain tasks may be performed by sailors:

> * " The fourth, upon the stocks thy vessel lay,
>   Soon with light keel to skim the watery way."

And on the twenty-ninth,

> " And on thy dark ocean way
>   Launch the oar'd galley—few will trust the day."

He enumerates as unlucky the 4th, 5th, 13th, 16th, 19th and 24th.

Sunday has generally been thought a lucky day to sail or to fish, perhaps on the principle that "the better the day, the better the deed." In Scotland and England, it is regarded as a lucky day for sailors and fishermen. †At Preston-Pans, England, it was a favorite day to sail for the fishing-grounds, up to a recent date. Of the Isle of Man we read: ‡"Fishers would not go out Saturday night or Sunday. § A tradition existed that during one Sunday evening, when boats were out fishing, a great storm came up and destroyed many boats." ‖ Bishop Hall says of his superstitious man, "He will never set out to sea except on Sunday." ** If an Icelander's seal-skins be mended with thread and needle on Sunday, he will be drowned.

Concerning Monday, nautical tradition is silent, so it may be accredited an ordinarily lucky day. As to Tuesday, Spanish sailors seem to have regarded it as unlucky, judging from the proverb " El Martes, ne te casas, ne te embarques, ne de te mujer apartarse" (Tuesday, don't marry, go to sea, or leave your wife).

A Saxon MS. in the Cotton Library reads:†† "If the kalends of January fall on a Tiwesday, ships abroad are in danger."

* Works and Days.
† Choice Notes, p. 271.
‡ Robertson.— Isle of Man (1791).
§ Jones.— Broad, Broad Ocean, p. 241.
‖ Characters of Virtue and of Vice.
** Powell and Magnusson.—Icelandic Legends.
†† Hampton.—Medii Ævi Kalendarium.

Ancient Irish chronicles record that a certain king was not allowed to sail on a marauding expedition on Tuesday, or to go in a ship the Monday after Bealtaine (May-day).

Wednesday was consecrated to Odin, who, as Hnickar, was the Northern mariner's chief deity. Hence it was a lucky day to undertake a voyage. And so with Thursday, which was also dedicated to a favorite deity (Thor) with the Northern warlike mariner.

Saturday seems also to have generally borne a good character. But we are told in an old English work,* "Certayne craftsmen will nocht begin their worke on Satterday; certain schipmen or mariniers will not begin to sail on the Satterday—quhilk is plane superstition."

But Friday is of all days the one proverbially unlucky for sailors. Its bad character on shore is well known, and we should not wonder that it also obtained such at sea.

As Marryat says of one of his heroes: "His thoughts naturally reverted to the other point, in which seafaring men are equally bigoted, the disastrous consequences of sailing on a Friday; the origin of which superstition can easily be traced to early Catholicism, when, out of respect for the day of universal redemption, they were directed by their pastors to await the 'morrow's sun.'"

Southey says, "Many a ship has lost the tide which might have led to fortune, because the captain and crew thought it unlucky to sail on Friday."

The earliest account of this superstition that I find is in the "Itinerary" of Fynes Moryson (1553), who, speaking of the king of Poland at Dantzig, says:† "The next day the king had a good wind, but before this, the king and the queen, whilst sometimes they thought Monday, sometimes Friday, to be unlucky days, had lost many fair winds."

‡ Cooper says of a certain hero: "As for sailing on Friday, that was out of the question. No one did that in 1798, who could help it." Brand tells that a London merchant said, in 1790, that no one would begin any business or voyage on Friday.

§ Thatcher writes, in 1821: "Seldom would a seaman then sail on Friday." And Cheever, in 1827: "He (the sailor) will never go to sea on Friday, if he can help it."

* Hamilton's Catechism, 1531, in Jones' Credulities, p. 110.
† In Brand.—Popular Antiquities, Vol. III.
‡ Pilot.
§ Superstitions.

*Olmstead also writes, in 1841: "There has been a singular superstition prevalent among seamen about sailing on Friday; and in former times, to sail on this day would have been regarded as a violation of the mysterious character of the day, which would be visited with disaster upon the offender. Even now, it is not entirely abandoned; so if a voyage, commenced on Friday, happens to be unfortunate, all the ill luck of the voyage is ascribed to having sailed on that day. An intelligent shipmaster told me that, although he had no faith in this superstition, yet so firmly were sailors formerly impressed with superstitious notions respecting the day, that, until within a few years, he should never have ventured to sail on a Friday, for the men would be appalled by dangers which they would think light of on common occasions."

† Chaplain Rockwell says there were, in 1847, commanders in our navy who would not sail on Friday, and who would try to sail on Sunday. Officers have been known to refuse to begin a tour of duty on that day, in joining a new ship.

‡ Wellesley, earl of Dundonald, got under weigh on Friday, in 1848, but was recalled by the port admiral, and did not sail until the next day. This was in order to take a supplementary mail, but the crew firmly believed the admiral did it to avoid sailing on Friday.

Lord Littleton said he knew a naval officer who instantly quitted a room where thirteen happened to be, on Friday. Byron thought it an unlucky day, but sailed for Greece on Friday, and lost his life there.

§An assistant at a bathing machine in Scarborough, England, told a correspondent of "Notes and Queries" that most accidents happened on Friday, and especially on Good Friday. He had not worked on the latter day for years, nor would he do so.

It is still thought an unlucky day to sail in Suffolk, England. ‖ The Registrar General of Scotland reported, not many years ago, that many less ships sailed on Friday than on any other day.

** In Welsh folk-lore, the fairies rule on that day, and especially control the water, making it rough and stormy.

* Notes of a Whaling Voyage.
† Sketches of Foreign Travel (1847).
‡ Jones.—Credulities, p. 109.
§ Jones.—Credulities, p. 107.
‖ Grant.—Mysteries, p. 398.
** Sikes.—British Goblins and Welsh Folk-lore.

Spaniards deem it unlucky to sail on Friday, and Italians say, "Venerdi, non si sposa, non si parte" (Friday, don't marry, don't travel). * In Russia, St. Friday, or Mother Friday, is personified, and any work, especially washing and ironing, done that day, will offend her, and be unlucky. †In Wallachia, it is a woman's holiday, and you must not work with steel or a pointed needle.

‡ Finn and Breton sailors deem it an unlucky day to sail.

§ Gloucester fishermen still believe it an unlucky thing to sail on Friday. ‖ Brewer says, however, regarding this day: "In America, Friday is said to be a lucky day, and many of their greatest political events have been consummated on that day."

Columbus sailed on Friday, discovered land on Friday, and the Pilgrims landed on the same day, on which also Washington was born.

Friday was also linked with the mermaid superstitions. Under certain circumstances the apparition of a mermaid was a favorable omen to the seaman; and a tempest-tossed vessel, "spoken" by a mermaid on a Friday, would assuredly reach her destined harbor in safety. The superstition is well illustrated by an old ballad of the sea,—

marine, while *Thatcher gives it no particular home. The
story is, that the keel of a ship was laid on Friday, she was
launched on Friday, named Friday, commanded by Captain
Friday, sailed on Friday, and was lost on Friday—some
say was never heard from after a certain Friday.

† A writer in "Harper" tells the same story as among the
traditions of Wilmington, Delaware, in its palmy shipping
days, but there are amusing variations. The keel is laid on
Friday, although the builder's wife dreamed it was bad
luck. It was launched on Friday, christened for that day,
and sent to sea in command of Captain Friday. Just a
week from that time, it was seen foundering at sea. The
wife, when she heard of it, said: "I told thee so, Isaiah!
This is all thy sixth-day doings. Now thee sees the consequences. *Thee never had the vessel insured.*"

Many instances are told of disasters on Friday, strength-
ening the sailor in his belief. The English ship "Captain"
sailed on Friday, and was lost with her great crew. It is
said the admiralty did not venture to send the next ship
sailing after her loss, the Agincourt, to sea on that fatal day.

‡ The Amazon, a West India packet, the troop-ship Bir-
kenhead, and the packet Golden Gate, sailed on this unlucky
day, and were lost, with great sacrifice of life.

The United States ship Idaho left New York, on a cruise
to China, on Friday, much to the disgust of the old sailors.
Three weeks afterward, a fire broke out in the after magazine, and this was accredited to her sailing on Friday, and
her subsequent encounter with a terrific typhoon, and the
loss of her sails and spars, were cited as confirmatory facts.

The ill-fated Huron sailed on Friday, and this list could
be extended at will.

Friday undoubtedly got its bad name among christians
from its being the day of the crucifixion. Char-Freitag, or
"sad Friday," is the German name for Good-Friday. It is
named after Freya, a Norse goddess powerful at sea, and, in
southern tongues, after her prototype Venus. Both these
are goddesses of love, and women being so unlucky at sea,
this day, consecrated to the female deities, would also be
unlucky.

Omens have been seen, in many pages of this work, to
affect the sailor's estimate of the future, and to influence his

actions to a remarkable extent. Such omens were universally regarded in antiquity. The pilot says to Cæsar—

> * "A thousand omens threaten from the skies,
> A thousand boding signs my soul affright."

† The Grecian fleet at Mycale was only induced to engage the Persians, by the favorable omen of propitious sacrifices. ‡ A Basque poet says,—

> "The boatmen, ere his sail he spreads,
> Watched for an omen there,"

and Triptolemus says of Shetland boatmen: §"They are aye at sic trash as that, when you want a days' work out of them—they have stepped ower the tangs, or they have met an uncanny body, or they have turned about against the sun, and there is naught to be done that day."

These omens were derived from various sources. Prominent among these were the meteorological indications, numerous examples of which we have seen, in speaking of the wind-raisers. Clouds, sky, wind, waves, etc., were eagerly watched for such signs as were thought to indicate the course to be pursued, to gain success in any endeavor.

Lightning was thought by the ancients to be an evil portent. ‖ Cabrias, the Athenian general, feared to engage in a sea-fight, because of intense lightning, and postponed sailing against the enemy.

** Eclipses of the sun and moon were also dire portents of evil, and Virgil has been quoted in a previous chapter as testifying to their influence on the mariners of antiquity. †† Nicias lost his liberty and his life, because he failed to sail in support of the Athenians, having been delayed by the bad omen of an eclipse. ‡‡ In Iceland, a crescent moon with the horns turned toward the earth, indicates a wreck during that moon.

To the legions of Aulus Plautius, when about to invade Great Britain, in 43 A.D., there was a happy omen shown by a meteor moving toward the fleet.

§§ Fishermen in Kerry, Ireland, will not go to sea until

* Rowe.—Lucan's Pharsalia.
† Herodotus.—History.
‡ Webster.—Basque Legends.
§ Sir W. Scott.—Notes to Pirate.
‖ Jal.—Glossaire Nautique, Augures.
** Tylor.—Primitive Culture. Vol. II., p. 370.
†† Jurien de la Gravière. La Marine des Anciens, 1880.
‡‡ Powell and Magnusson.—Icelandic Legends.
§§ Notes to Hayes' " Ballads of Ireland."

the first star appears. In Wiesland, if clouds come from
the sea on St. George's day, fish are sure to be abundant
that year.

* Aubrey says Charles II sailed for France from Ports-
mouth, when a storm came up, and the ship put back. Sunshine and calm then intervened, but when the king again
embarked, a second gale appeared. It was deemed a bad
omen.

† In an account of the shipwreck of the England of
Newcastle, the narrator says they saw an aurora borealis
in the Gulf of St. Lawrence, of a yellow and orange color,
and all thought it portended violent tempests, but none
came for some days.

‡ Bede says he had remarked the sparkling of the sea,
and thought it a portent of storms.

§ It was said in Cornwall that the defeat of the English
fleet by the Dutch was foretold by a rain of blood on the
stones of St. Denis' church.

Tacitus says the seas were blood-red, and that human
forms were cast on shore, just before the war between the
Romans and the Britons, 60 A.D.

‖ We also read, in the account of the transfer of St. Cuthbert's body: "And being vpon the sea in a shippe, by myricle marveillous, iij waves of water were turned into blood."
A storm ensued.

** Jones quotes from a Cottonian MS., concerning a
stream in Yorkshire, where, when the waves were quiet,
"there is a horrible groninge, heard from that creek, at the
least six myles in the mayneland, that the fishermen dare
not put forth, though thyrste of gain drive them on, bould-
ing an opinion that there is a greedie beaste, raging for
hunger, and designs to be satisfied with men's carcasies."

†† On our own coast, a recent writer tells us: "The raging
sounds of the rising or falling of the sea are tokens that
presage disaster or good tidings."

‡‡ When, in a storm, the surge passes over the decks, and
gives out a hollow and deathly sound, it is said, in Pomerania, to be a sign that the weather will be fair and good.

* Miscellany.
† Chambers' Miscellany.
‡ De Rerum Natura.
§ Bottrell.—Traditions and Fireside Stories of West Cornwall.
‖ Chronicles of the Monastery of Durham.
** Credulities, Past and Present, p 64.
†† Harper's Magazine, 1860.—"Saline Types."
‡‡ Tenne.—Volksaagen aus Pommern, p. 347,

Such omens have also been derived from animals. The storm-raisers, especially, as the dolphin, cat, halcyon, etc., were carefully watched for indications of coming changes. Birds, always the favorites of the augurs, furnished many omens. When, as the poet sings,—

> "The sea-birds, with portentous shriek,
> Flew fast to land,"

it was time for the fisherman to moor his boat.

Irish fishermen in Tralee bay regard the presence of sea-gulls in great numbers as signs of herring shoals; * and we have already seen that the osprey and fishhawk were auspicious visitors.

The albatross was a good omen to the ancient mariner.

> † "At length did cross an albatross,
> Thorough the fog it came,
> As if it had been a Christian soul,
> We hailed it in God's name."

> "And a good south wind sprung up behind,
> The albatross did follow."

‡ The incident from Shelvocke's voyages, referred to in a previous chapter, is here given: "We had not the sight of one fish of any kind since we were come to the southwest of the Straits of Lemaire, nor one sea-bird, except a disconsolate black albatross, who accompanied us several days, hovering about us as if he had lost himself, until Sam Huntley, my second officer, observed, in one of his melancholy fits, that the bird was always hovering near us, and imagined, from its color, that it might be an ill-omen; and, being encouraged in his impression by the continued season of contrary weather, which had opposed us ever since we had got into these seas, he, after some fruitless attempts, shot the albatross." It is not unlucky always to catch an albatross. Says a sailor, speaking of one,—

"No, we had no ill-luck after the bird's death. If you shoot one and kill him, you may look out for squalls; but to catch him with a piece of fat pork and let him die on deck is a different think altogether, you know."

§ Pomeranians say that birds coming aboard at sea should not be chased or taken, for, as you lay hands on the birds, you will have to lay hands to the sails, in the storm that will come.

* See Chapter VII.   † Coleridge.—The Ancient Mariner.
‡ Shelvocke's Voyages (1719), q. by Low.—Maritime Discovery, II, p. 146.
§ Toeppe.—Volksagen aus Pommern, p. 349.

Swallows and other land-birds also furnished omens.
*Lloyd **says**: "By swallows lighting upon Pirrhus' tent,
and on the masts of Marcus Antony's ship, sayling after
Cleopatra to Egypt, the soothsayers did prognosticate that
Pirrhus should be slain at Argos in Greece, and Marc
Antoninus in Egypt."

†Jal says Horticius Mancinus, a consul, conceived a bad
idea of the result of a coming battle, for a like reason.
‡Shakspeare alludes to this superstition in "Antony and
Cleopatra."

§It is related that a cock on board of Rodney's flag-ship,
in his victory in 1782, crowed at each broadside fired at the
enemy, and this was deemed a happy omen by the seamen.
At St. Domingo, it is said that the coop of a cock, kept on
the poop of the "Superb," was destroyed by a shot. The
bird at once mounted on the spanker-boom, and crowed at
each broadside, until his perch was shot away, when he
hopped about the deck unterrified by the din and carnage
of battle. It was thought an omen of success. A cock on
board one of the vessels at Fort Fisher crowed loud and
often, and this, too, was taken as a good sign.

‖Lloyd says Themistocles was warned of a victory over
Xerxes by the crowing of a cock. The cock is a noted bird
in folk-lore, and will crow at Ragnarök, at the last day.

**Melville says there was, some years ago, a superstition
that it was an ill omen for ravens to perch on the masts of
a ship, at the cape of Good Hope.

Many superstitions connected with animal omens have
been related in previous chapters. Those concerning the
hare and the cat were wide-spread. In England, Scotland,
France and Austria, fishermen say it is an unlucky omen to
meet them when going to the boats, except in the case
where they preceded them to the boats. It was also an ill-
omen in Preston-Pans, England, to meet a pig when on
the way to the boats.

††An old work tells us the instinct of rats leaving a ship
is because they cannot be dry in it. A writer in the " Shipping Gazette," in 1869, says: " It is a well-authenticated fact

* Stratagems of Jerusalem, in Jones' Credulities, Chapter I.
† Glossaire Nautique.—Augure.
‡ Act IV, Scene 10.
§ Life of Rodney, in Jones' Credulities, p. 64.
‖ Diall of Daies.
** Moby Dick.
†† Athenian Oracle.

that rats have often been known to leave ships in harbor previous to their being lost at sea. Some of those wiseacres who want to convince us against the evidence of our senses, will call this superstition."

* Burnes says of the Mohammedan sailors of Sinde: "They are very superstitious; the sight of a crocodile below Hydrabad is an evil omen, which would never be forgotten."

† Melville says men in a whaler, hearing sounds at night in the water, some said they were the souls of drowned men, others that they were mermaids. They were found to be seals, and were then declared ill omens; and on the loss of a boat's crew soon after, a Manx sailor declared that these cries were their spirits calling them.

‡ The appearance of mermaids, as we have seen above, always portended disaster. In Brittany, the siren is called Marguerite mauvais-temps (bad-weather Margaret). They say,—

"When the siren doth commence to sing,
Then the sailor must begin to weep."

There are many ill-omened actions avoided by sailors, and others deemed fortunate, which are done by them to secure good luck.

Chinese and Japanese junk sailors think it a good omen to cross the bows of a foreign vessel, and frequently give great trouble in crowded channels, and incur considerable danger, from this cause.

Hawaiian fishermen deem it a bad omen if a fish-hook catch in the tail of a fish.

Various interpretations of dreams have been recorded as omens. § In England, to dream of a smooth sea is thought to indicate a good and prosperous voyage, but of a rough and boisterous sea, a stormy and unprofitable journey.

To see a dolphin in your dreams, portends the loss of your lady-love, and to dream of drowning, was a sign of good luck. To dream of an anchor, the sign of hope, was always esteemed a happy omen. ‖ A dream of fish indicated rain, while one of wading or bathing in the sea was indicative of future bliss.

Many places were thought ill-omened, and sailors hesi-

* Travels into Bokhara, Vol. II, p. 347.
† Moby Dick.
‡ L. F. Sauvé, in Mélusine, March, 1885.
§ Grant.—Mysteries, p. 479.
‖ Saxon Leechdoms, Wortcunning, etc.

tated to visit them. Bab el Mandeb, at the mouth of the Red Sea, was one of these. *Says Moore,—

> " The vessel takes its mournful way,
> Like some ill-destined bark that steers
> In silence through the Gate of Tears."

† Richardson says: " It received this name from the old Arabians, on account of the dangers of the navigation, and the number of shipwrecks by which it was distinguished."

. When first discovered, and for many years afterward, this bad character clung to the Cape of Good Hope, notwithstanding its change of name.

‡ Voltaire says of another cape: " The Cape of the Caba Rumia, which is in our tongue, the Cape of the Wicked Christian Woman; and it is a tradition among the Moors that Caba, the daughter of Count Julian, lies buried here, and they thought it ominous to be forced into that bay; for they never go in otherwise than by necessity."

Such beliefs have doubtless given us many of our geographical names, and the Devil may have been supposed to dwell in many of the places named after him.

§ It is thought an ill-omen among Vancouver's Island tribes for any one to pronounce the name of a certain mountain, while passing it in a canoe.

In 1799, a djerme named L'Italie, during the time of war in the Mediterranean, ran ashore in the Nile, with her load of prisoners and wounded, and, being attacked by the Arabs, was blown up by her captain. Napier took her loss as a bad omen for Italy's cause.

It was thought by the soldiers of Ptolemy Soter's army a bad omen when they found an anchor in a marsh, but he deemed it a good one.

‖ Lichtenstein tells us that the king of the Koosa Kaffirs broke off a piece of the anchor of a stranded ship. He soon after died, and the natives ever afterward saluted the anchor, and thought it an ill omen to touch it.

Auguries were in antiquity common alike to seamen and landsmen. Astrological indications have often influenced the lot of the mariner, not only in antiquity, but, as we shall see, in later days. Seamen frequently consulted the augurs,

---

* Lalla Rookh.
† Notes to Moore's Poems.
‡ General History. See also Don Quixote, Chapter XLI.
§ Farrar.—Primitive Customs.
‖ Travels in South Africa.

diviners and sibyls, without whose advice no event of importance was undertaken Soothsayers attended the armies and fleets, carefully watching every omen for indications of success or defeat. Augurs carefully inspected the entrails of the victims sacrificed, and noted each sign, from the murmur of a stream or the flight of a bird, to an eclipse of the sun or moon.

* Plutarch says, " The murmuring of a wave or a bird, or the driving of a thin cloud, is a sign to pilot of a stormy heaven and troubled sea."

He also says the Melians cast away their ships in obedience to an oracle, and that the Pelasgi often settled where their ships had been wrecked, deeming it an augury of their success. A seal designated the site of Phocea (seal town).

In later times, when there were no oracles, augurs or soothsayers to consult, the astrologers and sorcerers took their places, and even in modern times, weather-prophets receive considerable attention from mariners.

† Metellus tells of a woman who consulted a sorceress as to the fate of her son at sea. Melted wax was poured into a vessel of water, and assumed the form of a ship with a man floating beside it, indicating that the absent sailor was drowned.

‡ Lodge speaks of a " Divell who persuades the merchant not to traffique because it is given him in his nativitie to have losse by sea."

§ Falero, the Spanish astronomer, refused to accompany Magellan on his voyage around the world, saying that his calculations had made him doubtful of the result.

Lily, the astrologer, is said to have predicted many disasters at sea.

‖ Old Norse chronicles inform us that Thorold, on a voyage to Iceland, determined the site of his future colony, by throwing overboard two wooden columns of a temple of the gods, landing where they were carried by the current.

** Père Dan tells us how Barbary corsairs augured of victory or defeat, before engaging in battle. A man took an arrow in either hand, calling the one Christian, the other Moslem. The clerk of the ship then performed a certain

* "Socrates' Dæmon," in Morals, Goodwin's Trans.
† De Diis Sanagitarum (1560).
‡ Incarnate Devils (1596).
§ Goodrich.—Man upon the Sea, p. 227.
‖ Erbryga Saga.—Mallet, Northern Antiquities, p. 518.
** History of Barbary; in Jal, Glossaire Nautique.

ceremony, and read an invocation, when, it was said, the arrows approached each other, and continued fighting until one dropped down, and thus augured the defeat of one side.

* Wright tells of a certain fortune-teller, Alice West, who, in 1613, had great repute, "And saylers' wives came ordinarily to her whilest shee lived in Saint Katherine's, to know when their husbands would come home."

† Aubrey says an English merchant consulted a Barbary wizard concerning his ships at sea, and the latter assured him of their safety, by showing him in his hand a ship under full sail.

‡ A work by John Gadbury alludes to the use of astrological figures to predict the voyages of ships from English ports. He claimed that, in one instance, at least, the prediction was verified, the ship having suffered disaster. In another case, he claimed a fortunate result, as predicted. This was indicated, he says, in this manner: "As, indeed, under so auspicious a position of heaven, it had been strange if she had missed so to have done; for herein you see Jupiter in the ascendant, in sextile aspect of the sun, and the moon, who is lady of the horoscope, and governor of the hour in which she weighs anchor, is applying *ad Trinum Veneris.*

In 1712, Whiston, the English astronomer, had predicted the destruction of the world, on the appearance of a certain comet. It was so implicitly believed that the captain of a Dutch ship, off London Docks, threw his powder into the Thames, to keep it from exploding.

§ An odd instance of the so-called power of prophecy is told. A certain ship, the Xanthe, was to sail from an English port on an excursion on a certain day, and, in order to keep servants from going in her, a storm was advertised to befall her,—and actually occurred!

‖ In a modern Greek tale, sailors' wives sit on the strand and throw stones in the water, auguring of their husband's return by the wavelets thus created.

A certain Canadian weather-prophet, Wiggins, predicted a great storm on a certain day in 1882, which he said would destroy ships at sea. A New York newspaper says: "Captain Parsons, of the ship John R. Bergen, which lies at the

* Old English Tract.
† Miscellanies (1696).
‡ Nauticum Astrologicum (1710), in Brand, Popular Antiquity, Vol. III, p. 341.
§ Grant.—Mysteries. p. 547.
‖ Folk-lore Record (1879).

dock in Jersey City, had been trying to ship men for three days,' and was unable to get a crew on board. He attributed his failure to the superstition of sailors, and their fear of putting to sea before the term of Wiggins' predicted storm had passed."

* Drake says no ship of the Gloucester fishing fleet would then put to sea, although the loss was great. The same author says of a celebrated Salem witch, Moll Pitcher, who lived in 1752–1800, " The common sailor and the master, the cabin-boy and the owner, equally resorted to her humble abode to know the luck of a voyage. It is asserted that many a vessel has been deserted when on the eve of sailing, as a consequence of Moll's unlucky vaticination."

We also learn that in the Shetland Islands, even to this day, † " Spey wives and dealers in charms and incantations still ply a roaring trade. There are drunken old hags in Lerwick itself who earn their livelihood by imposing upon the credulity of ignorant sailors and silly servant-girls."

" Wraiths and portent receive implicit credence. Many of the survivors of the great storm of 20th July, 1881, assert that they owed their safety to the warnings they had received. A woman washing her husband's clothes in a burn sees his trousers fill with water, and infers from that an intimation of his approaching death."

To insure luck, not only were sacrifices and prayers made, but various charms have been used by seafaring men to insure them safe voyages, or a plentiful supply of fish.

Runes were used by the old Norse sailors for this purpose,‡ and have been described in a previous chapter. Runhofdi was their inventor, and they were engraved on oar, rudder or ship.

Such charms to control the storm-spirit were known in antiquity. § Assyrian fragments, recently deciphered, contain charms for controlling the seven evil storm spirits. Greek sailors used formulæ for invoking the winds, called Anèmo-Kostai. One is still extant, composed by Simonides. Inscriptions of a votive character were written on the ships themselves, or on the sails. ‖ Plutarch says, " Like those ships that have inscribed on them 'a prosperous voyage,' 'a protecting providence,' or 'preservation against danger,'

* Legends of New England, p. 243.
† Good Words, 1885.
‡ See Chapter III.
§ Records of the Past.
‖ Morals.—Goodwin's Translation.

and yet, for all that, endure storms, and are miserably shattered and overturned."

*Ships in the middle-ages carried such votive sentences, painted or engraved on a tablet which was affixed to the poop, just as the name of the ship is now placed in merchant vessels. This was called the "Dieu Conduit" (God leads).

Instead of these inscriptions, some figure or letter, or symbolic representation, was often substituted for it. †On the sails of Egyptian vessels, as depicted on the monuments, are seen painted representations of the sacred Ibis, or Vulture, and on the prow, as well as on the rudder, were the sacred lotus and eye.

The eye is still painted on the prows of Chinese junks, although it is, as they allege, for the ship to see her way by. "No have eye, how can see? no can see, how can sabee?" was the well-known response of a junk captain to a sneering "Fanqwei," who asked him the reason of its existence.

The cross, or a relic of it, was one of the most popular charms at sea. St. Helena, as we have seen,‡ calmed the angry Adriatic, by throwing in a piece of it. Portuguese and Spanish sailors used to carry with them small crosses or rosaries, that had been blessed by the priests, as charms against storms and disasters. A cross-bun was taken to sea by Sunderland fishermen, and one version of the Flying Dutchman's tale accounts his delivery as affected by a return to him of the cross, on which he had sworn.

§ Holy water, as we have seen, was also effectual as a charm. According to a French authority, St. Vincent calmed an angry sea with it.

Portuguese sailors called these crosses, relics, etc., carried by them to sea as charms, by the name of *fetiçao*, and the name fetish is since given to charms of this nature, supposed to influence fate or the weather. These fetishes are common among primitive people, and are often used to control the elements. Du Chailin says African tribes use a fetish to appease Noumba, who dwells in the ocean.

Relics of the saints were also powerful as charms. Besides the numerous instances met with previously in these

* Jal.—Glossaire Nautique. Aubin.—Dictionnaire de la Marine.
† Wilkinson.—Manners and Customs of the Egyptians.
‡ See Chapter II.
§ See Chapter III.

"NO HAVE EYE, HOW CAN SEE?"

457

pages, we learn that *Turketal, a famous Anglo-Saxon chancellor, had a thumb of St. Bartholomew, warranted to preserve him from storms and tempests. Although it was thought that the presence of a dead body on shipboard would raise a gale, there was yet a belief in the efficacy of human charms, and it frequently occurred that a dead man's hand and other human relics were carried to sea, as charms against shipwreck.

Animal charms were of the same class, and were more frequently used. †Pliny says the skin of a sea-calf was a protection against lightning, and ‡Augustus is said to have worn one for this reason. §Esquimaux fasten a seal skin to the prows of their canoes, as a charm against bad weather and storms. Foxes tails and eagles' beaks served equally well. In an Esquimaux tale, an old woman gives a man a charm, made of a merganser's skin, which, when nailed to the prow of his boat, causes it to fly swiftly over the waves. In another tale, a gull's wing aids a man to raise a spell, by which a calm is brought about.

Each feather picked up during the wren hunt on the Isle of Man, was a charm against wreck and disaster.

‖Sea shells were popular charms among the Indians of our own coast, and Negroes of the gold coast wear fetishes, consisting of a bag of shells as large as a hen's egg, which they believe brings them luck, and keeps them from storms at sea. The eyes of cuttle-fish, in Peru, and whales and sharks' teeth, in Fiji, were equally efficient charms. Fish charms were used by Columbia River Indians.

**Two bones found in the head of a fish, the Sciæna Aquila, were powerful charms with the Romans, and, if given or loaned, not sold, were of great virtue in storms.

Fish amulets were very common during the middle ages. These were stones having a fish engraved upon them, and bearing generally the word *Ichthus* (fish), signifying the Savior. Sometimes the reverse bore the words, "May'st thou save us." These were especially powerful against shipwreck. They were denounced by the fathers of the Church, the Council of Laodicea (366) prohibiting clergymen from wearing them, and a later council (in 721),

* Turner.—Anglo-Saxons.
† Natural History. Bk. II, ch. 56.
‡ Suetonius.—Octavius. ch. 90.
§ Rink.—Traditions of the Esquimaux.
‖ Tyler.—Primitive Culture. Vol. I.
** Jones.—Credulities, p. 155.

interdicted their use entirely. A recent traveler says they are still seen and used as charms in parts of Bosnia.

* Women in Berlin often carry a fish-scale, as a charm, in their purses.

† An odd charm for the toothache was

"An eel, a spring-back,
True indeed—true, in sooth, in sooth,
You must eat the head
Of said spring-back."

‡ Reginald Scot says a bone from the carp's head stanches blood.

An old fish amulet has engraved on it the bark of St. Peter, sailing over a fish (Leviathan, or Satan) with doves (the faithful) perched on mast and stem.

In a Scotch invocation of the fifteenth century we read,

" In holy kirk, my haip is maist,
That holy schip."

A stone with a ship engraved on it was a favorite charm in Scotland, during the middle ages, against shipwreck.

§ Aleuts made a powerful charm, by wearing a belt of sea weed, in magic knots. A pebble thrown up by the sea was also a marvelous charm, whose power no animal could resist.

A widespread superstition has for centuries prevailed concerning the caul—the thin membrane enveloping the heads of some new-born children, and it was regarded as a fortunate omen to the possessor, to be carefully preserved, and was thought to indicate by its condition the health of the wearer. The old dramatists give examples of this belief. ‖ Face says to Dapper:

"Ye were born with a caul o' your head";

and another speaker has it,—

** " Were we not born with cauls upon our heads?
Thinkest thou, Chichon, to come off twice a-row
Thus rarely from such dangerous adventures?"

* Blind.—Contemporary Review, August, 1882.
† Shortland.—New Zealand.
‡ Discovery of Witchcraft.
§ Bancroft.—Native Races, Vol. III, p. 144.
‖ B. Jonson.—Alchemist, 1610.
** Digby.—Elvira, in Brand, III, 118.

Mariners have likewise preserved the tradition of its efficacy as a charm and preventive against drowning and shipwreck. The first notice we have of it in this connection is in a rondeau by Claude de Malleville (1797). *It has been long used as a charm against drowning in Iceland, where it is called a *Fylgia*, or tutelary spirit, part of the soul being thought to abide in it. †In Scotland, it is called a Sillyhoo, or Hally-how. Scotch fishermen and sailors implicitly believe in its efficacy. "Many an emigrant has gone to the possessor of such a powerful charm, got a nail's breadth of it, sewed it with all care into what was looked upon as a safe part of the clothes, and wore it during the voyage, in the full belief that the ship was safe from wreck, and would have a prosperous voyage."

‡Marryat alludes to the superstition: "A sailor here (in Shetland) passes off a diamond for a caul, to avoid being robbed of it." §He tells also of a sailor who has a caul sewed up in his canvas trousers, which he values at twenty pounds. The dominie calls it a vulgar error that it would save from drowning, but receives the sage response, "A vulgar error saving from Davy Jones' locker is as good as anything."

‖In an old English will of 1658, Sir John Offley leaves a caul as a valuable legacy. They are frequently advertised for sale in English papers. **One reads: "To the gentlemen of the navy, and others going long voyages, at sea. To be disposed of, a child's caul, worth twenty guineas." ††Another: "To persons going to sea, a child's caul, in a perfect state, to be sold cheap." ‡‡Another advertiser announces his caul as "having been afloat with its late owner forty years, through all the perils of a seaman's life, and the owner died at last in his bed, at his place of birth."

Besides these, there were notices of cauls for sale in the London *Times*, February 20, 1813, and one in the *Western Daily News*, of Plymouth, February 9, 1867, offering one for five guineas, and three in the Liverpool *Mercury*, in 1873, ranging in price from thirty shillings to four guineas.§§

*Thorpe.—Northern Mythology, I, 114.
†Gregor.—Folk-lore of Scotland.
‡Phantom Ship.
§Jacob Faithful.
‖Brand.—Popular Antiquities, III, p. 114, note.
**London Morning Post, August 25, 1779. Jones, p. 112.
††London Times, February 21, 1813. Jones, 112.
‡‡London Times, May 8, 1848. Jones, p. 112.
§§Jones.—Credulities, p. 112.

I saw a notice in the Chicago *Times*, of November, 1883, of an advertisement of a caul for sale, taken from an English paper.

*Sir Hugh J. Rose says: "Ship captains coming into Cadiz harbor, I have found, sometimes preserve a child's caul on board, as a charm against shipwreck."

†It was customary, says Gibbons, among mariners of the south of Europe a century ago, to suspend a child's caul in the cabin of a ship to save her from sinking, and these curious membranes were much sought after by credulous mariners.

Coral was long thought efficacious as a charm. ‡Isidore of Seville says it is a charm against lightning and hail. It was also an amulet against fascination, and was thought to turn pale when the wearer was sick.

Ovid says it will stop bleeding. Orpheus says,—

"The coral, too, in Perseus' story named,
Against the scorpion is of might proclaimed,"

alluding to a superstition that it counteracted the poison of a scorpion's sting; and also to Ovid's story that it was reddened by the blood of the Gorgon Medusa's head, shed by Perseus.

Lucullus says it exhales a moist odor, that preserved anyone against lightning.

Another old writer says it is soft when it is first gathered, hardening gradually; and Reginald Scot tells us, §"The corall preserveth such as beare it from fascination or bewitching, and in this respect they are hanged about children's necks. But from whence that superstition is derived, and who invented the lie, I know not, but I see how readie the people are to give credit thereunto by the multitude of coralls that waic employed."

‖The Romans entertained this superstition, that coral protected a child from the effects of the evil eye. Ferdinand I. of Naples wore such a charm, and used to point it toward anyone supposed to be noxious. Many Neapolitans still believe it will turn pale when the wearer is ill.

**Another old English writer asserts that it stops bleeding at the nose, and checks dysentery.

*Spain.
†Boxing the Compass (1883).
‡Jones.—Credulities.
§Discoverie of Witchcraft (1580).
‖Jones.—Broad, Broad Ocean, p. 145.
**C. Leonardi.—Speculum Lapidarum (1717).

Amber was a favorite amulet in ancient times.　* Amber necklaces are enumerated by St. Eloi, in the seventh century, as remains of heathen superstition.

† In Iceland, a stone called the oskastein (wishing-stone) is used by fishermen at sea.　It is obtained by marking a raven's egg, three days before hatching, seething it in water, and replacing it under the bird.　When the brood hatches, the stone is found in the egg.

‡ An old work quoted by Jones tells us that "a wood-pecker and a sea-dragon under its feet, on the stone den-trites," was a good charm to open locks or tame wild beasts, and that "a quail and a sea-tench, engraved in a gem, would render one invisible."

That well-known charm, the horseshoe, has long been a favorite with the mariner.　§ They are often nailed to the masts of the boats of western England, and are occasionally seen among the fishing-boats on our own coasts.

| They were regarded as a great security in Scotland, and were thought better if from a "wraith horse"—the fabled progeny of a water-stallion.　** In Pomerania, a horseshoe or half a nail in the deck, forward of the mainmast, will protect from lightning.

†† Thatcher says they were used by sailors in 1821. ‡‡ Cheever says of the sailor, about that time, "He still insists that the horseshoe shall be nailed to the foremast, as a protection against the evil one."　Rockwell records their occasional use in 1841.

§§ Bunches of garlic are hung about Greek and Turkish vessels, as charms against storms, or the evil eye, and laurel as a charm against lightning.　Tiberius Cæsar is said to have worn a chaplet of laurel, for this reason.

Cornish fishermen keep bits of sea-weed, "lady's tree," in their houses, as charms.

|| A turf from the churchyard was thought, in Iceland, a sure preventive of sea-sickness.

** Scotch fishermen passed their boats through a bight of the halyards to counteract the evil effects of witchcraft.

* Jones.—Credulities, p. 170.
✦ Maurer.—Islandische Sagen.
‡ The Magick of Kiran. King of Persia, and Harpocration (1685).
§ Folk-lore Record, Vol. III.
| Gregor.—Scotch Folk-lore.
∞ Tenne.—Volkssagen aus Pommern, p. 347.
✦✦ Superstitions (1821).
‡‡ Sea and Sailor (1826).
§§ Jones.—Credulities.
| Maurer.—Islandische Sagen.　　　✦✦✦ Gregor.—Folk-lore of Scotland.

Galway fishermen use charms to prevent drowning. They are of various objects, hung in a bag about the neck,—there often being as many as six in one bag.

Lord Bacon said a man might be safe at sea, if he only wore a planet ring.

* Meg Merrilies gave the boatswain a charm, written on a parchment, carried in a bag about his neck, which would save his ship from destruction.

† Under the keel of an old Spanish ship, whose wreck was found in the Orkneys, in 18—, was a coin, dated 1618, wrapped in canvas, and evidently placed there as a charm.

English fishermen in many localities, when they wound the hand with a fish-hook, carefully preserve the latter from rust, as a charm to cure the hand.

STERN OF EGYPTIAN SHIP.

‡ Chinese have charms of strips of red cloth on the rudder and sails, and pieces of red paper with characters or sentences on them, are pasted on each thwart and seat in the boats. Gilt-paper images of boats and ships are placed near the compass as charms.

Old pieces of nets are hung about the junks to catch spirits, and priests are supposed to use them also for this purpose.

Images were early placed on the prows or poops of ships, and were at first, as we have said, of a sacred nature. Phœnician vessels carried representations of the Pataikoi, or Cabiri, and Greek vessels bore the images of their pro-

* Sir Walter Scott.—Guy Mannering.
† Notes and Queries
‡ Gray.—Chinese.

teeting gods. *Early Egyptian sculptures show us vessels
carrying at their prows and sterns the sacred ram, or the
Ibis head.

† Ovid says, " The waves dash against the figures of the
deities," and names Minerva (Athene) as the protecting or
tutelary goddess of his ship, which bore her image on the
poop. ‡ Paul's ship had Castor's image on it.

§ Lucan says,—

" No golden gods protect the shining prow,"

and the Romans always carried their *Lares,* or tutelary gods,
to sea with them, and finally affixed them to some part of
the poop, naming them *Tutelæ.* In Lucan's description of
a great ship, there are said to be niches there, reserved for
the gods. This custom of carrying the images on the poop
deck doubtless made it more sacred, as it is to this day reserved on all ships for the use of officers and passengers.
On Chinese junks a similar reason has made the *prow* the
post of honor.

These images were replaced in the middle ages by those
of the saints, for whom the ships were named. In addition,
streamers and pennants carrying the same name, were also
used.

The axe-like prow of the Venetian gondolas is the shining
blade of St. Theodore, their patron saint.

| Edward III. of England embarked, in 1350, on board
the Thomas, and an image of that saint was sent with him,
to insure protection. A figure of the Virgin, captured on
board a Spanish ship, was sent to the same monarch, in
1370.

** Da Gama, when asked by the Zamorin of Calicut to
give him the golden image of the Virgin which his ship carried, answered "that the image was not of gold, but of
wood gilded; but, nevertheless, as it had preserved him at
sea, he desired to be excused from parting with it."

St. Francis Xavier found in his day (1560) images in
Chinese junks, where meat and drink was placed before
them, and incense burned. †† Images of Tienhow are still
carried in these junks, and on the shrines are written these

* Dümichen.—Die flotte einer Könige Ægyptiens (1860).
† Fasti.
‡ Acts XXXVIII, 7.
§ Pharsalia.—Rowe's Translation.
| Jones.—Credulities, p. 59.
** Jones.—Credulities, p. 60.
†† Jones.—Credulities.

sentences: "Wherever this ship may sail, O Goddess, grant her a prosperous voyage," "Enable us by trading to acquire wealth," "When on the wide water, continue, O Goddess, to show us thy favor."

Norse ships carried images of wood shaped like dragons, serpents, etc., on their prows, and the law prescribing their removal to prevent frightening the landvaettir, has already been alluded to.

We read the following remarkable legend of these images:

*"Thorir had a large ship built in the wood, and prayed Bishop Sigurd to hallow it, and he did. Thereafter, Thorin fared out to Iceland, and caused the ship to be broken up, when he grew weary of sailing, but the beaks of the ship he had set up over his outer door, and they were there long afterward, and were so full of weather-wisdom, that the one whistled before a south wind, and the other before a north wind."

The belief of the sailor and the fisherman in these many omens, lucky signs, auguries, etc., are survivals of ancient superstitions—reminiscences of the many impositions practiced on credulous people by Chaldean magicians and astrologers, Greek and Roman augurs, mediæval sorcerers, and cunning charlatans of all ages.

They are, for the most part, fragments of a system of signs and tokens, by which shrewd men pretended to guess the future. Such beliefs still survive in nearly every land, among the mass of the people. Every collection of folk-lore will be found full of them. Beliefs in regard to luck are equally ancient in their origin. Certain persons or animals were deemed unlucky, because of their supposed influence on the weather or good fortune of the believer, generally through some implied connection with evil spirits. Certain days were unfortunate, because of their supposed connection with some evil influence, either in a conjunction of planets, or by the supposed diabolical character of the day itself, derived from deeds done in it, or from the deity from which it was named. Certain places were alike unlucky because they were thought to be the abode of evil spirits. Such beliefs are common to savage, uncivilized and uneducated minds, and are also shared by many persons of considerable intelligence.

*Grettir Saga.—Morris and Magnusson, p. 125.

30

CHAPTER XIV.

MISCELLANEOUS LEGENDS.

"The burying waters close around their head,
They sink! forever numbered with the dead."
                    Falconer.— The Shipwreck, Canto III.

"The second night, when the new moon set,
O'er the merry sea we flew,
The cockle-shell our trusty bark
Our sails of the green sea-rue."
                                        Hogg.

THERE are many superstitions connected with drowning, and with drowned bodies. Death by drowning was particularly abhorred in antiquity, when it was thought that fire must burn the body or earth cover it, and when the sea was particularly feared and detested by many, because it swallowed up the bodies of those perishing therein. As this was the abode of Typhon, and the quencher of the beneficent sun, and also, early in the middle ages, the purgatory of souls, it was considered especially unfortunate to be buried in it. This idea is manifested in the traditions of the proximity of the sea-bottom to Hades, of St. Brandan's burning islands, and in the name, still extant, of Davy Jones' locker at the bottom of the sea.

Sometimes, in antiquity, a badge was tied or fastened to the body, so as to identify it if found—very much as modern sailors tattoo the body.

There was in antiquity, and during the middle ages, an almost universal belief that devils and demons abode at the bottom of the sea, and lay in wait for people, and sometimes dragged them down. These beliefs have been fully discussed in a preceding chapter.* Water-spirits, mermaids, and such folk, were also thought to seize people, or entice them below. This subject has also been treated at length.†

These ideas led to a belief that the spirits of the drowned still inhabit the waters after their death. ‡In Brittany, these spirits are called criers, and they returned in the shape of birds. Teutonic nations believed there was a land at the bottom of the sea, where the spirits of the drowned abode. Burmese say a demon, Ruuhu, devours the drowned. In Russian belief Rusalkas,§ or water sprites, are the spirits of drowned people.

Sometimes, however, their end was not so lamentable. In Mohammedan belief, drowned persons are martyrs. In Mexican legend, they went to the greatest of three heavens, and in Greenland traditions, they reside in the lower, or ocean heaven. Brazilian Indians said the souls of drowned persons lived apart from the rest; and, in German belief, they haunt rivers and wells.

∥Widows in Matamba, Africa, duck themselves to drown their husbands' ghosts, which thereafter live on the ocean.

** The prevalent idea that demons lurked in the depths, to entrap the unwary bather, led to a further widespread superstition that it was unsafe to attempt to save the life of a drowning man. †† "The belief that some harm is sure to come to him who saves the life of a drowning man is unintelligible, until it is regarded as a case of survival of culture. In the older form of the superstition, it is held that the rescuer will, sooner or later, be drowned himself; and thus we pass to the fetichistic interpretation of drowning as the seizing of the unfortunate person by the water-spirit or nixy, who is, naturally, angry at being despoiled of his victim, and henceforth bears a special grudge against the bold mortal who has thus dared to frustrate him."

It is also probable that the inhumanity or cruel policy of wreckers, who believe that "dead men tell no tales," assisted the growth of these ideas.

These fears of evil results from aiding drowning people prevailed in many parts of Great Britain. Sir Walter

* See Chapter II.
† See Chapter IV.
‡ L. F. Sauvé, in Mélusine, February, 1885.
§ Ralston.—Songs of the Russian People.
∥ Tylor.—Primitive Culture, Vol. II, p. 28.
** Jones.—Credulities, pp. 67, 658.
†† Fiske.—Myths and Myth-Makers, p. 215.

Scott says they were, in his day, in full force in Shetland
and in the Orkneys.   Bryce, the pedlar, says, in the
"Pirate": "To fling a drowning man a plank may be the
part of a Christian, but I say, keep hands off him, if ye
wad live and thrive free frae his danger."   "Are ye mad!
You that have lived sae lang in Zetland, to risk the saving
of a drowning man?   Wat ye not if you bring him to life
again he will be sure to do you some capital injury."

*So in Scotland.   Sailors and fishermen in many Scotch
villages feared to pick up the body of a drowned person on
the beach, believing that the one so doing would meet with
death in the same manner.

English seamen fear to pick up any object on the coast,
washed ashore from a wreck, for fear lest the drowned
owner may claim his property and them with it. †Scotch
fishermen fear to go to sea in a boat from which persons
have been drowned.

‡Some years ago, a man fell overboard from a Russian
ship in Leith docks.   The crew tried to rescue him at first,
but when they found that he would surely drown, they ran
away, fearing to haul out the body.   §Barry tells the following: "A drunken man walked into the water and was
drowned, no one trying to save him.   On his clothing being
afterward examined, no cross was found about his neck.
He was declared by the villagers to be 'drowned because
he had no cross on his neck.'   It is generally believed here
that you must wear a cross when you go to bathe."   The
cross here replaces the steel, supposed in Norse legend to
deter a Nyck from approaching.

‖A still more curious incident is related by Ellrick: "I
myself saw a fellow fall overboard and drown, after a long
struggle, during which neither the crew of the vessel nor
his comrades made the slightest efforts to save him.   While
he was battling against the angry waves, the crew stood
quite composedly on deck, and said in chorus, 'Jack! Jack!
give in!   Dost thou not see that it pleases God!'"

**Similar things are recorded of Bohemian fishermen, in
1864, who say that "Waterman" will drown them, and take

*Grant.—Mysteries of All Nations, p. 396.
†Jones.—Credulities, p. 67.
‡Grant.—Mysteries, p. 398.
§Ivan at Home (1870).
‖Sketches of Austria, in Jones' Credulities, p. 63.
**J. V. Grohman.—Aberglauben und Gebräuch aus Böhmen, p. 12.

away their luck in fishing. They also pray on the river-bank, and offer wax candles and bread.

The Chinese have a repugnance toward aiding drowning men. They say the soul of a drowned person is in a kind of ocean purgatory, whence it is released only by finding some one to take its place. * In a Chinese tale, "The Fisherman and his Friend," the hero refuses to aid a woman who is drowning, for this reason.

†The Hong Kong authorities were obliged to insert a clause in junk charters, requiring them to save life, if the necessity occurred. ‡Gray tells of many instances that came under his observation, where Chinese refused to aid drowning men, claiming that their spirits flitted along the water, demanding a sacrifice. Salt was thrown into the place where any one was saved from drowning, to appease their spirits.

§Hindoos would not save any one who fell into the sacred Ganges, but would help him to drown, if near by, and it was a sin to try to save yourself.

| Kamtchatdales would not speak to a man rescued from drowning, take him into their houses, or give him food. **It was a sin to save a drowned man, a good deed to aid in drowning him.

††Koosa Kaffirs pelted them with stones, or else ran away from drowning men. Thèal says they think people are drowned by spirits, and they would not try to save a boat's crew from death by drowning.

Fijians used to eat those rescued from a watery grave. ‡‡Malay islanders will not save drowning men.

Death by drowning having been so universally thought an undesirable end, we find charms for avoiding it used frequently, and have treated the subject of the *caul*, so commonly used for this end, as well as other charms used for the same purpose, at some length in the last chapter. Indians of Queen Charlotte's Sound used a fetish of fish-bone; and African tribes generally use such charms. These were especially worn by bathers, in the hope of keeping away the cramp. Various curious charms have been used

* Gdes.—Chinese Tales by Ping Sung Ling.
✦ Black.—Polk-Medicine, p. 28.
‡ China.
§ Ward.—Hindoos, VII, p. 318.
| Kracheninckow.—Voyage to Siberia, Part II, p. 72.
** Steller.—Kamtchatka, 274.
†† Lichtenstein.—South Africa, Vol. I, p. 259.
‡‡ Bastian.—Mensch, Vol. III, p. 210.

for this.   Rings made of the nails or screws of a coffin were
deemed especially efficacious for this purpose.   Bacon says:
" There are two things in use to prevent the cramp, viz.,
rings of sea-horse teeth, worn upon the finger, and fillets of
green rushes tied about the calf of the leg, the thigh, etc.,
where the cramp usually comes."

* Part of a will in the "Ordinary," by Wm. Cartwright,
in 1651, has this clause, " I, Robert Monk, the —— of——
give to thee, Joan Pollock, my biggest cramp ring."

These were considered more valnable after being blessed
by a sovereign, and we have several notices of this ceremony
in England, which was only discontinued by Edward VI.

A manuscript of Cardinal Wiseman gives the formula
for blessing these.   Prayers used for the same purpose are
given by Dr. Pegge.†

‡ A writer of the time of Henry VIII. says, " The Kynge's
majestic hath a gret helpe in this matter, in hallowinge ye
crampe rynges, and so given without money or petition."
" The Kynges of Englande doth halowe every yere cramp
rynges, ye which rynges worne on one's fynger doth helpe
them whych hath the crampe."

The patella, or knee-bone, of a sheep, or even of a human being, was also worn for the same purpose.   § In
Northamptonshire, England, shoes and stockings were
placed in the form of a cross; and boys wore an eel-skin
about the leg.

Many hugged themselves with the delusion that they
were not born to be drowned.   Says Cicero: " He that is
born at the rising of the dog-star cannot be drowned in the
sea."

So Gonzales, in " Tempest,"—

> " I have great comfort in this fellow,
> Methinks he hath no drowning mark upon him."

And Proteus, in " Two Gentlemen of Verona,"—

> " Go, go, begone, to save your ship from wreck
> Which cannot perish, having thee aboard,
> Being destin'd to a drier death on shore."

The same idea is involved in the superstition that a ship
would not be lost with a king on board, as related in the
last chapter.

* Brand.—Popular Antiquities.
† Curialia Miscellanea.
‡ Andrew Boorde, in Brand, Popular Antiquities, Vol. III, p. 230.
§ Brand.—Popular Antiquities, Vol. III, p. 325.

We have also seen in a previous * chapter many instances of a belief in the appearance of the spirits of drowned persons. It is thought in many places that these apparitions are real, and these ghosts are frequently heard calling their names, especially near a scene of wreck. † In Cornwall, fishermen avoid a wreck in stormy weather, believing that ghosts haunt it. In Penrose, they are often heard "hailing their own names" in the gale, and it is known as the "calling of the dead." Fishermen on the Norfolk coast say that when anyone is drowned, a voice is heard, portending a squall. A Cornish legend is told of a man who was walking on the sea-coast, when he heard a voice say, " The hour is come, but not the man." Soon after, a dark figure leaped over the cliff into the sea.

‡ Lord Teignmouth records similar beliefs as existing in the parish of Ullsvang, in Norway: "A very natural belief that the voice of a person drowned is heard wailing amidst the storm, is apparently the only acknowleged remnant of ancient superstition still lingering along the shores of the fiord.

§ I have already chronicled the Danish belief that the spectres of drowned persons, called "Strand Varsler," promenade unconsecrated beaches. A peasant was seized by one of these, who would be carried to a church to be baptized, but he evaded the ghost. A woman, who took a ring from a dead body on the beach, was chased by a Strand Varsler. A similar belief is that in the "Gongers," ghosts of drowned persons, prevalent in Norway. We have seen many traditions of islands, such as Poëlsetta, Hörum, Heligoland, Great Britain, etc., inhabited by the spirits of the drowned. At Sent, on the Breton coast, the skeletons of the drowned are said to promenade the beaches. We read in the "Gudrun Lay": " Gloom arose, winds blew, and ever there came upon the winds a sound of grievous mourning and lamentation, for the drowned lay restless in their graves."

A certain South American tribe, if the body cannot be found, catch the soul, thus: "A line is stretched across the river, so that the soul shall not escape down the stream. A bag is set on the bank, distended, and near it some food. A feast is held there, and it is believed that the soul will come out to partake of it, and be caught."

* See Chapter VIII.
† Bottrell.—Traditions and Fireside Stories of West Cornwall (1870).
‡ Reminiscences (1880).
§ See Chapter VIII.

Fijians say you should not bury a limb in the sea, or the body will surely follow it.

It has also been widely believed that the bodies of the drowned may be found, by floating some object or other,—and that they would come to the surface at a certain specified time.

*Sir Thomas Browne says it was believed in his time that the body would float on the ninth day, and he did not question the statement. He also says that women float face downward, a notion entertained by Pliny,† who said that they did so that they might hide their shame. Both aver that men's bodies float face upward.

‡Pigafetta, in his account of the voyage of Magellan, records that the bodies of Christians, when thrown overboard from the ships, floated face upward, toward heaven, while those of Mahommedans, on the contrary, were turned face downward.

It has been widely believed that the position of a drowned body would be indicated by floating a loaf of bread down stream, when it would stop over the spot where the body was. It was necessary to put in the loaf a little quicksilver, or, some said, a lighted taper. An old account of thus finding a body in Kennet river, near Hull, is given in the "Gentleman's Magazine": §"After diligent search had been made in the river for the child, to no purpose, a twopenny loaf, with a quantity of quicksilver put into it, was set floating from the place where the child, it was supposed, had fallen in, which steered its course down the river upward of half a mile, before a great number of spectators, when, the body happening to lie on the contrary side of the river, the loaf suddenly tacked about, and swam across the river, and gradually sank near the child, when both the child and the loaf were brought up with grabbers ready for the purpose."

‖Henderson says this was practiced near Durham, England, so late as 1860. It was also believed that the body would float on the ninth day, when the gall-bladder would burst, and a cannon was often fired over the water for the purpose of breaking it.

Ideas similar to these are held in many parts of England

* Pseudoxica Epidemica (1646).
† Natural History.
‡ Goodrich.—Man upon the Sea, p. 228.
§ Vol. XXXVII. p. 140.
‖ Folk-lore of the Northern Countries of England, p. 59.

and Scotland. * A wooden club is said to have served as well as the loaf, in Eton. † In Ireland, a body is said to have been found by the use of a bundle of floating straw, with a paper containing certain characters written on it by the parish priest.

‡ In France, loaves consecrated to St. Nicholas, with a lighted wax taper in them, were used for this purpose, and in § Germany, a piece of bread, with the drowned person's name on it. A wooden bowl in St. George's church, on the Weser, is said to have served as well. In Bohemia,‖ a fresh cut loaf with a lighted taper in it was used.

It is believed in many parts of America, that the body may be found by means similar to these. ** Sir James Alexander says: " The Indians imagine that, in the case of a drowned body, its place may be discovered by floating a chip of cedar wood, which will stop and turn round at the exact spot. An instance occurred within my own knowledge, in the case of Mr. Lavery, of Kingston Mills, whose boat upset, and three persons were drowned, near Cedar Island, nor could the bodies be found until this experiment had been tried."

†† A writer in "Notes and Queries " claims that it is a scientific fact that a loaf and quicksilver indicate the position of a body, as the weighted loaf is carried by the current just as the body is.

‡‡ In Norwegian streams, those in search of a dead body row to and fro with a cock in the boat, who will crow when it is over the spot where the corpse lies.

§§ Near Samland, Prussia, the Rufen, or sound of a certain bell, will cause the sea to give up its dead.

In Java and China, a live sheep thrown into the water is thought to indicate the position of the body, by sinking near it.

Many other superstitions connected with dead bodies have been related in preceding chapters. It was believed that they were potent storm-raisers on board ship, and it is still believed that their presence at sea bodes no good.

* Choice Notes, p. 41.
† Choice Notes, p. 42.
‡ Mélusine, February 5, 1885.
‖ Folk-lore Record, 1879.
‡ Wuttke.—Deutsche Volksberglauben, p. 389.
** L'Acadie (1849), Vol. I, p. 19.
†† J. Baillie, December, 1883.
‡‡ Liebrecht, Zur Volkskunde, p. 331.
§§ Frischbier.—Preussisches Wörterbuch, in Mélusine, February 5, 1885.

*Aubin says it was believed unlucky to bury a body at sea from the port side, only animals being thus treated.

†Grant and Melville say it is held to be unlucky, on board merchant ships, to wear a dead man's effects until the voyage is over. But this does not hold true on board of our men-of-war, where the effects of a dead comrade bring high prices at the usual auction.

The narrative of the loss of the "Wager" furnishes us with a remnant of antique beliefs in regard to unburied bodies. The crew of that vessel found the body of a sailor who had been murdered, and left unburied. "The body had never been buried, and to such neglect did the men now ascribe the storms which had lately afflicted them; nor would they rest until the remains of their comrade were placed beneath the earth."

‡Epes Sargent says it was believed in the middle ages that the compass-needle would not traverse, with a dead body in the same boat. §So Browne asserts that Eusebius Nierembergius, a Spanish Jesuit, wrote that the human body was magnetic, and, if laid in a boat, and set adrift, would go to the northward by its own attraction.

This brings us naturally to the superstitions concerning the compass, and the loadstone. Besides dead bodies, there were many other substances which were thought to affect the quality of the magnet.

Pliny, Ptolemy and Plutarch all say that garlic destroys its attractive powers, and the former asserts that a diamond or a needle dipped into mercury, had a similar effect on the loadstone. Gilbertus, a middle-age writer, declares, on the other hand, that a needle touched to a diamond would become magnetic.

Various strange ideas have been entertained concerning the variation of the magnetic needle. When Columbus discovered that the needle changed its variation, and began to point to the eastward, his crew became terrified, thinking it portended great evils. ‖The Chinese declare that the needle, in the seventeenth century, pointed south, and that it has since reversed.

**Browne says: "Now the cause of this variation may be

* Dictionnaire de Marine (1702).
† Grant.—Mysteries, p. 327. See also Dana, Two Years Before the Mast, Chapter VI.
‡ Note to Rogers' Columbus.
§ Vulgar Errors.
‖ Tylor, Vol. I, p. 375.
** Sir Thomas Browne.—Pseudodoxica Epidemica.

the inequality of the earth variously disposed of, and differ-
ently mixed with the sea." Local attraction, he says, "may
proceed from mutations of the earth by subterranean fires,
fiends, mineral spirits, or otherwise."

This phenomenon of local attraction has given rise to
many curious stories of loadstone mountains, rocks, etc.
Pliny speaks of a loadstone mountain which attracts ships,
and Serapion says boats in Ceylon were not nailed together,
but sewed with thongs of leather, to prevent injury to them
on approaching the loadstone mountain, as iron nails would
would be drawn out and the boat fall to pieces.

Middle-age writers continued and elaborated these
legends. * The ship of the Third Calendar was endangered
by being driven by adverse winds near this mountain, and
was finally lost, all the nails being drawn out by the attraction. El Kazwini and El Wardee again vouch for the
wonderful story-teller, as they relate equally marvelous
things of the wonderful mountain, adding that shoals of dead
fish are found near it. In Persian story, Aboul Foueris is
wrecked upon a magnetic rock.

† Ogier the Dane, in middle-age legend, sails with one
thousand knights, and is wrecked by a storm. They take
to the boats, and are again wrecked, being cast upon
Avalor Island, by the attraction of the loadstone mountain
or castle. ‡ According to the Gudrun Lay, a fleet of Danes
is mysteriously stopped at sea by the attraction of a rock
called Gyfers.

§ A poem written in the twelfth century by Henry of
Valdeck, tells us that Duke Ernest, while sailing in the
Kleber Meer, encountered there a rock named Magnes, and
his ship was dragged down "among many a wreck of keels,
whose masts stand like forests."

Magnus Magnussen reported that his ship, during his
voyage to discover Greenland, was stopped by a loadstone
at the bottom of the sea, in deep water, and with a fresh
breeze blowing.

| That redoubtable traveler, Sir John Mandeville, tells
us this tale: "In an isle clept Crues, ben schippes withouten
nayles of iren, or bouds, for the rockes of the adamandes;
for they be alle fulle there aboute in that sea, that it is

* Lane.—Arabian Nights, I. pp. 161-207.
† Keary.—Outlines of Primitive Belief, p. 452.
‡ Ludlow.—Popular Epics of the Middle Ages, p. 231.
§ H. Von Valdeck.—Herzog Ernest von Bayern's Erhötung (Ed. 1869), p. 65.
| Voiage and Travaille.

marveyle to spaken of. And gif a schipp passed by the marches, and hadde either iren bandes or iren nayles, anon he sholde ben perishet. For the adamande of this kinde draws the iren to him; and so wolde it draw to him the schipp, because of the iren, that he sholde never departen fro it, ne never go thens."

Cadamosto, the Venetian traveler, speaks of the load-stone mountain.

The accounts of Pliny, Serapion and the Arabians place this mountain in the south, while Avalon and the other load-stone rocks of the northern legends were to the north.

*Sir Thomas Browne, in discussing the variations of the needle, gives us the key to the origin of the whole myth, as †Tylor has observed. This variation was supposed to be caused by polar mountains, ‡men "ascribing thereto the cause of the needle's direction, and conceiving the affluxions from these mountains and rocks invite the lilly toward the north." That the mountain should be in the south accords with the Chinese idea that the needle points south. As these supposed mountains caused the needle to vary, the myth that mountains existed elsewhere that would attract iron to them would easily arise.

The loadstone was often thought to possess other remarkable powers. Pliny says it would, if preserved in the salt of a remora, draw gold out of a well. §A small bit of loadstone used as a charm, in Scotland in 1699, was said to have saved a boat from sinking.

‖A magnet used by the English admiral Somers, and still preserved by his descendants, is thought a charm against drowning.

The loadstone was also thought a cure for the gout, if carried in the pocket.

There are many superstitions connected with stones, some of which have been already referred to. **An upright stone in Iona Island is said to confer the power of steering well to any one who will stretch his arm along it. ††At Innesken, near Mayo Island, a stone is kept, which, as late as 1851, was brought out and importuned to bring wrecks

* Vulgar Errors, II, p. 3.
† Primitive Culture, I, p. 374.
‡ Browne.—Loc. cit.
§ Folk-lore Record, 1875.
‖ Jones.—Credulities, p. 160.
** Jones.—Broad, Broad Ocean, p. 243.
†† Notes and Queries, February 7, 1852.

along. It was cylindrical, and was carefully wrapped in flannel. * Massey says it was an image of Neevoungee, an ancient deity.

† It is said in Iceland, that if a stone be thrown into the sea, the waves arise, and ships will be lost.

There are many nautical legends connected with bells. Sailors say that the bell of a sinking ship will toll as she goes down, even if it be firmly lashed in place.

‡ In St. Leven churchyard (Cornwall) a bell is said to ring the half-hours in the grave of a Captain Wetherell, who died at sea. But those who go on purpose to hear it will meet with bad luck; and a sailor who heard eight bells strike, was lost at sea soon afterward, or, as the sailor-phrase still has it, " It was eight bells with him," that is, the end of his long life-watch.

§ Fishermen near St. Monan's, Scotland, alleged, some few years ago, that the bell, hung on a tree near the sea, had a baneful effect on the fishing, and finally had it removed.

‖ There is a legend of Giltstone Rock, near Hartington, England. A slaver sailed at the sound of the Christmas bells, and was long absent, gaining great wealth by his nefarious occupation. On his return, as he entered with a fair wind, the bells again rang the Christmas chimes, when the wind suddenly changed, and the vessel was wrecked on the rock.

Southey's ballad, " The Inchcape Bell," is well known. Sir Ralph, the Rover, removed the bell placed on the Inch-cape Rock by the good abbot, and was afterward wrecked on account of the absence of its warning tones.

> " But even in his dying fear
> One dreadful sound could the Rover hear,
> A sound as if with the Inchcape Bell
> The devil below was ringing his knell."

Sunken bells like these are believed to sound in many parts of the world.   ** The maritime legend of Tintagel bells, still current in Cornwall, has been related.

†† Welsh stories are told of submerged bells in Lake Crumlyn, which are said to be rung by fairies.

* Book of the Beginnings.
† Powell and Magnusson, Icel. Legends.
‡ Bottrell.—Traditions and Fireside Stories of Cornwall.
§ Jones.—Credulities, p. 98.
‖ Jones.—Credulities.
** See Chapter III.
†† Sikes.—British Goblins and Welsh Folk-lore, p. 389.

* A legend is also told of "St. Goven's Bell," in Pembrokeshire. That saint lived in a cell in the rock near the coast, and a chapel was afterward built near the spot, with a bell in its open belfry. A pirate crew stole this bell, but a storm arose and wrecked their boat. The bell was mysteriously conveyed into the center of a stone, at the brink of a well near the chapel. It is still fabled to ring, when the stone is struck.

Mariners say the sound of a submerged bell is often heard near Blackpool, England. So they are heard in pools near Crosmere, when storms agitate the surface. † A vessel carrying the bell of St. David's in Pembrokeshire sank with it, and its sound is still heard, according to local legends.

There is an abundance of stories of such sunken bells in various parts of Europe. There is hardly a lake or a pool in Germany and Austria, in which, it is said, these sounds are not heard generally at night. ‡ In the Opferteich, near Moringen, they toll from 12 to 1, and no fish can live therein. These are the bells of a Knight Templar's castle, sunk on account of the crimes of the order. A bell is said to lie in the Kahlebysee in Schleswick, which sank there, with the ship of the pirates, who were carrying it away. A set of bells was stolen one Easter morning from Newkirk.§ The robbers got to their ships with them, but at the call of the priest of their church, they sank to the bottom, carrying the ships with them, and are still heard every Easter morning. Another of these stolen bells broke through the ice, and sank.

‖ The legend of the Bells of St. Ouen has also been related.

** At Cammarana, in south Italy, there is a legend that Saracens once pillaged the town and carried off a bell and an image of the Virgin. But the impious act caused them to lose their boat, and the bell sank, and is still heard to ring on the anniversary of that day.

†† The bell of Ivekoft Church, Sweden, sank, into a morass when the church was burned, and is said to have tolled at night for many months, disturbing every one. Two fish-

---

* Jones.—Credulities, p. 100.
† Sikes.—British Goblins and Welsh Folk-lore, p. 341.
‡ Thorpe.—Northern Mythology, Vol. III, p. 118.
§ Wolf.—Nederlandsche Sagen.
‖ See Chapter III.
** Pitre.
†† Jones.—Credulities, p. 98.

ermen tried long to fish it up, but only succeeded by invoking the aid of the Virgin and St. Olaf.

Sailors have often declared that bells could be heard from
the submerged churches of Port Royal in the West Indies.

There are other miscellaneous legends connected with
bells. *St. Pol de Leon, a Brittany saint, is said to have
caused a silver bell, coveted by a certain lord, to navigate
its way from England. This bell was famous afterward for
miraculous cures. St. David and St. Mardoc are likewise
said to have caused bells to sail on the water at will.

† Bell-string acre in Lancashire, England, is so named
because it was given to buy a silken cord for a bell whose
tones warned the donor, a sea captain, of danger, and saved
him from wreck.

It has been suggested, with some reason, that these tales
of sunken bells owe their origin to the sounds made by fish.
There are several species of fish which make musical sounds,
some of which, as the drum-fish found on our southern
coast, may be heard at quite a distance.

There are also many traditions of cities, towns, castles
and churches buried below the waves.

‡ Says an old poet,—

> " Ships riding in Alexandria bay
> Are lost on tops of houses and there stay."

§ Breton peasants have many traditions of sunken cities.
Berbido and *Is* are the most celebrated ones. The latter was
sunk for its crimes. When it rises, Paris will sink. Bells
are heard, steeples appear at low tide, and houses are seen
beneath the waves.

‖ Such legends are told of several places on the coast of
England. Lyonesse, or Leownesse, is a famous sunken
city near Land's End.

> " Between Land's End and Scilly Rocks
> Sunk lies a town that ocean mocks,"

says an old poem.

Fishermen still tell of seeing the walls of the houses
occasionally, and some aver that they have fished up win-

* Jones.—Credulities.
† Jones.—Credulities, p. 105.
‡ Heywood.—Hierarchin of the Blessed Angels (1635).
§ L. F. Sauvé in Mélusine, April 1, 1885.
‖ Bottrell.—Traditions and Fireside Stories of West Cornwall.

dows. There are said to be signs of a remarkable subsidence here, and trees are often seen growing in the water.

There is also a tradition that St. Michael's mount was once mainland, and that part of it was submerged.

*Sounds of revelry are often heard from a spot near Cudden point, where a certain lord of Pengerswick, a cruel landlord and oppressor of the poor, sank with his guests while dining in a boat off a silver table, which boatmen say they often see.

A certain bay at another place on the south coast of England is said to be the site of a former city which sank there. †A Cornish diver found such a city beneath the waves, and a company was formed to explore it.

There is said to be a submerged city, Kilkokeen, in the Shannon river. It was said that, in 1823, a boat's crew of fifteen men were seen in church, who came from this subaqueous village, to receive spiritual consolation. The legend further relates that a ship came into the river one night, and anchored here at the wharves of a fine city. The next morning, one of the inhabitants came aboard, and engaged them to go to Bordeaux; and the day after their return with a rich cargo, the city sank and never reappeared.

‡There are also Irish legends of a buried city near the cliffs of Maher, in County Clare, called Inclidon. If you can fix your eyes on it (which can only be done from one spot), you will be rich. Lake Inchoquin is also said to contain a city, sunk because of the crimes of its inhabitants. Giraldus says there is also such a city in Lough Neagh, which was traditionally at first only a fountain. So Moore sings,—

> " On Lough Neagh's bank, as the fisherman strays
>   When the clear, cold eve's declining,
> He sees the round towers of other days
>   In the wave beneath him shining."

§There is a tradition in Ireland that O'Donoghue revels in his castle below the waters of Killarney lake.

The apostle of Ireland, St. Patrick, is said to have turned the inhabitants of a certain town, who had mocked

* Hunt.—Romances and Drolls of the West of England.
† Bottrell.—Traditions and Fireside Stories of West Cornwall.
‡ Choice Notes, p. 29.
§ Croker.—Killarney Legends, p. 32.

him, into fish, and sunk their town beneath the waters of a lake.

*A Celtic story represents a man as visiting one of these towns below the water. One in Loch Eam was traditionally submerged by the overflow of St. Columba's well. In Gaelic legend there exists a land, Tir-fa-lorn, below the waves; and there are other traditions of buried cities.

Manx sailors assert that they frequently hear cattle lowing, dogs barking, etc., beneath the waves.

† Welsh tales of a town below Crumlyn lake, and another in Langorse pool, are still told, and bells are heard from them.

German legends of sunken cities are also abundant. ‡ These are usually said to be inhabited, and bells are heard from them, and people seen occasionally, while a wash is at times hung out just above the surface. It is said that many of these were sunk for the crimes of their inhabitants. Such cities also exist in the Rhine, according to popular legends.

§ A famous legend is told of the city of Stavoreen, Holland. According to this, there lived there a certain rich virgin, who owned many ships. One day, she entertained a wizard, but gave him no bread. He predicted her downfall in consequence thereof, saying that bread was the most useful thing. A shipmaster was, soon after, bidden to procure the most valuable cargo in the world. He chose a load of wheat; but, when he arrived with his cargo, the owner bade him throw it overboard. He begged to be allowed to give it to the poor, but was refused, and it was thrown into the sea. The wheat sprouted, a bank grew up, and the harbor was forever ruined.

∥ Büsen, on the Holstein coast, was traditionally swallowed up by the waves for the sins of its inhabitants.

> "At times, when the low water falls,
> The sailor sees the ruined walls,
> The church tower peeps from out the sand,
> Like to the finger of a hand.
> Then hears one low the church bells ringing,
> Then hears one low the sexton singing."

*"Groach de l'Ile de Lok." Campbell.—Tales of W. Highlands.
†Sikes.—British Goblins and Welsh Folk-lore. p. 330.
‡Grimm.—Deutsche Sagen. See also Wuttke and Kuhn.
∥Wolf.—Nederlandische Sagen.
§Max Müller.—Chips from a German Workshop, Vol. IV.

31

* Vineta, near Rügen Island, on the Danish coast, is said also to have been swallowed up by the waves in ·1183. Wilhelm Müller wrote a poem on the subject.

In Japanese story, a large tortoise carried a fisherman down to a city in the sea, and returned him thence, long after his friends were dead.

Numerous stories of habitations below the waves have been related in the chapter on Mermaids and Water-sprites, and the whole idea may doubtless be traced back to Atlantis, the submerged island which Pluto says Neptune overwhelmed because of the crimes of its people.

> "From its deep-rooted base the verdant isle
> Stern Neptune shook, and plunged beneath the waves,
> Its impious inhabitants."

Geological changes, involving subsidence of the land, submergence of cities beneath the waves, or changes in the coastline, have been numerous, and these tales are simply traditions of such changes, often invented to account for the occurrence of such phenomena, only to be explained to the unenlightened, by the theory of a punishment or vengeance for some sin.

Among miscellaneous legends are the following:

† A bank formerly existed near Tenby, England. It has disappeared, and with it the fish, formerly abundant. Fishermen claim that this is because of some enormity committed by the inhabitants of Tenby.

‡ There is a superstition among English sailors that all those born at sea belong to Stepney Parish.

§ Cardinal Ximines dropped into the sea a manuscript, during a storm, and it is asserted that it found its way to the shore, sound and dry. It must have been a sermon.

There are many superstitions and legends connected with ships, boats, and voyages that have not already been spoken of. Legendary, mythical, magical and wonderful ships have abounded in all ages. The oldest traditions of these are connected with the Deluge myth, and the Ark is the type of mystical vessels, abundant in after ages.

Although nearly all nations and peoples of the globe have legends of the Deluge, but few particularize the ship, where it is at all mentioned. Its biblical name, tebah, is

* Max Müller.—Chips from a German Workshop, Vol. III.
† Jones.—Credulities.
‡ Notes and Queries.
§ Jones.—Credulities.

referred by lexicographers to the old Egyptian *tba*, chest, and it is called chest in many places. This ark was 525 feet long, 87.6 broad, and 52.6 high. Vessels of these proportions have been built, notably in Holland, and possessed great carrying capacity.

Many traditions concerning the biblical ark are reported. * Berosus, and Syncellus say fragments of it were preserved in the Georgian mountains, and bitumen was taken from them, to be used as charms. El Kazwini says a temple constructed out of the planks of the ark long covered the spot where it rested, enduring until the time of the Abassides. Epiphanius says the same. Josephus says pieces of it were reported as existing in his day, and † El Macin tells us that the Emperor Heraclitus visited the remains of the ark on El Djudi. ‡ Benjamin of Tudela says Caliph Omar carried the ark away in 640, and placed it in a temple on an island in the Tigris.

§ Ibn Abbas, commentator on the Koran, says Noah was bidden to build the ark in the shape of a bird's belly, of the wood of a plane-tree which he had brought from India, and whose growth in twenty years, furnished abundant material. Various times are stated in Mussulman legend as having been occupied in its construction, the term extending from ten to one hundred and twenty years. ‖ Oriental legends say the ark made the tour of the world in six months. Jewish Rabbins said it was miraculously lighted up by a shining stone.

** Many of the Christian fathers asserted that the wood of the Ark was to be seen in the Koord country, and Prévoux says a piece of it is shown in the town of Chemna, in Arabia. †† Rawlinson saw bits of wood brought from Jebel Joodee, the Ararat of the modern Armenians, by pilgrims.

Marco Polo says there was a tradition in his time that the Ark still rested on a mountain in Armenia. In 1670, one John Stroan went up Ararat, until, he said, he saw the Ark visible, a speck in the distance above him.

The Chaldean account of the flood, by Nicholas of Damascus, calls the Ark a *scaphos*, or boat.

* Cory.—Ancient Fragments, p. 26.
† Baring-Gould.—Legends of the Patriarchs and Prophets, p. 126.
‡ Itinerary, in Baring-Gould's Legends of the Patriarchs and Prophets, p. 126.
§ Baring-Gould.—Legends of the Patriarchs and Prophets, p. 102.
‖ Baring-Gould.—Legends of the Patriarchs and Prophets, p. 117.
** Baring-Gould.—Legends of the Patriarchs and Prophets, p. 126.
†† Notes to Rawlinson's Herodotus.

* Berosus, quoting Alexander Polyhistor, says: "Ea commanded him (Xisuthros) to build a ship. He obeyed, and built a ship five stadii long and two broad. And out of the wood of this ship, which stopped in Armenia, the inhabitants of that country made amulets."

THE ARK ON MOUNT ARARAT.

We should not forget that a beam of the wood of the Ark is said to be in the Lateran church at Rome.†

‡George Smith translates from Chaldean records: "Ea came in a dream, saying, 'Make a vessel, and do it quickly.

* Cory.—Ancient Fragments.
† Baring-Gould.—Legends of the Patriarchs and Prophets, p. 134.
‡ The Chaldean Deluge.

Six hundred cubits shall be the measure of its length, and sixty cubits the measure of its breadth and height. Launch it upon the ocean and cover it over with a roof.' "

Various Assyrian, Babylonian and Greek legends relate to the Ark, calling it *Ploion, Schedia, Larnax, Kibotos,* etc., and the Noah, Xisuthros, Hasisadra, Deucalion, or Tamzi (the sun).

* Lucan says: "He (Deucalion) placed himself, with his children and his wives in a great chest," and a chest is graven on a medal of Apamea, of the second century. Pausanius says Ogyges, king of Bœotia, escaped the flood in a vessel.

† According to the Book of Enoch, a cow fabricates a ship, and comes out of it a man, after the deluge.

‡ In Hindoo legend, Manu built an ark at the command of Vishnu, a divine fish, and tied it to the fish's horn, and was saved thereby.

§ Bergelmir (Mountain Giant), the Norse Noah, escaped from Ymir, or chaos, in a luthr, or ark.

‖ Welsh legends name several Noahs, and the Ark is called Ked, or Avanc (*beaver*).

Gutzlaff found a representation of the Ark in a Buddhist temple, in China.

In Japanese story, Hiruko, who, as the third child of the first god-man, was the Noah, had an ark of camphor-wood, made by his parents in his third year.

A Javanese colony is locally represented as having been founded by Noah, who came to Palemberg in the Ark, with his forty sons.

The Fijian ark was, according to some, the rind of a large fruit, the *shaddock*, while others say it was a canoe, a double canoe, two single canoes, or a double jointed canoe.

Qat, the Banks Island Noah, built a canoe containing eight people. A canoe also served Marerewana, the Guiana Noah, and also the Carib flood man. The Marquesas ark was a *house*. In a Peruvian myth, it was a floating mountain.

Painted Mexican representations of the Ark still exist. The Codex Chimalpopeca** says the Noah (Coxcox) was

* De Dea Syria.
† Baring-Gould, op. cit. p. 113.
‡ Katapanha Brahmanana, in Lenormant.
§ Thorpe.—Northern Mythology, Vol. I, p. 142.
‖ Davies.—Celtic Researches, p. 163.
** Lenormant.—Beginnings of History.

commanded to "hollow out a great bald cypress, and you shall go into it when the water begins to rise towards the sky."

* Tezpi, the Michoacan Noah, had a vessel, and Teocepactli, a raft.

Jamaica Indians told the Spaniards that their ancestor built a ship, and passed safely through the flood.

There are various traditions of arks among North American legends. † In Cherokee story, a dog saves a man in a canoe, and Manabozho, according to the Ojibways, escaped on the trunk of a tree. ‡ Szenkha, the Pimas Noah, saved himself on a ball of resin, and Thlinkeets escaped the flood in a great floating building.

The Papagos say Montezuma made a boat, while their Cayote ancestor saved himself on a reed.

A raft served to save the Sibka Koloshes and Dog-rib Indians, and a bark canoe, the Mandan Noah. § In Caddoque legend, the Deluge vessel is traditionally made of the nail of the little finger, by blowing on it in the hollow of the right hand, and saying, "Nail, become a canoe, and save me from the wrath of the moon."

‖ In Kamtchatkan traditions the Ark is a raft. A tradition among the ** Voguls of Siberia is as follows: Their ancestors speak, "Let us cut a poplar-tree in half, hollow it, and make of it two boats; we will then twist a rope, five hundred feet long, and bring one end to the earth, and fasten the other to the prows of the boat." The legend further relates that the boat was lost, because they forgot to melt tallow and put on the gunwale of the boat, and so the cable was chafed in two.

The next great legendary voyages in course of time are the Argonautic Expedition, and the Wanderings of Ulysses. Enough has been said of these, to show their character, as embodiments of myths of the soul voyage, and at the same time, of the mystic course of the sun. The Argo has also been spoken of as a speaking-ship. The legend of the voyage is well known. At first, the heroes led by Jason, who sought the famous golden fleece (the sun's rays?), went eastward through the Black Sea, but the route was after-

* Mueller.—Americanische Urreligion. p. 515.
† Schoolcraft.—Algic Researches, p 358.
‡ Bancroft.—Native Races. Vol. III. p. 79.
§ A. Jones.—Traditions of North American Indians. pp. 21-23.
‖ Baring-Gould.—Legends of Patriarchs and Prophets. p. 118.
** Regally, in Lenormant. Beginnings of History.

ward extended to the Ægean and western Mediterranean. The wonderful ship stuck in launching, like Hringhorn, but was finally moved by Orpheus (the wind). Castor and Pollux sailed in the ship, which carried fifty heroes. Another legend of the ship reports that Danaus sailed from Egypt in one along with his fifty daughters.

These ships are of the same class. * "Whatever then the Argo may be, it is clearly the bright vessel in which the children of the sun go to seek the lost light of day." Of a like nature is, perhaps, the mystic ship (one story says a real ship) in which Dædulus and Icarus voyage, as the latter loses his life by approaching too near the sun, thus melting the wax on his wings, i. e., the cloud is dispersed by the sun's rays.

These cloud vessels existed, in popular fiction, during the middle ages.

They were then believed to navigate the upper air, and a sea was supposed to exist there. † Gervase of Tilbury, a mediæval English writer, says that in 1211, people coming out of a church on a dark cloudy day, saw a ship's anchor in a pile of stones, with a cable reaching up above the clouds. Voices were heard from the aërial ship, and presently a man slid down along the cable, but lost his life in the close atmosphere. An hour afterward, two shipmates cut the cable and sailed away, leaving the anchor hooked to

accidentally let his knife fall overboard from the aërial ship. At the same instant, it fell through the open roof and stuck in the table in his own home in Bristol, directly beneath him. "Who, then," he says, "after such evidence as this, will doubt the existence of a sea above this earth of ours, situated in the air, or over it?"

The venerable Bede says there are waters in the celestial regions.

We find all the Celts believing in this cloud-sea, and it was thought possible even to sail over the earth margin to it. *So Sir Francis Drake was thought to have "shot the gulf," and safely returned thence.

The world was, by the uneducated in his time, thought to be a solid plane, with another over it, and thus he could sail from one to the other. Vendean peasants believed in this cloud-sea, and thought that birds found their way to paradise through it.

Similar ideas seem to have been held by other people. The Japanese have a tradition that their ancestors came from the skies in a boat. †New Zealanders say the upper firmament is solid, and that the water is let through holes. Malays say their ancestors came from heaven in a great ship, built by the Creator. ‡Greenlanders say there is a heaven below the waters, and another above the air; and there is a legend of a man who went in a kayak to where the ocean met the upper heaven. Cosmos Indico pleustes says the waters of heaven rest on the firmament just above the earth. Hebrew tradition seems to point in the same direction, for we are told that the Creator divided the waters which were above the firmament from those which were under it. Sea and sky are everywhere confounded in early Aryan lore.

In the middle ages, mysterious ships abounded. By far the greater portion of these were death-barks, and have been described in a previous chapter.

Faust, the great German magician, built a glass ship, but could not sail it without the assistance of a Nix, or familiar spirit.

§A legend somewhat like that of Danaus was reported of the settlement of Great Britain. According to this, the

* Jones.—Credulities. p. 4.
† Grey.—Polynesian Mythology.
‡ Rink.—Tales and Traditions of the Esquimaux.
§ Brewer.—Dictionary of Phrase and Fable.

thirty-three daughters of Diocletian of Syria were set afloat in a ship, after the murder of their husbands, and came to Britain, the youngest, Albia, giving her name to the land of their choice.

Many mystical vessels are described in the German legends of the middle ages. *In the story of Hagen, Hettel builds a ship for Hilda, capable of holding three thousand marines. Other curious barks are alluded to in fairy and folk-lore tales, and an account of some of these has already been given. In a Scotch poem, "The Legend of the Lady Beatrice," occurs a ship manned by fiends; and in †"The Dæmon Lover," such a diabolic vessel is given to win a bride:

> "She sets her foot upon the ship,
> No mariners could she behold;
> But the sails were o' the taffetie,
> And the masts of beaten gold."

New Zealanders, ‡ Fijians, Samoans and Hervey Islanders have traditions of mysterious voyages in great ships, which they say were undertaken by their primitive ancestors, when their countries were colonized.

Such tales, of ancestral gods coming in ships or canoes, are abundant, and may contain in them an element of truth, but many give evidence of being sun-myths.

The ship of legendary deluges became a symbol in early Christian art. § It is often figured as the church militant. St. Ambrose says it is the church, and the mast is the cross. St. Augustine says the ark is the figure of the city of God. In a French church, Christ is shown carrying the church in a ship. Early churches were even built in the form of a ship, and in old French the name for the *nave* of a church and the ship were the same (*Nef*). "A ship entering port was a favorite heathen emblem of the close of life," says Lindsay.

The bark of St. Peter in a storm is also symbolical, and the celebrated picture in the porch of St. Peter's is an example of this symbolism. Ships of St. Nicholas and St. Ursula, often seen, are doubtless symbols of Christian qualities, but forgetful worshipers invented later legends, to explain their presence with those saints.

---

* Ludlow.—Popular Epics of the Middle Ages.
† Scotch and English Legendary Ballads.
‡ Ellis. Polynesian Researches. Gill.—Myths and Songs of the South Pacific.
§ Lindsay.—Early Christian Art.

A Mosaic in the Vatican, by Giotto, represents the church as a ship, commanded by Christ, and devils as winds are trying to overthrow her.

*In pictures in the Catacombs, the ship is the church, resting on the fish, Christ, who also steers. The dove fills the sails, and the prophets, as doves, keep lookout aloft.

In St. Calixtus, is the ship of the world, and Jonah, being cast into the jaws of a monster. In another, this ship strugles with the stormy waves of life, and the hand of God is stretched to aid her.

The ship often typifies certain qualities or actions in the legends of Argo, Isis, and in other ancient representations. Many events in the lives of the saints are also typified by the presence of a ship in paintings. The Ship of State is a frequent figure, as is beautifully exemplified in Longfellow's poem. A modern instance of the typical use of the ship is in the arms of the city of Paris. The isle of Paris is, or was, ship-shaped, and so the ship was adopted to represent it in the coat of arms. A ship is marked St. Jude's and St. Simon's days in the Runic calendar, as they were fishermen. It is frequent as an inn sign in maritime towns, and a ludicrous instance is that of an inn in London, where a ship and a shovel are intended to typify Sir Cloudesly Shovel. The ship occurs as a hieroglyphic character; Norse gods swore by board of ship. In Japan it is lucky to dream of sailing in a ship.

†A boat of glass was the symbol of initiation into the Druidical mysteries, probably typifying the Deluge or the universal redemption. An old Welsh adage was, "All must come unto the ship of the world."

The moon was also represented as a ship. Manichæans called the half-moon "Navis vitalium aquam" (ship of the living waters). The Egyptian Isis boat was double prowed, and says ‡ Bryant, the ancients often described the Ark as a double-prowed ship, and called it Mea, and Selene, or the moon.

§ In English weather-lore, the moon, with her horns up or on her back, is a boat, and hence contains water, and it will not rain. In old legends, the moon is a mermaid, or a silver boat, sometimes both, and Isis, patron of navigation, is also the moon.

* Palmer.—Early Christian Symbolism, p. 53.
† Davies.– Celtic Researches.
‡ Ancient Mythology.
§ Dyer.—English Folk-lore.

These legendary and mythical ships have been the subjects of much speculation by mythologists. Many of these conjectures and ideas concerning them have been recorded in other places. We have seen that the sun, the moon, the clouds and the world, have been regarded by them as typified by the legends and myths concerning the ship. We have also seen that the horse and ship were closely connected in these legends. As also remarked, the ships Skidbladnir and Hringhorn have been regarded as typifying the summer and winter,—or nature in her growth and in her decay. As Cox says: "The Argo, the Shell of Aphrodite, the Panathenaic ships are descendants of the Yoni, symbol of fertility." The same idea, we have seen, was also believed to be represented in Wades' boat, Guingelot. The worship of Priapian deities was undoubtedly extended, and the analogy of *pelvis* (Latin for thigh) to *pleva* (Sanscrit for ship), has been urged to support this theory, which is extended by Cox so as to include the various boats of sacred ceremonies, the forbidden lotus, the goblets of various myths, the boat-shaped cup of the Holy Grail, famous drinking horns, the salt-grinding queen, and even Aladdin's

CPSIA information can be obtained
at www.ICGtesting.com
Printed in the USA
LVHW08s0224260918
591389LV00008B/359/P